TEACHING AS A REFLECTIVE PRACTICE

The German Didaktik Tradition

STUDIES IN CURRICULUM THEORY

William F. Pinar, Series Editor

TEACHING AS A REFLECTIVE PRACTICE

The German Didaktik Tradition

Edited by

IAN WESTBURY
University of Illinois at Urbana–Champaign

STEFAN HOPMANN
Norwegian University of Science and Technology, Trondheim, Norway

KURT RIQUARTS
*Institut für die Pädagogik der Naturwissenschaften
an der Universität Kiel, Germany*

2000

LAWRENCE ERLBAUM ASSOCIATES, PUBLISHERS
Mahwah, New Jersey   London

Lawrence Erlbaum Associates, Inc., Publishers
10 Industrial Avenue
Mahwah, New Jersey 07430

Cover design by Kathryn Houghtaling Lacey

Library of Congress Cataloging-in-Publication Data

Teaching as a reflective practice : The German didaktik tradition /
edited by Ian Westbury, Stefan Hopmann, Kurt Riquarts.
p. cm. -- (Studies in curriculum theory series)
Includes bibliographical references and indexes.
ISBN 0-8058-2920-2 (alk. paper)
1. Education--Germany--Philosophy. 2. Teaching. 3. Curriculum
planning. I. Westbury, Ian. II. Hopmann, Stefan. III. Riquarts,
Kurt. IV. Series: Studies in curriculum theory.
LB14.7.T393 1999
375'.001--dc21   99-16280
                                          CIP

Printed in the United States of America
10 9 8 7 6 5 4 3 2 1

Contents

Preface

Several years ago one of us (Ian Westbury) shared with an American colleague, Walter Doyle of the University of Arizona, a copy of a paper by Arnold Kirsch (see chap. 15, this volume) on "simplification" in mathematics teaching that he had been given at a seminar in Germany, and had found to be quite fascinating. Doyle got back to Westbury quickly, agreeing that the paper was indeed very interesting, but he went on to ask where it came from and what it represented. Westbury told him that the paper had been described to him as a model of classical "Gymnasium didactics"—although he was later to understand that it was more correctly seen as an example of *Fachdidaktik*, that is, subject Didaktik. Predictably the question that followed was "What is 'Gymnasium didactics'?" and Westbury had to say that he didn't know.

At that time Walter Doyle was working on the kind of understanding that needs to be developed within curriculum studies of the issues around the *transformation* of concepts and bodies of content as they are moved from a curriculum to the classroom. For Doyle, Kirsch's paper was to become a key exemplar of and support for his emerging idea, and he was to cite it several times. But the question he had asked when he first read Kirsch's paper nevertheless remained. What was this "Gymnasium didactics" that we were told Kirsch's paper represented?—with the implication that there might be much, much more written on "transformation" and "simplification" in the German literature on didactics than was available in the English-language literature on curriculum.

Eventually, at a conference at the University of Oslo in 1990, Westbury was able to ask "What's didactic?" in a conversation with Bjørg Gundem of the University of Oslo and Stefan Hopmann, a speaker at the conference and then a member of the research staff of the Institut für die Pädogogik der Naturwissenschaften (IPN), the Institute for Science Education, at the Christian-Albrechts Universität, Kiel. They told him that didactics, or *Didaktik*, was the long-standing heart of thinking about teaching and teacher education in Germany; that "Gymnasium Didaktik" was one, but only one, part of the tradition; that it was a body of thought that had had, in recent years, a complex relationship with the "curriculum" tradition as that tradition had been imported into Germany in the 1960s; that in the

1980s there had been renewed interest in the traditional Didaktik and there was a contemporary "Didaktik-renaissance" in Germany; but that many issues around the relationship between the Didaktik tradition and the American curriculum tradition remained to be explored. These issues were of great interest to Gundem and Hopmann.

As a result of these discussions in Oslo, a "Didaktik meets curriculum study group" was formed, consisting of Walter Doyle (University of Arizona), Bjørg Gundem (University of Oslo), Sigrun Gudmundsdottir (Norwegian University of Science and Technology, Trondheim), Stefan Hopmann (formerly of the IPN, Kiel; now the Norwegian University of Science and Technology, Trondheim), Rudolf Künzli (Didaktikum, Aarau, Switzerland), Roland Lauterbach (University of Leipzig), Peter Menck (University of Siegen), Kurt Riquarts (IPN, Kiel), and Ian Westbury (University of Illinois at Urbana-Champaign). This group gave itself the tasks of, on the one hand, illuminating, for the Anglo-Saxons in the group, what Didaktik was and, on the other hand, exploring the relationships between curriculum and Didaktik as traditions of thought embedded in different educational cultures that seemed, or might be seen, to address similar questions, but in different ways. We were able to secure support for three seminars and conferences in Europe—in Aarau, Switzerland, Kiel, Germany, and Oslo, Norway—to discuss these issues.

As a result of these meetings, two volumes in English have appeared exploring the relationship, since the 1960s, between curriculum and Didaktik in Germany and Scandinavia: Stefan Hopmann and Kurt Riquarts (Eds.), *Didaktik and/or Curriculum* (Kiel: Institut für die Pädogogik der Naturwissenschaften an der Universität Kiel, 1995); and Stefan Hopmann and Bjørg B. Gundem (Eds.), *Didaktik and/or Curiculum: An International Dialogue* (New York: Peter Lang, 1998). This volume addresses the second task that the Didaktik meets curriculum group set itself: to present an introduction to Didaktik for English-speaking readers that draws on a range of writing associated with the *bildungstheoretische Didaktik* tradition. We believe that this volume is of great potential significance for English-language students of the curriculum if only, by highlighting another way of discussing issues of curriculum and teacher education, it throws light on the assumptions, characteristics, and perhaps weaknesses, of curriculum thought.

This activity was supported by grants from the Deutsche Forschungsgemeinschaft (German Research Council) to the IPN at Christian-Albrechts Universität, Kiel, and by the institutions involved: the Didaktikum in Aarau, IPN, and the Faculty of Social Sciences and the Institute of Educational Research at the University of Oslo. Much of the work of translation that lies at the heart of this volume was supported by the Spencer Foundation, Chicago, Taylor & Francis Ltd. of London, England, through the *Journal of Curriculum Studies*, and IPN. The intense day-to-day communication required by a project such as this one was generously supported by our institutions: the University of Illinois at Urbana-Champaign, IPN, the Norwegian University of Science and Technology, Trondheim, and the University of Oslo. Needless to say, we are grateful to these agencies and institutions for the support that made this book possible.

In addition to these institutional acknowledgments, we need also to express our appreciation to many, many people: to Jürgen Baumert, who as Managing Director of the IPN supported this project from its beginnings; to Gillian Horton-Krüger, who prepared most of the translations included here; to Klaus Witz of the University of Illinois at Urbana-Champaign, who not only volunteered to translate a paper when funds for translation had run out, but also answered innumerable questions about references and proofed much of the German included in the text of this volume; to Jörg Biehl of the IPN, who hunted for many elusive references as well as preparing the biographical statements included in Part II; and finally, to Lana Bates and Debra Gough of the College of Education at the University of Illinois at Urbana-Champaign who keyed many of the chapters as well as drew, and redrew, the graphics.

Many publishers graciously gave their consent for our use of their copyrighted material in this volume. Specific acknowledgments are made in the text.

Finally, we need to thank Bill Pinar, the editor of the series in which this volume appears, and Naomi Silverman of Lawrence Erlbaum Associates, for their support for this (we believe) important, but out-of-the-ordinary work. When Ian Westbury first sought support for translations from American funding sources, we were always asked what Didaktik was! Our answer was that we needed the project to find out. The understandable response was that it was difficult to support funding something when it wasn't clear what it was. Rebecca Barr of the Spencer Foundation, Bill Pinar, and Naomi Silverman found ways out of this Catch 22!

Ian Westbury
Stefan Hopmann
Kurt Riquarts

TEACHING AS A REFLECTIVE PRACTICE

The German Didaktik Tradition

INTRODUCTION

Starting a Dialogue:
A Beginning Conversation Between
Didaktik and the Curriculum Traditions

Stefan Hopmann
Kurt Riquarts

When Klaus Westphalen in Kiel, Karl Frey in Zurich, or Bjørg Gundem in Oslo want to explain to their student teachers how to prepare lessons, they all use the same term: in German *Didaktik,* and in Norwegian *didaktikk.* This word, in English *didactics,* originates from the Greek *didaskein,* which meant "to teach, to be a teacher, to educate." *Didaktikos* meant "apt at teaching" or "instructive" and *didaskaleion* was a school. In modern German, *Didaktik* is generally defined as the art or study of teaching, with *didaktisch* as the adjective and *Didaktikum* denoting a teacher-training institution. This usage dates from 17th-century pedagogy, particularly as set out by Wolfgang Ratke (Ratichius; 1571–1670) in Germany and the Bohemian bishop Jan Amos Komensky (Comenius; 1592–1670), both of whom used the Latinized term *didactica* for their theories of teaching. These theories were discussed throughout Europe.

Since the days of Comenius and Ratke, Didaktik has been the most important tool for planning, enacting, and thinking about teaching in most of northern and central Europe. Indeed, it is impossible to understand German, Nordic, and central European schooling without appreciating the role and impact of Didaktik. However, except for brief periods, Didaktik did not have a comparable importance in the English-speaking world where the issues Didaktik addresses are presented in the different framework of "curriculum and methods" or "curriculum and instruction." For this reason, it is difficult to translate Didaktik conceptions and theories into English—not only because of differences in languages, but because there are fundamental cultural differences in understandings of teaching, schooling, and the teaching profession. Why then "starting a dialogue"? Because we share Ian Westbury's belief (see chap. 1) that both traditions can offer each other substantial insights and knowledge, especially in those areas where each tradition has its own shortcomings.

Curriculum theory has taught the Didaktik tradition important lessons on the relation of school and society, on the nature and scope of educational planning, and on the many other issues around teaching and schooling as socially constructed realities. We believe that the Didaktik tradition can, in its turn, support the recent move of curriculum theory toward issues of reflective teaching, curriculum enactment, and teacher thinking by its rich, systematically developed knowledge about these very issues. And the Didaktik focus on content as the core of teaching also fits perfectly well with the recent awareness of curriculum theorists that "subject matters" (Stodolsky, 1988).

However, to make the dialogue fruitful, we do have to be aware of the differences between the curriculum and the Didaktik traditions. The history of this dialogue between these traditions, as we sketch it in the following discussion, provides more examples of misunderstanding and misrepresentation than well-informed interaction. But our recent experience (see, e.g., Gundem & Hopmann, 1998; Hopmann & Riquarts, 1995) has convinced us that a fresh start is worthwhile—and possible.

Traditions

In Comenius' shortest definition, given in his *Didactica Magna*, Didaktik contains three elements, *omnes omnia docere,* that is, "teaching everything to everyone." To teach "everything" meant relating the microcosmos of instruction to the macrocosmos of the world. Such teaching required knowing what the *content* of instruction should be like, where it comes from, and how it is used: in short, to have a representation of content that followed its natural or social appearance. Furthermore, teaching is possible only if instruction takes care of the progress of learning and the development of the learner. Comenius supplied a theory of the *learner* based on natural stages of development. Finally, *teaching* has to be aware of both the content and the learner. In the Comenian tradition, it is the teacher's responsibility to take care of the natural and/or social stages common to all successful instruction. Developed, for example, by Johann Friedrich Herbart, this tripartite conception has been a core concept in the development of Didaktik.[1]

---

[1]See *Allgemeine Pädagogik aus dem Zweck der Erziehung abgeleitet* by J. F. Herbart (1806) (translated as "General pedagogy derived from the purpose of education" by H. M. and E. Felkin as part of *The Science of Education* [London, 1904]).

In Germany and the Nordic countries, we are used to presenting its components—the content, the learner, and the teacher—as the *Didaktik triangle*, a tool to structure the field of Didaktik research and theory (see chaps. 1 and 2, this volume).

The rise of mass schooling, sparked by the Lutheran school reformation in the 16th century, brought about a situation in which Didaktik became the common approach for planning lessons and legitimizing schooling in central and northern Europe. The reorganization of school and the school inspectorates in Austria, Prussia, and southern Germany in the 18th and early 19th centuries, with the accompanying expansion of teacher education, brought home the need for a theoretical system that would enable state directives to be translated into classroom practice by teachers. Didaktik became the conventional way to fill this frame of reference, to construct as well as to translate these guidelines, and was developed and taught at the new teacher-training institutions, the precursors of which had been set up in the 17th and 18th centuries, that were rapidly spreading throughout Europe.

Two sources especially influenced the content of Didaktik until the late 18th and early 19th centuries. On one side were the curriculum guidelines issued by governments or other state institutions. Although most of the requirements of these guidelines could not be met in most schools, they set a level of aspiration that schools had to contend with, forcing teachers and supervisors either to explain deviations or to prove correspondence. On the other side, the expansion of teacher education created a market for supporting literature. The first books of this kind were—like the very popular one, edited in 1796 by August Hermann Niemeyer—compilations of methodological knowledge, guides of the how-to-do-good-instruction style that are still successful in the educational market. However, method was not understood in the reduced fashion predominant today. In fact, the search for the "best method" meant the notion (held by almost all educators from Comenius to Pestalozzi) that there is a *natural* way of teaching and learning that is in accord with the nature of content. This older tradition laid the ground for the belief, firmly held by most models of Didaktik today, that method is not just a mode of application, but a crucial factor *induced* in any level of educational reasoning.

The most developed historical example of this approach, and one that opened new perspectives, was Herbart's. It combined classical rhetorical education with modern psychology. Like Comenius, Herbart distinguished three layers of education: *government, discipline,* and *instruction.* Government means sustaining order by leadership and command. Discipline, or *character,* is the general compliance to order inside and outside school that teachers try to implant. Whereas government is based on direct intervention and discipline on the self-control of the learner, instruction mediates between both, the teacher and the student, *by means of content;* that is, it educates by developing the learner's knowledge of obligations, opportunities, and choices. In Herbart's view *instruction* is *education by content*. Combining both, he created the model of *educating instruction* as the core of schooling, a notion that has been at the core of German Didaktik to the present day.[2]

There was a double irony in Herbart's success. First of all, he strongly opposed any notion of state curriculum making. For him, the state was too distant from what happens in schools and instruction. Yet his Didaktik was successful because of state curriculum making and because of the gap between legislation and the local needs of teachers and students. Second, it was not Herbart's sophisticated arguments that permeated teacher education and schooling, but the simplifications developed by his followers, the so-called Herbartians like Tuiskon Ziller and Wilhelm Rein. The most important contribution of Herbartianism was to extract Didaktik from general educational theory, turning it into a discipline of its own, dealing with *instruction under the conditions of schooling* as distinct from other instructional settings like self-education or education in the family. But in doing so, the Herbartians changed Herbart's analytical tools into schematic sequences preforming any hour and minute of teaching. The conventional prejudice against something being "didactic" can be traced back to the practical impact of the Herbartians. Whereas Herbart argued for an active interplay of all components, the content, the teacher, and the learner, Herbartians like Ziller reduced the content to a fixed array of school subject matter to be poured over passive learners. The rules dictated, for instance, that every lesson should follow the same formal pattern, that is, the five formal steps of *preparation, presentation, association, generalization,* and *application.*

Needless to say, this tendency toward a schematic, rigid approach to instruction did not remain unchallenged. Beginning with Rudolf Hildebrandt's (1824–1894) legendary criticism of the killing boredom of Prussian school routine, a new mode of thinking emerged, later expanding into "reform pedagogy," that was directed at a multifaceted education of a kind actually appropriate for children. Reform pedagogy was then and is still an international movement while Herbartianism was to vanish into the archives of educational historians—though its ideas are still operative today as formulaic knowledge, albeit unconsciously on the part of its users.

In the German-speaking part of Europe, Herbartianism was supplanted by a theory of education and teaching, *bildungstheoretische Didaktik,* and by a development of this Didaktik, *geisteswissenschaftliche Pädagogik* (human-

---

[2]It has to be stressed that "discipline" has nothing to do with drill or formal education: Discipline is following one's own moral judgment. Rusk (1969) translated *government (Regierung)* as "orderliness or teacher's control of pupil's behavior" and *discipline (Zucht)* as "character training or self-discipline."

science education), which was rooted in a specific branch of reform pedagogy and built on the philosophy of Wilhelm Dilthey (1833–1911). Some of the most influential Didaktik models of today are rooted in these traditions. The renewed Didaktik did not, however, find any followers outside the German-speaking countries. Didaktik thus became an almost purely German affair, even the Didaktik theories that have an explicit connection with Anglo-Saxon research on teaching like the so-called *Berlin School* of Didaktik—introduced by Paul Heimann, Gunther Otto, and Wolfgang Schulz—and the models of Didaktik build around concepts of communication and everyday life (as provided by the Frankfurt school of sociology and some other approaches). To understand this, we have to differentiate between problems of export and import.

EXPORTING AND IMPORTING DIDAKTIK

To start with the latter, the difficulties of import: Why, for instance, did the Americans of the late 19th century cherish Herbart, but not his reform-pedagogical critics? Why were they ignorant of the rising tide of Bildung-centered Didaktik? We have to keep in mind that the overwhelming success of Didaktik was bound to certain institutional environments. Only where there was a need to integrate state curriculum making, centralized teacher education, and local schooling, that is, only in centralized school systems like those of Prussia, was there a growing need for a theory regulating the interplay of these levels. In the United States, with its traditionally locally controlled school system, there was no need for such complicated efforts of mediation between different levels of decision making and control.

What Americans like G. Stanley Hall and John Dewey did take from Herbart was in fact not the whole of Didaktik, but the educational psychology grounding it. Thus Herbart became one of the fathers of the American spelling of pedagogy as educational psychology. The fragmentation of American educational science, separating curriculum studies from pedagogy, was fundamentally opposed to the holistic approach of reform-pedagogical Didaktik. But *content* was lost in American curriculum studies—as well as in pedagogy—by this fragmentation.

The history of educational thinking is only one in a bundle of constraints that kept modern Didaktik outside the United States. Other factors include the general ups and downs of U.S.-European and especially U.S.-German relations. Thus the First World War and, even more, the Nazi Reich and the Second World War had a devastating impact on the import of German educational theories (except for those brought in by emigrants). Moreover, the Germans had problems exporting their theory self-confidently, because— unlike German educators in the 18th and 19th centuries—20th-century German educators did not value their own school system as the best in the world. If one had to name a second key word of German reform pedagogy, alongside Bildung, it would have to be *crisis,* the constant belief of German educators that they are in trouble, lasting trouble, dangerous trouble.[3]

Even though Americans were not interested in our Didaktik, we took on curriculum. We did it in one of our crises, the one that was said to be the looming educational catastrophe of the 1960s. The issues at stake were the economic competitiveness of West Germany and the cultural stress grounded in the social and political race between the East and West. The political background was not much different from what is familiar to Americans from the educational policy debate following the Sputnik shock, the Conant and Rickover reports, and so on, in the late 1950s and early 1960s.

Bildung-centered Didaktik was still predominant then in a highly developed, very sophisticated form, *Didaktik analysis.* Following the Second World War, almost all professorships in teacher education—if not already occupied by exponents of traditional Didaktik—had gone to a young and liberal breed of reform-pedagogical innovators, renewing Didaktik in many ways and fashions. The strong objections of educators, as well as the public, were not so much directed against the renewal of Didaktik as such, but centered on whether the conventional wisdom of Didaktik could be sufficient to meet the challenges of tomorrow. Conventional Didaktik dealt with state-issued guidelines, implementing and adopting them on a local level. What was lacking was a research program going beyond the interpretation of the guidelines and directed toward active planning of the educational future of German society. Because curriculum researchers seemingly understood curriculum making as an interwined process starting from the needs of society and moving down into every single classroom, the American curriculum tradition seemed to be far ahead, and much more appropriate, for meeting the needs of a rapidly changing society.[4]

Once again there is an obvious irony, the fact that curriculum theory gained its biggest success on the Continent and in Germany at a time when, in the United States, it was said to be "moribund" (Schwab, 1978). But we

---

[3]The close connection of pedagogy and crisis can be tracked back to the 18th-century Enlightenment when pedagogy was constituted as a scientific discipline (see Koselleck, 1973). It fits nicely that German pedagogy is just now regaining strength on the international market; our educational system never looked as bright and glorious to ourselves as it does right now, compared with the educational disasters of the East. And, at the same time, there is a rising tide of centralization in curriculum making and control by assessment all over the English-speaking world, creating a demand for the kind of pedagogy we have to supply.

[4]The most important critic introducing the turn toward "curriculum theorizing" was Saul B. Robinsohn; see the translation (Robinsohn, 1992) of his *Bildungsreform als Revision des Curriculums* [Educational reform as curriculum revision].

Germans did not really care for this all-American debate. We took curriculum research and planning as the long expected cure-all for everything we had not come to terms with in recent years. What was lacking, however, was a truly comparative discussion. Most researchers and administrators just took on the curriculum perspective, leaving behind Didaktik as the model of the past.

The curriculum fever did not burn for very long. One reason was once again provided by the institutional structure: The central condition for curriculum making, that all levels from curriculum planning down to classroom interaction are systematically interwined, did not fit into the still-predominant system of state curriculum making separated from local planning and instruction. Second, inside teacher education and school administration, Didaktik analysis and its patterns of content transformation remained strong enough to stall any attempt to replace them in favor of—let us say—Mager or Bruner. Curriculum planning as found in the United Kingdom or the United States could not be adapted to the German structures without losing its identity. Although curriculum research had done much to enhance the quality of teaching and learning, it could not fulfill the expectations thrust upon it. The curriculum movement did not become moribund like the U.S. field; it simply died almost everywhere, quietly and without mourning.

Once again there was no truly comparative discussion! Many of those involved in curriculum studies continued publishing books, but now calling their efforts Didaktik—as if nothing important had changed. Karl Frey is probably the best known example of this conversion (see Frey, 1971; Frey, Frey-Eiling, & Landolf-Marazzi, 1990). And those who had held on to Didaktik in the unfriendly 1970s felt confirmed: Curriculum planning was not a better tool, and where it differed most—in creating one unified approach to all levels of curriculum making—it failed most obviously. This may be an oversimplifying summary, but it pinpoints the course of the turnabout: from Didaktik forward to curriculum and back to Didaktik again—as if the curriculum movement had been just a kind of first love: hot and fierce, but short.

Yet, Didaktik did not come out of the "wonder years" of curriculum love unchanged. It changed in two respects. First, and most important, the exponents of Didaktik accepted the critique made by the curriculum movement, that it had been all too naïve when working with state regulations (see, e.g., Adl-Amini, 1986; Klafki, 1977, 1980). Today there is a consensus among all versions of Didaktik that Didaktik has to be critical, and even resistant, if state requirements do not fit into what Didaktik believes is good for the students. And second, and no less important, Didaktik has recovered its old strength as a mediator between the content, the teacher, and the learner by a radical turn toward the content. *Subject-matter Didaktiks,* that is, the Didaktik produced and delivered inside the boundaries of school subjects, have spread all over the scene, gaining institutional and intellectual support in universities, teacher training, curriculum making, and schooling. Today, almost every student teacher has compulsory training in the field of subject-matter Didaktik.

And, surprisingly enough, it is this turn toward the content that raises the possibility of a second attempt at comparison of curriculum and Didaktik. And this time the necessity to mingle both traditions is seen on both sides of the Atlantic. What do teachers know about the content they are teaching? What do students see and comprehend when confronted with a content, a subject, or a field of study? Are there different teacher–student relations, different tasks of classroom management depending on the content at stake? Subject-matter Didaktik and curriculum research, as represented by Lee Shulman, Miriam Ben-Peretz, and Walter Doyle, are dealing with the same set of questions. What all these efforts have in common is the strong belief that we need an integrative approach, as intended by Herbart and Comenius, that can do justice to each corner of the Didaktik triangle: the teacher, the content, and not least, the learner who has to come to terms with this ever more complicated world.

REFERENCES

Adl-Amini, B. (1986). Ebenen didaktischer Theoriebildung. In D. Lenzen & A. Schrunder-Lenzen (Eds.), *Enzyklopädie Erziehungswissenschaft: Handbuch und Lexikon der Erziehung, Band 3, Ziele und Inhalte der Erziehung und des Unterrichts* (pp. 27–48). Stuttgart: Klett-Cotta.

Frey, K. (1971). *Theorien des Curriculums*. Weinheim, Germany: Beltz.

Frey, K., Frey-Eiling, A., & Landolf-Marazzi, E. (1990). *Allgemeine Didaktik: Arbeitsunterlagen zur Vorlesung*. Zürich: Verlag der Fachvereine.

Gundem, B. B., & Hopmann, S. (Eds.). (1998). *Didaktik and/or curriculum: An international dialogue.* New York: Peter Lang.

Hopmann, S., & Riquarts, K. (Eds.). (1995). *Didaktik and/or Curriculum*. Kiel, Germany: Institut für die Pädagogik der Naturwissenschaften an der Universität Kiel.

Klafki, W. (1977). Zum Verhältnis von Didaktik und Methodik. In W. Klafki, G. Otto, & W. Schulz (Eds.), *Didaktik und Praxis* (pp. 13–39). Weinheim, Germany: Beltz.

Klafki, W. (1980). Zur Unterrichtsplanung im Sinne kritisch-konstruktiver Didaktik. In B. Adl-Amini & R. Künzli (Eds.), *Didaktische Modelle und Unterrichtsplanung* (pp. 11–48). Munich: Juventa Verlag.

Koselleck, R. (1973). *Kritik und Krise: Eine Studie zur Pathogenese der bürgerlichen Welt* (Suhrkamp Taschenbuch Wissenschaft, Vol. 36). Frankfurt: Suhrkamp.

Robinsohn, S. B. (1992). A conceptual model of curriculum development. In H. Robinsohn (Ed.), *Comparative education: A basic approach* (pp. 125–144). Jerusalem: Magnes.

Rusk, R. R. (1969). *The doctrines of the great educators* (4th ed.). New York: St. Martin's Press.

Schwab, J. J. (1978). The practical: A language for curriculum. In I. Westbury & N. J. Wilkof (Eds.), *Science, curriculum and liberal education: Selected essays of Joseph J. Schwab* (pp. 287–321). Chicago: University of Chicago Press.

Stodolsky, S. S. (1988). *The subject matters: Classroom activity in math and social studies*. Chicago: University of Chicago Press.

Westphalen, K. (1975). *Praxisnahe Curriculumentwicklung: Eine Einführung in die Curriculumreform am Beispiel Bayerns*. Donauwörth, Germany: Auer.

DIDAKTIK AS A REFLECTIVE PRACTICE

1

Teaching as a Reflective Practice: What Might Didaktik Teach Curriculum?

Ian Westbury

Ian Westbury is a professor of curriculum and instruction at the University of Illinois at Urbana-Champaign. He is general editor of the *Journal of Curriculum Studies*.

> *How learning is organized, how it is perceived, how issues about it are debated are always rooted in the particularities of national histories, of national habits, and national aspirations.*
>
> —W. A. Reid (1998)

As Stefan Hopmann and Kurt Riquarts note in their Introduction to this volume, Didaktik is a tradition of thinking about teaching and learning that is virtually unknown in the English-speaking world. Although the core of this volume is taken up with texts from Didaktik, intended to introduce readers to this tradition in its own words, we also argue in the pages that follow, implicitly if not explicitly, that this German tradition of curricular and pedagogical thought is worth the sustained and serious attention of those who work within the "Anglo-Saxon"—as our European colleagues phrase it—educational and curriculum traditions. We argue that Didaktik provides ways of thinking that highlight some very important, and universal, educational questions that are not well defined in the English-language curriculum tradition. In addition, we propose that Didaktik suggests ways of thinking about, and some practical approaches to, some of the core tasks of preservice and inservice education of teachers, which many recognize are not being well handled in American teacher education. In this introductory chapter to this volume, I sketch one version of the case that I have asserted in these sentences and, at the same time, seek to outline a framework for reading the chapters that follow.

But is it possible that there are ways of discussing the curriculum and teacher education that are different from those we Anglo-Saxons know and that our ways of thinking about the curriculum, and our practice of teacher education, might learn from? Hopmann and Riquarts outline a case for this difference in their Introduction to this volume. However, Wolfgang Klafki (1995; see also chaps. 5 and 8, this volume), one of the most distinguished contemporary scholars in the Didaktik tradition, has suggested that curriculum, that is, American curriculum theory, and Didaktik are not far apart, not least because they are concerned with the same set of issues:

- Teaching and learning goals.
- The topics and contents that follow.
- Organizational forms and teaching and learning methods and procedures.
- Teaching and learning media.
- Prerequisites, disturbing factors, and unintentional auxiliary effects.
- The ways in which learning results and forms can be controlled and evaluated.

One implication of this kind of listing is that Didaktik can be more or less straightforwardly assimilated to the categories of English-language curriculum theory. I, on the other hand, argue here, with Hopmann and Riquarts, that, although Didaktik and curriculum theory do address similar issues or topics, there are fundamental differences in the ways in which traditional American curriculum theory and Didaktik have posed, and then sought to answer, the questions that flow from these topics. These differences provide, if nothing else, directions for elaboration within the curriculum tradition. In addition, there is a body of issues that are addressed within the Didaktik framework that are simply not asked within the curriculum tradition—but are very important. Didaktik also has highly developed (and highly usable) approaches to the education of teachers that flow from its starting points that are also not found in the Anglo-Saxon tradition of teacher education. It is these features of Didaktik, and the different way of thinking about curriculum that they represent that makes this German tradition of educational thought so interesting for Anglo-Saxons. But what are these differences, and why do they occur?

In the American case, the dominant idea animating the curriculum tradition has been *organizational,* focusing on the task of building systems of schools that have as an important part of their overall organizational framework a "curriculum-as-manual," containing the templates for coverage and methods that are seen as guiding, directing, or controlling a school's, or a school system's, day-by-day classroom work. These manuals replicate, in place after place, the somewhat open categories of the national, institutional curriculum; but, it is seen as a major responsibility and task of each school system to decide, for itself and after appropriate public deliberation, what the larger national curriculum means for this place in the light of its circumstances. The resulting curricula are sometimes progressive in spirit and sometimes not so progressive, but that difference is not essential. What is essential is the idea that public control of the schools means that, whatever the character of the curriculum that is developed for a school or school system, teachers as employees of the school system have been, and are, expected to "implement" their system's curricula—albeit with verve and spirit—just as a system's business officials are expected to implement a system's accounting procedures or pilots are expected to follow their airline's rules governing what they should do (see Westbury, 1994). Teachers are, to use Clandinin and Connelly's (1992) apt metaphor, seen as more or less passive "conduits" of the system's or district's curriculum decisions. Curriculum as a field of study within American education has traditionally sought to address, and to prescribe for, the problems involved in developing and implementing curricula seen in this way.

In the German case, on the other hand, the state's curriculum making has not been seen as something that could or should explicitly direct a teacher's work. Indeed, teachers are guaranteed professional autonomy, "freedom to teach," without control by a curriculum in the American sense. The state curriculum, the *Lehrplan,* does lay out prescribed content for teaching; but, this content is understood as an authoritative selection from cultural traditions that can only become educative as it is interpreted and given life by teachers—who are seen, in their turn, as normatively directed by the elusive concept of *Bildung,* or formation, and by the ways of thinking found in the "art" of Didaktik.

Thus, Didaktik is centered on the forms of reasoning about teaching appropriate for an autonomous professional teacher who has complete freedom within the framework of the *Lehrplan* to develop his or her own approaches to teaching. Didaktik, as a system for thinking about the problems of the curriculum, is not centered on the task of directing and managing the work of system of schools or of selecting a curriculum for this school or this district. Instead Didaktik, as Wallin (1998) put it, provides teachers with ways of considering the essential what, how, and why questions around *their* teaching of *their* students in *their* classrooms. These are, of course, the core issues that are the heart of a *reflective* practice of teaching! Within Didaktik the range of possible answers to these questions is further elaborated to become, in turn, frameworks for structuring, and sometimes assessing, the larger *rationales* teachers have for their classroom work. The centrality Didaktik gives to such rationales for teacher thinking reflects its starting point that every teacher must, necessarily, assume a role as reflective educational (and curriculum) theorist in order to teach anything, anywhere. Table 1.1 spells out these core assumptions of the German Didaktik and contrasts them with the core assumptions of the Anglo-Saxon curriculum tradition.

As I have suggested, it is these starting points around Didaktik, and the ways in which they are elaborated and worked out in relation to the idea of Bildung, that makes this tradition so interesting to those from outside its northern and middle European worlds. Didaktik offers ways of thinking about issues that have been, to this point, barely identified, and certainly not elaborated, in American educational theory. We argue in this volume that a better-developed relationship between curriculum and Didaktik would promise a great deal for Anglo-Saxon educational theory, curriculum studies, and teacher education. However, seeing the promise of Didaktik takes work—because, as Reid (1998) pointed out, the Didaktik tradition, like the curriculum tradition, is rooted in the particularities of a national history, national habits, and national aspirations.

TABLE 1.1
Didaktik and Curriculum Compared

Level	Curriculum	Didaktik
1. Lesson Planning		
core question	how	what and why
content as	object	example
aims as	task	goal (direction)
lesson plan as	course action	frames of reference
teaching as	enactment	licensed
2. Research		
focus	individual teacher teacher thinking (interpretative)	art of teaching, Didaktik analysis (hermeneutic)
assessment of successful teaching	student achievement (scores & standing)	professional appropriateness, reflection
3. Theory		
function	preparation	initiation
sequence	subject matter comes first	Bildung comes first

Note. From Hopmann and Riquarts (1995). Copyright © 1995 by Institut für die Pädagogik der Naturwissenschaften (IPN). Adapted by permission.

In the balance of this chapter, I explore these claims—and, in so doing, frame this book—by, first, offering interpretations of the "traditional" Anglo-Saxon curriculum theory and Didaktik individually as ideal-types, and then comparing them. I conclude by outlining a framework that offers a way of seeing the constructive relationship between the two traditions that we need—when we come to know each other better.

Curriculum Theory and Research

> For American students, the world that education should help to create is presented as objectified. . . . The social and cultural world is [seen as] an objective *structure*. . . . The task of curriculum [is] to present this structure to students, and help them determine what place they will occupy in it. The premises behind such reasoning are, firstly, that culture and society can be rendered in facts to be learned and, secondly, that, for students, the question of how they are to relate to society and culture is one that they have complete freedom to answer for themselves. (Reid, 1998, p. 13)

If we start our analysis by staying close to the practical curriculum work found in the world of American schools, all of the essential elements of curriculum studies can still be readily described within the framework outlined in the core text of the field, Ralph Tyler's (1949) *Basic Principles of Curriculum and Instruction,* that is, the Tyler *Rationale.*[1] In the text of the *Rationale,* but also in the nested national-to-local praxis it symbolizes, there are two distinct themes and several subthemes; and although these aspects of curriculum thinking are generally seen as fused, they reflect different strands in American curriculum theory—and become different issues in practice.

First, there is the assumption that Reid (1998) identified, that the world that the school seeks to reflect is objective and can be "rendered into facts to be learned" (p. 13)—an assumption that leads inevitably to (and at the same time is a result of) a *managerial* framework for, first, curriculum development and specification and, later, for the control and evaluation of the effectiveness of educational "service delivery." The core curriculum technologies of planning, objective writing, instruction, test development, and curriculum evaluation follow from the larger framework.

This structure is seen as *rational* in that it is assumed that it is possible to specify a set of orderly steps setting out how an optimal curriculum can be developed. In the *Rationale,* this rationality is value-neutral and framed by the steps of assessing (a) subect-matters and the "needs" of students and society and (b) screening what emerges from this analysis by way of a

---

[1]For recent, sympathetic, interpretations of the Tyler *Rationale,* see Hlebowitsh (1992) and Airasian (1994).

normative and a psychological analysis. The conclusions of such analyses provide the basis from which the goals of a school can emerge, which are in turn transformed into courses and units with their behavioral objectives—from which instructional methods, forms of student assessment, and curriculum evaluation follow. This evaluation provides, in turn, feedback to the curriculum developers and teachers about the quality and appropriateness of their work. What happens in classrooms as a curriculum is *transformed* into teaching is not seen as a major problem. It is assumed that teachers can, or should, faithfully implement the curriculum if it is well developed and teachers are appropriately prepared to use it.

The second strand in the Tyler *Rationale,* and in American curricular thought more generally, gives the field its reforming, as distinct from its managerial, themes. This second strand, which emerged in the 1920s and 1930s, contains three disparate aspects: First, curriculum work incorporated into itself the progressive movements of that period for the reform of the pedagogy of the elementary school; second, it picked up the set of tasks associated with the emergence of mass terminal secondary education as distinct from the elite preparatory secondary education of the 19th and early 20th centuries. This transition required both ideological and public legitimation of the curricular changes that were seen as the necessary concomitants of a "new" school intended to serve new classes of pupils, and the communication of the social inventions that accompanied the new school of the American 1930s, the comprehensive, "democratic" high school. The curriculum field took on this task of ideological legitimation of the new ways for teachers and the task of "teaching" teachers and school administrators how the new ways might work.

These communicative, educational tasks of the curriculum field, which necessarily involved some distance from existing institutional categories and the organization of the then-school, were taken up aggressively by the new class of university "intellectuals" who addressed the curriculum "problem." With the entry of these intellectuals to the center of the activity, curriculum studies assumed its modern form: It became an expert endeavor that sought to support, rationalize, direct, and legitimate changes being undertaken in the schools, or changes that *should* be undertaken in schools. Although this movement identified itself with the curriculum, and with the work of progressive schools districts, schools, and teachers, the target was still the "system," albeit a reformed system (see Doyle & Westbury, 1992; Westbury, 1992).

The three primary themes circling around all American discussions of curriculum follow from this history and its embedded cultural understandings and institutions. First, as the formal plan of work for a publicly determined and centrally managed, community- or nationwide *service delivery system,* all discussion of the curriculum is framed in terms of conceptions of public "needs," with the school being seen as the agency for satisfying those needs by way of its structured (and codified) programs. No other conception is available within the dominant curriculum theory tradition or its policymaking mate. Second, curriculum thinking is inextricably associated with notions of "modernization" and "reform" of the schools. Both the reforming rhetorics and the systemic technologies that are the focus of much of traditional curriculum theory exist to change and redirect schools as institutions, not to maintain and support them or to nurture the ongoing, routine work of their teachers! Finally, within the managerial perspective of curriculum, teachers are always the invisible *agents* of the system, seen as "animated" and directed *by* the system, and not as sources of animation *for* the system. This starting point leads to a view that existing teachers are a (if not the) major brake on the innovation, change, and reform that the schools always seem to require. As I suggest in the concluding pages of this chapter, it is this view of the teacher as a cipher for the formal curriculum that represents perhaps the major source of internal tension within contemporary, "progressive" curriculum theory and practice. And, as I have been foreshadowing, it is their respective views of the teacher, and the role the teacher is given within their theoretical and institutional systems, that represents the most dramatic difference in viewpoint between Didaktik and curriculum theory.

DIDAKTIK

> For European students, [the world that education should help to create is presented] as subjectified. . . . There are things to be learned . . . but students *should* be encouraged to "plot their own course." (Reid, 1998, p. 13)

> The "Didaktiker" does not begin by asking how a student learns, how a pupil can be led toward a body of knowledge, nor does he or she ask what a student should be able to do or know. . . . The Didaktiker looks first for the point of a prospective object of learning in terms of Bildung, asks what it can and should signify to the student, and how students themselves can themselves experience this significance. (Künzli, chap. 2, this volume)

The institutional and ideological form of the American (public) school system, and thus the institutional context for the American form of the curriculum and curriculum studies that I described earlier, emerged in the large cities of the United States in first half of the 19th century—and was a response to the problems associated with creating an effective administrative system for urban mass elementary education (see Kaestle, 1973a, 1973b). The core structures and institutional context of the contemporary German school system are associated historically with the *Gymnasium* or academic secondary school, with the last decades of the 18th century and the first decades of the 19th century, and predate both Germany's urbanization and the emergence of the educational and curricular "systems" of the Anglo-American world. This German world was, in Grafton's (1983) wonderful words, "a homely tapestry of Biedermeir, *Bildung,* and *Besitz* [i.e., property], populated by the large provincial burghers of small provincial cities, and only occasionally blackened by the smoke of a small factory" (p. 159). The very different contexts of emergence of Didaktik and curriculum studies in socially and culturally embedded systems for schooling lie at the heart of the intellectual and practical differences between the two fields. Let me briefly trace some of the tributaries that have flowed into modern Didaktik.

The German states developed systematized educational administrations in the 18th century and, in the first decade of the 19th century, extended the scope of this administration to the curriculum, and after 1830 to teacher education for the Gymnasium and the elementary school. But these states did not assume responsibility for the direct management of the preexisting networks of schools adminstered by churches, towns, and foundations, but, rather, their initial focus of concern, the *Lehrplan* or the state-prescribed curriculum, was a set of guidelines to regulate the subjects and topics to be taught in these schools. Schools, and later individual teachers, were *licensed* to teach the topics outlined in the *Lehrplan;* thus, schools and classrooms had instructional plans, but schools and local administrative units did *not* have curricula! The management of schools, and teaching and planning for teaching, was thus decoupled from the idea of a curriculum.

Given the prior existence of long-sanctioned networks of schools that the state did not have the power to control, administrative expediency played an important role in the development of these institutional patterns. But, at the same time, the traditions associated with the larger context of the German professions—traditions that are very different from those of the English-speaking world—also played an important role in the emergence of the modern Didaktik.

The framework for all German professions was (and is) heavily dependent on the state and on the idea of professional licensing. Licensure gives a state-sanctioned right of autonomous practice by professionals within the state's legal and administrative frameworks. The prerogatives symbolized by such licensure are, in turn, derived from the German system of higher education and state examination of professionals. Within this framework, higher education and the state worked together to form a structure that, in Jarausch's (1990b) words:

> Imparted the general liberal education (*Bildung*) that is necessary for an elevated social position, a modicum of abstract scholarly knowledge (*Wissenschaft*) that is necessary for generalized problem solving, and some degree of

trade training (*Ausbildung*) facilitating subsequent practical learning. The complex system of two tiers of state examinations, with the first testing scientific information and the second checking its application to practice, elevated all German academic vocations above lesser pursuits. (p. 14)

Just as "the law" provides the framework and the rationale for a lawyer's professional work, Didaktik was to emerge to provide rationales within the terms of which "professional" teachers could reason about, and if necessary defend, their interpretations of the *Lehrplan* as the authoritative administrative framework for their professional work. And over time Didaktik became, as Hopmann and Gundem (1998) pointed out, the common "language by which state administrators, principals, teachers, and all others involved in the process of education, could communicate about how to work within the framework" (p. 341) of the *Lehrplan*.

The form and manner of the intertwining of the state and the university around the professions in early 19th-century Germany also meant that the professions, and particularly Gymnasium or academic secondary school teachers and teachers in pedagogical seminaries, were influenced, in ways not found at any time in American public schooling, by "cultural" issues. The complex strains of influence that followed from this were central in the formation of the ideology of modern German teachers and teaching, and played a decisive role in the creation of both the intellectual and the professional framework around teaching that was to determine the essential character of both traditional and modern Didaktik. One strand of this influence was quite fundamental.

In the middle years of the 18th century, *Staatswissenschaften,* the sciences of the state, dominated both educated public opinion in the German lands and were the cutting edge of university change and reform.[2] These state sciences reflected a larger interest in practical and utilitarian images of the social order, the economy, and human nature. Thinking about education, *Pädagogik* was seen from this viewpoint as a form of inductive science that sought to develop an understanding of the universal principles governing human growth, and the "art" of applying those principles. The 18th-century *Staatswissenschaften* were, of course, the precursors of the "sciences" of society, that is, sociology and economics, and the individual, that is, psychology, that emerged in their modern form in the 19th century and, of course, became the sciences that American school leaders and researchers were to use, in the 20th century, to justify and rationalize their reforms of schooling.

However, in Germany, in the last years of the 18th century, a "new" creed emerged to contest the ideology of *Staatswissenschaften*. Instead of celebrat-

---

[2]For an extensive discussion of *Staatswissenschaften* in the 18th and 19th centuries, see Lindenfeld (1997).

ing the prosperity, order, and opportunity that was possible in a properly constituted state, the new generation of neo-humanists would write that:

> The true end of Man, or that which is prescribed by the eternal and immutable dictates of reason, and not suggested by the vague and transient, is the highest and most harmonious development of his powers to a complete and consistent whole. (Humboldt, 1969, p. 16)

This movement, with the word *Bildung* or "formation" as its "embodiment,"[3] was decisively important for the future of German thinking about teaching and schooling, and of the German professions and culture more generally.[4] It overwhelmingly captured the heart not only of university humanists and classicists, and the Gymnasium teachers and other professionals who graduated from their classes and seminars, but also much of German culture. Indeed, Louis Dumont's (1994) fascinating study, *German Ideology,* explores the idea of Bildung with its ebbs and flows as "representative of the entirety of German culture" in the 19th and 20th centuries:

> The German intellectual not only ignores society *(Gesellschaft)* in the narrow sense of the word, but at the same time, in his inner life, he thinks of himself as an individual and devotes all his care to the development of his personality. This is the famous ideal of *Bildung,* or "self-cultivation." . . . Here then is a duality which is both characteristic and at first sight puzzling. On the one

---

[3]*Bildung* is a noun meaning something like "being educated, educatedness." It also carries the connotations of the word *bilden,* "to form, to shape." *Bildung* is thus best translated as "formation," implying both the forming of the personality into a unity as well as the product of this formation and the particular "formedness" that is represented *by* the person. The "formation" in the idea of "spiritual formation" perfectly captures the German sense. I am indebted to Klaus Witz of the University of Illinois at Urbana-Champaign for this explication of Bildung.

As Lindenfeld (1997) wrote, "Embodiments are unit-ideas or symbols which serve to condense or fixate a variety of meanings or shades of meaning in a single unit. . . . By virtue of their simplicity, embodiments can be apprehended quickly and shared by diverse groups within a culture" (p. 7).

[4]In 1808 Friederich Immanuel Niehammer, a school councilor in Munich, elaborated a conception of Bildung as *the* rationale for a reformed secondary school, a move that La Vopa (1988) saw as the key step marking both the crystallization of a new educational ideology and the point "at which an emergent ideology was patterning in formulaic statement—the kind that could be incorporated into state laws and applied in organizational blueprints for schools" (p. 264).

Culturally, the ideal of Bildung gave a new twist to the traditional Lutheran concept of "vocation" and, in so doing, gave ideological legitimacy and a sense of purpose to secondary school teachers as they sought to separate themselves from the clergy to become members of an autonomous profession. It gave a new purpose and a new pedagogy to the classical curriculum and a new role for Greek in that curriculum as the core of "general human education." It condemned all older pedagogies, and the kind of rationalist Pädagogik that reduced the student (and teacher!) to "subject," the passive object of external manipulation.

hand, there is quiet survival, in modern times, of the community, that is to say, of a holistic feeling and orientation. . . . On the other hand, there is a pronounced inner development of individuality, a jealous interiority devoutedly attended to. (pp. 19–20)

Under the impulse of neo-humanism, this formative "inner development of individuality" was seen to occur as a result of the encounter of the individual with beauty and character in literature, in societies, and in cultures, and particularly the classical Greek culture. However, the actual form of this encounter in schools and universities in the first half of the 19th century was via teaching the methods necessary for the detailed, careful reading of the texts that embodied that culture, teaching that was pointed toward the independent, scholarly analysis of those texts to create new knowledge of the ancient world. The graduates of such teaching were socialized to image themselves as scholars teaching potential scholars the skills needed to do highly disciplined "research" (Grafton, 1983).

However, in the last decades of the 19th century a new generation of Bildung-centered teachers in *Gymnasien,* in pedagogical seminaries for elementary teacher education, and in university-based pedagogical seminaries for Gymnasium teachers began to articulate new conceptions of the teacher's role—although it was one that continued to draw heavily on the then century-old ideal of Bildung. Thus, beginning around the midcentury, Gymnasium teachers began to image themselves not as potential scholars in their own right but, rather, as cultural leaders who had as their central responsibility the task of teaching in a way that would and should breathe life into a school and a middle- and upper-class social culture that was seen as a dry and formulaic (Pyenson, 1983). This new self-conception of the Gymnasium teacher fused with the widespread acceptance of a "genetic," "heuristic" teaching practice that saw understanding as a process of becoming to be nurtured by teachers as they refined and clarified simple ideas in the classics, physics, math, and so on, in ways that permitted students to easily grasp them. If students were taught in this way it was believed that they could and would actively participate in their own formation and be led to the comprehensive worldview that was immanent in, say, the sciences, mathematics, or Greek and Latin literature.

In the same period, both pedagogical seminaries and state examinations to prepare and initially license elementary school teachers and state examinations for the further licensing of school leaders were being institutionalized. The need for a "content" for these institutions stimulated a different kind of exploration of the ideas of Bildung and the educational theories of Herbart, Pestalozzi, Froebel, and the like—which resulted in the emergence of an *allgemeine Didaktik* (i.e., a general, "whole-curriculum" Didaktik as distinct from the *Fachdidaktik,* i.e., subject-based Didaktiks, of the Gymnasium). It was from these seminaries that the first systematic compilations of Didaktik thought were to emerge; for elementary teachers, and for the teacher educators who worked alongside them, this Didaktik, a body of professional knowledge specific to their work, was crucial to their eventual professionalization.

The modern *bildungstheoretische* (Bildung-theory) and *kulturtheoretische* (culture theory) Didaktik traditions that Künzli describes in chapter 2, this volume, emerged in the last years of the 19th century and the first decades of the 20th century out of these streams of thought about the art of teaching. This new Didaktik brought together, and elaborated within the crucible of a new discipline of *Pädagogik,* or education, the central ideas and approaches of both the elementary school–based *allgemeine Didaktik* and the secondary school–based *Fachdidaktik*—as well as many elements of turn-of-the-century German culture. Thus, for the group around Herman Nohl (1879–1960) at the University of Gottingen, the *Geisteswissenschaft* (human-science) perspective of Wilhelm Dilthey, with its emphasis on the necessity of a hermeneutic orientation in research in the human sciences, provided the starting point for a highly elaborated version of *bildungstheoretische Didaktik,* the *geisteswissenschaftliche Pädagogik,* that is, human-science theory of education (see Weniger, chap. 6, this volume), that had at its center both an explicitly hermeneutic Didaktik as well as the period's concerns for a "progressive" reform of the school. The most developed, practical form of this human-science Didaktik is represented in this volume in Wolfgang Klafki's "Didaktik Analysis as the Core of Preparation of Instruction" (see chap. 8, this volume; see also chap. 5), but we also see its hermeneutic orientation in both "Didaktik as a Theory of Education" (see chap. 6, this volume) by Erich Weniger, Noel's succcessor as leader of the *Göttinger Schule,* and Heinrich Roth's "The Art of Lesson Preparation" (see chap. 7, this volume).

Although the forms of schooling and teaching associated and legitimated by the ideal of Bildung were to change in the course of the 19th and 20th centuries,[5] Bildung-centered humanism as an idea and ideal insulated much of German education from both empiricism and the idea that education, that is, Pädagogik, could be a science until well into the 1960s. And contemporary *bildungstheoretische Didaktik,* and the subject-matter Didaktiks that flow from it, continue to be centered on the idea of Bildung and on the ideal of the teacher as a reflective professional working within, but not directed by, the

---

[5]The idea of Bildung has provided German educational thought with a stable language that can be turned in ever-new directions: Thus, as Ringer (1990) noted, in Weimar Germany "The modernists asked themselves, for example, how the ideal of self-cultivation might be relevant to the experience of a factory worker, or to a much enlarged system of secondary schooling, or to sources of Bildung other than those of classical antiquity" (p. 18). And, as seen in Klafki's chapter (chap. 5, this volume), postwar didacticians continued to reformulate and extend the neo-humanist legacy so that it could direct thinking about the democratic, egalitarian, and in the 1960s and 1970s, critical tasks of both elementary and secondary schooling.

framework provided by the "text" of the state curriculum, the *Lehrplan*. It continues to search for ways of offering students an experience that can assist their development of a comprehensive worldview. It continues to seek the explication of generalizable forms of teacher thinking and reflection, and examples of such thinking, to support the search for ways in which classroom practices and environments can support a personal and subjective encounter by students with potentially educative (in the sense of Bildung) subject matters, forms of social life, tradition, and the like. In the words of Wolfgang Klafki (see chap. 8, this volume), one of the leaders of the post–World War II restoration and extension of the Weimar period's *geisteswissenschaftliche Pädagogik:*

> The task of Didaktik analysis . . . is . . . to establish as the pedagogically crucial elements of the material those parts "on which its internalization [one could also say, its power to penetrate] depends or, inversely, in which the form of subjective Bildung is fulfilled and perfected." . . . In other words, Didaktik analysis is to indicate wherein the general substance of specific content of education lies.

To do this, Didaktik provides models of teacher thinking, the elaborated forms of *Didaktik analysis* seen in chapter 8, this volume, which can be institutionalized in teacher education and can, when internalized, structure reflection on the *transformation* to active life in the classroom of the educational potential that is available in the *Lehrplan*. Although contemporary Didaktik seeks to do this with a more critical stance toward the *Lehrplan* than is found in the classical *bildungstheoretische Didaktik* tradition, the underlying Bildung-centered starting point of the traditional Didaktik remains. And although *Fachdidaktik*, the Didaktik of subject-based teaching, has assimilated the frameworks of one or another psychology, it has, as we see in the chapters by Peter Reinhold (chap. 17, this volume) and Michael Neubrand (chap. 14, this volume) in Part IV, maintained its links with traditional Didaktik with its overriding concern for the formative potential of subject matter. Didaktik in all its forms is teacher rather than system centered: Its focus, and ideal, is on the role of the teacher in "forming" rather than "instructing" his or her students and, to do this, celebrates the individuality of each teacher as an active, reflective curriculum maker and theorist rather than seeing the teacher as an agent of a workplace manual of best practices, that is, a curriculum or curriculum package.

DIDAKTIK AND CURRICULUM THEORY

To this point I have attempted to set out the context and character of the curriculum and Didaktik traditions separately. Now let me try to sketch the differences I see between the two systems more systematically. They are, as I have indicated, very different in their environing contexts, in their starting points and methods, and in the work they seek to do—but mapping these differences lays out a richly textured territory.

Let me begin by summarizing the argument of the previous sections about the institutional contexts of curriculum theory and Didaktik. In the American world, there is a vision of a system of schools with clear public purposes and well-articulated curriculum, and a consequent strong and overt formal control over teachers as *employees* of the system. In this context, "professionalism" is a contested and attenuated aspiration for American secondary or elementary teachers, and this is reflected in the language used to describe teacher education: Teachers are "trained" and "certified" to teach the curriculum—and then retrained and "inserviced." Teachers are not "licensed" as self-determining professionals who work within a larger institutional framework that directs, but does not control the details of their work.

As I have noted, in the United States the role of the system in prescribing what teachers do—*as employees*—has been traditionally symbolized by the notion of the curriculum as an authoritative and directive manual of teaching tasks to be undertaken and procedures to be used. It is the responsibility of the elected governing authorities of each school system to determine the curricula (and the textbooks that will be used) that instantiate and symbolize the public values and goals of the school system—although more recently external testing has been the preferred mechanism of symbolic and organizational control. Traditional American curriculum thought has found its problems, and derived its language, from the framing assumptions that this context creates; traditional curriculum ideology, scholarship, and practice is the servant of this larger institution—as is symbolized by its preoccupation with "curriculum *implementation*."

In Germany, on the other hand, teaching in the Gymnasium, or academic secondary school, was firmly "professionalized" by the mid-19th century—and, as Jarausch (1990b) observed, the German professional ideal, which was to spread from academic secondary teachers to other kinds of teachers, centers on an effort to establish a "middle ground of *expert self-determination*" (p. 217, emphasis added) against bureaucratic, that is, systemic, regulation. Like lawyers and engineers:

> [Teachers] expected autonomy of practice, with their "professional" decisions reviewed not by clients or employers, but by peers in a system of self-discipline. To justify such privileges, these callings embraced an ethos of public service, which was linked to central social values such as law, knowledge, and progress. (Jarausch, 1990b, p. 219)

For the teacher the *Bildungsideale* is the "central social value" of teaching as a profession.

Didaktik is the institutionalized framework within which both generalist and subject teachers, and the profession of teaching, has pursued, and pursues, its aspiration to professional self-determination. Didaktik, as a body of theories and frameworks that order the considerations involved in planning for and thinking about Bildung-centered, formative teaching, provides the language for teacher reflection—and, as such, is a necessary and principal focus of formal teacher education. And although the *Lehrplan,* the state's framework for teaching, provides the institutional *context* for the teacher's work, this context is seen as embedded in the more fundamental social value of a *Bildungsideale* and the art of Didaktik analysis and reasoning, which serves to marry the resources the culture has for formation, represented in the *Lehrplan,* with the ideal of Bildung as both a process and an end.

Through and by way of Didaktik reflection each and every teacher must determine, as an expert professional, what must be done in this setting, with this material, with these students, in the light of the values associated with Bildung—or that is the ideal. In the thesis that is part of the Second State Examination, every teacher must demonstrate how they marry, using the languages provided by one or another form of Didaktik analysis, the values represented by the teacher's role as a public servant working within the framework of the *Lehrplan,* understandings of the ideals embedded within Bildung, and the formative "needs" of their students (see chap. 13, this volume, for an example of such a thesis). In this world "curriculum change" takes place as the schools are "reformed," as teachers make their independent judgments—in the light of *their* sense of the central social value associated with Bildung—that a new way is preferable to an old way.

These different contexts for teaching in the American and German worlds also provide the starting points within which curriculum and Didaktik *as intellectual traditions* have found their tasks. We can see what these differences mean when we compare these traditions using as the framework for the analysis the elements of a slightly modified version of the classical formulation of the *Didaktik triangle* (see chap. 2, this volume). I suggest that the different understandings of the enveloping topic of *subject matter* seen in the two traditions lead to very different interpretations of the meaning of the elements of the triangle (see Fig. 1.1; the figure replaces the "teacher" in the traditional formulation with "agent").

For Didaktik, with its Bildung-centered, humanist roots, there is a basic distinction between the external, objective aspects of the subject matters to be taught in the school and their inner, formative meaning:

> An entity is educative if it leads to an experience of values, creates intellectual needs, spiritualizes vital drives, forms attitudes, sparks moral understanding. . . . The educative moments of the object are those that attract vital interests, that capture feelings and emotions, but that in the dealings with the object—and

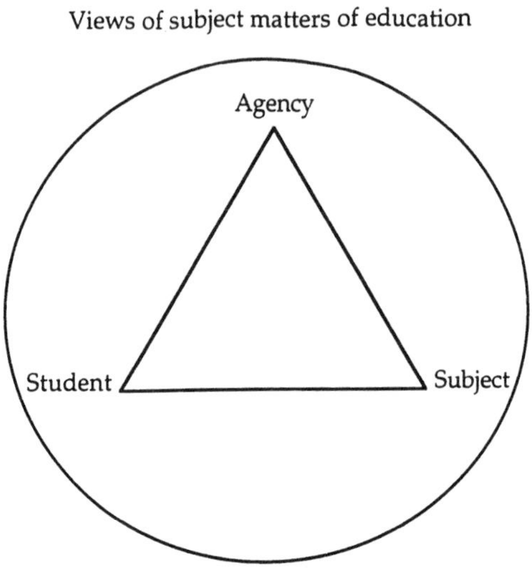

Views of subject matters of education

FIG. 1.1. The Didaktik and curriculum triangle.

this is the crucial point—transform: direct and bind them to higher values, in other words, moralize and spiritualize. (Roth, chap. 7, this volume)

There are many metaphors for those activities that help to bring together the general and the individual, the objective and the subjective, for example, "reciprocating," "exchanging," "unifying," or "encountering." The objective side is perceived as factual, as independently valid; the subjective side is spontaneous in the acquisition of reality. *It is these two factors that enable the teacher to function as a link.* (Menck, chap. 10, this volume, emphasis added)

An individual teacher is the *only* agent of such exchange and encounter by his or her students, and thus the animating heart of any realization of a *Bildungsideale*. The *Lehrplan* prescribes the traditions and topics, the "objects" in Roth's words, or the "general" and the "objective" in Menck's words, that will provide the content of teaching. But each teacher must understand this content as a reflection of the communal values that it represents, reflects, and might nurture, *and* be constantly aware of the subjective self-formation that teaching seeks to support. The deliberative reflection that this conception of formation requires is at the core of the Didaktik tradition of theory building and praxis.

For curriculum theory, on the other hand, the curriculum and its subject matters do not have the dualism that is the heart of the idea of Bildung as formation through contact with a culture and its objects. The topics of the curriculum are bodies of information, repositories of skills and objective understandings, or ways of knowing, that can be specified, stand apart from the learner and the teacher, but can be "taught" using appropriate methods.

And, of course, there is the clear implication that the efficacy of a curriculum and of teaching can be rationally evaluated. Thus the task of the curriculum maker is to build an organizational and/or curricular framework or program that optimizes the match between the educational and social goals of the school system, subject matters and topics, and the objective "educational needs" of students—while minimizing the problems that the idiosyncrasies of individual teachers pose for the effectiveness of the total system.

For curriculum, the central construct is, therefore, the abstracted, objective concept of *agency,* a school system that seeks to institutionally transmit appropriate understandings of content seen unproblematically as this or that view of and authoritative selection from a larger, objectively valid subject matter. The central questions are: What knowledge is of most worth for this *kind* of student? How might the most appropriate and effective *instructional structuring* of that knowledge be determined? and How might that determination be implemented in this *agency* or school system? As the systematic, institutional program planning and evaluation that seeks to answer these questions is undertaken, a fourth necessary and central topic is added to the three terms of the Didaktik triangle, *milieu:* Effective curriculum building needs to understand the appropriate functional matches between the "purposes" of education and the larger social and economic context or milieu and link those understandings to a school's programs. Figure 1.2 seeks to summarize this interpretation of the central concerns of curriculum theory.

For Didaktik, on the other hand, it is the individual teacher who nurtures the *self-formation* that is at the heart of Bildung: Human individuality can be

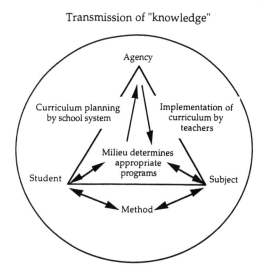

FIG. 1.2. The curriculum triangle.

nurtured only by people—no abstracted and institutional "system" can support individual, interior formation. Thus Didaktik gives to each and every teacher the reflective task both of discerning what formative value is available for his or her students in this or that element of the *Lehrplan* and of developing his or her own teaching plans to instantiate those values. The core of the teacher's professional work to discerning in what way, and how, such a web of potential interactions might be productively engaged—and to search for ways and means for such engagement. Didaktik seeks to explicate, and then find a usable framework for thinking about, teacherly reflection and deliberation around such a task. Thus *teacher* and *teacher planning* are the key terms in Didaktik's interpretation of the triangle. Figure 1.3 summarizes this interpretation of the central concerns of Didaktik.

CAN DIDAKTIK TEACH CURRICULUM?

If the analysis summarized in Figs. 1.2 and 1.3 has succeeded in capturing the hearts of Didaktik and curriculum theory, we have in these traditions the very different frameworks for thinking about "curriculum" summarized in Table 1.1. Seen separately, the two traditions reflect, most centrally, very different imagings of the work of schooling and teaching, and they offer different interpretations of the idea and ideal of "education." But when they are seen comparatively, the two frameworks have complementary thrusts. Curriculum seeks to provide a structured framework for thinking about

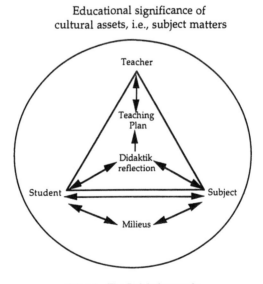

FIG. 1.3. The Didaktik triangle.

institutional issues—when, for example, the questions circle around the institutional forms that are needed to realize collective aspirations; Didaktik, on the other hand, seeks to provide a framework for teacher thinking about the most basic how, what, and why questions around their work.

Curriculum addresses the "system" and the "needs" of the larger social and cultural order. Didaktik, with its starting point in a vision of the teacher transforming the bodies of content reflected in a *Lehrplan* into an educative subject matter for the classroom, has developed rich frameworks for thinking about education and children's life worlds and, particularly, about the reflective *transformation* of subject material into teaching that reflects a *Bildungsideale* for this class and these students. *It is a teacher's rather than policymaker's or system administrator's framework.* And in its institutionalized aspects, as seen both in its elaborated models for Didaktik analysis as a starting point for reflection on practice and in the role of these models in teacher education and teacher licensing, Didaktik instantiates models of teacher thinking and practices in teacher education to support its image of this thinking that are completely absent from the Anglo-Saxon tradition.

But the differences between Didaktik and curriculum that I began this chapter discussing remain and provoke interesting and fundamental questions: Is there a way, or a circumstance, in which the forms of thinking associated with Didaktik and traditional curriculum theory can be seen as usefully complementing each other? How? Or must they remain separate? And, if they complement each other, what different potentials do they offer for addressing the bewildering variety of questions around curriculum studies? Before I can consider these questions I must explicate the elusive term, *curriculum*.

Following Doyle (1992, 1995[6]), curriculum, and the related discussion and argument, can be seen occurring at two distinct levels of schooling: (a) the *policy* and *programmatic levels*, that is, at institutional levels, and (b) the *classroom* level. At the *institutional level* curricular discussions emerge in two basic arenas:

- At the intersection between schooling, culture, and society, the *policy level.*
- In the analysis of content for and in school tracks and their "subjects" and in the construction of appropriate content for classroom use, the *programmatic level.*

At the *classroom level,* curricular reflection, discussion, and argument is seen as the programmatic curriculum is further elaborated and connected to the

---

[6]Based on a parallel analysis of the curriculum, Hopmann and Künzli identify *political, programmatic,* and *practical* levels of curriculum action. These words capture somewhat different aspects of the notions Doyle articulated. Hopmann and Künzli are currently undertaking an empirical exploration of these "levels" in a European cross-national study.

events of the classroom and the worlds of real flesh-and-blood students. It is at this level that curriculum and pedagogy merge.

In curricular discussions at the institutional and programmatic level, we can see two major foci of concern:

- The form of the ideal curriculum or curricula that are seen as defining the connection between schooling and both a culture and a society.
- The nature and character of the curricular structures and programs that translate the abstract curriculum into the organizational frameworks that are the ultimate basis for a system of schools and their work.

Discussion of curriculum at the intersection of schooling and society centers on images, metaphors, and narratives as broad typifications of what can happen in a school. Such typifications are fundamentally important because they embody conceptions of what is desirable in social and cultural orders, what is and should be valued and sought after by members of a community. Curriculum planning at the institutional level, and the public processes involved in such planning, is a social form for both clarifying social and cultural norms and responsibilities around schooling and bringing larger social values to bear on the special role schooling is to play in realizing social and cultural ideals. In another sense the *variety* of typifications around the institutional curriculum available at any time provide, as one or another language is embraced, languages that school people can use to redefine the curriculum to meet changing social and cultural circumstances.

The programmatic or organizational curriculum, as a framework for organizing schooling as "educational" service delivery, involves complex processes through which one or another curricular vision or typification is translated into an operational framework for systems of schools, and for understanding what social, cultural, and educational images mean for the character of work in classrooms. At this level the process of constructing curricula-as-programs is grounded in arguments that rationalize the selection and arrangement of subject-matter content for schools of particular types *and* the transformation of that content into school subjects appropriate to those schools or school types. Thus, the organizational curriculum looks backward (or upward) to typifications of the ideal curriculum, but it also depends on the understandings that emerge from implicit and explicit theories of content that link the aims of education to the images of the activities of teaching. *But this link between the organizational curriculum and teaching is not direct and addresses an image of teaching rather than teaching itself.* At this level teaching is characterized, as Doyle (1992) noted, as dependent on, or as an instantiation of, the organizational curriculum or the program.

However, at the classroom level, curriculum is a sequence of events, initiated by the teacher and jointly developed by teachers and students, that reflects a view of the organizational curriculum as a potentially educative (or, in the language of Didaktik, "formative") experience for students. Such events require and depend on societal, teacher, and student interpretations and understandings of culture and schooling, how they are constructed, how they affect the curriculum, and thus what the institutional curriculum actually comes to be in the events of teaching. *Teachers are the essential interpreters of that institutional and programmatic curriculum and its Bildungsideale—in Germany—or its educational ideal—in the English-speaking world.* They guide students through its topics, shape the views of that curriculum that are allowed, and, important to note, define the tasks that students are to accomplish and that instantiate the classroom curriculum. Teachers everywhere are the only "authors" of curriculum events.

This conceptualization provides a way of gathering the threads of this speculative chapter together—and also provides a starting point for reading the later chapters of this book. Thus, and as I have emphasized throughout this chapter, American curriculum theory (and practice) is a search for a way of ordering, intellectually and in praxis, *institutional curricula:*

- At the intersection between the society and the culture and the school, that is, the interaction between social and cultural understandings and the tasks of schooling.
- As a search for ways to manage and regulate the decisions that the society and polity has made about the curriculum within the schools seen as a service delivery system.

However, the American preoccupation with the institutional curriculum has meant that the classroom curriculum has been neglected in American writing and thinking about the curriculum. Teachers are imaged as agents of the decisions made at organizational and programmatic levels. The role of the teacher as an interpreter and author of the curriculum has been uncertainly seen in the dominant traditions for thinking about the curriculum.

In recent years, of course, the traditional curriculum theory, as I have described it in this chapter, has been subjected to sustained criticism originating from a wide variety of theoretical perspectives—and one result has been a new focus on the role of the teacher as an active maker of the classroom curriculum. As Doyle (1994; see also Doyle, 1995) wrote, reflecting this shift in concern and its rationale:

> Teaching and teacher education can never be treated solely as a matter of technical proficiency. Teaching is, at its core, an interpretive process grounded in conceptions of what one is teaching and what value that content has for students and society. . . . *To teach effectively, teachers must be responsible curriculum theorists.* (p. 8, emphasis added)

To use a different image, teachers must be "reflective."

It is, of course, just such a starting point, with its focus on the classroom curriculum as an instantiation of the curriculum as something with formative potential, that has been at the heart of Didaktik. *Didaktik represents a sustained attempt to work out what it means for teachers to be Doyle's "responsible curriculum theorists"* as they think about their work.

Although there are real problems—which must be acknowledged—in any mapping of the specifics of the Didaktiks and Fachdidaktiks set out in the chapters of this volume into the Anglo-Saxon conceptual framework, the *general* orientation that underlies Didaktik does confront the central issues opened up, *but not resolved*, by the contemporary shift in American curriculum theory. *All Didaktik approaches—particularly the Didaktik associated with the human-science, cultural philosophy paradigm, i.e.,* geisteswissenschaftliche Pädagogik *(see Weniger, chap. 6 and Klafki, chap. 8 this volume)—address, frontally and head-first, Doyle's assertion that "teaching is, at its core, an interpretative process" and show what one highly developed elaboration of such a conception can mean.* Didaktik gives the image of the teacher as a "reflective practitioner" a meaning that it does not have in the Anglo-Saxon work that invokes this phrase by unpacking Doyle's (1992) concept of "*transformation*":

> The doing of both curriculum and pedagogy involves transforming content in some way. . . . A central issue for inquiry at the intersection of curriculum and pedagogy is the grounds on which such transformations, especially at the classroom level, are made. . . . a curriculum is not simply content, but a theory of content, that is, a conception of what the content is, what it means to know that content, and what goal one is accomplishing when one is teaching the content. (p. 507)

The chapters in Part III of this book—for example, those by Roth (chap. 7), Klafki (chap. 8), and Wagenschein (chap. 9)—illustrate Didaktik's theoretical and prescriptive exploration of this "central issue for inquiry" most directly—although in different ways—and, in doing so, show what a classroom- and teacher-centered conception of curriculum as a theory of content can mean. The chapters in Part IV show these same issues being worked out in a different way—at a variety of levels of teaching practice and in scholarly exploration of *possible* classroom practice. Together the chapters in Parts III and IV offer curriculum theorists a rich and exciting image of the curriculum theory that the American curriculum "reconceptualism" has been searching for, but not found.

Thus although, as I have suggested, Didaktik and curriculum as institutionalized traditions find their starting points at different levels on what may be seen as a continuum of concern—and are, therefore, clearly and profoundly complementary—they are, nevertheless, in fundamental tension because of their very different culturally embedded starting points. Each tradition is firmly located in the particularities of each culture's "national histories, of national habits, and national aspirations"—to recall Reid's (1998, pp. 11–12) words.[7] Thus, Didaktik and curriculum theory address different issues and begin with different contextual assumptions. These starting points lead to different understandings of even the word *education* itself with, on the one hand, that word's "subjectified" connotation in the German tradition and its "objectified" interpretation in the American tradition. As a result, any attempt to yoke Didaktik and curriculum too firmly within the common framework suggested by a notion of a curriculum continuum engages these tensions—with the result that, were we to see the two traditions merely as two sides of the same coin, they would be in tension at almost every point at which they might connect. Yet despite this reality, when seen as a tradition that addresses the classroom curriculum, and the necessary role of the teacher as a curriculum theorist or reflective practitioner, Didaktik has intensively explored what has been, to this point, a void in American curriculum theory. In addition, the Didaktik tradition offers forms and models for well-honed practices of teacher education and teacher development that can renew and enrich the education of teachers who are not well served within the assumptions of traditional curriculum theory. In other words, there *are* important lessons to be learned from Germany's Didaktikers.

ACKNOWLEDGMENTS

An earlier version of his chapter was published with the title "Didaktik and Curriculum Theory: Are They Two Sides of the Same Coin?" in Stefan Hopmann and Kurt Riquarts (Eds.), *Didaktik and/or Curriculum*, IPN 147 (Kiel: Institut für die Pädagogik der Naturwissenschaften, 1995), and this revised version of that paper is published here with the permission of the Institut für die Pädagogik der Naturwissenschaften.

The work reported in this chapter was supported, in part, by the Spencer Foundation, Chicago. The opinions expressed here do not, of course, reflect the views of the Spencer Foundation. I must also acknowledge my indebtedness to Stefan Hopmann for the assistance and guidance he gave through-

---

[7]Thus although much of the contemporary curriculum theorizing in the United States is setting its sights on the classroom curriculum, policymaking around the curriculum, and most of the thinking around such policymaking, has maintained the traditional focus on the *system* and the use of the instruments and practices of the traditional curriculum theory—although with a firmer and more comprehensive sense of the system than is found in the older tradition (see, e.g., Goertz, Floden, & O'Day, 1996). We see in this continuing preoccupation an instantiation of the assumptions that have always circled around American schooling with its central awareness that classroom curricula *aggregate* to create collective and institutional phenomena and effects.

out the writing of this chapter. Walter Doyle provided crucial insights when I was losing sight of the issues. Tone Carlsten, Tomas Englund, Peter Menck, Bill Reid, Francis Schrag, and Max van Manen provided very helpful comments on earlier drafts of the chapter. Needless to say, none of these colleagues is responsible for what I have made of their help!

REFERENCES

Airasian, P. (1994). The impact of the taxonomy on testing and evaluation. In L. W. Anderson & L. A. Sosniak (Eds.), *Bloom's taxonomy: A forty-year retrospective* (93rd Yearbook, Part 2, of the National Society for the Study of Education, pp. 82–102). Chicago: University of Chicago Press.

Clandinin, D. J., & Connelly, M. F. (1992). Teacher as curriculum maker. In P. W. Jackson (Ed.), *Handbook of research on curriculum* (pp. 363–401). New York: Macmillan.

Doyle, W. (1992). Curriculum and pedagogy. In P. W. Jackson (Ed.), *Handbook of research on curriculum* (pp. 486–516). New York: Macmillan.

Doyle, W. (1994, April). *Why Didaktik might be of interest to Americans.* Paper presented at the annual meeting of the American Educational Research Association, New Orleans (Tucson, AZ: College of Education, University of Arizona).

Doyle, W. (1995). Studying the enacted curriculum. In S. Hopmann & K. Riquarts (Eds.), *Didaktik and/or Curriculum* (pp. 267–288). Kiel, Germany: Institut für die Pädagogik der Naturwissenschaften an der Universität Kiel.

Doyle, W., & Westbury, I. (1992). Die Rückbesinnung auf den Unterrichtsinhalt in der Curriculum- und Bildungsforschung in den USA. *Bildung und Erziehung, 45*(2), 137–157.

Dumont, L. (1994). *German ideology: From France to Germany and back.* Chicago: University of Chicago Press.

Goertz, M. E., Floden, R. E., & O'Day, J. (1996). *Systemic reform* (Pub. No. ORAD 96-1322). (Washington, DC: U.S. Department of Education, Office of Educational Research and Improvement.

Grafton, A. (1983). Polyhistor into *Philolog:* Notes on the transformation of German classical scholarship, 1780–1850. In C. Schmitt (Ed.), *History of universities* (Vol. 3, pp. 159–192). Amersham, England: Avebury.

Hlebowitsh, P. S. (1992). Amid behavioral and behavioristic objectives: Reappraising appraisals of the Tyler *Rationale. Journal of Curriculum Studies, 24*(6), 533–547.

Hopmann, S., & Gundem, B. B. (1998). Didaktik meets curriculum: Towards a new agenda. In B. B. Gundem & Stefan Hopmann (Eds.), *Didaktik and/or curriculum: An international dialogue* (pp. 331–353). New York: Peter Lang.

Hopmann, S., & Riquarts, K. (1995). Didaktik and/or curriculum: Basic problems of comparative Didaktik. In S. Hopmann & K. Riquarts (Eds.), *Didaktik and/or curriculum* (IPN 147, pp. 9–40). Kiel, Germany: Institut für die Pädagogik der Naturwissenschaften an der Universität Kiel.

Humboldt, W. von. (1969). *The limits of state action* (J. W. Burrow, Ed.). Cambridge, England: Cambridge University Press.

Jarausch, K. H. (1990a). The German professions in history and theory. In G. Cocks & K. H. Jarausch (Eds.), *German professions, 1800–1950* (pp. 9–26). New York and Oxford, England: Oxford University Press.

Jarausch, K. H. (1990b). *The unfree professions: German lawyers, teachers, and engineers, 1900–1950.* New York: Oxford University Press.

Kaestle, C. F. (1973a). *The evolution of an urban school system: New York City, 1750–1850.* Cambridge, MA: Harvard University Press.

Kaestle, C. F. (1973b). *Joseph Lancaster and the monitorial movement: A documentary history* (Classics in Education, No. 47). New York: Teachers College Press.

Klafki, W. (1995). On the problem of teaching and learning contents from the standpoint of critical-constructive Didaktik. In S. Hopmann & K. Riquarts (Eds.), *Curriculum and/or Didaktik* (IPN 147, pp. 187–200). Kiel, Germany: Institut für die Pädagogik der Naturwissenschaften.

La Vopa, A. J. (1988). *Grace, talent, and merit: Poor students, clerical careers, and professional ideology in eighteenth century Germany.* Cambridge, England: Cambridge University Press.

Lindenfeld, D. F. (1997). *The practical imagination: The German sciences of the state in the nineteenth century.* Chicago: University of Chicago Press.

Pyenson, L. (1983). *Neohumanism and the persistence of pure mathematics in Wilhelmian Germany* (Memoirs of the American Philosophical Society, Vol. 150). Philadelphia: American Philosophical Society.

Reid, W. A. (1998). Systems and structures or myths and fables? A cross-cultural perspective on curriculum content. In B. B. Gundem & S. Hopmann (Eds.), *Didaktik and/or curriculum: An international dialogue* (pp. 11–27). New York: Peter Lang.

Ringer, F. (1990). "Bildung" and its implications in the German tradition, 1890–1930. In W. Nijhof (Ed.), *Values in higher education: "Bildungsideale" in historical and contemporary perspective* (pp. 1–22). Enschede, Netherlands: University of Twente, Department of Education.

Tyler, R. W. (1949). *Basic principles of curriculum and instruction.* Chicago: University of Chicago Press.

Wallin, E. (1998). Changing paradigms of curriculum and/or Didaktik. In B. B. Gundem & S. Hopmann (Eds.), *Didaktik and/or curriculum: An international dialogue* (pp. 127–146). New York: Peter Lang.

Westbury, I. (1992). Curriculum studies in the United States: Reflections on a conversation with Ulf Lundgren. In D. Broady (Ed.), *Education in the late 20th century: Essays presented to Ulf P. Lundgren on the occasion of his fiftieth birthday* (pp. 117–140). Stockholm, Sweden: Stockholm Institute of Education Press.

Westbury, I. (1994). Deliberation and the improvement of schooling. In J. T. Dillon (Ed.), *Deliberation in education and society* (pp. 37–65). Norwood, NJ: Ablex.

2

German Didaktik: Models of Re-presentation, of Intercourse, and of Experience

Rudolf Künzli
Gillian Horton-Krüger (Trans.)

Rudolf Künzli is director of the Didaktikum in Aarau, the teacher education college of the canton of Argau, Switzerland. He is editor (with B. Adl-Amini) of Didaktische Modelle und Unterrichtsplanung (Munich: Juventa).

What Is Didaktik?

There is no uniform or even homogeneous conception of the object, method, and system of Didaktik within German educational research or teacher education[1] and, indeed, the word itself is used with a variety of meanings.[2]

---

[1]The adjective "German" is used here to denote a linguistic and cultural area. It is not intended to refer to a geographical entity, and certainly not to a particular nation or state. "German Didaktik" therefore refers to the contributions, past and present, within a more or less explicit German-speaking tradition.

[2]The Greek root of the word *Didaktik* means the action of showing and indicating. *Didaktike techne,* or Didaktik, would thus be the art of showing, of pointing and drawing attention, of allowing something that does not simply demonstrate itself, or cannot be understood, to be seen, perceived, and recognized. In keeping with this original meaning of the word, Didaktik can be used to mean the science of such actions of demonstrating or, more specifically, as the science of instruction—Didaktik as theory of instruction and the embodiment of knowledge about instruction. On the other hand, it can also be used to refer to the more or less binding set of rules governing skilled teaching and reflecting the professional ability of the teacher. No strict delineation is made between the meanings, that is, between "theory of instruction" and "art of instruction." There is, therefore, some justification for saying that the *Great Didactic* of Comenius (first published in 1638) and the *Neue Lehrart* (A New Way of Teaching) of Wolfgang Ratke, or Ratichius (first published in 1612), together with J. F. Herbart's decisive *Allgemeine Pädagogik aus dem Zweck der Erziehung abgeleitet* (1806) (General Pedagogy Derived From the Purpose of Education), have continued to influence German pedagogical approaches in their scope and in their claim to synthesize the theory and the craft.

The various views and schools of Didaktik differ significantly, and may even be considered to encompass those German-speaking educationalists whose work is not specifically termed Didaktik but is, nevertheless, Didaktik in all but name, and is understood as such by their colleagues. In the 1970s and 1980s, under the influence of a more empirical approach to instructional research (*realistische Wende* or "realistic turn" was the term coined for this by Heinrich Roth, 1967) and a growing interest in American curriculum studies, German Didaktik became ideologically suspect and tended to be considered outdated.[3] This has now changed: Didaktik has been rejuvenated and reinstated as a fashionable concept (Hopmann & Künzli, 1992; see also Hopmann & Riquarts, Introduction, this volume), a development that gives an indication of the paradigmatic character of the Didaktik approach to the problem of organized teaching in the German-speaking world.[4] This chapter presents a short synopsis of the tradition, a discussion of the significance and the application of German Didaktik, and a description of its theories and instruments.

Didaktik developed primarily as the discipline of teacher education, and preservice teacher training is traditionally the context in which its theories are produced and applied. This explains the high status of "models" within Didaktik, mostly theories of Bildung condensed into instruments of training and development.[5] More recent works present Didaktik as a multiperspectival concept, although there is still no clear formal definition.

Jank and Meyer (1990) spoke of Didaktik as the theory and practice of teaching and learning. Klafki (1971) identified four applications:

In view of the Herbartian concept of "educating instruction," the two concepts of "Didaktik" and "Pädagogik" can be read as largely synonymous, which is what happened in Herbartian teacher education. Compare Adl-Amini, Oelkers, & Neumann (1979).

[3]The two prominent works in the vanguard of this development were Robinsohn (1967) and Frey (1970). Curriculum was seen as a modern competitor to Didaktik, as a body of theory that was more able to assimilate the new demands being made on research and science by schools, administration, and teacher education. Those who continued to use the term *Didaktik* did so in conjunction with the term *curriculum*. A characteristic example is the entry entitled "Curriculum-Didaktik" by Klafki (1974, pp. 117–128), one of the leading figures of Didaktik, in the 1974 *Wörterbuch der Erziehung*. Later, however, the term *curriculum* began to lose currency and, as early as 1983, the two-volume dictionary of basic pedagogical terms edited by Lenzen (1989) defined the term *allgemeine Didaktik*, yet had no entry at all under *curriculum*, although the editor himself had previously been a representative of the curriculum movement.

[4]I use the term *organized teaching (organisiertes Lehren)* instead of *instruction* or *teaching* to indicate that Didaktik can be understood as being independent of the level and the organizational form of teaching and its instruments employed on this premise.

[5]The formation of schemata, presented mainly in the form of tables and figures (see Memmert, 1977), is an essential element of this tradition, and their use simply as formulae or recipes for teaching is, therefore, a much-discussed problem within Didaktik (see Grell & Grell, 1979; Meyer, 1986).

- Didaktik as a science of teaching and learning.
- Didaktik as a "science of instruction," or a "general theory of instruction."
- Didaktik as theory of educative contents *(Bildungsinhalte)*, of their structure and selection, their teaching and learning objectives, and the teaching and learning tasks that can be assigned to them, or as theory of the "categories of Bildung."
- Didaktik as "theory of the control of learning processes," as "economics of mediation."

Each of these conceptions has its proponents. Kron (1993) claimed to identify five basic dimensions of Didaktik:

- Didaktik as the science of the processes of mediating culture in specific societies.
- Didaktik as social science.
- Didaktik as comprehending, explanatory, action-oriented social science.
- Didaktik as teaching and learning processes of any kind in any place.
- The contents of teaching and learning processes as the cultural and social values and norms of society.

But, to simplify and summarize, Didaktik can be said to deal with the following questions:

- What is to be taught and learned? (i.e., the content aspect).
- How is "content" to be taught and learned? (i.e., the mediation or method aspect).
- Why is "content" to be taught and learned? (i.e., the goal aspect).

However, we may identify the more or less explicit predominance of the content aspect over the other aspects of instruction as the fundamental characteristic of German Didaktik, controversial though this often proves.[6] Even issues of goals and interaction appear to be subsumed under the content aspect.

More specific differentiations have been made to characterize a number of theories of Didaktik. There are descriptions of Didaktik in a "wider" or

---

[6]The controversies on this subject, now notorious, are summarized in the collection *Didaktik-Methodik* (Adl-Amini, 1981). The main protagonists were W. Klafki and the members of the "Berlin School" of Didaktik around Paul Heimann (see *Didaktik als Theorie und Lehre,* 1970), later including Schulz and Otto. The "Berlin Model" that emerged has influenced teacher education in Germany for decades.

"narrower" sense, referring in the first case to the conception of Didaktik as an instrument of instructional guidance and an aid for the preparation of instruction and, in the second, to the whole of organized teaching and learning, particularly, to curricula and their justification and interpretation in terms of *Bildungstheorie,* or educational theory. Klafki in particular popularized a differentiation of this kind in the tradition of Willmann (*Didaktik als Bildungslehre,* 1957) and Weniger (*Theorie des Lehrplans und der Bildungsinhalte,* 1990). These works are fundamental to German Didaktik, not least because they were the starting point for Klafki's (1959; 1964) theory of "categorical education" *(kategoriale Bildung),* which he transposed into a model of Didaktik analysis for use in teacher education, a model that has become highly influential (see chap. 8, this volume).

German Didaktik as an academic discipline is characterized by a differentiation between the general *(allgemeine Didaktik)* and the specific, that is, focusing on specific teaching subjects *(Fachdidaktik).* This division reflects the theoretical and historical background. General Didaktik is not to be understood as a merely formal theory of method for the art of teaching, devoid of content. However, it does insist, in contrast to subject-specific Didaktik, that the question of content should not be automatically predetermined by the disciplines, but that it is the task of Didaktik to identify the contents that are significant for Bildung through an analysis of the whole life of a culture. In this tradition, which may be termed the *classical Didaktik,* the individual academic disciplines play only a marginal role: They are neither the main source of content, nor even a source of criteria to govern the choice of contents and their mediation. This separation has significant consequences for the organization and sociology of the academic disciplines at German-speaking universities.[7]

Theoretical and Historical Background of Didaktik

In its specifically German configuration, Didaktik is the historical product of a development in the early 20th century, when human-science research confronted its Herbartian precursors on the one hand and a program of "experimental" educational research on the other. This confrontation dominated Didaktik from the turn of the century to the 1920s, the era in which Pädagogik, or education, was institutionalized as a university discipline. The human-science, cultural philosophy paradigm, that is, *geisteswissenschaftliche Pädagogik,* proved dominant and was assimilated by the postwar pedagogical studies of the 1940s and 1950s. It remained a determining force, despite a wide range of developments and modifications, and has been able

---

[7]For their French-speaking counterparts, in contrast, Didaktik as a general entity is virtually unknown. It is the Didaktik of individual disciplines that is relevant, both in research and in the actual training of teachers. See Chevallard (1991).

to assert itself up to the present alongside the empirical approaches gradually developing from the 1970s onward (Thiersch, Ruprecht, & Herrmann, 1978).

In the light of this history, the demise of human-science pedagogy that was widely proclaimed at the end of the 1960s (Dahmer & Klafki, 1968) may be interpreted, in retrospect, as the beginning of a critical reconstruction in the light of philosophical debates around the Frankfurt School and neo-Marxism, as well as a manifestation of hermeneutics, drawing increasingly on phenomenology and ethnomethodology. It was less the objective obsolescence of human-science Didaktik that gave rise to this proclamation of the end of a paradigm than the fact that a new generation of educationists was beginning, albeit hesitatingly at first, to confront the fascist involvements of their forebears.

Looking back to the origins of German Didaktik we realize that, on the one hand, the problems of bridging theory and practice became more and more intensified and, on the other hand, Pädagogik sought a certain independence as an academic discipline. The compartmentalization of knowledge about the processes of learning and development meant the loss of the coherent frame of reference in the Herbartian conception of pedagogy, exacerbating both the problem of how to mediate theory and practice and the problem of independent pedagogy. Both issues can be regarded as core points in the formation of a paradigm for pedagogy determined by the human sciences and cultural philosophy (Oelkers, 1982). Herbart's concept of "pedagogical tact" does not suffice as a unifying practical asset if the relevant theories in the individual disciplines are themselves heterogeneous and divergent and, outside the Herbartian concept, the idea of pedagogy as an independent science lost its foundation.

The solution that emerged from this discussion was to make practice itself both the starting point and the referential framework for theory (*reflexion engagée*; Flitner, 1966) and to transpose the mediation of both theory and practice to the educated *(gebildet)* individual. The theoretical basis for this solution is the concept of a theory of Bildung directed by cultural philosophy, which guarantees the independence of pedagogy from theories specific to individual subjects and overcomes the empirical means-to-an-end restriction.

The concept of Bildung has proved a stable source of orientation for this approach. Bildung is not determined by separate academic disciplines, but by life as a whole and the individual's share in this whole. The program of human-science pedagogy is thus the interpretation of life in the context of cultural philosophy. It follows from the work of Wilhelm Dilthey, the founder of the historical-systematic human sciences, without adopting his concept of science itself. At the center is an interpretation of the life world in terms of cultural philosophy. For Theodor Litt (1967), as well as for Eduard

Spranger (1980), pedagogical work revolves around a theory of assets of education *(Bildungsgüter)*, which gives a theory of pedagogical action in relation to the question of "personal transfer of ideational contents from person to person."

In this tradition, the question of the mediation of theory and practice, indeed the question of Didaktik itself, becomes the question of the educated personality *(gebildete Persönlichkeit)*. It was Erich Weniger (1990; see also chap. 6, this volume) who set out the Didaktik manifestation of this concept of pedagogy most clearly. For him Didaktik is the "theory of intellectual encounters between the generations," which requires "existential concentration" in the person of the teacher.

The preeminence of this focus throughout Didaktik must be seen as representing Didaktik's specific contribution to the treatment of the problems described earlier. In the perspective of Didaktik, Bildung is a concept beyond mere knowledge and skills, but is a forming of the individual through active participation in the cultural assets and in their productive acquisition. The initial task is *not* to ask how a student learns or how a pupil can be led toward a body of knowledge, nor to ascertain what a student should be able to do or should know. Instead the initial task of the Didaktiker is *to seek the character-forming significance of the knowledge and skills that a culture has at its disposal.* This is the focus of attention when considering the object, and it is this focus that determines the range of approaches available to teaching, and its context and interconnections. The essential, fundamental question of Didaktik is *Why is the student to learn the material in the first place?* No objectives are worth teaching or learning that cannot be said to contribute at least indirectly to Bildung. The first task is to find the point of a prospective object of learning in terms of Bildung, then to ask what it can and should *signify* to the student, and how students can themselves *experience* this significance.

Bildung serves Didaktik as a cipher in its concern to synthesize into a consistently coherent whole everything happening within instruction (see Diederich, 1988). All other questions and problems—for example, of class management, individual or group learning, teaching methods, individual learning rates, appropriate representation, and so on—are subordinate to this central concern and only gain significance when the question of educative substance *(Bildungsgehalt)* is at issue. Educational psychology and instructional research tend to be peripheral concerns.

Following the decline of the Herbartian model, this had the consequence for teacher education that the training of teachers in their academic disciplines became preeminent in the preparation for a teaching career—at least with respect to upper secondary education—despite efforts to professionalize the craft of teaching. Teacher education of this kind culminates in an understanding and acquisition of elements of culture and in their exemplary representation. In Spranger's model, teacher education converges on, and is fulfilled, in the Bildung of the teacher. Erich Weniger took this idea further with the demand that the teacher must represent the contents he or she is to teach in "existential concentration."[8]

The history of the professionalization of teachers and of the establishment of chairs of Pädagogik, or education, at universities is another fringe condition helping to explain the development of German Didaktik. In contrast to the Anglo-Saxon and Romance countries, education in Germany was established as part of philosophy and the historical-cultural sciences. Psychology, sociology and social science did not become recognized frames of reference for the new discipline.

In other words, Didaktik is a discipline that has been, and continues to be, influenced by place and application. Theories and models of Didaktik emerge in and for preservice teacher education. They tend to have the character of guides for the preparation and planning of instruction—and the market gives a wide choice. This literature includes a large number of more or less helpful compendia and compilations in which the most useful elements of the available knowledge about organized learning are brought together to create a standard of the teachers' craft. These compendia hope to facilitate, if not good instruction, at least good preparation of novice teachers. The frequently eclectic character of these practical "manuals" is typical of the field. This eclecticism tends to negate the dogmatism and prescriptive nature of the work, and is also an expression of uncertainty about theory on the part of most of the authors, and of the field as a whole.[9]

Given this condition of Didaktik, forms have developed that are actually regional variations, with schools and traditions crystallizing around important centers of teacher education. It is notable that the only two really widespread forms of German Didaktik that proceed from the child's learning, namely Hans Aebli's (1951) *Grundformen des Lehrens* (Basic Forms of Teaching) and Walter Guyer's (1952) *Wie wir lernen* (How We Learn), originated in Switzerland, on the edge of German-speaking culture. The first can be considered as an applied Didaktik based on Piaget's work, the second as an outcome of the confrontation with John Dewey's pedagogy. But neither of these variations, although they are among the most influential texts in

---

[8]On the issue as a whole, cf. Prange (1991, particularly chap. 4).

[9]A variety of this compilation literature is the synoptic representation of various Didaktik approaches and models, where something is proffered as Didaktik for the classroom that is in reality simply a more or less professional review and arrangement of products of Didaktik thought. These are a type of (more or less intelligent) compendia for the academic examination business.

teacher education, is included in Kron's (1993) new *Grundwissen Didaktik*
(Basic Knowledge of Didaktik), which the publishers describe as a standard
work of Didaktik—and not, interestingly enough, of German Didaktik. This
also applies to the work of Klaus Prange who, in his *Bauformen des Unterrichts* (1983), made a significant attempt to reconstruct Herbartian traditions
and to give practical guidance for instruction. In this he was swimming
against the current of theories of method and interaction influenced by
German Reform Pedagogy *(Reformpädagogik)*. Prange's work does not fall
within the span of German Didaktik as such, in that it appears to owe more
to an older Kantian and more recent Anglo-American tradition of pragma-
tism, and thus proceeds from the concept of experience, and not from any
concept of Bildung or life.

MODELS OF DIDAKTIK

In the following, I consider some of the most significant "models" of German
Didaktik. Models are tools (i.e., forms, heuristics, rules, schemata, classification patterns, and interpretative views) for the design, and possibly also
for analysis, of instruction and its planning and preparation. Their instru-
mentality varies, as does the level of instructional planning at which they
aim. Models range from theories about general education for the future, for
the structuring of curricula and teaching media, and for the daily preparations of the individual teacher.

The Didaktik triangle[10] (see Fig. 2.1) is a schematic representation that
covers the various models, not only in outward terms, but also as an
explanatory, classifying arrangement. Three basic strands, represented by
three variants of Didaktik, can be identified, each with its own emphasis in
theory and practice. The variations result from differing emphases when
viewed from one or two points of reference. Thus the *representation axis*
joining teacher with content can be treated in two different ways: (a) as a
doctrinal interpretation, which gives content priority over the teacher, or
(b) as a *magisterial* interpretation, which gives the teacher priority over
content. Similarly, the *experience axis* can be viewed (a) as an *objective*
approach to interpretation, with the objects of experience rated particularly
highly, or (b) as a *subjective* approach to interpretation, which brings the
more informal aspect of learning to the fore. The *classroom relations axis*
may be seen in terms of (a) a *charismatic* interpretation, in which the teacher
is emphasized as a role model, or (b) a *democratic* interpretation, in which
the asymmetry of the teacher–student relationship is transformed, with

---

[10]The theoretical significance of this triangle has been demonstrated. Compare Paschen
(1979).

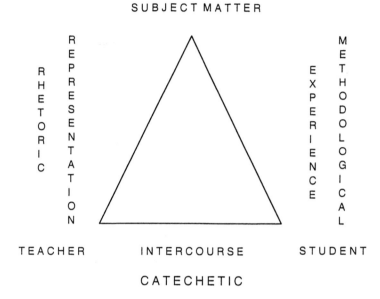

FIG. 2.1. The Didaktik triangle.

pedagogical intent, into a quasi-symmetrical relationship. For reasons of simplicity, I sketch only the three main types without discussing the individual variations.[11]

Models of Presentation

Where cultural objectifications are at the center of the teaching process, we have a culture-theory Didaktik *(kulturtheoretische Didaktik)*.[12] Both the predominance of the teaching matter and the ability of the teacher to guarantee the appropriate teaching of subject matter are the fundamental characteristics of this Didaktik approach. To a large extent this is also the position of human-science pedagogy *(geisteswissenschaftliche Pädagogik)*. Within this perspective, the foremost task of school instruction is cultural induction,

---

[11]The reader will easily be able to recognize and reconstruct the connections and intervals between the magisterial interpretation of representation and the charismatic interpretation of classroom intercourse, to compare and contrast the objective interpretation of experience and the doctrinal interpretation of representation, or the democratic interpretation of classroom intercourse and the subjective interpretation of experience. These transitional areas are, of course, recognized and propagated by the authors in the available models. Typifying and cataloguing them is more a question of representation than of construction.

[12]The classical expression of Didaktik as instructional theory is manifest in catechetical teaching, in which the unconditional validity of the matter and its presentation by the catechist guaranteeing orthodoxy are central.

the introduction of the students to their culture and to participation in that culture.

The classical representatives of this position are Eduard Spranger (1973), Wilhelm Flitner (1965), and Erich Weniger (1990). Wolfgang Klafki (see chap. 8, this volume) is a contemporary proponent, and it is his elaboration of the *kulturtheoretische tradition* that can be regarded as today's embodiment of Didaktik. This model operationalizes the fundamental tenet that the core of Didaktik, both for the theorist and for the teacher, is to approach, *with the will to understand,* the knowledge and skills handed down by cultural tradition, and to analyze its future significance and validity. Peter Menck's (1986) "Didaktik of object construction" may be included in this tradition. The group around Herwig Blankertz (see Blankertz, 1971), known as the *Münsteraner Schule,*[13] was responsible for the "structured framework approaches" *(Strukturgitteransätze),* which were particularly popular in the 1970s; these approaches developed a Didaktik for specific teaching subjects within the context of medium-range curriculum development. They are object and culture analyses that are highly elaborated theoretically and take up and develop the cultural philosophy tradition of Bildung, but with reference to social criticism. Another version, eclectically enriched and subsequently highly influential in teacher education, was presented by Meyer (1986), although his strong emphasis on the components of experience and encounter mean that it can be assigned to this model only insofar as Meyer stems from the *Münsteraner* group around Blankertz.

Models of Classroom Intercourse

If the *teacher–student relationship* is judged of greater importance for Didaktik reflection, we have a *communicative Didaktik.* The historical model is the Socratic method. The models of Werner Loch (1969), Klaus Mollenhauer (1972), and Horst Rumpf (1976) all have their theoretical roots in the pedagogy of Martin Buber (1953), Friedrich Bollnow (1959), and M. J. Langeveld (1966), influenced by phenomenology and existential philosophy. The same is true of Klaus Schaller's (1971) "communicative Didaktik." The reception of G. H. Mead's (1975) sociophilosophical, sociopsychological work (particularly through the work of Jürgen Habermas, 1987, and the Frankfurt School) was a decisive impetus for this work. These models were given more detail by Rudolf Biermann (1978) and Rainer Winkel (1986). *Communicative Didaktik works on the students' conceptions of facts and phenomena.*

Martin Wagenschein's (see chaps. 9 and 16, this volume) Didaktik (1968), Socratic in genre, is one of the most influential models of communicative

---

[13]*Münsteraner Schule* is the name given to the group, including Wolfgang Klafki, Peter Menck, Klaus Mollenhauer, and others, around Herwig Blankertz, who himself had been a member of the Göttingen group around Erich Weniger.

Didaktik, far beyond its place of origin. Unlike the other models of Didaktik, it is a model for specific teaching subjects, developed and exemplified wholly in relation to physics and mathematics. In a series of examples in the manner of a Socratic exchange, Wagenschein demonstrates the student's initial incomprehension. The student is then guided toward the phenomenon, first to take note with wonder, then to understand. Wagenschein gradually evolved this instructional method into a model of Didaktik, and his followers later compiled a series of further examples (see Berg and Schulze, 1995). It is a form of Didaktik that is itself organized and disseminated as an exemplary model.

Models of Experience

The third of our three axes is *experience,* joining student and learning content; this axis leads to a Didaktik oriented to theory of learning and experience. The classical forebear of this model is a research-based theory of method, the attempt to stylize the student learning process, construing this as a research process. Paul Heimann (1970) and Heinrich Roth (1963; see also chap. 7, this volume) proposed two powerfully effective models of instructional analysis and planning in which attention is channeled toward the formal structure of the "path of learning" *(Lernweg),* its steps and its preconditions. Here observations are, of course, influenced by the relevant findings of educational psychology. These models are widely seen as countermodels to the *kulturtheoretische* "Didaktik analysis" of the Weniger school.

Hans Aebli (1968), from Switzerland, is closely associated with the German reception of Jean Piaget's work. His "basic forms of teaching" are well on the way to becoming classic material in German-speaking teacher education. Aebli's Didaktik can be read as an independent Piagetian Didaktik for teachers and he (perhaps in conjunction with Heinrich Roth) achieved for German Didaktik, albeit on a more modest scale, what Jerome Bruner achieved for Anglo-Saxon pedagogy, the access to psychology and thus to empirical instructional research.[14]

The models of Klaus Giel (1975) and Gerhard Hiller (1980) also deserve particular mention. Their joint work draws on anthropological theories of play, aiming at reconstruction of the dimension of human experience. An elementary work for primary teaching, however, developed from this base, was not especially successful in terms of practical application, although this does not negate the fundamental significance of the construct for Didaktik thought.

---

[14]It is also appropriate to mention the models of Manfred Bönsch (1991) and Wilhelm H. Peterssen (1982, 1989), with their markedly practical approaches. They absorb in particular the pragmatic schools of thought within Reform Pedagogy and progressive education, a fact that accounts to no small degree for the current popularity of their books.

As I have already noted, Klaus Prange's (1983) *Bauformen des Unterrichts* (Forms of Building Instruction) is an attempt to reconstruct the rhetorical Herbartian tradition. The work is based on a systematic development of the idea of the *significance of experience* as a fundamental concept of pedagogy.

Concluding Remarks

The renaissance of general, *allgemeine Didaktik* following the curriculum movement of the 1970s and 1980s can be seen as a reconquest and re-acquisition of Didaktik's stock of pedagogical reflection, whereas the curriculum movement, with its references and obligations to social science, was mainly perceived as imported theory. In contrast to its French counterparts, German Didaktik has not yet adequately succeeded in merging with research in specific teaching subjects. *Allgemeine Didaktik* remains wary of the empirical. The real weakness of German teacher education, even today, is the parallel existence of this general Didaktik on the one hand and subject-specific instructional methodology on the other, with little connection between the two. A number of projects currently underway, however, have set their sights on a consistent integration of the two entities.

ACKNOWLEDGMENTS

This chapter was prepared with the support of a grant from the Spencer Foundation.

REFERENCES

Adl-Amini, B. (1981). *Didaktik-Methodik.* Weinheim: Beltz.
Adl-Amini, B., Oelkers, J., & Neumann, D. (eds). (1979). *Didaktik in der Unterrichtspraxis: Grundlegung und Auswirkungen der Theorie der Formalstufen in Erziehung und Unterricht.* Bern and Stuttgart: Haupt.
Aebli, H. (1951). *Grundformen des Lehrens: Ein Beitrag zur psychologischen Grundlegung der Unterrichtsmethode.* Stuttgart: Ernst Klett.
Aebli, H. (1968). *Psychologische Didaktik: Didaktische Auswertung der Psychologie.* Stuttgart: Klett.
Berg, H. C., & Schulze, T. (Eds.). (1995). *Lehrkunst und Schulvielfalt, Vol. 2: Lehrkunst: Lehrbuch der Didaktik.* Neuwied: Luchterhand.
Biermann, R. (1978). *Interaktion im Unterricht: Didaktische Ansätze, Beiträge, Perspektiven.* Darmstadt: Wissenschaftliche Buchgesellschaft.
Blankertz, H. (1971). *Curriculumforschung: Strategien, Strukturierung, Konstruktion.* Essen: Neue Deutsche Schule Verlagsgesellschaft.
Bollnow, O. F. (1959). *Existenzphilosophie und Pädagogik: Versuch über unstetige Formen der Erziehung.* Stuttgart: W. Kohlhammer.
Bönsch, M. (1991). *Variable Lernwege: Ein Lehrbuch der Unterrichtsmethoden.* Paderborn: Schöningh.

Buber, M. (1953). *Reden über Erziehung*. Heidelberg: L. Schneider.

Chevallard, Y. (1991). *La transposition didactique: Du savoir savant au savoir enseigné avec un exemple de la transposition didactique*. Grenoble: LaPensée sauvage.

Dahmer, I., & Klafki, W. (Eds.). (1968). *Geisteswissenschaftliche Pädagogik am Ausgang ihrer Epoche— Erich Weniger*. Weinheim and Basel: Beltz.

Diederich, J. (1988). *Didaktisches Denken: Eine Einführung in Anspruch und Aufgabe, Möglichkeiten und Grenzen der Allgemeinen Didaktik*. Weinheim and Munich: Juventa.

Flitner, W. (1965). *Grundlegende Geistesbildung: Studien zur Theorie der wissenschaftlichen Grundbildung und ihrer kulturellen Basis*. Heidelberg: Quelle and Meyer.

Flitner, W. (1966). *Das Selbstverständnis der Erziehungswissenschaft in der Gegenwart*. Paderborn: F. Schoningh.

Frey, K. (1970). *Theorien des Curriculums*. Basel: Beltz.

Giel, K. (1975). Vorbemerkungen zu einer Theorie des Elementarunterrichts. In K. Giel (Ed.), *Stücke zu einem mehrperspektivischen Unterricht: Aufsätze zur Konzeption* (Vol. 2, pp. 8–181). Stuttgart: Klett.

Grell, J., & Grell, M. (1979). *Unterrichtsrezepte*. Basel: Beltz.

Guyer, W. (1952). *Wie wir lernen: Versuch einer Grundlegung*. Zurich: Rentsch.

Habermas, J. (1987). *Theorie des kommunikativen Handelns*. Frankfurt a. M: Suhrkamp.

Heimann, P., Otto, G., & Schulz, W. (1970). *Unterricht: Analyse und Planung*. Hanover: Schroedel.

Hiller, G. G. (1980). Ebenen der Unterrichtsvorbereitung. In B. Adl-Amini & R. Künzli (Eds.), *Didaktische Modelle und Unterrichtsplanung* (pp. 119–141). Munich: Juventa.

Hopmann, S., & Künzli, R. (1992). Didaktik Renaissance. *Bildung und Erziehung, 45*(2), 117–135.

Jank, W., & Meyer, H. (1990). *Didaktische Modelle: Grundlegung und Kritik*. Oldenburg: C.v. Ossietzky University.

Klafki, W. (1959). *Das pädagogische Problem des Elementaren und die Theorie der kategorialen Bildung*. Weinheim: Beltz.

Klafki, W. (1964). Didaktische Analyse als Kern der Unterrichtsvorbereitung. In H. Roth & R. Blumenthal (Eds.), *Didaktische Analyse* (pp. 5–34). Hanover: Schroedel.

Klafki, W. (1971). Didaktik. In H.-H. Grothoff & M. Stallmann (Eds.), *Neues pädagogisches Lexikon* (pp. 225–232). Stuttgart: Kreuz-Verlag.

Klafki, W. (1974). Curriculum-Didaktik. In C. Wulf (Ed.), *Wörterbuch der Erziehung* (pp. 117–128). Munich and Zurich: Piper.

Kron, F. W. (1993). *Grundwissen Didaktik*. Munich and Basel: Reinhardt.

Langeveld, M. J. (1966). *Einführung in die theoretische Pädagogik*. Stuttgart: Klett.

Lenzen, D. (Ed.). (1989). *Pädagogische Grundbegriffe*. Reinbek: Rowohlt.

Litt, T. (1967). Das Wesen des pädagogischen Denkens. In T. Litt, *"Führen" und "Wachsenlassen": Eine Erörterung des pädagogischen Grundproblems* (pp. 83–109) Stuttgart: Klett.

Loch, W. (1969). Enkulturation als anthropologische Grundbegriff der Pädagogik. In E. Weber (Ed.), *Der Erziehungs- und der Bildungsbegriff im 20 Jahrhundert* (pp. 122–140). Bad Heilbrunn: Klinkhardt.

Mead, G. H. (1975). *Geist, Identität und Gesellschaft: Aus der Sicht des Sozialbehaviorismus*. Frankfurt: Suhrkamp.

Memmert, W. (1977). *Didaktik in Grafiken und Tabellen*. Bad Heilbrunn: Klinkhardt.

Menck, P. (1986). *Unterrichtsinhalt, oder Ein Versuch, Unterrichtsgeschehen als Prozess der Konstitution von Inhalten zu verstehen*. Frankfurt: Peter Lang.

Meyer, H. (1986). *Leitfaden zur Unterrichtsvorbereitung*. Berlin: Cornelsen.

Mollenhauer, K. (1972). *Theorien zum Erziehungsprozess*. Munich: Juventa.

Oelkers, J. (1982). Zur Grundlegung der geisteswissenschaftlich-kulturphilosophischen Pädagogik in den zwanziger Jahren. Ein Problemaufriss. In J. Oelkers & B. Adl-Amini (Eds.), *Pädagogik, Bildung und Wissenschaft* (pp. 9–53). Bern and Stuttgart: Haupt.

Peterssen, W. H. (1982). *Handbuch Unterrichts-planung: Grundfragen, Modelle, Stufen, Dimensionen*. Munich: Ehrenwirth.

Peterssen, W. H. (1989). *Lehrbuch der allgemeinen Didaktik.* Munich and Vienna: Oldenbourg.

Prange, K. (1983). *Bauformen des Unterrichts.* Bad Heilbronn: Klinkhardt.

Prange, K. (1991). *Pädagogik im Leviathan, Versuch über die Lehrbarkeit der Erziehung.* Bad Heilbrunn: Klinkhardt.

Robinsohn, S. B. (1967). *Bildungsreform als Revision des Curriculum.* Neuwied: Luchterhand.

Roth, H. (1963). *Pädagogische Psychologie des Lehrens und Lernens.* Hanover: Schroedel.

Roth, H. (1967). Die realistische Wendung in der pädagogischen Forschung. In H. Röhrs (Ed.), *Erziehungswissenschaft und Erziehungswirklichkeit* (pp. 179–191). Frankfurt: Akademische Verlagsgesellschaft.

Rumpf, H. (1976). *Unterricht und Identität: Perspektiven für humanes Lernen.* Weinheim: Juventa.

Schäfer, K.-H., & Schaller, K. (1971). *Kritische Erziehungswissenschaft und kommunikative Didaktik.* Heidelberg: Quelle & Meyer.

Spranger, E. (1973). *Philosophische Pädagogik: Vol. 2. Gesammelte Schriften* (O. F. Bollnow & G. Bräuer, Eds.). Heidelberg: Quelle & Meyer.

Spranger, E. (1980). Zur Theorie des Verstehens und zur geisteswissenschaftlichen Psychologie. In Hans W. Bähr (Ed.), *Gesammelte Werke: Vol. 6. Grundlagen der Geisteswissenschaften* (pp. 1–42). Tübingen: Niemeyer.

Thiersch, H., Ruprecht, H., & Herrmann, U. (1978). *Die Entwicklung der Erziehungswissenschaft.* Munich: Juventa.

Wagenschein, M. (1968). *Verstehen Lehren: Genetisch, Sokratisch, Exemplarisch.* Weinheim and Basel: Beltz.

Weniger, E. (1930). Die Theorie des Bildungsinhalts. In H. Nohl & L. Pallat (Eds.), *Handbuch der Pädagogik, Band 3: Allgemeine Didaktik und Erziehungslehre* (pp. 3–54). Berlin and Leipzig: Julius Beltz.

Weniger, E. (1952). *Didaktik als Bildungslehre, Teil 1: Die Theorie der Bildungsinhalte und des Lehrplans.* Weinheim: Beltz.

Weniger, E. (1990). Theorie der Bildungsinhalte und des Lehrplans (1930/1952). In E. Weniger, *Ausgewählte Schriften zur geisteswissenschaftlichen Pädagogik* (pp. 199–294). Weinheim and Basel: Beltz.

Willmann, O. (1957). *Didaktik als Bildungslehre, nach ihren Beziehungen zur Sozialforschung und zur Geschichte der Bildung.* Freiburg: Herder.

Winkel, R. (1986). Die kritisch-kommunikative Didaktik. In H. Gudjohns (Ed.), *Didaktische Theorien* (pp. 79–83). Hamburg: Bergman & Helbig.

BILDUNG: DIDAKTIK'S CENTRAL IDEA

3

Theory of Bildung[1]

Wilhelm von Humboldt
Gillian Horton-Krüger (Trans.)

Wilhelm von Humboldt's fragment, "Theorie der Bildung des Menschen," was probably written in 1793 or 1794. Earlier, in a letter written in November 1793, Humboldt had remarked on the absence of anything more than an embryonic theory of Bildung. The fragment develops a few general principles for such a theory.

I

A substantial and exquisite piece of work could be produced if someone were to undertake to portray the peculiar faculties that the various fields of human knowledge require in order to expand successfully; the proper

---

[1]Translation of Wilhelm von Humboldt, "Theorie der Bildung des Menschen." In Wilhelm von Humbodt, 1969, *Werke in fünf Bänden: Vol. 1. Schriften zur Anthropologie und Geschichte* (Andreas Flitner & Klaus Giel, Eds.) (pp. 234–240). Darmstadt: Wissenschaftliche Buchgesellschaft.

Translator's Note: In preparing for the present translation, two main problems were identified for which no comfortable solution could be found. These were the term *Bildung* itself and the question of inclusive language. As noted several times in this volume, although the word *Bildung* is conventionally translated as "education," this is not an adequate translation; it does not cover the connotations the word has in German. As in the rest of this volume, we have chosen to leave the term in German in order to avoid inappropriate connotations.

With respect to inclusive language, we have chosen to adhere to the practice with which Humboldt would have been familiar. Today it is alienating to use the generic terms *man* or *mankind,* and consistently male pronouns, when referring to "a person" in general. In this instance, we have chosen to be source oriented. Although the use of an inclusive term such as *men and women* might be more acceptable to a modern readership, it would convey a view of the world that would not reflect that of Humboldt.

spirit in which they must be worked on and the relationship in which they must be placed to one another in order to accomplish, as a whole, the development of mankind. The mathematician, the naturalist, the artist, indeed even the philosopher commonly commence their business without knowing its real nature and without viewing it in its entirety; and indeed only the few later attain this higher standpoint and this more universal view. In an even worse position, however, is the person who does not choose one field exclusively but wishes to draw on them all for the benefit of his education. In the embarrassment of such choice and lacking the skill to utilize any of these fields beyond its narrow confines to his own more general end, he will sooner or later be forced to surrender himself to chance alone and to use whatever he takes up for inferior purposes only, or as a mere toy to pass the time. Herein lies one of the preeminent reasons for the frequent, not unjustified, complaints that knowledge remains idle and the cultivation of the mind unfruitful, that a great deal is achieved around us, but only little improved within us, and that the more generally and more immediately useful development of principles is neglected in favor of the higher scientific education of the mind that is suitable for only the few.

At the convergence point of all particular kinds of activity is man, who, in the absence of a purpose with a particular direction, wishes only to strengthen and heighten the powers of his nature and secure value and permanence for his being. However, because sheer power needs an object on which it may be exercised and pure form or idea needs a material in which, expressing itself, it can last, so too does man need a world outside himself. From this springs his endeavor to expand the sphere of his knowledge and his activity, and without himself being clearly aware of it, he is not really concerned with what he obtains from the former or what he achieves outside himself by means of the latter, but only with his inner improvement and elevation, or at least with the appeasement of the inner unrest that consumes him. In pure, ultimate terms, thought is never more than an attempt of the mind to be comprehensible to itself, whereas action is an attempt of the will to become free and independent in itself. Man's entire external activity is nothing but the striving against futility. Simply because both his thought and his action are not possible except by means of a third element, the representation and cultivation of something that is actually characterized by being nonman, that is, world, he seeks to grasp as much world as possible and bind it as tightly as he can to himself.

It is the ultimate task of our existence to achieve as much substance as possible for the concept of humanity in our person, both during the span of our life and beyond it, through the traces we leave by means of our vital activity. This can be fulfilled only by the linking of the self to the world to achieve the most general, most animated, and most unrestrained interplay. This alone is the yardstick by which each branch of human knowledge can be judged. For in each case, the only true path is that on which the eye is able to follow steady progress toward the final goal, and here alone may the arcanum be sought that animates and makes fruitful those things that would otherwise remain eternally lifeless and vain.

At first glance, the linking of the self to the world may appear to be not only an incomprehensible expression, but also an overextravagant idea. On closer inspection, however, the latter suspicion at least will disappear, and it will be seen that once the true endeavor of the human spirit is perceived (embodying both its greatest vitality and its greatest impotence), it is impossible to stop at anything less.

What do we demand of a nation, of an age, of entire mankind, if it is to occasion respect and admiration? We demand that Bildung, wisdom, and virtue, as powerfully and universally propagated as possible, should prevail under its aegis, that it augment its inner worth to such an extent that the concept of humanity, if taken from its example alone, would be of a rich and worthy substance. And the demand does not stop here. It is expected that man leave a visible impression of his worth on the constitutions he forms and even on inanimate Nature around him, indeed that he should breathe his virtue and his strength (in such might and dominance are they to permeate his being) into his progeny. For only in this way may the acquired merits be perpetuated, and without these, without the comforting thought of a certain sequence of elevation and Bildung, human existence would be more transient than the existence of a flower that, upon withering, has at least the certainty of leaving behind the germ of its likeness.

Although all these demands are limited to man's inner being, his nature drives him to reach beyond himself to the external objects, and here it is crucial that he should not lose himself in this alienation, but rather reflect back into his inner being the clarifying light and the comforting warmth of everything that he undertakes outside himself. To this end, however, he must bring the mass of objects closer to himself, impress his mind upon this matter, and create more of a resemblance between the two. Perfect unity and constant interplay are contained within him; thus he must apply both to Nature. Within him are several faculties to represent one and the same object to himself in various guises: now as a concept of reason, now as an image of the imagination, now as an intuition of the senses. Using all of these as so many different tools, he must try to grasp Nature, not so much in order to become acquainted with it from all sides, but rather through this diversity of views to strengthen his own innate power, of which they are only differently shaped effects. But it is precisely this unity that determines the concept of the world, a concept that encompasses both the diversity of ways in which the external objects touch our senses and the independent existence through which these objects influence our feelings. For only the world comprises all conceivable diversity, and it alone possesses so complete an independence that it counters the obstinacy of our will with the laws of Nature and the decisions of Fate.

What man needs most, therefore, is simply an object that makes possible the interplay between his receptivity and his self-activity. But if this object is to suffice to occupy his whole being in its full strength and unity, it must be the ultimate object, the world, or at least (for only this is in fact correct) be regarded as such. Man seeks unity only to escape from dissipating and confusing diversity. In order not to become lost in infinity, empty and unfruitful, he creates a single circle, visible at a glance from any point. In order to attach the image of the ultimate goal to every step forward he takes, he seeks to transform scattered knowledge and action into a closed system, mere scholarship into scholarly Bildung, merely restless endeavor into judicious activity.

II

This all would be most vigorously promoted by a study of the kind mentioned previously. Determined to observe and compare the various kinds of human activity in the directions they give to the mind and the demands that they make of it, such work would lead directly to the convergence point that everything must reach if it is to affect us. Under its guidance, our observation would take refuge from the infinity of objects in the narrower circle of our faculties and their diverse combinations; as though in a simultaneously brightening and mustering mirror, the image of our activity, which we otherwise glimpse in fragmented form and through external successes only, would be revealed to us in direct relation to our inner Bildung. The man concerned only with the heightening of his powers and the elevation of his personality would find an excellent lesson in this work, which would set out before him, simply and comprehensibly, the influence that every business of life can exercise on our inner Bildung.

At the same time, however, the person who pursues a single task will only there learn to conduct his business in its proper spirit and with an awareness of its greater signification. He no longer wants only to prepare knowledge or tools for men's use, no longer wants merely to help further just a part of his Bildung; he knows the goal that is set for him; he sees that, executed in the right way, his business will give the mind its own, fresh view of the world and through this its own, fresh self-determination, so that he can achieve a full measure of Bildung from this, his own perspective; it is this he strives to achieve. If, however, he works only for power and its enhancement, he may satisfy himself only when he expresses his own power perfectly in his work. However, the ideal becomes greater if one measures the exertion it requires rather than the object that it is to represent. The consuming purpose of genius everywhere is only to satisfy the inner compulsion. The sculptor, for example, does not actually wish to present the image of a god, but to express and make fast the fullness of his plastic imagination in this figure. Every business of life has its own characteristic intellectual attitude and in this lies the true spirit of its perfection, in this alone lies the genuine spirit of its completeness. There are always several external means of conducting any of life's business, but only this intellectual attitude can determine the choice among them, can determine whether it is to find a lesser or greater degree of satisfaction.

The procedure of our mind, particularly in its more mysterious effects, can be fathomed only by deep reflection and unceasing observation. But even this achieves little, unless at the same time attention is paid to the difference between minds and to the variety of ways in which the world is reflected in different individuals. The work I describe would therefore have to portray this diversity and should not overlook anyone who has distinguished himself in any field and through whom it has acquired a new form or a broader concept. These would have to be portrayed in their complete individuality, showing the whole of the influence their times and their nation had exerted on them. Thus one would survey not only the diverse ways in which every single field can be treated, but also the sequence in which the one gradually arises from the other. However, because this sequence is repeatedly interrupted by the influence of national character, of the period and of external circumstances in general, this would yield two different series with constant mutual influence: one comprising the changes that any intellectual activity gradually acquires as it proceeds, the other comprising the changes that the human character undergoes in particular nations and periods, as well as in general, through the occupations that it takes up; in both would be seen the deviations where individuals of genius suddenly disturb this otherwise uninterrupted natural progression and suddenly pitch their nation or their time into other directions offering new vistas.

Only by proceeding step by step and finally surveying the whole can one reach the point of explaining completely to oneself how human Bildung manages to progress evenly and endure, yet without degenerating into the monotony by which physical Nature goes through same transformations time after time, without ever producing anything new.

4

On Wilhelm von Humboldt's Theory of Bildung

Christoph Lüth
Gillian Horton-Krüger (Trans.)
Dedicated to Wolfgang Klafki for his 70th birthday.

Christoph Lüth is Professor of Philosophy of Education and Pedagogical Anthropology at the Universität Potsdam. His fields of research are history and philosophy of education, 20th-century educational policy, Didaktik, and hermeneutics. He is coauthor of *Erziehung der Menschengeschlechter: Studien zur Religion, Sozialisation und Bildung in Europa seit der Aufkärung* (1996) and *Vervollkommnung durch Arbeit und Bildung?* (1997).

Ten years or so ago, in conversation with a colleague in New York whose specialty was philosophy of education, I mentioned Wilhelm von Humboldt. The name was obviously new to my acquaintance. Who was this man? When did he live? These questions astonished me—until I realized that Wilhelm von Humboldt is virtually unknown as an educationist in the United States. I explained that he lived from 1767 until 1835 and that in the German-speaking world his role can be compared to that of Dewey in the United States. Americans, it seems, are more likely to be familiar with his younger brother, Alexander (1769–1859), the naturalist. Wilhelm von Humboldt is known, if at all, only as a philologist. If he does find mention as an educationist, he is represented only as an advocate of a traditional form of classical education: "Humboldt promoted general education in the classics to enable the individual to become independent of the constraints of his or her social milieu" (Pinar, Reynolds, Slattery, & Taubmann, 1995, p. 810). In the face of such views of Humboldt, an examination of his theory of education as an historical tributary of 20th-century German educational theories (cf. Klafki, 1967) can make a useful contribution to the current exploration of the historical dimension in curriculum theory (Pinar et al., 1995).

The first two sections of this chapter contain a brief biographical sketch and an appraisal of the fragment "Theorie der Bildung des Menschen" (ca. 1793/1794; see chap. 3, this volume). In the third and final section I discuss Humboldt's earlier writings, pluck out a few strands of thought that were later developed in his theory of education, and touch on his contribution to the Prussian reform of education (1809–1810).

BRIEF BIOGRAPHY

Humboldt's life is a blend of the contemplative and the active. He was born in Potsdam and educated by tutors. He then studied law, as well as philosophy, history, classical philology, and physics (at the universities of Frankfurt an der Oder and Göttingen, 1787–1789) and made the usual journeys for young men of his station: to the Rhine, to Paris (shortly after the French Revolution), and to Switzerland. After qualifying in law (Berlin, 1790) he entered the legal and diplomatic service, but left after a brief spell in 1791, unable to continue within such a narrow-minded and dry environment. There followed a period as a private scholar of political theory, humanist philology, aesthetics, and philosophy (influenced by Kant and Schiller). In the final phase of his life (1820–1835) he was again a private scholar, mainly at his estate at Tegel, near Berlin, now concentrating on language studies, an area that had interested him earlier and found expression in such works as *Die Vasken* (1801) on the Basques.

Between these two phases, Humboldt was again in public service, first as Prussian ambassador at the Vatican (1802–1808), later as director of the education section within the Ministry of the Interior (1809–1810). It was during this latter period that he made his contribution to school and university reform within the framework of the sweeping Prussian reforms of that period. There followed a series of diplomatic missions to Vienna (1810–1813) and later, in the period of readjustment after the Napoleonic Wars, to Prague, Chatillon, Vienna again, Paris, and Frankfurt am Main (1813–1816). Later he was ambassador to London (1817–1818), and in 1819 he was appointed a minister in the Prussian government. This last post was Humboldt's for only a short time: A difference of opinion with Chancellor Hardenberg over his call for participation of "the estates of the nation" in legislation led to his dismissal from public service in late 1819.

Humboldt's wide-ranging interests, and his role in the political and intellectual history of his time, are amply reflected both in his published works and in his letters. His collected correspondence comprises more than 12,000 letters and replies involving more than 1,000 people and 111 institutions. Although it is impossible to characterize this complex person in just a few words, he can be seen as a key figure in the transition from the Enlightenment to Romanticism and German Classicism. In what was to remain a fragment of an autobiography (1816), Humboldt wrote of his blend of the contemplative and the active:

> I was always loath to mix with the world and longed to stand free as a spectator, an examiner, and naturally I have felt that only the most unconditional self control could attain such a point outside the world as I desired. (Humboldt, 1960–1981, Vol. V, p. 6; all subsequent references to Humboldt's writings are to this edition)

All the same, Humboldt judged himself to have been active in the world: "As far as the world is concerned, instead of separating myself from it, I have endeavored to know and to see as much of it as possible, wanting alienation from the world only from a position in its very midst" (V, p. 7).

THEORY OF HUMAN BILDUNG

In his letter of November 1793 to Christian Gottfried Körner (1756–1831), Humboldt complained that there was no more than an embryonic "theory of human Bildung" (V, p. 172).[1] In the fragment given this name, written presumably in 1793 or 1794 (cf. V, pp. 316–321), a few "general principles" (V, p. 173) of such a theory are developed. In the following I present the main train of thought in the fragment, henceforth referred to as "the 1793 fragment" or simply "the fragment," before discussing the principles with reference to some of Humboldt's earlier and later works.

Humboldt began by considering the contribution of the individual disciplines to the Bildung of humankind. He did not pursue the question in any detail, but made suggestions for work of this kind. The important aspects, as he saw it, were the "peculiar faculties" that are a presupposition to work in each field, as well as the relationships between the disciplines. He saw the justification of his plan in the fact that little heed is generally paid to such questions by scholars, and even less by those who acquire and apply science eclectically in their preparation for a career. Humboldt saw in the absence of inquiry into the preconditions for the disciplines and their interrelationship an explanation for much of the then-contemporary criticism of scholarly pursuits. Although a great deal was being achieved by the application of science, humankind was not being improved. Trenchantly he observed that the application of science was accomplishing a great deal "around us," but improving little "within us." The contrast of "without" and

---

[1]From this point, as in the title, I use the word *Bildung* rather than the conventional translation *education*. The reader who can accept "Weltanschauung," "Schadenfreude," and "Zeitgeist" as entries in *Webster's Dictionary* will, I am sure, accept Bildung in preference to any translation that is in constant risk of calling up false association (see Hopmann & Riquarts, 1995). The noun *Bildung* is derived from *bilden*, to form or, in some instances, to cultivate. In the few cases where the adjective *bildend* would be used in German, I use *formative*.

"within," a typical configuration in Humboldt's reflection, concerns us later. It is this criticism, reminiscent of Rousseau's first *Discourse* (1750) on the question of moral improvement through the development of the arts and sciences, that provides Humboldt with his justification for addressing the sciences' contribution to Bildung.

Humboldt emphasized a principle or theory of Bildung in support of the criticism. People are in the center of "all particular kinds of activity." Thus it is imperative to inquire which "peculiar faculties" are required of a person engaging in a particular discipline and to explore the interaction of the different fields of human understanding in Bildung. In a further principle linking the theory of Bildung and anthropology—more of this connection later—Humboldt spoke of people's striving ("inner unrest") to train their powers through exercise and to secure value and continuance for their being. In both cases, people need the world. Here, then, attention is directed back toward the world, but this time from within the person, who thus remains the center. The striving of humankind reveals itself in thought and action:

> In pure, ultimate terms, thought is never more than an attempt of the will to become comprehensible to itself, whereas action is an attempt of the will to become free and independent in itself. People's entire external activity is nothing but endeavor against futility.

Identifying this form of endeavor, Humboldt looked beyond the humanities and sciences and referred to action in general. Later he described a further activity, the cultivation of nature, as an expression of humankind's endeavor. Despite the importance of these extensions for his theory of Bildung (cf. Lüth, 1985), in the 1793 fragment Humboldt spoke primarily of the humanities and sciences when referring to human activity. Through the exercise of activities (thought, actions, external activity) men and women are to understand their rational operations and make their will "free and independent" through action. But the focus is not only on the powers of humankind, but also on the results obtained through the agency of these powers. Through such results, humankind wishes to secure "value and continuance," quality and quantity. The world, which is processed through thought and action, is thus no longer considered simply as necessary subject matter for thought and action, but also as matter in which human fulfilment can be found. This second thought is explored more closely. It is not only a question of internal Bildung, but it is also the "ultimate task of our existence" to create something permanent through knowledge and action, which is not to be random but should extend the content of "the concept of humanity in our person." This means that a new defining property is to be added to our concept of what is human. The pyramids in Egypt, for example, were built to demonstrate what absolute rule and self-deification (by the pharaoh) mean. Or, to take an example from the present, if gene technology can serve to intervene in the ontogenetic process, then this represents a new scientific attitude toward human nature, and thus extends what were previously reckoned to be the characteristics of a human. By formulating the task so that a person is to extend "the concept of humanity" through activity, it becomes clear that Humboldt's theory of Bildung has a normative side. We return to this later.

After emphasizing the importance of results for the continuance of achievement in the history of humankind, Humboldt returned to the "inner being of man," that is, to human powers. He did this to avoid the danger of men and women becoming alienated from themselves as they gain knowledge of the world ("nature"). It is, Humboldt admitted, human nature to look to the external objects. But the important consideration in this outward drive is that men and women do not lose themselves, but rather reflect back into their innermost selves the "clarifying light and the comforting warmth of everything that they undertake outside themselves." The point of this activity is to gain knowledge of nature. We explore one and the same object in nature through various receptive faculties such as sense perception and active faculties such as reason and imagination ("self-activity"; in Kant "spontaneity"). In correspondingly varying guises the object appears to us as "intuition of the senses," as concept, as image. These different aspects serve, above all, to enhance the faculties through application. As Humboldt presupposed that the different faculties are simply different manifestations of one and the same power, he maintained that it is a question of strengthening our "own innate power." This is further emphasized by the fact that the receptive and active faculties, that is, receptivity and self-activity, are in a state of "constant interplay," and thus form one unity. This epistemological standpoint can be traced back to Kant: The active faculties of reason receive matter to be processed through sensory perception, whereas the matter assimilated by sensory perception is ordered or structured by reasoning activity.

Humboldt interchanged the terms *nature* and *world* without making his differentiation clear. He appeared to regard "world" as a concept covering more than "nature" (cf. Menze, 1965): society, history, other people, cultural products, and so on. This would explain why he spoke not only of "laws of nature," but also of "decisions of fate"—meaning, for example, history—that are in opposition to the obstinacy of our will. It is a consequence of this broader comprehension of "world" that social action and state constitutions play a role in the 1793 fragment. But it is apparent that Humboldt was using the scientific treatment of nature as an example to elucidate what the development of the faculties through scientific knowledge means and how this is comprehended through reflection. In this respect, the world does play a role in his theory of Bildung, the world as nature (for a different view see Menze, 1965). That the activity of the naturalist is meant only as an example can also be concluded from the fact that Humboldt cited the mathematician, the artist, and the philosopher, as well as the naturalist, in his plan for a study of the faculties required for scientific work.

The enhancement of the faculties through the comprehension of nature shows what Humboldt meant when he postulated that humanity should not become alienated from itself but should let "the clarifying light and the comforting warmth" reflect back into inner being. Through the application of their various faculties men and women develop them. The metaphor "clarifying light" intimates that the rational operations become clearer if they are applied in the analysis of an object. They are provoked by having, for example, to use terms to describe the diversity of the objects, then to categorize and explain them. This diversity is present only in nature and, therefore, it is nature that we must address. Although the risk of alienation is present, this is humankind's only opportunity to develop its faculties further (cf. Wagner, 1995).

A degree of alienation remains by virtue of the fact that in forming a conception of nature people distance themselves a little from their previous state. This modification and advancement of mental activity through scientific knowledge is later expressly emphasized. Men and women do not lose themselves if they retain an awareness that their faculties are developed through their conception of nature. Humboldt described a process of mutual adaptation, with nature adapting to the conceptual forms of humanity (sensory perception, reason, imagination) and humanity's conceptual forms having to adapt to nature in its diversity, whereby a greater resemblance between the two is created.[2]

According to Humboldt, reference back to one's own faculties safeguards against the loss of self "in infinity," in a never-ending progression of confrontation with the world (= nature). In this way, "scattered" knowledge and

---

[2]It therefore evidences prejudice on Horkheimer's part—as on Litt's before him—when he accused Humboldt of furthering internalization through concentration on the individual. Such concentration, maintained Horkheimer, puts an end to the "substantial Bildung of the individual" and thus to the individual himself (Horkheimer, 1953/1978, p. 26). I suggest, however, that Horkheimer himself characterized the process of Bildung in a manner quite in keeping with Humboldt's approach, while purporting to refer to Bildung only as interpreted by the "realistic genius of Goethe and Hegel" (Horkheimer, 1953/1978, p. 26). For Horkheimer, Goethe and Hegel had recognized that Bildung is a process of externalization, or simply of experience, that takes place and achieves fruition solely in devotion to the matter, in intellectual work, and in practice aware of itself. Only in objective work can the individual progress beyond the randomness of his very existence (cf. Horkheimer, 1953/1978). This is precisely Humboldt's theory of Bildung through alienation.

action can be "unified." The circle is completed by the return to the individual's own faculties. The decisive point for the theory of Bildung is the understanding that only in this way can "mere scholarship" be transformed into "scholarly Bildung" and the "ultimate goal" (i.e., Bildung through extension of the "concept of humanity in our person") be fulfilled. Scientific activity does not, therefore, automatically induce Bildung—only under this specific condition.

In the second part of the 1793 fragment, the work Humboldt envisaged at the beginning is presented as a method of avoiding humankind's alienation from itself. The method is summarized, elucidated further, and thus highlighted. In the analysis of the various intellectual activities, attention would once more be directed away from the objects of science to the inner being of humanity, that is, to our faculties. The infinite mass of objects would be exchanged for the narrower circle of humanity's faculties and the interplay between them. An image of human activity would be revealed, no longer in fragmented form, dependent on external successes, but as in a "simultaneously brightening and mustering mirror" in direct relationship to our inner Bildung. In this way the "procedure of our mind" can be "fathomed by unceasing observation of itself." This approach, though deeming individuals to be dependent on the world in the development and recognition of their abilities (i.e., powers), can be termed *anthropocentric* (for a different view see Wagner, 1995) in that attention to the world is followed by a return of focus to the individual. Thus people are in the center.

At the end of his plan for a study of human mental faculties, Humboldt added that attention should be paid to the diversity of those faculties that arises out of the diversity in the minds of those acquiring the world through science. This brings individuality to the foreground, a point we address in more detail later. The fragment concludes with a sketch of the influence of individuality on the progress of the sciences, as well as "the influence of national character, of the period and of external circumstances in general"— an early sociological perspective—on the individuality of the scientist.

We have already seen that the 1793 fragment contains some statements that point beyond the narrower circle of scientific activities. There is reference to the activity of the artist, counted among the "various fields of human knowledge" because the artist, for example when creating a sculpture of a deity, does not so much seek to create a concrete shape as to express "the fullness of his plastic imagination." The main concern is, therefore, the extension and the knowledge of this faculty of imagining in plastic terms. But this activity is on the borderline of the various fields of science. Humboldt went beyond this demarcation line when he cited other areas of human activity besides science: action and humankind's "whole external activity." These other activities are also in view when Humboldt spoke of the state constitutions that have been created. Humboldt's earlier works also reflect his close study of constitutional issues: his investigation of the "new French Constitution" following the French Revolution (Humboldt, 1791, Vol. 1, pp. 33–42) and his treatise on the limitation of state activity to the guarantee of internal and external security, which was to become well known within the tradition of political liberalism.[3] In the 1793 fragment, Humboldt also spoke of the processing of nature by men and women as a process of Bildung. Broadly, he regarded any of life's business as a possible factor in Bildung.

Let us now look to other works of Humboldt to yield further statements on the nature of humanity and the process of Bildung. I use questions arising from the study of the fragment as a framework on which to paint a broad-brush representation of Humboldt's work *before* and *after*. Thus we can shed more light on the fragment itself by relating it to the theory of Bildung as developed by Humboldt up to that point, as well as pursuing the subsequent route of the theory and exploring its role in educational policy (*Bildungspolitik*).

THE THEORETICAL AND POLITICAL CONTEXT OF BILDUNG

The title of the fragment promises more than the text actually provides. A "theory of human Bildung" is developed only in its most rudimentary principles. It therefore comes as no surprise to learn that the work was not given its title by Humboldt, but by Albert Leitzmann, who first published the fragment, in 1903.[4]

We can identify three questions:

- What does Humboldt say about human nature?
- What is the structure of the process of Bildung?
- What role is played by subject matter and objective in the process of Bildung?

All these questions artifically separate what belongs together in the theory of Bildung, and in the process recorded and determined by this theory. This is most obviously the case in the second and third questions. But even the question about the nature of man and its anthropological reply is closely related, as we see later, to theory of Bildung.

---

[3]Humboldt, *Ideen zu einem Versuch, die Grenzen der Wirksamkeit des Staats zu bestimmen*, 1792 (see also Humboldt, 1969, Vol. 1, pp. 56–233).

[4]He derived the title from the letter to Körner cited earlier.

NATURE OF MAN—ANTHROPOLOGY

The *anthropocentric thesis* that humankind is in the center "of all particular kinds of activity" fits the fact that Humboldt had already dealt with anthropological issues well before this fragment. He wrote in 1791:

> Of all images that history offers, none attracts keener or more general attention than the image of man in the diversity of his lifestyles, each determined by the composition of nature inanimate and animate nature surrounding him, under whose constant influence he lives. (Vol. 1, p. 43).

At roughly the same period in which our fragment was written—perhaps somewhat later, according to dating—Humboldt was working on a study "On the Difference Between the Sexes and Its Influence on Organic Nature" (1794), later followed by his essay "On the Male and Female Forms" (1795), his great draft "Plan of a Comparative Anthropology" (1797), and his study "On the Concept of Humanity" (1797). But in other fields, too, his questioning often led him back to anthropology.

Concept of Power. In the tradition of faculty psychology, Humboldt distinguished three groups of powers: physical powers, intellectual powers, and moral powers. Given his repeated efforts to trace connections—social relations and their role in Bildung are just one example—it is not surprising that he comprehended all the various powers as different sides of one and the same power, a concept he expressed at an early date with respect to the relationship between body and mind: "But we are not mental substance alone; we are in connection with the world of the senses outside us, are dependent on their changes, are swept along in the perpetual flow of all things physical" (Humboldt, 1790, Vol. 1, p. 18)

In keeping with this, Humboldt later saw the Greeks as a synthesis of Nature and Idea:

> Just as humans are only able to reach up toward heaven by virtue of being firmly rooted on earth, so is no property within him [the Greek], no matter how sublime, anything other than the fruit of natural instinct refined by the implantation of godly ideas. (Humboldt, 1807, Vol. 2, pp. 104–105; cf. also Vol. 2, pp. 114–115)

It would therefore be false to see only the Idealist in Humboldt. In the same work, he referred to the unity of all the powers:

> All in the universe is one and one is all, else there is no unity at all within it. The power pulsating in the plant is not merely a part, but the whole power of nature, else there is an insurmountable cleft between it and the rest of the

world, and the harmony of the organic form is irretrievably destroyed. (Humboldt, 1807; Vol. 2, p. 96)

The pantheistic character of this view of the world is unmistakable.[5]

This dynamic conception of human beings as a concentration of coordinating powers is expressed in the 1793 fragment in the "inner disquiet" of people straining outward to external objects. Partly drawing on sensualism as propounded, for example, by Condillac, Humboldt had earlier explained this endeavor as a response to sensations. Sensations give life and aspiration to the soul; "left unsatisfied, they spur to action" (Humboldt, 1792, Vol. 1, p. 132). From the idealistic point of view, Humboldt later explained this aspiration as a longing springing from the autonomous mind. He regarded the drive to achieve Bildung, forcing its way to the outside, as something still quite close to organic life, as an expression of vital power. Humankind characterized in this way continues to be flexible within itself. The character of an individual is "in continuing activity," as the powers are never stationary (Humboldt, 1797/1798, Vol. 1, p. 444). Thus the whole of humankind is an "eternally active and effective whole" (Humboldt, 1797, Vol. 1, p. 44), always aspiring to new thoughts and actions and thus "never completed, . . . an infinite object" (Humboldt, 1797/1798, Vol. 1, p. 422).

If all powers are taken into consideration, it is only consistent to understand character not as a specific, lasting attitude, or a moral one, but as the particularity of the whole human being. Philosophical anthropology "conceives character as the sum of all those particularities which distinguish man—considered as a physical, intellectual and moral being—both universally and, in particular, as one being from the other" (Humboldt, 1797/1798, Vol. 1, p. 436). In keeping with this holistic conception of man, Humboldt in later years demanded in the school plans he developed during his association with Prussian educational policy, that all human powers should be practiced at every school.

As the powers are the same in all humans, people differ from each other solely in the interrelationship of the powers and in their movement. In his search for individual differences, Humboldt offered some evocative characterizations of people (e.g. of Napoleon, whom he saw in person; Frederick II; Caesar; Alexander the Great) and of national characters (French, English,

---

[5]In the historical dimension, too, unity is recognized through the continued effect of the powers. "The most remote past exists only in the present moment, and the whole universe would be destroyed if its effect could be destroyed each time" (Humboldt, 1806, Vol. 2, p. 28). This "metaphysical-a priori concept of power" (Menze, 1965, p. 97) can be traced back to the monadology of Leibniz (1646–1716). According to Leibniz, monads are single substances of power that contain "the whole universe as a notion within them" (Windelband, 1957, p. 363). As remote as such a notion may seem to us today, we must take it into consideration if we wish to understand Humboldt's theory of powers.

German) but was also careful to point out that the powers that reveal themselves solely in their effects can only be approximately recognized.[6] In the end, Humboldt maintained that we realize that we cannot know anyone fully:

> Humanity is more than and something different from the sum of speech and actions and even the sum of emotions and thoughts; . . . Up to a certain point, a person's plans and reasoning can be developed and dissected without undue difficulty; but when the moment comes to consider where the thought or the decision originated, we are suddenly transported to the boundary of an unknown world from which only single disjointed apparitions suddenly arise, while the world itself remains swathed in impenetrable darkness. And yet it is these very first springs, these inner powers, that define the true essence of the individual and set everything else in motion. (Humboldt, 1797/1798, Vol. 1, pp. 475–476)

ANTHROPOLOGICAL POINT OF DEPARTURE FOR PROCESSES OF BILDUNG

From this perspective, humankind's expressions (i.e., thoughts, actions, feelings) can be seen as continuing—never quite successful—attempts at self-understanding. The scientific activities addressed in the 1793 fragment are an example of this. They, Humboldt claimed, are simply attempts to understand ourselves. Processes of Bildung are a means of externalizing, of concretizing certain powers and reflexively reacquiring the expressions.

This is the point at which humanity, innately aspiring to Bildung, transcends a state that had existed and thus fulfills its aspiration. Humboldt expected empirical and philosophical anthropology to support this process in two ways. First the figures with relevant influence, such as statesmen and teachers,[7] should use the knowledge we have of empirical and philosophical anthropology. Empirical study of the nature of the individual, maintained Humboldt, allows the individual's opportunities for development to be estimated—today this is what we expect of pedagogical diagnostics. The philosophical charting of a target combines these developmental possibilities to produce an ideal for the person in question: "The setting up of an ideal itself requires conscientious observation of reality. For this ideal is nothing other than nature expanded in all directions and freed of all restricting obstacles" (Humboldt, 1797, Vol. 1, p. 351). Before an implementable ideal can be set

---

[6]Not even the process of the hermeneutic circle can change this, according to which an overall impression of a person can be gained from the recognition of individual traits whereas the overall impression can be adjusted in its turn by the knowledge of the individual (Humboldt, 1797/1798, Vol. 1, p. 463).

[7]One wonders whether this represents an appreciation of worth for statesmen or teachers!

up, it must link up with empirical human observation. I return later to the question of the ideal when I deal with the objective of Bildung.

Second, Humboldt expected anthropological studies on the difference between individuals to have repercussions that contribute to the Bildung of the observer. Cognitive treatment of individual variation differentiates the consciousness of the observer. And consciousness differentiated in this way affects the observers themselves (Humboldt, 1793, 1797).

We have already touched on processes of Bildung. In the next section we consider a few conditions of these processes and their structures.

PROCESSES OF BILDUNG: STRUCTURE AND REQUIREMENTS

I begin with Humboldt's statements on the structure and conditions of the process of Bildung before exploring its subject matter and objectives. Like Humboldt, I start with the individual. I refer to the relationship between the internal and the external touched on in the 1793 fragment, then move beyond the scope of the fragment to examine the role of social relationships in the process of Bildung, before finally examining liberty and diversity of life situations as preconditions for processes of Bildung.

The question of how the individual relates to the external (world) through externalization (scientific knowledge, action) and thus acquires Bildung did not concern Humboldt only in the 1793 fragment. It is a recurring topic of his earlier and later work on the theory of Bildung and can be seen as a manifestation of the old problem of the relationship between the *vita contemplativa* (contemplative life) and the *vita activa* (active life). Despite Humboldt's own waverings between the active power of the individual and the importance of the product as an expression of these powers in certain matters, the significance of both sides for the Bildung of the individual becomes clear (cf. Lüth, 1985; Menze, 1965). Of particular interest here is the passage in his study "The Eighteenth Century" (1797/1798) in which Humboldt criticized the inclination of his age toward purely cerebral activity and sentimentalism and called for action. In according such importance to the internal (the powers), Humboldt did not mean that the products of activity are unimportant, but simply that no individual can express himself wholly in his products. It is thus a question of the dignity and freedom of the individual. This is not to be confused with his works:

> Only what we are is completely our own. What we do depends on coincidence and circumstance. Every person . . . is more than his work, because he never succeeds in reaching the ideal he carries in his mind, although in another sense his work is more than he is, as it is a fruit of his collected and exalted

powers, which are otherwise dispersed and less active. (Humboldt, 1797/1798, Vol. 1, pp. 453–454).

We have not so far discussed the role that social relations play in Bildung. In a letter (1793), Humboldt emphasized that a theory of Bildung in which life and social contacts play a major role is the most important part of a comprehensive theory of human development (Humboldt, 1793, Vol. 5, p. 173). Even earlier Humboldt had said that education alone does not suffice. More important are the "circumstances that accompany a person throughout his life" (Humboldt, 1792, Vol. 1, p. 108). "Circumstances" are situations and other people. Here Humboldt was probably interpreting the observations he made in Berlin social circles such as the Salons.

Relations with other people serve to overcome possible bias in character, with one acquiring "the richness of the other" (Humboldt, 1792, Vol. 1, pp. 64–65). One condition is named: These connections must "spring from the innermost being"; that is, they must correspond to a person's inclinations and developmental potential. On the other hand, these relations must retain such a degree of independence that individual development is possible and mere emulation of others precluded: "For, as one person cannot adequately comprehend the other without this intimacy, in the same way independence is necessary to transform what has been comprehended into one's own essence" (Humboldt, 1792, Vol. 1, p. 65).

A third condition for such formative *(bildend)* contacts, already presupposed here, is an optimum degree of difference between the individuals: "a difference that is not so large as to preclude comprehension of one another, but not so small as to preclude admiration for what the other possesses and a wish to transfer it to oneself" (Humboldt, 1792, Vol. 1, p. 65). This process of acquisition corresponds structurally to the process of alienation in the treatment of science and humanities we have already examined. Involvement with the particularity of others means alienation from the self, but this is ultimately a fruitful process because the individual is strong enough to transform what he is assimilating "into his own being" (Humboldt, 1792, Vol. 1, p. 65). This assimilation, with the counterassertion of independence through modification, requires effort (power) (Humboldt, 1792). The individual must absorb yet still remain independent. This interlocking of beings is not to transform one into another, "but to open up routes of access from one to the other. What an individual already possesses must be compared with what is received from the other and modified accordingly, but not oppressed by it" (Humboldt, 1792, Vol. 1, p. 82).

Wagner (1995) highlighted the nature of this process as crisis. The foreign individual actively impinges on the assimilating individual. This impingement is another factor in the latter's Bildung, as it activates his power.

In the contacts sketched here it is not a question of imitation, but of self-assertion. It is, however, quite a different matter if the mechanism of self-assertion is interrupted by moral transgression or the abandonment of truth. Thus "anything that cannot exist in parallel" must be destroyed by social contacts (Humboldt, 1792, Vol. 1, p. 82).

This enrichment of individuality through relationships with others is one aspect. Humboldt discerned another: Social relations can also lead to a more sharply defined contrast, and thus to further development and a more precise definition of individuality. A character exposed to "pure and determined characters" is itself formed "in purity and determination" (Humboldt, 1797, Vol. 1, p. 349). Contrast contributes as well as resemblance, and "that greater and more beneficial friction" comes into play that Humboldt noted in the "more numerous particularities" in ancient Athens (Humboldt, 1807, Vol. 2, p. 85). In his famous concept of university (Humboldt, 1810), Humboldt was later to call for "antagonism and friction" among professors to facilitate productive debate and prevent ossification. An extreme case of such contrasts and opposing forces, which Humboldt recognized is war, which for this reason contributes, as he believed, to Bildung. Fortunately he restricted this premise, not intending it to mean that wars should be initiated for this express reason. But even without this extreme example of antagonism, it is clear that the oft-propagated image of Humboldt as a serenely detached classicist is merely fiction.

The processes of Bildung through social relations are described in a presupposition of liberty. Only in a state of freedom can individuals assert their independence which, as has been shown, is a condition for formative (*bildend*) acquisition or repulsion of foreign influences. Therefore Humboldt (1792) postulated freedom as a precondition of Bildung and used this to justify the exclusion of the state from any influence on processes of Bildung (cf. Lüth, 1988). State influence would lead to uniformity and "alien behavior" in the nation (Humboldt, 1792), in short the very opposite of the independence discussed. And work can contribute to Bildung only in the absence of control by any form of a welfare state. Any activity not chosen by men and women themselves in which they are "restricted and directed" remains alien to them. Such activity is not accomplished "with human power, but with mechanical skill" (Humboldt, 1792, Vol. 1, pp. 77). Only in liberty can "every business" educate (*bilden*), as Humboldt said in the 1793 fragment and as he had already argued in his constitutional essay (1792; cf. Lüth, 1985).

The second external condition for Bildung, in addition to freedom, is "diversity of situation" (Humboldt, 1792, Vol. 1, p. 64). This diversity represents the potential stimulus for the further development of the individual. Diversity is provided by a variety of situations: "The more man opens himself to these, the more new sides will be stimulated and the livelier his inner activity will be in developing these new sides and aligning them as part of his whole" (Humboldt, 1797, Vol. 1, p. 346). The matter already considered (world) contains this diversity as a necessary condition for Bildung.

PROCESSES OF BILDUNG: MATTER AND OBJECTIVES

We have already seen the central role of subject matter in every process of Bildung as: (a) a means of expressing, exercising, and intuiting powers, (b) a potential stimulus for human development, (c) a counterpart to mark out the boundaries of the individual, and (d) a means of objectivizing ideas and powers in order to leave traces in the world and thereby create tradition and stimulus for others. Humboldt did not offer any detailed Didaktik discussions, for example, on instructional matters, simply a few remarks in his school plans (1809) and in his university plan (1810). The decisive point is his demand that the various subjects of instruction should educate or form *(bilden) all* of the learner's powers. This does not, however, exclude the setting of individual emphases. Indeed, he advocated a form of specialization in the recommendation that power should be exercised "upon as small a number of objects as possible and, as far as possible, on all sides" (Humboldt, 1810, Vol. 4, p. 261). In keeping with this view, in the 1793 fragment Humboldt assumed that men and women acquire the same object through a variety of faculties.[8]

In his university plan, Humboldt underlined the significance of science as matter for Bildung. The task of the university is "to process science in the deepest and broadest sense of the term" and to address it as "matter which is appropriately prepared, by its nature and not by design, to be used in the service of intellectual and moral Bildung" (Humboldt, 1810, Vol. 4, p. 255). This thought provides a link with the theory of Bildung through science that Humboldt put forward in the 1793 fragment. As long as it can serve not only intellectual but also moral Bildung, it fulfills the demand, also echoed by Humboldt, for "formation of character" (Humboldt, 1793/1794, Vol. 1, p. 235). Schelsky (1978) and Habermas (1963) argued that moral Bildung of this kind presupposes a particular type of science, namely idealistic philosophy,

---

[8]In view of this significance of matter Klafki, in his famous essay "Kategoriale Bildung," quite rightly criticized a particular reception of Humboldt's theory of Bildung, encapsulated in the ideology of the German Gymnasium, as one-sided. Summarizing this ideology Klafki pointed out: "The essential aspect of Bildung is not the assimilation and acquisition of *contents,* but the formation, development, maturation of physical, spiritual and mental *powers*" (Klafki, 1967, p. 33).

and that the modern, empirical, and analytical sciences can no longer contribute to moral Bildung.

What is the goal of education (i.e., Bildung)? Humboldt never proposed a particular aim in relation to content. He neither saw a particular constitutional arrangement as a focus of orientation—indeed he advocated continuing change in the arrangement of the state through confrontation between the developing individuals and the existing state—nor did he address himself to particular social groupings. There is no definition of objectives in either religious or classical terms. Humboldt admired the Greeks in particular, as the collection of statues at his home at Tegel clearly shows, and he regarded study of the classics as a significant contribution to the extension of human knowledge, as his school plans confirm. Yet such studies must not—as Pinar et al. (1995) assumed—be allowed to divert attention from the urgent concerns of the present, but should offer ideas for liberation from current circumstances through political restructuring in the present. For Humboldt, the Greeks were not an ideal to be imitated in classicist mannerisms, but their uniqueness could be a source of inspiration to create new individuality in the present.

But if no objective can be defined in relation to content, in other words if Humboldt disassociated himself from all given social, political, and cultural orders, the question arises whether any objective for Bildung can be discerned in Humboldt's writings. This could be seen to echo Humboldt's own question whether any objective can be discerned for the development of humankind as a whole. He discussed the contrasting views that humankind strives toward a particular objective through the "guidance of a wise power" (Humboldt, 1791, Vol. 1, p. 44) and that it is impossible to make any pronouncement on the future development of humankind because the "whole fabric" of human action is largely obscure (Humboldt, 1791, Vol. 1, p. 52). Humboldt himself believed that no plausible justification had yet been put forward for either of these views (Humboldt, 1791, 1793). Neither the philosopher nor the historian had answered convincingly whether the conflicting and unifying powers led humankind into eternally returning circles or to one great infinite goal.

It is paradoxical that Humboldt regarded the question of humankind's objectives as unanswered, yet continually inquired as though an objective existed. In his study of the 18th century, written just as the century was ending, he asked: "Where do we stand? What portion of its long and arduous progression has humankind now accomplished? Is humankind progressing toward the ultimate goal? And how far has it already progressed in this direction?" (Humboldt, 1797/1798, Vol. 1, p. 376).

In an apparent acceptance of such an objective, he spoke of a step-by-step development of the human mind—of the individual and of humankind as a whole—from one-sidedness of individual powers to a perfection of all powers

(Humboldt, 1797/1798). He mentioned progress (in poetry, morals, intellect; Humboldt, 1797) and a perfection of man (Humboldt, 1792). "Step," "progress," and "perfection" assume a goal of some kind toward which development is directed. And it fits here that in the 1793 fragment Humboldt assumed a "certain sequence in the ennoblement and Bildung" of humankind. He expressly mentioned an "ultimate goal of nature" in relation to humankind (Humboldt, 1792, Vol. 1, p. 141), supported by the passing on of achieved faculties (Humboldt, 1797).

The hypothetical assumption, that a goal has been set and that humankind cannot but move closer to it, is later relinquished. It depends on the reason of individuals, he said, whether they tread the path of "uninterrupted progress toward perfection" (Humboldt, 1797/1798, Vol. 1, p. 381). Human reason has given men and women the task of overcoming arbitrariness in their subsequent actions. Thus the question of goal orientation is transferred to people's own reason. Following the break-up of political order in the French Revolution, Humboldt advocated this orientation to humankind, to human reason, in order to locate a standpoint within men and women themselves. If everything outside is precarious, then "the only safe refuge is within us." This is reminiscent of the statement in the 1793 fragment that humanity is at the center of all activity. Such an orientation to human reason is also the message of Humboldt's famous tenet on the goal of Bildung: "The true aim of humankind—dictated not by changing whim, but by eternally unchanging Reason—is the highest and most proportional Bildung of its powers to form a whole" (Humboldt, 1792, Vol. 1, p. 64). This is a typical statement of the Enlightenment. The "true aim of human kind" is set down by reason, not by other agencies (such as God, the government, the estates).

In this well-known formula for proportional, that is, harmonious Bildung of the powers, only one statement can be immediately understood. *All* powers of humankind are to be formed or educated *(gebildet)*. Later, when drawing up his school plans (1809), Humboldt also referred to general *(allgemeine)* Bildung, distinguishing general from "special" Bildung as required, for example, for a particular occupation. Specialized Bildung has a one-sided orientation to the requirements of the work, whereas general Bildung is to be oriented to all human powers and their development. This distinction between one-sided Bildung steered from the outside and Bildung guided from within by the powers of men and women themselves already occurs in the earlier works (see Humboldt, 1790, 1797/1798, where he lamented the one-sided nature of education in the 18th century in contrast to the "harmonious education of all powers" in Ancient Greece), but is only developed later in the political discourse on the requirements of vocational education.

We must bear in mind the nature of vocational education at that time—unscientific skill training—if we are to understand why Humboldt defined general Bildung further as having to lead toward understanding of the acquired knowledge. Through general Bildung, "the powers, i.e., man himself, are to be strengthened, purified and regulated" (Humboldt, 1809, Vol. 4, p. 188). Special Bildung is simply a medium for the acquisition of the skills that are to be applied:

> For human beings, every piece of knowledge, every skill which is not sublimated by complete insight, is dead and unfruitful. Such knowledge must often be restricted to the results, leaving their reasons uncomprehended, because the skill must be there and time or talent for insight is lacking. (Humboldt, 1809, Vol. 4, p. 188).

Clear as this statement on the education or formation (Bildung) of all powers may be, it still poses two problems:

- How can a harmony of all powers be conceived if Bildung, according to Humboldt, proceeds through one-sided points of emphasis?
- How can individuality and diversity be achieved—a central objective in Humboldt's theory of Bildung—if the goal is apparently always identical, namely the harmonious (= proportional) Bildung of all powers to form one whole?

By "harmony of all powers" Humboldt meant the "correct balance of all powers" as the basis for virtue (Humboldt, 1790, Vol. 1, p. 15). In this sense, he criticized an overweighting of sensibility that is even morally only wholesome in the right ratio to the exercise of intellectual powers. Thus higher perfection is achieved only through the conjoining of the powers of reflection and sensation, "in proportionate degrees of strength" (Humboldt, 1792, Vol. 1, p. 141). Humboldt located a balance of this kind in the Greeks: "the correct ratio of receptivity and self-activity, the inner fusion of the sensual and the intellectual, retention of equilibrium and symmetry in the sum of all efforts" (Humboldt, 1808, Vol. 2, pp. 69–70). These examples suffice to show the central role of Humboldt's goal of harmonious Bildung of all powers, which is also reflected in his school plans (1809) and his university plan (1810).

But how can such equilibrium of the forces be achieved? Only in exceptional cases would it be possible to exercise all powers to the same extent. As a rule, the various powers can only be exercised and thus trained in sequence:

> Each person is only able to work with one power at a time, or rather his whole being is at one time determined to one activity. Thus humanity appears condemned to one-sidedness by weakening his energy as soon as he spreads himself over several objects. (Humboldt, 1792, Vol. 1, p. 64)

It is, however, only an *apparent* condemnation to one-sidedness, for the concentration on the various powers in sequence allows training of all of them in the course of life. Of course, it must still be explained how equilibrium of the forces can be achieved in this way, if at various periods individual powers are emphasized. Humboldt saw the answer here in the endeavor to draw simultaneously on both the highlighted and the faded, and thus to unite the individual, individually exercised powers. This intertwining of the various periods is achieved by memory, which creates identity in the progression of life, linking the present with the past. The nature of the training of the powers as a sequence is reflected in human progression from childhood to adolescence, to adulthood and old age. And the same applies to humankind as a whole. Only in the course of history can the various, individually trained powers coincide to form a unity.

But how, in view of this goal of equilibrium of powers, are we to conceive of Humboldt's central goal of the diversity of individuals? Are we not dealing instead with monotonous uniformity? The only conceivable way out of this paradox (uniformity vs. individuality) is to recognize that the individual powers allow for variety of expression and combination. Humboldt identified, for example, different movements: "In the lively character [by which Humboldt indicated movement] imagination and emotion will infallibly prevail, in the slow character reason and reflection" (Humboldt, 1797/1798, Vol. 1, p. 445).

This is, of course, a step away from the postulate of equilibrium of the powers. This correction is important, because it is in the very deviation from the state of equilibrium that "the interesting characters, the most particular and diverse manifestations" (Humboldt, 1797/1798, Vol. 1, p. 441) originate. Humboldt cited three historical figures to illustrate his point: in Alexander the Great, will and imagination dominate; in Caesar, will and passion; and in Frederick II, will and reason.[9]

The diversity of individuals in the course of history serves to extend the "concept of humanity," as it is termed in the 1793 fragment, through the continued appearance of new manifestations of individuals. This does not only include the great figures of history, but also refers to the albeit small contributions of the majority of humankind. Only in the course of history can the greatest possible differentiation of the concept of humanity to an "ideal of humanity" (Humboldt, 1797, Vol. 1, pp. 339–340) be achieved. It is a communal effort of humankind. This goal can be achieved only by enhancing the powers of individuals and of humankind. Thus it is "highest" or "most exalted" Bildung that is postulated (Humboldt, 1792, Vol. 1, p. 64). But as long as Bildung proceeds through the active acquisition of the products of

---

[9]The differences between individuals by virtue of various combinations of differently emphasized powers can be explained in the same way that differences between words, sentences, and texts can be explained by different combinations of the same set of letters.

other individuals, it cannot be complete in this sense. No individual can acquire the products of such "totality of individuals" (Humboldt, 1797, Vol. 1, p. 340), not even if the products are intended to serve only in the training of the powers and not in the acquisition of matter. This was recognized by Simmel (1986), who referred to a "store of objectivized mind which expands to unforseeable dimensions. . . . [The subject] becomes entangled in general contexts whose totality it can't escape, but whose particular implications it can't master" (p. 216). He saw Humboldt's conception of Bildung (the acquisition of such products) as overburdened and doomed to failure. It could be countered, however, that in the face of such incalculability of products, Bildung is only possible as a communal effort, through "division of labor."

With the aim of "totality of individuals" the future is open, as it cannot be ascertained in advance which individualities will emerge. To this extent, any form of teleology is relinquished (cf. Benner, 1990). This argument that the diversity of individuals is enhanced by the "well-nigh boundless interconnection of all nations and continents" (Humboldt, 1792, Vol. 1, p. 88) anticipates the thoughts of the French anthropologist Lévi-Strauss (1985). In his essay, written for UNESCO, Lévi-Strauss defended his antiracist position that cultures can bring forth only a "cumulative history" by combinations of their achievements, and that the resulting highly differentiated "world culture" must take the cultures of the so-called third world into account.

With respect to the assumption that Humboldt anticipated a form of postmodernism in the arbitrariness of life forms, individuals, and plurality, it must be ascertained that Humboldt wished to restrict this maximum diversity by principles of ethics, aesthetics, and science (truth). He described his "blueprint" for a state as follows:

> I have tried to locate the most advantageous situation for people within the state. This, so it appeared to me, would have to encompass the most diverse individuality and the most original independence in parallel with the most diverse and most intimate union of several persons—a problem that only liberty of the highest kind may resolve. (Humboldt, 1792, Vol. 1, p. 211)

As we have seen, Humboldt developed his theory of Bildung from the postulate that the reason he presupposed for it is axiomatic or rhetorical, "eternally unchanging" (Humboldt, 1792, Vol. 1, p. 64), as Humboldt claimed when justifying his formula of the harmonious Bildung of all powers. With a different conception of reason, it was inevitable that his theory of Bildung and the school and university reforms that it guided would be criticized. This is not the place for a review of reception and criticism up to the present,[10] but the topicality of Humboldt's theory of Bildung and his concept

---

[10]Compare Litt (1960), Menze (1965, 1985), Kawohl (1969), and Lüth (1982). For university reform compare Lundgreen (1997). For reception compare, for example, Klafki (1967).

of school and university is reflected in the fact that they continue to be chosen as points of reference, with argument developed in favor or against accordingly.

ACKNOWLEDGMENT

This chapter was first published in a slightly revised form in the *Journal of Curriculum Studies* and is reprinted by permission of the copyright holder, Taylor & Francis Ltd., London.

REFERENCES

Benner, D. (1990). *Wilhelm von Humboldts Bildungstheorie: Eine problemgeschichtliche Studie zum Begründungszusammenhang neuzeitlicher Bildungsreform.* Weinheim: Juventa Verlag.

Habermas, J. (1963). Vom sozialen Wandel akademischer Bildung. *Merkur, 17,* 413–426.

Hopmann, S., & Riquarts, K. (1995). Didaktik und/oder Curriculum. Grundprobleme einer international vergleichenden Didaktik. In S. Hopmann & K. Riquarts (Eds.), *Didaktik und/oder Curiculum Zeitschrift für Pädagogik* (Supplement 33, pp. 9–34). Weinheim and Basel: Beltz Verlag.

Horkheimer, M. (1978). Begriff der Bildung. Immatrikulationsrede Wintersemester 1952/1953. In J.-E. Pleines (Ed.), *Bildungstheorien: Probleme und Positionen* (pp. 22–27). Freiburg im Breisgau: Verlag Herder. (Original work published 1953)

Humboldt, W. von. (1960–1981). *Werke in fünf Bänden* (A. Flitner & K. Giel, Eds.). Stuttgart: J. G. Cotta'sche Buchhandlung.

Humboldt, W. von. (1969). *The limits of state action* (J. W. Burrow, Ed.). Cambridge, England: Cambridge University Press.

Kawohl, I. (1969). *Wilhelm von Humboldt in der Kritik des 20. Jahrhunderts.* Ratingen bei Düsseldorf: A. Henn Verlag.

Klafki, W. (1967). Kategoriale Bildung: Zur bildungstheoretischen Deutung der modernen Didaktik (1959). In W. Klafki, *Studien zur Bildungstheorie und Didaktik* (pp. 25–45). Weinheim and Basel: Verlag Julius Beltz.

Lévi-Strauss, C. (1985). Rasse und Kultur. In C. Lévi-Strauss, *Der Blick aus der Ferne* (pp. 21–52). München: Wilhelm Fink Verlag.

Litt, T. (1960). Berufsbildung und Allgemeinbildung. In T. Litt, *Berufsbildung, Fachbildung, Menschenbildung* (pp. 9–46). Bonn: Bonner Universitäts-Buchdruckerei.

Lundgreen, P. (1997). "Mythos Humboldt" today: Teaching, research and administration. In M. Ash (Ed.), *German universities past and future: Crisis and renewal* (pp. 127–148). Providence, RI: Berghahn Books.

Lüth, C. (1982). Wilhelm von Humboldts Schulpläne im Licht kontroverser Interpretationen. *Pägadogische Rundschau, 36,* 259–276.

Lüth, C. (1985). Arbeit und Bildung in der Bildungstheorie Wilhelm von Humboldts und Eichendorffs: Zur Auseinandersetzung Humboldts und Eichendorffs mit dem Erziehungsbegriff der Aufklärung. In H.-G. Pott (Ed.), *Eichendorff und die Spätromantik* (pp. 181–201). Paderborn: Ferdinand Schöningh.

Lüth, C. (1988). Der Übergang von der privaten zur staatlichen Erziehung bei Wilhelm von Humboldt. *Informationen zur Erziehungs- und Bildungshistorischen Forschung, 33,* 33–64.

Menze, C. (1965). *Wilhelm von Humboldts Lehre und Bild vom Menschen*. Ratingen bei Düsseldorf: A. Henn-Verlag.

Menze, C. (1985). Ist die Bildungsreform Wilhelm von Humboldts gescheitert? In G. Heintz & P. Schmittner (Eds.), *Collectanea philologica: Festschrift für Helmut Gipper zum 65. Geburtstag* (pp. 381–401). Baden-Baden: V. Koerner.

Pinar, W. F., Reynolds, W. M., Slattery, P., & Taubmann, P. M. (1995). *Understanding curriculum: An introduction to the study of historical and contemporary curriculum discourses.* New York: Peter Lang.

Schelsky, H. (1978). Bildung in der wissenschaftlichen Zivilisation (1963). In J.-E. Pleines (Ed.), *Bildungstheorien* (pp. 113–129). Freiburg im Breisgau: Verlag Herder.

Simmel, G. (1986). Der Begriff und die Tragödie der Kultur. In G. Simmel, *Philosophische Kultur: Über das Abenteuer, die Geschlechter und die Krise der Moderne* (pp. 195–219). Berlin: Verlag Klaus Wagenbach. (Original work published 1911)

Wagner, H.-J. (1995). *Die Aktualität der strukturalen Bildungstheorie Humboldts*. München: Deutscher Studien Verlag.

Windelband, W. (1957). *Lehrbuch der Geschichte der Philosophie* (H. Heimsoeth, Ed.). Tübingen: J. C. B. Mohr.

5

The Significance of Classical Theories of Bildung for a Contemporary Concept of Allgemeinbildung

Wolfgang Klafki
R. Macpherson (Trans.; revised by W. Klafki)

Wolfgang Klafki is a Professor Emeritus of Education at the University of Marburg.

At the beginning of this essay it seems appropriate to recall—in the sense of critical recollection—at least some aspects of the period of German philosophical-pedagogical thought in which the concept of Bildung, and its interpretation as Allgemeinbildung, became, for the first time, a central focus of reflection.[1] We discuss the period between, roughly, 1770 and 1830, a time normally described by historians of philosophy, literature, and education as a web of relations—deeply fraught with tensions—linking the later part of the Enlightenment, philosophical-educational idealism, the classical period of German literature, neo-humanism, and at least certain undercurrents of Romanticism.

In this period, when many aspects of the concept of Bildung unfolded, most reflection on education was bound up with more or less general discussions on the philosophy of history, culture, art, politics, and anthropology—as with Lessing and Wieland, Herder and Fichte, Schiller and, to a large degree, Humboldt, and, in Goethe above all, as a theme of poetic creation, autobiographical reflection, and conversation or correspondence with contemporaries. Or it was—most clearly in Hegel's works—an integrated element of a total philosophical system. However, in Pestalozzi, and also in Kant and Herbart, Schleiermacher, Froebel and Diesterweg, reflections on a

---

[1]For histories of the concept of Bildung, see the studies by Franz Rauhut and Ilse Schaarschmidt in Klafki (1965). See also Dohmen (1964–1965) and Weil (1930).

theory of Bildung emerge within contexts that are identified in advance as specifically educational, but in such a way that the links with more comprehensive or contiguous problem contexts remain preserved.

In view of the fact that the contributions of this period, which are fundamental for our context, are often fragmentary theoretical *approaches,* one may talk of theories of Bildung in this period only as a simplification. Thus, an appropriate degree of reservation must be observed, in light of the differing variants, secondary currents and phases of the period, when I write later—sometimes presenting things in simplified terms—of "the classical phase" of philosophical–educational thought and the like. *Bildungstheorie* is used in the singular when it is a question of common characteristics of the *bildungstheoretische* thinking of this period, whereas the plural, *Bildungstheorien,* is used when the aim is to recall various emphases and stresses.

But why, it may be asked, shouldn't one let these theoretical-historical connections rest and turn immediately and directly to urgent contemporary and future problems of education? These contemporary problems in fact constitute the central theme of this chapter. Two points should be briefly made to address this question.

First, no present-day attempt to interpret the concept of Bildung or Allgemeine Bildung afresh—and (by the way) also no position that seeks to maintain the inappropriateness of those concepts for discussions about aims among present-day educationalists—can sidetrack the history of the problem. *Each and every* contemporary contribution to our problem would have to make sure of its own historical implications in order to be fully informed.

But, second, in whatever way concepts of Allgemeinbildung that are developed in the light of the tasks of the present day and the foreseeable future may turn out, the quality of such drafts will depend, *inter alia,* on whether the problem level and the degree of sophistication of reflection regarding a theory of Bildung that has already been achieved has been maintained.

However, it is also important to stress that we still find ourselves in the overall context of a bourgeois society, in which, at the point of decisive breakthrough, the classical *Bildungstheorien* were developed in response to the historical situation of the time, that is, in response to the dangers and the possibilities of the bourgeois subject. Given this, a critical review of those educational concepts would seem to be promising even for our present day. Of course, the undeniable historical distance means that we cannot expect that a straightforward adoption and application of the ideas of that era would be possible today. Even if the yield of a critical reappraisal of that spiritual heritage were to be rich, we would have to transfer it to a new conception, one that would do justice to the tasks and possibilities of our time. And, of course, such a process of transfer would also have to take into consideration the history of *Bildungstheorie* after the decades around the turn of the 18th and 19th centuries, a history that in its dominant features, at least until the emergence of the progressive education movement, I would interpret largely as a history of decline. But that task cannot be accomplished in this essay.

In the following pages, I outline an interpretation of general characteristics of classical *Bildungstheorien* and how they relate to each other. Such an interpretation should not be merely a repetition of the utterances of writers about themselves but the result of a comparative and synoptic interpretation. The framework of central concepts and their relations to each other that I offer is not to be understood as a deductive connection; the individual concepts or conceptual groups reinforce each other. The elements of this framework are found in different degrees in the authors I discuss, and their interpretation is offered not only with reference to a variety of authors but also, in part, with reference to the same author in the form of a spectrum of interpretative variants. Of course, here I can offer only a brief, simplified sketch that must lack detail.

BILDUNG AS CAPACITY FOR REASONABLE SELF-DETERMINATION

The first element of Bildung is denoted in the basic texts by terms such as *self-determination, freedom, emancipation, autonomy, responsibility, reason,* and *independence*. Bildung is understood as a qualification for reasonable self-determination, which presupposes and includes emancipation from determination by others. It is a qualification for autonomy, for freedom for individual thought, and for individual moral decisions. Precisely because of this, creative self-activity is the central form in which the process of Bildung is carried out.

This was formulated by Kant in a uniquely meaningful way with reference to the self-determination of thought in the often-quoted opening sentences of his treatise answering the question, "What Is Enlightenment?" (1784): "Enlightenment is man's departure from an immaturity of his own making. Immaturity is the incapacity to make use of one's own reason without the guidance of another" (Kant, 1968, Vol. 8, p. 35). "Have the courage to use your own reason *(Verstand)* is thus the watchword of the Enlightenment" (Kant, 1968, Vol. 8, p. 35). And, as regards moral self-determination, Kant made a statement in his lectures on education that is very much in keeping with what he says in the *Foundation of a Metaphysic of Morals* and *The Critique of Practical Reason:* "Making himself better, cultivating himself and . . . developing morality in himself—this is what a human being must do" (Kant, 1963, p. 13). In this and the later texts of Kant, such cultivation is very often also called Bildung or *Selbstbildung* (self-formation) although he was not always consistent (Kant, 1963, pp. 124, 128).

Despite the controversies around the interpretation of Kant's principle of self-formation, the basic intention that makes itself felt in the conceptual complex of the classical period is a constant element in the classical theories of Bildung. Humankind must be understood as capable of free and reasonable self-determination; the realization of this possibility has been "assigned" as a destiny, but in such a way that only each person, by himself or herself, is able, in the end, to secure this destiny; and, finally, that education is simultaneously the path and the expression of such a capacity for self-determination.

Let me illustrate this with one further example: In Wilhelm von Humboldt's fragment *On the Spirit of Humanity* (1797) there is one thesis with the heading "Path of Reason" *(Vernunft):*

> It is the destiny of man that must be sought as the final goal of his aspirations and the supreme standard of judging about him. But the destiny of man [elsewhere even in this text this is called the task of his Bildung: author's note] as a free and independent being is contained in himself alone. (Humboldt, 1956, p. 65)

BILDUNG AS SUBJECT-DEVELOPMENT IN THE MEDIUM OF OBJECTIVE-GENERAL CONTENT

The semantic content of the classical concept of Bildung is not exhausted by a discussion of only self-determination. If one leaves it at that there is always the possibility of a misunderstanding that sees this concept of Bildung as ultimately the expression of an extreme, if sophisticated, subjectivism. It must be emphasized that the basic concept of subject- or self-determination is anything but subjective! This becomes clear as soon as we consider a second group of determinants. Here the central concepts are: *humanity, humankind* and *humaneness, world, objectivity, the general.* These concepts must be thought of as being amalgamated, or as being constantly in need of being amalgamated anew, with the first group of determinants. This means that reasonableness, capacity for self-determination, and freedom of thought and action are attained *only* in the processes of acquiring and examining the content of something that does not at first come from the person himself or herself, but is the objectification of activities in the culture—and this in the widest sense: in the objectification of activities in which possibilities of human self-determination, the development of human reason, human freedom, or else their opposites, have taken shape; in civilization's achievements in the satisfaction of needs, knowledge of nature and the world of humankind, political constitutions and actions, moral orders, systems of norms and moral action, forms of social life, aesthetic products or works of art, interpretations of the nature of human existence in philosophies, religions, and world views *(Weltanschauungen)*. It is crucially important that the Bildung that is to be gained in such processes of acquiring and discussing be attributed not only to a limited group in society, a specific class or intellectual élite, as their possibility and due, but be declared in principle to be valid for all human beings. According to the classical theorists Bildung is Allgemeinbildung: It is meant to be Bildung for *all*.

It was, above all, Wilhelm von Humboldt who, in the brief phase of his activity as educational politician (1809/1810), saw the implications of this basic conviction as he designed an educational system in the form of a graded comprehensive school system. His school plans show that he was not completely successful in transforming this central thought into a concept of school organization and teaching. But his basic demand (Humboldt, 1956) was that all instruction in the school, which he saw as a form of Allgemeinbildung, have "only one and the same foundation" because "in their nature the meanest day laborer and the most consummate scholar [must] originally have been attuned the same" (p. 77), or put differently, "that each and every person, even the poorest, [should receive] a complete education" (p. 74). This basic demand implicitly contains a fundamental criticism of society and a perspective that points far into the future.

It is nevertheless undeniable that there are two limitations of grave consequence in classical theory of Bildung.[2]

First, no thinker of this period displayed consistency in examining the economic, social, and political conditions needed for the realization of this general demand for Bildung. Second, all concrete interpretations of the principle of general Bildung—even those to be found in the classical theoreticians of Bildung—reveal a clear concentration on one half, the male half, of the humanity. There is no denying that the polarizing philosophy of the genders, developed in the intellectual confines of the classical period, was a historic advance on the way to the factual equality of girls and women, an equality that has not been achieved to this day. But that philosophy of the genders, which was based on the concept of the *equal value* of the genders and which perceived the entirety of humanity as being fulfilled only in the equally developed possibilities of women and men, that philosophy, allotting as it did supposedly suprahistorical "essential characteristics" of the male and the female, did in the end remain tied to conventional social role attributions and a traditional social consciousness.

Nevertheless, the utopian "leap ahead" that their authors *consciously* performed is striking.[3] Furthermore, the conviction of almost all classical

---

[2]See Graf (1925).

[3]It is my opinion—against Hans Weil (1930)—that in its initial phase the principle of Bildung of the German classical period was not the expression of historico-political and personal resignation.

theoreticians of Bildung that their perspectives on the future were not pure illusions was the result of a historico-philosophical approach to Western history as the exemplary precursor of a world-historical process: Seen on a large scale, human history is conceived of as the process of the liberation of man for self-determination and of the reconciliation of man's spirituality with his rootedness in nature, without it being forgotten that this process had to overcome numerous barriers, mistakes, and setbacks. There was a consciousness that the decisive phases of this process of humanization, for which a once-and-for-all conclusion was never conceived of as being possible, were still ahead.

This becomes especially clear when representatives of the classical theory of Bildung contemplated the problem of which contents should be selected for the process of Bildung they pleaded for—whether for institutionally regulated or for noninstitutionalized, personal processes of Bildung. It was not only a question around curricular proposals, such as those made by Schleiermacher or Humboldt as leading figures in the educational reform in Prussia (1809–1815); it was also a question in reflections that went far beyond, a result of the understanding that the process of Bildung is, in principle, unending. It was a process and task that embraced a person's entire lifetime. As was pointed out by Hans-Joachen Gamm (1980), Goethe is perhaps the most significant example of how, given the conditions of his time and his undoubtedly privileged social situation, one individual "has, so to speak, exalted Bildung to the law of his life" (p. 19).

The implicit questions dominating all these reflections on the content of Bildung are always the same. What objectifications of human history seem best suited to open a person who is engaged in his or her own Bildung *(Selbstbildung)* to the possibilities and duties of an existence in humanity? to being humane, oriented to self-determination guided by reason? and to a freedom that is reciprocally recognized, but also limited by the claims of the others? oriented to justice, critical tolerance, cultural multiplicity, the dismantling of forms of domination and the development of peaceableness, human interaction, and the experience of happiness and fulfillment?

In Herder's *Ideas on the Philosophy of the History of Humanity,* one of the great documents of the initial phase of the philosophy of Bildung and humanity, which dates from the period 1783–1791, the optimistic theory of history—the conception of an educationally committed Protestant theologian—culminates in one chapter, whose main section bears the title: "Humanity Is the Goal of Man's Nature, and God Has Put the Fate of Our Species Into Its Own Hands With This Aim in Mind" (Herder, 1982, Vol. 4). There one can read:

> Man has been made by God into a god on earth; he laid in him the principle of his own efficacy and from the very outset set this in motion through the

internal and external needs of his nature. Man was not able to live or maintain himself if he failed to learn how to use reason; as soon as he used this, the way was open to a thousand errors and failures, but also—and precisely via these errors and mistakes—to a better use of reason. The quicker he learns to recognize his mistakes, the more vigorously he goes about correcting them, all the more progress he makes, all the more his own humanity takes shape; and he must develop it or groan under the burden of his own faults for centuries to come. (p. 343)

In this respect the entire history of peoples and nations becomes for us a school of competition for the attainment of the loveliest garland of humanity and human dignity. So many glorious nations of old attained a more modest goal; why should we not reach a purer, more noble one? They were men like us: their mission—the molding of mankind in the best of all possible ways—is ours, according to our historical circumstances, our conscience, our duties . . . The Divine Power helps us only through our application, through our intellect, through our powers. (p. 346).

Earlier in the text one can read:

Thus in error and in truth, in his stumbling and in his standing up again, man is simply himself: a weak child, but still a being that is born free; even if he is not yet reasonable, still he is at least capable of superior reason; if he is not yet gebildet [formed] for humanity, still he is capable of becoming gebildet. (pp. 65–66)

In Humboldt as well this world-historical horizon of a humanization process conceived of as task or duty describes the objective side of the Bildung of the subject: The formative process is understood by him as a mediation process—open to the front—of subjects with the historical and natural world. This is how Humboldt's fragment, Theory of the Bildung of Man (1793; see chap. 3, this volume), is phrased: "This can be fulfilled only by the linking of the self to the world to achieve the most general, most animated, and most unrestrained interplay." The integration of the individual subject in greater historical, cultural, and social contexts, which are interpreted with the prospect of man's future history in mind, can be clearly sensed when one reads in the same text:

What do we demand of a nation, of an age, of entire mankind, if it is to occasion respect and admiration? We demand that Bildung, wisdom and virtue, as powerfully and universally propagated as possible, should prevail under its aegis, that it augment its inner worth to such an extent that the concept of humanity, if taken from its example alone, would be of a rich and worthy substance.

Finally, Hegel interpreted the mediatory structure of the subject and the objectively general in the process of Bildung so that the subject "comes" in the other (the "other" means here the objective, the general) "to himself," to fundamental reasonableness, to concrete *universality*. However, this formulation signals a difference, important in terms of theory of Bildung, that sets Hegel apart from thinkers such as Herder, Schleiermacher, and Humboldt. In Hegel one pole of the dialectical relationship—the other, the objective, the general—is given a clear emphasis in comparison with the developing subject. Along the same lines are formulations like the following: In the formative process the individual "has" to work off his "mere subjectivity" (Hegel, 1952, p. 269); he "has" to "form himself" *(sich anbilden)* according to the objective already existing, "to make [himself] according to it" (Hegel, 1961, p. 272; cf. pp. 312 f.). The philosophical backdrop of such theses is provided by the metaphysics of the absolute spirit developed in Hegel's logic, a speculative draft—as magnificent in conception as it is problematic—purporting to reveal the structure of the world-historical process, in which the absolute, by passing through various mediatory stages of the subjective and objective spirit "comes to itself."[4]

To summarize: If the formative process was initially characterized as Bildung for all to gain the capacity for self-determination, a second determinant must now be kept in mind. Bildung is possible only in the medium of a general, that is, of historical objectifications of humanity, of humaneness and its conditions, with an orientation to the possibilities of, and obligation of, humanitarian progress. To put this in the spirit of a sentence of Kant's (1963) lectures on education: "Children must be brought up not in accordance with the present-day condition of the human race but rather with a future and possibly better one: that is to say, the idea of humanity and its total destiny" (p. 14). Or, in Schleiermacher's (1957) variant, which Kant, one may assume, could not have objected to: Youth must come to possess "the capability to enter upon what it meets with, but also the capacity energetically to enter upon such improvements as might present themselves" (p. 31).

INDIVIDUALITY AND COMMUNALITY IN THE CLASSICAL CONCEPT OF BILDUNG

It is only with this background of the dialectical relationship between the capacity for self-determination *(Selbstbestimmung)* and an objective-general content that a third determinant of the classical concept of education becomes available for interpretation. Here the central concepts are *individuality* and *communality*.

---

[4]Compare Reuss (1982), pp. 21 ff. See also Nicolin (1955), and Litt (1953), especially the fifth chapter in Book 4, "Logik und Freiheit," pp. 288–304, and Theunissen (1982), pp. 16f., 27f.

This structure, still abstract, in which subjects are able to attain their capacity for self-determination via the stages of appropriating and examining the objectively-general, is individual in its concrete manifestations. This process of the formation (Bildung) of individuality is understood by the classical *Bildungstheorien* not as a limiting or breaking of the validity of the universal, but as the condition for the unfolding of the potential richness of the general. Humanity can be realized only in an individual way! But that signifies, at the same time, that the concept of individuality was not understood by the classical theoreticians as being "individualistic," as a self-centered isolation. Instead, it always denotes *fundamental individuality,* and is characterized by the relationship of the individual to the general.

It is, in Herder, Humboldt, and Schleiermacher most especially, that language, or rather the acquisition and use of language, is drawn on as one of the examples for this basic realization.

Language and language competence—as essential features of human existence—are apparent in the multiplicity of languages; each individual language, as a concrete-general, allows all who acquire it an infinite number of individual realizations, notwithstanding the regularity of the vocabulary and syntax. That is why language formation *(Sprachbildung)* also always means making it possible for every child, every young person, and every adult to experience and to practice language in actual realization and in reflection as a *possibility* of the formation (Bildung) of his individuality.

But because the basic element of language is communication, that is, the reciprocal exchange of information, consideration, or argument, individualization involves its polar counterpart, communality and interpersonal relations. Thus in the educational process the formation of individuality, of personal uniqueness, is not possible in the isolation of the individual person *from* others, but only in communication *with* them, where persons evolve *as* individuals, where they—in their individuality—bring themselves into such communication and give each other recognition.

What has been illustrated here by the example of language formation was seen by the classical theorists of Bildung as a *general* structural element of Bildung. This may be demonstrated by the example of Humboldt's concept of university studies. From his point of view—as well as from the points of view of Schleiermacher, Schiller, Fichte, or Hegel—such studies were able to provide only an adequate academic preparation for professions conceived of as "public offices" when the orientation to the particular professional area, for example that of the lawyer, the administrator, the teacher, the doctor, the member of the clergy, is continually related to the overall context of the advance of individual and social humanization. One would be expressing this in a very abbreviated manner if Humboldt's notion of the conditions of studies was conceived only in terms of the maxim "solitude and freedom" (Schelsky, 1963). "Solitude in freedom" characterizes only *one* pole of formative *(bildende)* studies: the demand on the student—while studying alone—to come to grips, as an individual, with the content and the knowledge of the discipline and reflect on its significance for the humane existence of humankind. The *other* pole is characterized by the demand that

> one should live a number of years . . . in close communion with people of kindred spirits and of similar age and with the awareness that at this same place a number of people are to be found whose Bildung is complete [this formulation is certainly not meant to be taken literally: author's note] and with people who are devoting themselves . . . to the advancement and spread of knowledge. (Humboldt, 1956, p. 70)

It is of great importance for the theory of Bildung that the polar relation of "individuality" and "communality" found in the classical period be extended to the level of nations, peoples, and cultures interpreted in a figurative sense as individualities, that is, as unique manifestations of potential humanity. The question of which specific possibilities and perspectives such "collective individualities" have brought into human history, and also the question of where their particular limitations and mistakes have lain—such as in the conquest, subjection, and extermination of other nations, cultures, peoples in, for example, the colonization process of modern times—provides the yardstick for a critical point of view, the yardstick for a universal-historical approach. It is only in this framework of understanding that the high standing of Greek civilization within the classical theories of Bildung can be adequately understood. For Humboldt and other neo-humanists the—undoubtedly idealized—Greek civilization was not a normative paradigm for the present and the future, but rather an *exemplum humanitatis,* an example of humanity. Through this unique, once-and-for-all historical example, it would be possible for a person who makes Greek civilization his or her own in a productive and formative manner to attain an awareness of the humanitarian tasks of the present.

By referring several times to the "universal-historical perspective," I have introduced the necessary supplementation of the individuality-concept by the element of communality. The utopian guiding concept of the classical theorists was a peaceful coexistence of peoples, nations, and cultures, a coexistence free of any power designs, a coexistence based on mutual recognition and reciprocity for, to echo Herder's words, "the promotion of humanity." The concepts "people" and "nation," and even "patriotism," were thus understood as being anything but "nationalistic" or *"völkisch."* Thus the humanistic philosophy of Bildung necessarily includes a perspective of peace education and peace politics. This is expressed in its most meaningful form in Herder's *Ideas on a Philosophy of the History of Humanity* and in his *Letters on the Advancement of Humanity.* The climax of the *Letters* (1793–1797) is an appeal—expressed in a positively imploring tone—for the cultivation of the "spirit of peace" and "disgust at war" and—in the same context—in a sense of outrage against colonial exploitation. And however different Kant's method of justification may be from Herder's, his *Idea of a Universal History, Cosmopolitan in Intent* (1784) develops no less decisively into the demand for a league of nations as guarantor of law and order in international relations. In his *Metaphysics of Morals* (1797), as well as in the minor text *On Eternal Peace* (1795), Kant developed an ethical argument that claims to put both the postulate "There must not be war" (Kant, 1968, Vol. 6, p. 354) and the thesis "Eternal peace [is] no empty idea but a duty" (Kant, 1968, Vol. 8, p. 386)—no doubt also a duty of cognitive and moral Bildung—on a philosophical-rational footing.[5]

Here the discrepancy is especially striking between, on the one hand, the standards of critical rationality and morality guided by reason found in the intellectual domain of German classicism and its *bildungstheoretiche* approaches and, on the other hand, the false consciousness that, in the 19th century and far into the 20th century, frequently had no inhibitions about passing itself off as "culture" or "Bildung." This ideology pushed progressive-liberal, republican, and cosmopolitan traditions into the background and largely condemned them to impotence. It distanced itself from the evolving labor movement for being a rebellious ganging-together of "the masses," lacking a "fatherland," "property," and "culture." And it completed, or at least permitted without demur, the metamorphosis from cosmopolitan-liberal national thought into a narrow nationalism, and its connection to economic and political imperialism. Finally, this ideology even gave ideological support to the initial preparations for, and later takeover of, Germany by the Nazis—or let its adherents look on this disastrous process uncomprehendingly, without putting up resistance. The universal horizons that the classical theory of Bildung had opened up had disappeared from the consciousness of the majority of the so-called "people of culture."

But how does the question of the general or universal, which is the substantial precondition for human self-determination, present itself today? This problem cannot be tackled by direct reference to the concrete attempts of classicism to answer the question. I think that the general or universal in Bildung, a universal that today can or must be defined as binding, will have to focus on problems that are the central concern of us all as well of the generations to come, that is, the key problems of our social and individual existence—at least as far as these problems can be foreseen.[6]

In his *Self-Realization and Universality* (1981), Michael Theunissen came to a similar conclusion—on the level of a philosophical critique of the con-

---

[5]Blankertz's last lecture was devoted to this theme. See Blankertz (1984).
[6]Compare Klafki, 1995, 1996a, 1996b.

temporary consciousness: "A self-realization that is to be a binding postulate must realize universality in that the individual subject pursues things [read "duties"; my note] that are reasonable in themselves in orienting himself to the totality of subjects that are like him . . ." (p. 45). In his following sentence, Theunissen discussed three of the most serious elements of what is pressing down on a worldwide scale as historical universality and that are, at the very least, a challenge to "the protracted education of man to perceive world problems": "The self-realization demanded by us is manifested today . . . in the anxieties about the worldwide exploitation of nature, in the consternation about those in the world who are starving, in efforts at preserving world peace" (p. 46).

THE MORAL, COGNITIVE, AESTHETIC, AND PRACTICAL DIMENSION IN THE CLASSICAL CONCEPT OF BILDUNG

One further, basic aspect of the classical notion of *Bildungstheorie* has already been touched on several times. Bildung, as understood in the classical theory, is Allgemeinbildung or *general* Bildung. It must be the development of *all* human "powers" (to use Humboldt's expression); the comprehensive Bildung of humanity; the Bildung of "head, heart, and hand" (to quote Pestalozzi's famous formula); or of the "many-sidedness of interests" (as Herbart put it). But this development must take place in such a way that the multidimensionality of the possibilities for human interaction with natural and human-historical reality must remain bound to the unity of the responsible person. How can the relative autonomy of the various dimensions of human activity *and* their interrelation be determined at one and the same time? And how can the person educating herself *(die sich bildende Person)* in this multidimensionality still gain, retain and, even better, constantly re-create the unity of her person? Struggling with this problem is an overriding feature of the classical period of educational thinking about Bildung.

There is general agreement that there are at least three main dimensions to this issue: a moral dimension, a dimension of knowing or thinking, and an aesthetic dimension. Here the influence of the basic division of Kant's philosophy, that is, the theory or critique of practical reason, theoretical reason, and aesthetic reason or the faculty of aesthetic judgment, is unmistakable.

It should be clear from my earlier discussion of the thought of classical theorists of Bildung that Bildung meant above all the awakening of self-determined *moral responsibility,* a *readiness for moral action,* and the *capacity for moral action.* Kant, Pestalozzi, Fichte, and Hegel showed complete agreement on this score. And even interpretations of Herder, Goethe, Humboldt, or Froebel that describe their concept of Bildung as being one-sidedly aesthetic, or even aestheticizing, miss the mark.

The significance of the *dimensions of knowing* or *thinking* for the classical theorists also resulted—as I have already emphasized—from their preservation of the basic impulse of the Enlightenment—"Dare to make use of your own reason or your own intellect"—and their attempts to take the impulse further. This conception of Bildung was thoroughly "science oriented," given the horizons of the sciences' state of development at that time. However, the distinction, developed by Kant, between the terms *Verstand* and *Vernunft* hints at an important differentiation. *Verstand* denotes instrumental rationality, through which knowledge and realization are produced in a never-ending process; the results of that process can then be technically applied, in principle, to any purposes whatsoever. *Vernunft* captures that reflective mode of rationality within which, on the one hand, the preconditions for rational realization and, on the other hand, justifiable goals in the use of knowledge and its realization are inquired into. For the classical theories of Bildung, this meant inquiring into the possibilities and limits of instrumental rationality for a humanely human existence.

At the end of the 18th century and the beginning of the 19th the emergence of the separate sciences and disciplines, their increasing differentiation, the elaboration of ever more complicated methodologies, the rapid expansion of the actual content of knowledge, all this was still in its early stages, or else lay ahead. The then-contemporary sciences of man, and of the sociohistorical world, could still, at least in part, be related relatively directly to the question of their *human* significance—which means to the Bildung of humankind. However, Herder, Pestalozzi, Schiller, Humboldt, and, above all, Hegel already saw the beginnings of that process, which was later named the "dialectics of enlightenment" by Horkheimer and Adorno, as the metamorphosis of an advance of knowledge, conceived of as an emancipation, into a new *unfreedom*. They saw reflective, sense-seeking reason lagging behind, or remaining powerless, in the face of the development of instrumental intellectual knowledge and its translation into machine technologies or systems of political-administrative control. And forms of a division of labor that could no longer be comprehended or influenced by individuals appeared to an increasing degree, and found their reflection in a fragmented consciousness. The classical thinkers intended, therefore, that cognitive Bildung, the Bildung of the cognitive capacity, should never promote instrumental rationality *without* reference to reasoned reflection on its human sense, or the responsibilities involved in its applications.

It is within these terms of this classical formulation that we can judge all modern forms of the naïve belief in science as well as the claims of a "scientific orientation" to learning that is unreflective insofar as science is reduced to its instrumental dimension. The same goes for the associated belief in technological progress.

However, that judgment does not imply an irrational hostility toward science or technology. The problems of the present and of the foreseeable future will not be tackled without instrumental rationality and the technologies based on it. But without reflective reason *(Vernunft)* we will only expand the arsenal of means, thus increasing the number of new dependencies, new specializations and fragmentations, providing new potentials for conflict, new dangerous environmental consequences, and, last but not least, accumulating the possibilities for the annihilation of humankind.

Instrumental rationality must be brought under the control of a reflective reason; such reason must present itself as being oriented in a scientific and rational-argumentative manner to insight and intersubjective realizability, and yet remain at the same time be fully conscious of the moral responsibility of humankind. General Bildung must impart the prerequisites for tackling these tasks of the present and future.

The third dimension of universality, or many-sidedness, named in almost all classical *Bildungstheorien,* is the *aesthetic.* It is a yet further aspect of the story of the decay of the classical concept of Bildung that Bildung has been largely reduced to the cognitive dimension—and this while eradicating the critical element—a process that even the endeavors of 20th-century progressive education have been able to counteract only to a limited degree. The discovery, which was inherent in the classical concept of Bildung, that the aesthetic dimension contains the possibility of specific experiences of meaning and freedom, and thus has to be an indispensable perspective of Allgemeinbildung, is not recognized or adequately realized, either theoretically or practically, to this very day.

It is possible to at least hint at the scope of the reflections on aesthetic Bildung in the classical *Bildungstheorie* by identifying some of the key concepts around which these reflections were unfolded: the cultivation of "sensitivity" *(Empfindsamkeit),* the refinement of the ability to feel in the face of natural phenomena and human expression; the development of imagination and fantasy, of taste, of the capacity to enjoy, and the faculty of aesthetic judgment; and the capacity to play, and for sociability *(Geselligkeit).* These key words make clear that the classical concept of the "aesthetic," and aesthetic Bildung, does not consist of only the area of the "great" in literature, theater, the plastic and graphic arts, and music, but embraces the whole spectrum of the aesthetics of daily life, from jewelry to furniture design, from clothes to folk music, dances as much as games, festivals, forms of human interaction and styles of sociability, and ultimately, to follow Schiller, eroticism as aesthetic cultivation of natural sexuality. Once again one can notice that this period's theoretical approaches to Bildung went far beyond the framework of school education.

In this chapter it is possible to explore only some of the key notions of the extensive efforts of the classical period to draw up a theory of aesthetic Bildung as seen in Schiller's *Letters on the Aesthetic Education of Man* (1795). It is crucial, even in Schiller's terminology, that *Erziehung* ("education," "upbringing") and Bildung should not denote different things, but that *Erziehung* be understood as conscious pedagogical aid to support Bildung.

It is initially surprising that Schiller began his arguments on the theory of art and the teaching of art from two mutually interlocking questions, one political, behind which stands the experience of the French Revolution, and the second moral, which derives from the reception of Kant's ethics.

Schiller conceived of the French Revolution, to whose basic ideas he adhered even after his disappointment at the turn things had taken, as the attempt to establish for the first time in human history a "state governed by reason" *(Vernunftstaat)*. He saw such a state as one whose legislation and social order were determined not by the particularistic interests of individual and group egotism, or by feudal and absolutist structures of domination, but by principles of reason universal to all men and by the ideals of freedom and justice. He felt it necessary to interpret the actual course of the French Revolution, above all the change to the so-called terrorist phase of Jacobin rule, as a proof that the social groups upholding the Revolution were still not yet mature enough to realize a state of reason, that they continued to be governed by impulses of a nature that reason had not cultivated. As a consequence the question was: How can people do justice to the lofty demands that are contained in the idea of a reasonable state governed by freedom, and become active supporters of such a state? But because a *Vernunftstaat* must be sustained by the reason of all its citizens, the political question is only a generalized form of the problem of how each and every human being can attain the capacity to realize the intrinsic possibility of self-determination by means of "practical," that is, moral, reason given that the rootedness of human beings in their primal nature is lasting and cannot be set aside once and for all.

It is with reference to both of these questions that Schiller developed his first tentative answer. There exists a preparation for the determination by reason in the experience of the "aesthetic condition," which he also called the condition of "play" or the "experience of the beautiful." In the productive reception of art in the broad sense, or in individual creativity, man experiences the synthesis of natural drives *and* reasonable substance, the latter being the authority for independent self-formation or self-legislation. In the "aesthetic condition" man makes the experience of the unity of content or matter *and* form; of spontaneity *and* regularity; of joy of individual expression *and* regulated cooperation with others; of opening individual subjectivity *and* empathetic participation in the subjectivity of others in a social life. In the pleasurable experience of the unity of reason-determined (here aesthetic) regularities *and* rootedness in nature, those who receive aesthetically or create aesthetically, even children, become spontaneously aware of freedom—which they must then assert, even against refractory nature if need be, in situations that involve morally relevant claims of reason.

However, in the framework of this argument, aesthetic experience is primarily a "means," a tool on the path to the formation of humanity's capacity for moral-political reason. In the *Letters on Aesthetic Education* there is a second line of argument that culminates in the often-quoted sentence: "Man is playing only when he is man in the full meaning of the word, and he is completely man only when he is playing" (Schiller, 1960, p. 41). Here the aesthetic condition is no longer interpreted as merely a preparatory medium for humanity's capacity for moral-political reason, but as a qualitatively specific human possibility with a value all of its own: the experience of happiness, human fulfillment, of a fulfilled present in which an expectation always emerges that goes beyond that present moment, a hope, a future possibility of the not-yet-realized "good life" of human existence. This difference between the two interpretations of the pedagogical significance of the aesthetic, a difference that is unresolved in Schiller's text, contains much food for thought in discussions of the sense and form of aesthetic Bildung as an element of a new conception of Allgemeinbildung.

In addition to the dimensions of the many-sided Bildung that have been discussed so far—the moral, the cognitive, and the aesthetic—there is still another dimension in the last element in Pestalozzi's graphic formula of "heart, head, and hand." Once again, though, it is necessary to stress that even Pestalozzi did not conceive of his distinctions as the agglomeration of part-*Bildungen,* but placed a heavy emphasis on the necessary interrelation of different elements in the unity of the person.

The metaphor of "hand" signals for Pestalozzi the *Bildung of the practical,* the *working abilities* of the child, the young person, and the adult. The "hand" is related to individual work in the social context, the domestic, agricultural, and industrial activities Pestalozzi emphasized for the social groups to which his pedagogical work was primarily addressed. But for the present discussion the crucial thing is not the details but two key ideas: On the one hand, the realization that the tackling of reality in the practical and workaday spheres is a fundamental component of personal development, provided that it does not degenerate into early drill and exploitation; on the other hand, the understanding that the demand for a comprehensive Allgemeinbildung can be realized only from the very earliest phases onward, albeit in a graded progression, and if the perspective of future professional activities and of later proof of such abilities is represented in the process of Bildung itself.

This central idea also recurs, at least implicitly, in the educational conception of the "Pedagogical Province" in Goethe's *Wilhelm Meister,* in Fichte's utopian educational model, and in Froebel. Here one difference to Humboldt becomes obvious. He too emphasized that Bildung must prove itself, not least in the way in which the mature person structures professional activities: whether they are performed on the basis of an insight into their purpose and their requirements, and human qualities are brought into them. However, Humboldt did not reflect in a consistent way on the conditions that would have to be met by professional activities if this demand were to be fulfilled. But, despite this limitation, Humboldt did recognize the significance of vocational Bildung, and thus demanded the expansion of a broad, sophisticated vocational education system. However, he thought it necessary to sharply differentiate a preliminary vocational orientation and a preparation for later professional specializations from basic Allgemeinbildung, both chronologically and institutionally. This conception was based on a static definition of the relation of the general and the particular, and Humboldt was implicitly contradicting the aims behind his idea of Allgemeinbildung. His interpretation would also leave no room for the evolution of an idea that makes its appearance in Pestalozzi—even if only in a rudimentary manner—and is later introduced into the discussion by Marx as "polytechnical education" *(polytechnische Bildung)*. Polytechnical Bildung is not in basic contradiction to the conceptual motifs of classical educational theory, but rather in a productive continuation of them.

In the course of the 19th century, completely different motifs from those that were central for Humboldt made themselves felt, motifs that have had a lasting effect in the public consciousness, in the organization of the education system, and even in areas like adult education. A dichotomy between the so-called "Allgemeinbildung" and "vocational training" *(Berufsbildung)* emerged and persists to the present. One of the central tasks in present-day work in *Bildungstheorie* and in future *Bildungspraxis* is to try to overcome this dichotomy, not only by a coupling of so-called Allgemeinbildung (general formation) *and* vocational training *(Berufsbildung)*, but also by integrating vocational training into a new conception of general Bildung. This would signify the permanent relativization and linking of every vocational or vocation-oriented specialization to the *general* interrelations of individual and social existence.

LIMITS OF THE CLASSICAL CONCEPT OF BILDUNG AND CONCLUSIONS FOR THE PRESENT

There is no doubt that the postulates that the classical theorists of Bildung formulated in the name of Allgemeinbildung—directed in a critical spirit against the realities of their time—contained far-reaching, indeed revolutionary, sociopolitical implications. We would be ignoring their consciously utopian anticipation if we criticized these theoretical approaches on the grounds that, at best, only their most primitive elements had, or would have had, any prospect of realization under the conditions of the time. However, we must inquire into the extent to which the thinkers of that period actually did expressly and emphatically reflect that problem in the context of the theory of Bildung. Such reflection can be found only in the work of Pestalozzi and Schleiermacher.

The limitations of the social and sociocritical horizons of Pestalozzi have been either pointed out or shown to merit further study in the discussion of the "political Pestalozzi." However, no thinker of the classical period experienced with such immediacy, and discussed with a comparable degree of concreteness, the bonds linking all educational endeavors to social reality, and especially the reality of the propertyless, small-holding, and lower-middle social strata. Here as well the significance and the limitations of Pestalozzi's *Bildungstheorie* are closely linked: With amazing practical and mental energy Pestalozzi struggled in the face of the limitations of social conditions of the common people to lay bare the possibilities of humane coexistence by means of *Menschenbildung,* the conditions for the realization of an interpersonally responsible, intrinsically satisfying life.[7] But although Pestalozzi's sociopolitical objectives and political action were aimed at the dismantling and surmounting of feudal-hierarchical power relations, his positive objectives amounted to a society organized according to vocation and social estate, a society whose members were to receive and accept forms of living and participation in public life that were graded differentially. He was to come to consider economic and social inequality as irrevocable, indeed God-given. This republican, who initially advocated of the ideas of the French Revolution, distanced himself from the factual Revolution because he did not think it possible to realize the principle of equality in the triadic formula *liberté, égalité, fraternité* with its radical implications. These implications did indeed go to the roots of the social system, but Pestalozzi—like many of his contemporaries—interpreted the period of the so-called Reign of Terror not as a temporary phase in the revolutionary process, but as a departure from its own original intentions, as an expression of a qualitative change of the Revolution into a new, inhuman form of domination.[8]

---

[7]And it was in a critical spirit that he recognized the eclipsing of the plight of people in these strata of the population—impoverished and exploited, even prior to the development of capitalistically propelled industrialization—in the consciousness of many luminaries of his age, as shown, for example, by his imploring but unheard appeal to Goethe in the "One Hermit's Evening Hour" ("Abendstunde eines Einsiedlers," Pestalozzi, *Works,* Vol. 1, p. 280).

[8]Compare Rang (1967), Froese et al. (1972), Friedrich (1972), and Krause-Vilmar (1978).

Of all the thinkers of the classical period, Schleiermacher is the one whose educational theory most cogently emphasized the contradictory relation between social inequality, on the one hand, and the possibilities of human development and Bildung on the other. He clung to the utopian intention of the French Revolution's postulate of essential equality, even after the disappointments over the actual course of that revolution.[9]

Schleiermacher distinguished between inherited *(angestammter)*, that is, socio-historically conditioned, and innate *(angeborener)*, natural inequality. His educational principle with regard to inherited inequality, a principle which has a moral foundation in the claim of each human being for the recognition of his or her own intrinsic value and the right to the complete development of individual possibilities, is as follows: Under *no* circumstances may education contribute to the strengthening of inherited inequality—although it is not in the power of education to *directly* change those social relations that produce inequality. Bildung can make only an indirect contribution, insofar as it endeavors to help the young to optimally develop their human possibilities—Schleiermacher said "the inner power"—and treats the external circumstances "insofar as they are characterized as signs of inherited inequality . . . as that which has gradually to disappear" (Schleiermacher, 1957, p. 41).

Once again it becomes clear: Here Bildung is understood as general Bildung *for all*, as the right of every person, without qualitative or quantitative gradations in status determined by social origins or future position in society. However, Schleiermacher did not draw the conclusion that education would have to be designed as "political education" in the sense that the young should be helped to perceive the causes of social inequality and that the attitude should be aroused in them, as well as capacities imparted to them, to work *actively* for the reduction of social inequality.

We must leave open the reasons that prevented Schleiermacher from drawing the conclusions inherent in his approach. *One* of the reasons may be discerned in his generally optimistic philosophy of history; even Schleiermacher—in this respect like Hegel—was convinced that the history of humankind was ultimately a history of the advance of humanity, a history of liberation, both from an uncomprehended dependence on forces of nature and from human-made limitations to developmental possibilities. This basic conviction did not prevent any of the thinkers we have been discussing from recognizing and criticizing numerous inhibitions, relapses, and serious mistakes as regards the process of humanization when they considered the historical past and their present in detail. However, Schleiermacher's conviction that the humanization of society and a resulting step-by-step reduc-

---

[9]Compare Klafki (1990).

tion of socially produced inequality would come about as a process of evolution, without turbulent crises, without harsh social conflicts and revolutionary upheavals, has not been realized. In the same way, this expectation has not been realized, that an increasingly enlightened middle class or a state that would offer its educated (*gebildeten*) citizens increasing opportunities for participation would become the supporters of such a social-evolutionary process.

When Schleiermacher wrote these reflections on education and social inequality, the short-lived Prussian reform movement in which he, like Humboldt, had played a leading role, had long been checked. The plans for educational reform that they had developed, and that could only have been the first steps on the path to the realization of educational goals that were far in advance of their time, were never realized in a consistent manner. And, at this time, the predominant sections of the middle classes were well on the way to integrating themselves into the restored authoritarian state, with the result that the concept of Allgemeinbildung degenerated into a social privilege. Bildung became wedded to property and came to be used, consciously and deliberately, as a mechanism of social delimitation against the "uneducated (*ungebildeden*), propertyless masses," who emerged in the aftermath of industrial revolution. As Bildung degenerated into a stabilizing factor of a class-based society in an authoritarian state, every possibility was also excluded of facing seriously that criticism—raised especially in Marx's early works—as regards the realities of bourgeois society and the contradictions of its self-interpretation (Heydorn, 1979, 1980a, 1980b), including its understanding of education.

Whatever has been achieved in the reduction of social and educational inequality since the final decades of the 19th century, and above all in our century, the task of reducing social and educational inequality has not been accomplished and can never be accomplished *once and for all*. The consequence for our own time must be:

- Allgemeinbildung as Bildung *for all* to develop the capacity for self-determination, participation, and solidarity.
- An outline and the critical discussion *of the general as that which concerns us all* in our epoch, and
- Bildung of *all* the dimensions of *humane capacities* that we can recognize today.

Allgemeinbildung must even now also be understood as *political Bildung*, as a capability for active participation in a process of ongoing democratization.

ACKNOWLEDGMENTS

This chapter was originally published with the title "Die Bedeutung der klassischen Bildungstheorien für ein zeitgemäßes Konzept allgemeiner Bildung" in *Zeitschrift für Pädagogik, 32*(4), 455–476. It was later published in Wolfgang Klafki (1985; 5th ed., 1996), *Neue Studien zur Bildungstheorie und Didaktik: Zeitgemässe Allgemeinbildung und kritisch-konstruktiven Didaktik* (Weinheim and Basel: Beltz Verlag), pp. 15–41. This translation is published with the permission of the original copyright holder, Beltz Verlag, Weinheim and Basel. An English version of the chapter with the title "The Significance of the Classical Theories of Education for an Up-to-Date Concept of General Education" appeared in *Education: A Biennial Collection of Recent German Contributions to the Field of Educational Research,* Vol. 36, pp. 7–31 (Tübingen: Institut für Wissenschaftliche Zusammenarbeit). This version is the basis of this chapter; however, the translation has been modified and abbreviated for this book by Wolfgang Klafki and Ian Westbury.

REFERENCES

Blankertz, H. (1969). *Bildung im Zeitalter der grossen Industrie: Pädagogik, Schule und Berufsbildunng im 19. Jahrhundert.* Hanover: Schroedel.

Blankertz, H. (1984). *Kants Idee des ewigen Friedens und andere Vorträge.* Wetzlar: Büchse der Pandora.

Dohmen, G. (1964–1965). *Bildung und Schule: Die Entstehung des deutschen Bilungsbegriffs und die Entwicklung seines Verhältnisses zur Schule.* Weinheim: J. Beltz.

Fröbel, F. (1951). *Ausgewählte Schriften* (Vols. 1 & 2, Erika Hoffmann, Ed.; Vol. 3, Helmut Heiland, Ed.). Düsseldorf: H. Kupper.

Friedrich, L. (1972). *Eigentum und Erziehung bei Pestalozzi: Geistes- und realgeschichtliche Voraussetzungen.* Europäische Hochschulschriften, Series 11, Pädagogik; Vol. 9. Berne and Frankfurt/M.: Lang-Verlag.

Froese, L. u-a (1972). *Zur Diskussion, der politische Pestalozzi* Marburger Forschungen zur Pädagogik, Vol. 4. Weinheim: Beltz.

Gamm, H.- J. (1980). *Das pädagogische Erbe Goethes: Eine Verteidigung gegen seine Verehrer.* Frankfurt a. M.: Campus.

Goethe, J. W. (1948). *Goethes pädagogische Ideen: Die pädagogische Provinz nebst verwandten Texten* (W. Flitner, Ed.). Bad Godesberg: H. Küpper.

Goethe, J. W. (1951). *Wilhelm Meister* (E. Trunz, Ed.). Hamburg: C. Wegner.

Graf, U. (1925). Das Problem der weiblichen Bildung. In H. Nohl (Ed.), *Göttinger Studien zur Pädagogik* (Vol. 2, pp. 6–18). Göttingen: Vanderhoeck & Ruprecht.

Hegel, G. W. F. (1952). *Sämtliche Werke,* Vol. 7: *Grundlinien der Philosophie des Rechts oder Naturrecht und Staatswissenschaft im Grundrisse* (H. Glockner, Ed.). Stuttgart: F. Frommanns Verlag.

Hegel, G. W. F. (1961). *Sämtliche Werke,* Vol. 3: *Philosophische Propädeutik, Gymnasialreden und Gutachen über den Philosophie Unterricht* (H. Glockner, Ed.). Stuttgart: F. Frommanns Verlag.

Herder, J. G. (1982). *Werke in fünf Bänden* (R. Otto, Ed.). Berlin and Weimar: Aufbau Verlag.

Heydorn, H.-J. (1979). *Über den Widerspruch von Bildung und Herrschaft* (Bildungstheoretische Schriften,Vol. 2). Frankfurt/M.: Syndikat.

Heydorn, H.-J. (1980a). *Zur bürgerlichen Bildung: Anspruch und Wirklichkeit* (Bildungstheoretische Schriften,Vol. 1). Frankfurt/M.: Syndikat.

Heydorn, H.-J. (1980b). *Ungleichheit für alle: Zur Neufassung des Bildungsbegriffs* (Bildungstheoretische Schriften, Vol. 3). Frankfurt/M.: Syndikat.

Humboldt, W. (1956). *Schriften zur Anthropologie und Bildungslehre* (A. Flitner, Ed.). Düsseldorf: Verlag H. Kupper.

Kant, I. (1963). *Ausgewählte Schriften zur Pädagogik und ihrer Begründung: Ausgewählte pädagogische Schriften* (H.-H. Groothoff, Ed.). Paderborn: F. Schöningh.

Kant, I. (1968). *Kants Werke: Akademie Textausgabe: Unveränderter photomechanischer Abdruck des Textes der von der Preussischen Akademie der Wissenschaften 1902 begonnenen Ausgabe von Kants gesammelten Schriften*. Berlin: de Gruyter.

Klafki, W. (Ed.). (1965). *Beiträge zur Geschichte des Bildungsbegriffs* (Kleine Pädagogische Texte, Vol. 33). Weinheim: Beltz.

Klafki, W. (1990). Gleichheit, Ungleichheit und Erziehung: ein Zentralproblem der Erziehungstheorie Schleiermachers. In F. Zubke (Ed.), *Politische Pädagogik: Beiträge zur Humanisierung der Gesellschaft* (pp. 17–38). Weinheim: Deutscher Studien Verlag.

Klafki, W. (1995). Education for Europe seen from an international perspective: Key problems as a central point for future-oriented educational work. In C. Kubina (Ed.), *The Europe schools in Hessen: A perspective for the school of tomorrow* (Materialen zur Schulentwicklung, No. 23, pp. 4–12). Wiesbaden: Hessisches Institut für Bildungsplanung und Schulentwicklung.

Klafki, W. (1996a). Grundzüge eines neuen Allgemeinbildungkonzepts: Im Zentrum: Epochaltypische Schüsselprobleme. In W. Klafki, *Neue Studien zur Bildungstheorie und Didaktik: Zeitgemässe Allgemeinbildung und kritisch-konstruktive Didaktik* (pp. 43–81). Weinheim and Basel: Beltz Verlag.

Klafki, W. (1996b). Core problems of the modern world and the tasks of education: A vision for international education. In *Education: A biennial collection of recent German contributions to the field of educational research* (Vol. 53, pp. 7–18). Tübingen: Institut für Wissenschaftliche Zusammenarbeit.

Krause-Vilmar, D. (1978). *Liberales Plädoyer und radikale Demokratie: H. Pestalozzi und die Stafner Volksbewengung.* Meisenheim am Glan: Hain.

Lessing, G. E. (1969). *Ausgewählte Texte zur Pädagogik* (D.-J. Löwisch, Ed.). Paderborn: F. Schöningh.

Litt, T. (1953). *Hegel: Versuch einer kritischen Erneuerung.* Heidelberg: Quelle & Meyer.

Marx, K. (1962). Zur Kritik der Hegelschen Rechtsphilosophie, Einleitung. In H. J. Lieber & P. Furth (Eds.), *Werke, Schriften, Briefe* (Vol. 1, pp. 488–505). Stuttgart: Cotta.

Marx, K. (1971). Die deutsche Ideologie. In H. J. Lieber & P. Furth (Eds.), *Werke, Schriften, Briefe* (Vol. 2, pp. 5–55). Stuttgart: Cotta.

Nicolin, F. (1955). *Hegels Bildungstheorie: Grundlinien geisteswissenschaftlicher Pädagogik in seiner Philosophie.* Bonn: H. Bouvier.

Pestalozzi, H. (1927). *Sämtliche Werke* (A. Buchenau, E. Spranger, & H. Stettbacher, Eds.). Berlin: W. de Gruyter.

Rang, A. (1967). *Der politische Pestalozzi* Frankfurter Beiträge zur Soziologie, Vol. 18. Frankfurt/M: Europäische Verlagsanstalt.

Reuss, S. (1982). *Die Verwirklichung der Vernunft: Hegels emanzipatorisch-affirmative Bildungstheorie* (Materialien aus der Bildungsforschung, No. 22). Berlin: Max-Planck-Institut für Bildungsforschung.

Schelsky, H. (1963). *Einsamkeit und Freiheit: Idee und Gestalt der deutschen Universität und ihrer Reformen* (Rowohlts deutsche Enzyklopädie 171/172). Reinbek bei Hamburg: Rohwohlt.

Schiller, F. (1960). *Briefe über die ästhetische Erziehung des Menschen von Friederich Schiller* (A. Rebel, Ed.). Bad Heilbrunn: J. Klinkhardt.

Schleiermacher, F. (1957). *Pädagogische Schriften* (E. Weniger, Ed.). Düsseldorf: H. Küpper.

Theunissen, M. (1981). *Selbstverwirklichung und Allgemeinheit: Zur Kritik des gegenwärtigen Bewußtseins.* Berlin: de Gruyter.

Weil, H. (1930). *Die Entstehung des deutschen Bildungsprinzips.* Bonn: F. Cohen.

SOURCES FROM THE DIDAKTIK TRADITION

6

Didaktik as a Theory of Education

Erich Weniger
Gillian Horton-Krüger (Trans.)

Erich Weniger, born in 1894, completed his first state (teacher certification) examination in history, German, and Latin and his doctorate in history in 1921 at the University of Göttingen, with a dissertation on the Prussian reforms of the beginning 19th century. After a year of teaching in a higher secondary school and completing his second state teacher examination, he returned as assistant to the University of Göttingen. Weniger was strongly influenced by his mentor Hermann Nohl, a major representative of the German *Reformpädagogik* and human-science pedagogy.

From 1929–1933 Weniger taught at the teacher training academies in Kiel, Altona, and Frankfurt. He first was suspended, and then dismissed, from his position by the Nazis in 1933 and, until the end of the Third Reich, centered his work on military education. In 1945, Weniger returned to Göttingen and worked for 3 years as director and professor at the teacher training college. He was appointed a professor at the University of Göttingen in 1948 and taught there until his death in 1961.

Weniger was involved in the rearming of the Federal Republic of Germany as a staff expert. He also was committed in school reform as a member of the German committee for the educational and school system *(Deutscher Ausschuss für das Erziehungs- und Bildungswesen)* from 1953 until his death.

Weniger's main fields of research were social education, military education, the theory of political education, teacher education, Didaktik, and the theory of Bildung.

His more than 400 publications include *Die Grundlagen des Geschichtsunterrichts: Untersuchungen zur geisteswissenschaftlichen Didaktik* [The Basis of History Teaching: Examinations From the Viewpoint of Human Science Didaktik]

(1926); *Wehrmachtserziehung und Kriegserfahrung* [Military Education and the Experience of War] (1938); *Die Erziehung des deutschen Soldaten* [The Education of the German Soldier] (1944); *Didaktik als Bildungslehre. Teil 1: Theorie der Bildungsinhalte und des Lehrplans* [Didaktik as Theory of Education. Part 1: Theory of Educational Contents and of the Syllabus] (1952); *Die Eigenständigkeit der Erziehung in Theorie und Praxis: Probleme der akademischen Lehrerbildung* [The Independence of Education in Theory and Practice: Problems of Academic Teacher Education] (1953); *Politische Bildung und staatsbürgerliche Erziehung* [Political Education and the Education of the Citizen] (1956); *Didaktik als Bildungslehre. Teil 2: Didaktische Voraussetzungen der Methode in der Schule* [Didaktik as Theory of Education. Part 2: Didaktik Preconditions of Method in School] (1960).

—Jörg Biehl

INTRODUCTION: THE TASK OF DIDAKTIK

Didaktik is primarily, and certainly in everyday terms, the study of teaching and learning, the study of instruction. But instruction is more than simply the interaction of teaching and learning. It encompasses widely differing factors in complex interrelationships. Didaktik subjects everything that happens in instruction to its observation. We call the structured context within which the growing generation is taught and knowledge is handed down the *order of teaching (Lehrgefüge).*[1]

The order of teaching is thus the specific connection of factors and elements in which adolescents—or indeed anyone engaged in a learning, assimilating, or developing process—interact with the world of values, with objective intellect, with society, with the adult generation, and with where education takes place. To this concept belongs the conscious will imposing itself on the structure. Order of teaching is the system that is imposed or simply used to achieve formative *(bildend)* encounters, or confrontation, with the intellectual, historical, and social world and to attain dominion over the natural world by recognizing one's place within it, as it were, to achieve acceptance of the world by the younger generation. As we show in this chapter, however, whatever is consciously desired and imposed is nonetheless tied to the precepts and influences of reality. It may be the case that nothing in the order of teaching is consciously desired beyond the will to use it, to fit with an educational intent into this structure of the world and life, everything else being predetermined.

---

[1]*Translator's note: Das Lehrgefüge,* translated here as "the order of teaching," encompasses the whole fabric of content and method. The concept of *Lehre* in Didaktik comprehends content and method, teaching and learning as one entity. Weniger restricted the term to the context of school.

Within the context of the Reform Pedagogy *(Reformpädagogik)* movement and modern theory of science, Didaktik of this kind is predestined to be located within the human sciences. This means that it proceeds from the actuality of the order of teaching, from the real-world educational situation, and not from theory or principles. Yet the context of meanings and effects that Didaktik tries to encompass is historical, that is, must not be comprehended from the superficial aspect of form alone. Moreover, the context changes over time, as a whole and in its component parts. In the educative *(bildend)* encounter between the generations in institutionalized teaching and learning, and in whatever other forms of introduction there may be to the intellectual world, it is to a large extent the progress and change of the historical world itself that is taking place. Processes of Bildung are not, say, merely concomitant and consequential phenomena of historical life: History is also happening within them. With the historicity of its object, Didaktik itself now becomes historical, that is, it cannot present insights of universal and eternal validity, but must always strive to understand the changing situation, and from there reshape the theory of action. . . .

Historical change in the order of teaching is accompanied by a change in the language in which Didaktik formulates its statements and gives its directives. Didaktik, too, is obliged to keep up with the times; it is bound to the changing and newly derived concepts in the historical work of Bildung. This linguistic "appropriateness" to the times is also expressed in the affinity between the concepts of Didaktik and the terminologies in which a particular period endeavors to express its most pressing concerns. . . .

To conclude this introduction, we now need to reflect on the relationship of Didaktik to the methodology of instruction. As these terms are nowadays often used synonymously, it would appear that consciousness of the singularity of Didaktik has been lost. . . .

Methodology is the study of methods to be applied in teaching. Method can mean either the objectively given way of comprehending a subject (scientific method) or the way given as a result of human dispositions and talents or inclinations and interests to enable a person to take possession of a particular subject matter. Method is always a secondary, a relative aspect, valid only under quite specific conditions. It is also susceptible to change over time. Method, therefore, can be described and taught only with reference to the preconditions of Didaktik. Of course, a theory of possible methods with a relatively high validity can then be developed. But the development of method must always proceed from and refer back to practical requirements. What is needed, therefore, is a human-science study of forms of instruction and Bildung, that is, of the structure of methods, referring, on the one hand, to the Didaktik of each teaching discipline and to general Didaktik as theory of education *(Bildungslehre)* and, on the other, to a reflection of the coherence of all educational and instructional measures in the course of education.

THE CURRICULUM *(LEHRPLAN)*

Any form of Didaktik that aims to proceed from the order of teaching must first ask itself from which point its subject can best be observed in order to be most representative of all its factors and elements. It may be argued that the order of teaching should be sought and portrayed at any point where teaching takes place. After all, as the whole is present in all of the component parts, it could be depicted through any one of the details. Thus it would seem appropriate to address oneself to the immediate pedagogical relationship and to gauge from this the whole, the structure of the order of teaching. But this would be a most arduous task, for although the whole is most certainly echoed in every lesson, in each of the teacher's questions, it would be both difficult and time consuming to infer the whole from each individual fact, and to represent it conceptually. Therefore we must ask whether the order of teaching has already been represented, possibly conceptually, at some point, and is already accessible to us. Only the analysis of such a conceptual representation and its confrontation with the educational reality we remember and observe can lead us deeper, and show what is missing and what defies codification, in other words what can be excluded or committed to a margin of free choice.

Such codification of the order of teaching is found in curricula *(Lehrplan)*. This is not to say that the Lehrplan always express the didactic substance, the inner context of the order of teaching, in an adequate and conceptually appropriate form. And educative *(bildend)* encounters between the generations are not restricted to the organized framework of the Lehrplan, but occur as part the whole breadth and variety of life itself. Yet the Lehrplan is the only conceptual order of teaching with the scope to subsume all given features, and relatively powerful in validating what is demanded. Even those aspects not themselves shaped in the Lehrplan can be understood and judged from its standpoint. We can more easily comprehend the irrational components of the process of Bildung if we see what can be directly determined and ordered through express directives, as are given by the Lehrplan. Thus, all reflection in Didaktik can be linked to a theory of the Lehrplan *(Lehrplantheorie)* and, as Aloys Fischer said, the struggle to create a new educational ideal and a reformed system of Bildung may be formalized as the struggle to design the Lehrplan. In this fight for the Lehrplan, which dates from the start of Reform Pedagogy, but to which the political and social movements of the time contributed, the position of Lehrplan was elucidated and at the same time changed, so today we are in a better position than before to comprehend the conditions determining the systematic structures of the order of teaching and the preconditions created by the existence of a systematic structure for educational action. Thus, the Lehrplan can be explored as an example to illustrate the whole issue of the content of Bildung, providing ready access to the way the categories of selection and concentration can best be obtained.

The task of Lehrplan is to establish the goals of Bildung, and to select and concentrate what used to be called instructional material, now referred to as the "assets" or "values" of Bildung, and that we prefer to term *contents of Bildung*. The Lehrplan stipulates what is to count in instruction. As a consequence every factor of human life, every social group, and every idea that wishes to exert broad and lasting influence on young people within the framework of school and organized learning must try to gain recognition and a position in valid Lehrplan. Any intellectual movement or tendency is, in the long run, recognized and secure as an influence on Bildung only if its goals and devices are accorded space in the Lehrplan. The fight for the Lehrplan is not, as would sometimes appear, an argument over the best instructional methods, or the selection and distribution of particular instructional matter. It is a battle of human influences and, as one-sided power decisions are impossible in human life today, the struggle is one of achieving a balance of forces in school and organized learning that corresponds to the relative positions of power held by the factors participating in the school. If a Lehrplan is "right" it expresses, as far as the outside world is concerned, the relative influences of the factors participating in Bildung and, as far as instructional practice is concerned, the degree of institutional and rational availability of the contents of Bildung through prescriptive and directive systematization—in other words, the extent to which intellectual influences or substances can be made available as rational teaching matter for the encounter with young people. This cannot, of course, always be inferred from the formulae and directives of the Lehrplan, because the very inclusion of a piece of teaching matter in the Lehrplan implies that a translation has been made, and a new relationship created that aims to subsume widely differing elements on the one level.

The Lehrplan has its own conceptual structure. . . . Everything that seeks inclusion has first to be transposed into this conceptual structure, and herein is revealed the inherent autonomy and arbitrary nature of a Lehrplan, its conservationist and leveling tendency, which is crucial with respect to innovations and can delay decisions over long periods. Once a Lehrplan is established, anything new must, to a certain extent, be adapted to fit the existing structure. . . .

To assess the significance of a Lehrplan, one must know how to read its language, and to retranslate it, in order to probe beyond the conceptual formulations, and to arrive at the actual elements of influence that, in an historical human context, refer to each other and to the order of teaching represented in the Lehrplan. Even a simple change in the arrangement of subject matter, such as the removal of ancient history from the final to the penultimate year of the academic secondary school, the Gymnasium, the exclusion of the Latin essay, the inclusion of natural science at all levels, and so forth, apparently effected for reasons of method, can express changes in the balance of power between the human influences, and may reflect major decisions.

These manifold, heterogeneous influences have come to bear on the Lehrplan over the course of time, which means that the smooth conceptual surface overlays different historical strata. The rank of the factors involved must, therefore, be ascertained, as their multiplicity is not simply a redundant by-product of history that reasoned reflection can sweep away leaving one single factor or a new order, but is in itself the very precondition for the emergence of any Lehrplan. Each factor must be assigned its legitimate place in the blend of the Lehrplan. The curricular significance of the great historical influences on Bildung, the position of science, religion, the state, and the professions in instruction, must be analyzed and, most important, the highest ranking and dominant influence ascertained.

To begin: The dominant factor in each school subject would appear to be an academic discipline. Each subject, it would seem, corresponds to an academic discipline, the structure and tenets of which determine the arrangement of school instruction. Every discipline, moreover, has an immanent set of objectives, an ideal of the perfection of its knowledge, of completeness, of the consummation of the attitude it demands. This would also seem to provide the goal of instruction, modified only by the particular conditions of school, especially the abilities of the students and the level of their intellectual development.

However, at this point a quarrel arises over the character of subject teaching in the school: The academic disciplines themselves tend to regard the teaching of the school subject as a preparation for the teaching of the academic subject, without which the instruction would be incomplete. But the school cannot admit that its entire efforts are nothing but preparation for later learning. . . . The school is obliged to ensure that all of its subjects are taught in a purposeful context and with an object in view that is complete in itself, and that the teaching achieves relative completeness and provides a real end in itself. On the other hand, it is inconceivable that school should achieve the same goals as discipline, without the attention to detail and the detours that the academic disciplines can make. Thus it is probable that school subject and discipline must first conjoin in relation to a third entity that instills meaning into both the purpose of a discipline and the goals of instruction.

The question therefore reaches beyond the individual subject, and it is here that the real difficulty begins: when a fixed order is superimposed on the subjects in the school system as a whole, when the sciences and cultural systems, the influences and ideals of Bildung, are presented in the individual subjects' need to be absorbed into a superordinate systematization. This is where the necessity for a Lehrplan in its true sense arises. None of the major subjects has an intrinsic awareness of its natural boundaries and of its particular service within the whole. Every subject has the drive to become the dominant factor for the Lehrplan.

Since the dissolution of the Encyclopaedia of the ancient and mediaeval world, with its qualitative and quantitative ordering of each discipline, the system of the disciplines does not in itself contain any criteria for choosing between the claims [of the different disciplines]. Indeed, modern curricula have developed only as a result of the breakdown of the old system of the liberal arts *(septem artes)* caused, on the one hand, by the increasing autonomy of the individual disciplines and, on the other hand, by the changing role of religion (there was no longer a religious world order, but specific religious instruction), of the absolute state, and of natural science.

The Lehrplan, since it emerged in its modern sense, is upheld and regulated by the state. The work of Paulsen, Spranger's studies of the relationship of politics and education in the modern world, Heubaum's research, Matthias' recollections from his years of practice, are all full of examples of how the state continually intervenes in curricula, how it forcibly juxtaposes opposing ideals or simply excludes . . . , how it allies itself with one philosophical system against others, . . . how it opposes a new ideal of Bildung and, if the progress of this ideal cannot be stopped, how it distorts the meaning by adding alien elements. . . . On the other hand, it may commit itself to a new ideal against the resistance of everything that has held valid up to that point. . . . This is not, however, a perhaps inevitable distortion of the true idea of Lehrplan, not an intervention of hierarchical power to promote causes outside the Lehrplan, though this might often have played a role. For the state, the Lehrplan is not only a purely administrative entity to ensure uniformity of control and mobility between schools within its territory, to achieve uniform entitlement to its services, and to assert certain specific individual demands. This is all involved, but the influence of the state is not restricted to this formal aspect, or to a formal decision between the other, "real" factors, the sciences, the church, the professions, pedagogy. The Lehrplan is more a vehicle through which the state can play "an active part in the education of the people, if it is important to enhance both the power of communality and the awareness of the latter" (Schleiermacher). Or as Lorenz von Stein described the true relationship: In modern times as the age of a system of civic Bildung, we recognize in teaching the basic traits of intellectual individuality and the power of public life. Through Lehrplan and official regulations, within the system of educational institutions *(Bildungsanstalten)* it provides, the state establishes the canon that is, in effect, the canon of human life itself, and that expresses within itself the organic process of Bildung that lies in the essence of personal development. Thus the state strives to represent its inner form within the cultural system of school and Bildung.

The conceptual precipitation of this, both expressing and directing, is the Lehrplan. It is pointless to say that school pursues culture or is a tool of the state. This is all true, of course, though secondary. Nor should the character of the power, with its dangers, that gives the state a certain predominance in the competition to shape school be denied. But, from the point of view of the state itself, school is first and foremost an expression of its intellectual condition, its historical position, its inner intellectual strength, which here finds immediate expression in the entity of Bildung.

The modern state no longer ranks above the values and views, or above the parties and social groups that embody them, in the manner of the old absolute state. The state itself has become the object in the struggle between views and social groups (as it used to be, admittedly, in secret), is shaped by them and, in its present constitutional form, is a continually changing expression of the division of power within the nation. . . . It is the idea of democracy that the state should be supported and developed by the operative powers of the nation in the order of their human influence. If, therefore, the state aims, like any other influence on Bildung, to ensure its present and continued existence through the educational system, the notion of perfection inherent in its form paradoxically compels it to qualify itself and its form and to confine the exercise of its power to the preservation of civic life and national culture. The state's vitality rests on the human powers of the people who support it, as political life is supposed to represent a decision, continually remade, regarding the best form of life, and as the coming generation will itself have to make responsible decisions about the form and life of the state. To use Schleiermacher's terms, the interest of the state in education depends on the awakening of the communal spirit, on the concurrence of individuals with the manifestation of the state and, at the same time, on the development of the younger generation in such a way that all skills are trained that are necessary for the upkeep of life in general in the state.

However, this freedom is restricted by the necessity of securing a form of state that makes such liberty possible, and thus we may observe the bipolarity of the democratic state system that poses a difficult task for the selection and systematization of the contents of Bildung. There is, of course, the particular danger that Lehrplan and school can become instruments of power wielded by the majorities ruling the state. In all events, the achievement of continuity in Bildung would appear to be particularly difficult. As early as the school reform of the 1890s, as Spranger has emphasized, the aim was no longer to work out an all-embracing state ideal of Bildung, but to equate the state idea of Bildung with the conservative ideal. Nowadays, these dangers have grown and it sometimes appears that, instead of having one regulatory factor in the Lehrplan that is more influential than the others from the outset, we have several factors struggling to dominate the Lehrplan—but via the medium of the state. Social groups and political parties, advocates of differing world views, not only want regard within the state, but dominion, and thus dominion over the school and the Lehrplan. The school would thus appear to be fully politicized. If in the long term clear decisions do not emerge from these struggles, an element of insecurity and unrest creeps into the school and the Lehrplan. They can no longer promote the development of their educative *(bildend)* potential, but depend on temporary compromises between the parties.

Given this situation of the modern state, recourse to any of the other influences—science, the church, industry, or the professions—is effectively barred. None of these, no matter how powerful, will be able to assert its authority over even the other influences, let alone over the state. Moreover, none of them, apart from the Catholic Church, represents a more closed system, surer of their ends and means, than the state. Not even in the areas of Bildung to which they directly relate and that they influence, such as the individual school subjects, does their existence contribute to finding criteria for the selection and concentration of contents.

THE FIRST STRATUM OF CURRICULUM: THE STATE AND THE INFLUENCES ON EDUCATION—THE IDEAL OF BILDUNG

At this point, the argument could almost appear to be leading to a justification of an omnipotent construct of state pedagogy to which all independent human life, all liberal educational effort must be sacrificed. In fact, the corollary is quite different. The difficulties that result from this seemingly absolute superiority of the state in education can be overcome, the dangers that spring from it for the freedom of education and for independent human life can be guarded against within the real situation, only by taking the true relations between the influences into account, in the task and organization of Bildung itself. But in these relations and in their historical development, in the structural change of the state and the other influences, it is inherent that, although the danger of an omnipotent state pedagogy certainly always threatens, the autonomy of pedagogy, the safeguarding of pedagogical behavior, and the freedom of pedagogical work is most strongly guaranteed by the relationship between education and the state, and would be more endangered under any other arrangement.

Perhaps this situation, symbolized by the transformation of rigid curricula into guidelines, can best be expressed as follows: By the very conditions of its existence, the state must have an effect in education by allowing dynamic freedom in this field, by affording opportunity for the dynamic influences on Bildung to influence the young, and and by securing them in the form of curricula. All other forces must, in order to become influences on Bildung, agree to a transposition of their aims and contents into the form of pure (purpose-free) Bildung. The state itself is this pure form of Bildung in the confrontation between influences on Bildung and the generations in the life world of school. Thus the state plays a double role in school. On the one hand it is one power among others that struggle to take effect and bear offspring. For this it has, like the other influences, preferred instruments in the context of Bildung—in this case history and civics—and all demands that it makes from the point of view of its concrete tasks as the state must first be transposed into appropriate forms. At the same time, however, the state as an educating entity *is* school and is represented by the singular order of educational processes *(Bildungsvorgänge)* within it.

This does not mean that such a position of the state is inevitable. The guarantors of this inner form of the state are never the institutions and curricula themselves, whose spirit can be misinterpreted and sabotaged, but living human beings who feel responsible for both the state and education. In curricula, the state gives responsible-thinking, civically and educationally oriented people the opportunity of showing the young its worth, and whoever wishes to serve the state and at the same time provide a truly worthwhile education must adapt themselves to this objective structure. The essence of what is expressed conceptually in the Lehrplan and institutionalized in the organizational structure requires the educator to come alive, and thus curricula are directed primarily at the teacher. They outline the human assets that the state must demand of its teachers. Indeed, each new Lehrplan should require fresh training of teachers and, as changes take place within the working life of a teaching generation, constant inservice education.

Curricula no longer contain the material that the students are to acquire and retain for testing. They contain only the human assets of the adult generation, of which the state knows it is the representative and in which it sees the human qualification of its existence. Again, this means that any absolute claim on the part of the state is restricted: It does not lay down contents of general validity as a superior authority, but always depends on the actual human assets of the nation, on the substance valid at the time. In practice, this means that the state codifies in the Lehrplan the assets of each adult generation, which means that Lehrplan today cannot be expected to last longer than a generation. These human assets that the curricula describe are not material. The material given in the Lehrplan is more a medium to express the pivotal human forces and contents. Thus the Lehrplan for the Gymnasium always contains more material than the teacher can cover, even in a more specialized area, whereas the Lehrplan for the elementary school always contains less than is required if the teachers are to present human substance effectively. On the other hand, general curricula . . . tend to become guidelines that determine only the scope and the fundamentals of Bildung and leave the rest, particularly selection, to the more specific curricula or syllabi of the regions or institutions, or to the teachers themselves.

The contradictions that maintain tension and momentum in the relationship between state and culture and that are the lifeblood of this relationship must be reflected in the Lehrplan and may not be eliminated. The Lehrplan indicates which of the opposing forces legitimate our present existence and, therefore, cannot be relinquished. It is these that should be alive in the teacher. The teacher represents the changing constellations of opposites in school, as the state does in life as a whole. The antinomies of the contemporary human situation are alive in the teacher, but at rest. In the teacher and in the educational community of school, the student is confronted with the human character of the age, despite all contradictions, and, beyond it, with human life itself. The student develops against this background, confronts the whole in the person of the teacher, and retranslates it into the movement from which it sprang.

Nothing is achieved, however, by the formal dialectical description of this whole as the unity of contradictions taking shape in the person of the teacher. Granted, the pedagogical attitude of the teacher may arise from the incontrovertible contradictions in our culture. The more difficult it is to obtain a uniform overall picture and the more the Lehrplan assumes the guise of a compromise between opposing forces, the less absolute and authoritative can the Lehrplan and teaching appear, and the more apparent it becomes that it is the child that must be the point of departure and the yardstick for the work. But this alone would not suffice, quite apart from the fact that a child orientation cannot really be stipulated in the Lehrplan. The educative *(bildend)* potential of the contents could not come to bear in their mere juxtaposition, given the constant instability of their relations. The common thread that binds them together in the Lehrplan needs to be defined, because it is in this context in which they are comprehended.

More is needed, therefore, than the mere statement of the balance of forces at the time the Lehrplan is developed. An ideal is required that governs how these forces are to be regulated in accordance with the will of the state, an ideal that encompasses the individual forms of dialectical unity still possible with respect to the differences in the teachers' personality structures, their disciplines, and their basic attitudes. The Lehrplan today is not only a synopsis of those past values deemed so important by the adult generation, represented by the state, that they must be passed on to the next generation through the medium of formal education. Any inventory of this kind would be purely historical and would immediately turn present into past. Rather, the Lehrplan tries to anticipate future development and expresses, in its picture of the future, the unity that is assumed in the teacher beyond any one-sidedness that may otherwise be in evidence.

Contemplation of the dynamic, educative substances *(bildende Gehalte)* of the present can proceed only from the *task* before us. The Lehrplan becomes comprehensible only in conjunction with the tasks, either expressly stated or tacitly assumed, that arise for the state in the field of education. . . . In formal terms this is always a twofold task: On the one hand the community is to be enhanced and awareness of community created; on the other hand, the inner strength and purity of the factors that give the modern state its dynamic quality and guarantee its continuance are to be maintained. In terms of content, however, the tasks in question here, and which form the initial basis for the Lehrplan, are not those that arise from the autonomous development of the disciplines—sciences, arts, and so on—with which only the adult, "educated" generation can be confronted. Nor do they concern the immediate fulfillment of political or cultural demands with the tools of education, but the development of education *(Erziehung und Bildung)* arising from the general situation of people, state, and culture, in which the continued socio-human life of people and state is secured. The general tasks of people and state are themselves applied to the Bildung of the coming generations, in other words on their humanity and human attitude.

THE SECOND STRATUM OF CURRICULUM: DOMAINS OF HUMAN EXISTENCE AND BASIC INSTRUCTION

To recapitulate, the following contribute to the forming of the Lehrplan: the state as educator; the powers within the state that influence education, that struggle to shape the state, to find expression within it, to gain status and independence, and that want to integrate the human and educational assets and the awareness of values of the adult generation into the order of teaching; the immediate, concrete task of Bildung that presents itself to the state and the powers within it; and finally the ideal of Bildung that is developed, in awareness of this task, from the given resources and intentions and that refers to future human attitudes. The structure of the Lehrplan can be understood only from this perspective and all reflection in Didaktik must proceed from here. Then, however, a *second* layer is revealed, independent of the first layer and restricted by it, which must ensure fullness and variety in contrast to the extreme concentration demanded by the conditions and tasks of the present.

Here the concern is to weave a fabric of ideas representing reality, to impart basic experiences in which the whole context of life becomes apparent, the network of "essential relations" in which life is lived. It is the categories for mastering the world and life itself that are to be taught in schools. Here then is the position of the schooling of functions and formal Bildung, but not only as a means of transmitting the elementary conditions of every attitude to life and the world in logical thinking, apperception, and association of thoughts—admittedly, this elementary area occupies a large part of the Lehrplan in practice—but also to achieve completeness of the world view and humanity. If, for example, the task of educating *(Bildungs-aufgabe)* at a particular period and the ideal of Bildung developed from it demand concentration on a one-sided human attitude, it falls to the second layer to guarantee the basic domains of thought in which human existence reaches fulfillment, not only to complement, not only because these human directions are interdependent and none of them completely dispensable in the balance of life, but also because future changes in the common task must be prepared for. The *Didaktik of the domains of human existence* treats the problems that arise here, the categorization of individual subjects according to domains of human existence and the relationship of all subjects to each domain, as well as the definition of the basic domains in their assertion of independence over any form of concentration, particularly those assigned to the sciences and the arts.

THE THIRD STRATUM OF CURRICULUM: KNOWLEDGE AND SKILLS

In Lehrplan and in teaching itself, the area occupying the most time and attention is one that can be assigned to a third layer and that may be summarily termed *knowledge and skills,* in contrast to the formation of views *(Bildung der Gesinnung)* and human attitude in the widest sense of the first two layers. Knowledge and skills often turn out to be a condition for work in the other layers and there are levels of instruction, parts of instruction, and whole subjects that appear in the knowledge and skills they endeavor to instill to serve only as preparation for more advanced studies and as pointers to other subjects. . . . The independent existence of the preparatory subjects is mediated. This can usually be seen most clearly in the classics, where students are first required to spend years practicing Latin grammar and unconnected translation to prepare them for the encounter with the ancient world later in their school career. Latin classes in the first and last grades have only the name in common.

This area poses difficult questions of method, particularly today, when many students do not go on to fulfill what instruction has been preparing them for, either because they leave full-time education or continue on a different path. There are occasions, too, where the subjects intended as the fulfillment of the instruction that has gone before are not even taught in the same section of the school system, but in other schools. In some cases, fulfillment comes only in vocational training, or indeed even in the living of life itself. Some curricular tasks have no longer anything to do with Bildung. They concern the out-of-school objectives of influences operating outside school as well as certain practical necessities of jobs, commerce, the Church (Hebrew!), and so forth. They are directed at schooling, training, mastering of material. For some reason or other, one must know or be able to do certain things. Here the influences shaping life do not want to become influences on Bildung, but simply demand a body of consolidated knowledge and mastered techniques. At times there is no attempt to dress these demands up as concerns of Bildung—"vocational education" or "formal education." School today must seriously fear that it will simply be mediated in this way. Industry and commerce in particular are not foreign to these tendencies, but many of the demands currently being made by the universities and colleges would have the same result in the end.

As these demands are founded in the structure of life; they cannot be rejected in their entirety. Preparatory steps in instruction must always be expected, but it is then the task of Lehrplan design and instructional method to imbue these demands with pedagogical significance and to find within them educative *(bildende)* features. If the experience of the great classical educationists and of Reform Pedagogy does not deceive, the solution to the problem lies in the practical proof that knowledge and skills are worthless and give no guarantee of their correct use unless they are supported by properly designed instruction, that is, by the human background as produced by the work in the first two layers of education. Rousseau and Schleiermacher developed the principles of true "preparation for life," which also apply here and, more recently, there have been Kerschensteiner's principles with their practical reference to the economy. We need to build on Pestalozzi's approach and design a form of elementary instruction that progresses holistically, drawing on the contents of the child's and the adolescent's life world, and thereby prepare for all legitimate demands of life and guarantee their fulfillment, as far as the school situation and the students' age will permit.

ACKNOWLEDGMENTS

Based on Erich Weniger (1952) *Didaktik als Bildungslehre, Teil 1: Die Theorie der Bildungsinhalte und des Lehrplans* (Weinheim: Beltz). An earlier version of this book was published under the title "Die Theorie des Bildungsinhalts" in Herman Nohl and Ludwig Pallat (1930), *Handbuch der Pädagogik, Band 3: Allgemeine Didaktik und Erziehungslehre* (Lagensalza: Julius Beltz), pp. 1–55. This essay was also published in E. Weniger (1975), *Ausgewählte Schriften zur geisteswissenschaftlichen Pädagogik* (Weinheim and Basel: Beltz Verlag), pp. 199–294. This translation is published with permission of the copyright holder, Beltz Verlag, Weinheim and Basel.

REFERENCES

Dilthey, W. (1924). *Die geistige Welt: Einleitung in die Philosophie des Lebens. Hälfte II: Poetik, Ethik und Pädagogik* (Gesammelte Schriften VI). Leipzig: B. G. Teubner.

Dilthey, W. (1927). *Der Aufbau der geschichtlichen Welt in den Geisteswissenschaften* (Gesammelte Schriften VII). Leipzig: B. G. Teubner.

Dilthey, W. (1934). *Pädagogik, Geschichte und Grundlinien des Systems* (Gesammelte Schriften IX). Leipzig: B. G. Teubner.

Freyer, H. (1928). Sprache und Kultur. *Die Erziehung, 3,* 65–78.

Hildebrand, R. (1807). *Vom deutschen Sprachunterricht in der Schule und von deutscher Bildung und Erziehung überhaupt.* Leipzig: Klinkhardt.

Joerden, R. (1925). *Das Problem der Konzentration der deutschen Bildung.* Göttingen: Vanderhoeck & Ruprecht. [Contains an excellent critical synopsis of relevant literature, particularly Reform Pedagogy and the crucial texts of Hildebrand, Nietzsche, Lagarde, Langbehn, Windelband, Troeltsch, Benz, Burdach, and Simmel, which for this reason are not specifically mentioned here]

Nohl, H. (1949). *Die Pädagogische Bewegung in Deutschland und ihre Theorie* (3rd ed.). Frankfurt/Main: Verlag Schulte-Bulmke.

7

The Art of Lesson Preparation

Heinrich Roth
Gillian Horton-Krüger (Trans.)

Heinrich Roth was born 1906. He entered the teacher training seminar in Künzelsau and completed his first state (teacher certification) examination; afterwards he moved to Erlangen where he studied psychology, education, philosophy, and geography. He again worked as a teacher before completing his doctorate at the University of Tübingen in 1933 with a psychological study on the "phenomenon of the group." From 1934–1942, Roth worked as an army psychologist; he was later conscripted to the German army and saw active service in the Soviet Union and in France.

After the war he joined his old seminar in Künzelsau, which was now an institute for teacher training. In 1955, Roth became professor at the College for International Educational Research *(Hochschule für internationale pädagogische Forschung)* in Frankfurt-on-Main. He later moved to Göttingen, where he held a newly founded chair in education. Roth died 1983.

Heinrich Roth opened German education, which was almost completely dominated by hermeneutics and philosophy until the 1950s, to empirical research. In addition to his work on empirical pedagogy, he was actively engaged in educational policy and school reform. Heinrich Roth was a member of the German Council for Education for which he edited *Talent and Learning*. He was also active in the teachers union and was a member of the editorial staff of the journal *Die Deutsche Schule* from 1956 until his death.

His major publications were *Pädagogische Psychologie des Lehrens und Lernens* [Pedagogy of Teaching and Learning] (1957); *Jugend und Schule zwischen Reform und Restauration* [Youth and School Between Reform and Restoration] (1965); *Erziehungswissenschaft, Erziehungsfeld und Lehrerbildung: Gesammelte Abhandlungen 1957–1967* [Education, the Field of Education and Teacher

Training: Collected Papers 1957–1967], edited by H. Thiersch and H. Tütken; *Pädagogische Anthropologie* [Pedagogical Anthropology] (Vol. 1, 1966; Vol. 2, 1971); *Begabung und Lernen: Ergebnisse und Folgerungen neuer Forschungen* [Talent and Learning: Results and Conclusions of New Research] (1969).

—Jörg Biehl

It is often forgotten that in a number of academic occupations the main work load lies in the preparation. How many hours and days might a conscientious preacher grapple with the words of the lectionary, whereas less than an hour is available for the sermon itself! The most typical example in this group of professionals is, however, the teacher. The primary school teacher must be as well versed in the art of preparation as the university teacher. But can anyone be said to have mastered this art? It often promises so much and yields so little. At times it leads its practitioners to despair; at other times it richly rewards them. In short, it is a difficult quantity to calculate. This is due to its focus on a future event. It seeks to predict. Mastering the art of preparation in effect means no less than knowing in advance what will stimulate the intellect. Can preparation achieve this? Are there hard and fast rules for the right kind of preparation?

I

It is generally said that the teacher must first have mastered the matter.[1] This would appear to make good sense. But what does *master* actually mean? Surely it cannot apply merely to the teacher's own acquisition of the matter as a school exercise. And where did this term *matter* originate when it is the object we are dealing with, the cultural asset, the distillation of human intellectual achievement, that cultural reality in which the human spirit assumes a definite form? It is not a question of "mastering the matter," but of developing a personal relationship with the cultural asset entrusted to our care, a relationship with a life of its own. The crucial point is the real and true inner relationship of a teacher to the deepest objective substance of the object to be dealt with. But how can the teacher achieve this relationship with the cultural asset?

It cannot be created by force, or by command, or by entrenchment, but is the fruit of a long intimate relationship with the very essence of a subject. Textbooks do not lead to such profound depths. It stands and falls with the personal encounter with the *original representatives* of the subject. They alone kindle the fire in the mind that leads to selfless, objective action and true meditation. The teacher, therefore, should turn to the original works,

---

[1]*Translator's note: Matter* translates Roth's term *Stoff.* Another possibility, *subject matter,* would seem to fit the context, but could be misconstrued as referring to school subject or even more narrowly to the contents of a syllabus.

should consult the most eminent experts! Herein lies the secret of preparation. The sources are not easily accessible. The task requires a great deal of searching and sacrifice of time and money, but its reward is to make the work of preparation an intellectual pleasure, an encounter with the vigorous minds of our time.

It is quite misplaced to think of the child or the adolescent at this early stage. First it is the *matter* that is important, an entity greater than ourselves, which is not compelled by us, but itself compels us: truth. At this point, it is not the child's possible relationship to the truth, but that of the *teacher* that is in the foreground. Nothing is more incorrect than the assumption that the immaturity of the child permits a superficial relationship with the cultural asset. The teacher's relationship to the object must always correspond to the teacher's *own intellectual level,* not the children's. And it must be the level at which the faculties of understanding are stretched to their utmost. Partial, distorted, or superficial knowledge is a betrayal of what reflection on the matter is all about: the grasping of true essence, of objective substance, of the existentially significant. Only reflection that penetrates so deeply liberates from the unimportant, the trivial, the peripheral. Only this reflection can pave the way for a change in the standpoint that has prevailed for centuries in relation to the object. Only this reflection liberates the object and enables it to be translated into the appropriate form for the people, for adolescents, and for children. This relationship to the eternal substance of the object, born of the object yet still free, is the prerequisite for all further consideration in the preparation of instruction.

II

Thus far, the dedication to the subject[2] required of the teacher is the same as the dedication demanded of any scientist, indeed any learner or seeker after the truth. It is the next step that characterizes the preparation of the teacher. Only the object, unadulterated and comprehended in all its depth, in its essence and individuality, in its pure, objective intellectuality may be held up for pedagogical treatment. And now *pedagogical reflection* as the second step of preparation is imperative, no longer seeking objective substance, but the particular educative (*bildsam*[3]) qualities of the object. The

---

[2]*Translator's note: Subject* translates Roth's term *Sache* at the risk of ambiguity. *Sache* may be defined as a development of object *(Gegenstand).* Whereas object is neutral, subject is infused with cultural values, with meaning. As in the case of *matter, subject* is not to be understood in its restricted sense of, for example, "school subject" or contents of a syllabus.

[3]*Translator's note:* The adjectives *bildsam* and *bildnerisch* are translated here as *educative.* They refer to the noun *Bildung,* which, for Roth, is personal development guided by reason. Where *educative, education,* and *educate* are used here to translate *bildsam* or *bildnerisch,* and the verb *bilden,* the German is given in brackets.

focus of reflection is now what justifies a cultural asset as an educative asset *(Bildungsgut)*.

How can this central pedagogical relationship be discovered? What constitutes the educative *(das Bildsame)* within the object? We should not temporize over this question. Uncertain answers have been given by various sides for too long. An entity is educative *(bildsam)* if it leads to an experience of values, creates intellectual needs, spiritualizes vital drives, forms attitudes, sparks moral understanding. This second step of preparation involves the discovery of the *pedagogical substance* of a cultural asset. The pedagogical substance lies in the power of an object to arouse interest and form attitudes. The facets of the object on which intellectual interests and attitudes can be developed are now the center of attention. It is a contemplation of the "humanity" of an object, its power to transform souls, its wisdom, its comfort, its tragedy, its greatness, its sublimation, and so on. The educative *(bildsam)* moments of the object are those that attract vital interest, that capture feelings and emotions, but that, in the dealings with the object—and this is the crucial point—transform: direct and bind them to higher values, in other words, moralize and spiritualize.

This contemplation of the pedagogical substance of an object is no less important than the comprehension of its purely objective substance. It requires the same degree of effort, but of a different, more personal kind. The pedagogical substance of a cultural asset unfolds itself only to those it has affected deeply and who are able to revive this sense of being affected again and again. Only those who themselves have been transformed by the object are sensitive to the rousing and transforming power of a cultural asset. If they wish to unlock the pedagogical substance of an object, they must ask themselves individually "How do I stand in relation to this object?" "How has it affected me?" "How has it gripped me? transformed, delighted, astonished or elevated me? frightened or burdened me? purified, improved, expanded me?" Without this personal focus, the pedagogical substance is very difficult to reveal. If this approach is not applicable, it may help to ask what the object might have meant to the writer, the creative worker, the craftsman, the discoverer, the creator? But in the end the question of the humanity of the object is decided in the issue of its significance for a society, for humankind as a whole. This is the ultimate touchstone for the pedagogical substance of an object, the central pedagogical criterion in the selection of cultural assets as educative assets *(Bildungsgüter)*.

Thus in pedagogical reflection everything depends on the comprehension of the human significance and educative qualities *(Bildsamkeiten)* of an object. This can succeed only through the teacher's personal relationship with the cultural asset. In their personal attitude toward the object, the students will often be more influenced by the teacher's relationship to the object than by the object itself. The teacher's personal attitude toward the cultural asset is transmitted to the student. A teacher who has not found the attitude toward a cultural asset with which he or she is comfortable tries only in vain to pass on this attitude to the students. And dissembling will achieve nothing. Sensitive children perceive the attitudes operating subconsciously, the inner involvement or the indifference. The authenticity of the teacher's cultural attitudes is crucial. It helps to see the object in the right relationship within the cultural whole. It helps to reveal its educative power *(bildende Kraft)*, its specific educational values *(Bildungswerte)*, within the framework of the educational whole. It hones the judgment of its popular and its academic significance. The nurture of cultural attitude is thus the teacher's foremost task. It grows from dealing affectionately with the great spirits of our culture.

III

The third necessary stage in preparation shifts the emphasis from the object to the child, the adolescent, the student, who is maturing and learning. This third step is *psychological reflection*. I must first know the person to whom I wish to say or to entrust something, whom I wish to convince or educate *(bilden)*. How misguided it is to seek to teach without knowing the person to be taught. How much more correct it is for a person to volunteer to advise in a delicate matter, reasoning that he or she knows the person concerned. Psychological reflection requires the teachers to know their students and to know human nature. This is a vast field. What does knowing one's students mean? It means knowing them as individuals and as a class. As individuals at their stage of development and maturity, in their personal characteristics; and as a class, in their origins, their social composition, their class spirit, their youth spirit. This is demanding a great deal and presupposes years of dealing with young people, the class, and the individual.

Knowledge of the students' and human nature can grow, however, only if I know about the psychological issues and adopt a psychological attitude. This demands that I turn away from the pedagogical, from the desire solely to teach, to supervise, to impart knowledge, and turn toward the child, listening and simply observing what emerges, what forces its way out in search of spiritual support—even in those instances where the adolescent is supercilious, mocking, amused, acting stupid, or feigning indifference. Psychological observation demands I know the young people from all sides, or at least from several sides, not only as students, but also as sons or daughters at home, as friends outside school, as the youth of today, as a generation. I must know my students accurately if I wish to impress them with my object, to hit the target, to enthrall them. It helps to think of a specific young person, one we know personally, perhaps more than one from different sections of the class, and to then ask ourselves how *this* student would react, follow, understand.

Psychological reflection requires that we do not deceive or allow ourselves to be deceived. In seeking to know the students, to know human nature, we seek to grasp the learners in their spiritual and intellectual *reality*. Just as they are, with all their imperfections. But it would be a poor sort of psychology if there were no wish to progress beyond this point. Psychological reflection in a pedagogical context demands more: It is directed at discovering the points in the child's mind to which teaching and education can connect with a positive effect. This means that the young people are to be perceived not only in their external reality but also in their inner *potential*. What is required here is feeling, sensing, understanding psychology, guided by affection, that seeks to ascertain how young people encounter the object spontaneously, in their natural life context, how they form their own relationships with it, how it matures for them. Reflecting in this way, we can ourselves become young again: We can experience as a young person how we were gripped by a book for the first time; how we understood Bach for the first time; how we first gazed in wonder at the stars on a clear night; how we asked after God for the first time. We discover how young people experience the world, ever new and ever different. We feel how our receptivity to the object must be complemented by readiness for contact with young people.

Psychological reflection is about the living relationship between the teacher and the young people. It is a question of whether the teacher can hear what the young are saying, can explore the object with the eyes and ears of the young, can see the object in human terms, that is, as an object borne of human interests, fashioned by human need, created for the sheer pleasure of creation or to overcome suffering, that must always perform the same demanding task for the young. It all depends on the teacher's ability to sense the often hidden striving of young people for participation in cultural life, and then to open it up and bring it to life for school.

This psychological understanding grows out of an open relationship with the young, out of listening to the child and the adolescent, observing and opening up psychologically. It is not the objective substance of the object that is decisive in psychological reflection, nor its educative power *(bildnerische Kraft)*, but its purely human facet: the object in the perspective of what it will become, continually developing out of the child's natural interests and feeding the child's natural thirst for education, as an eternal process of cultural and human renewal. In the course of such reflection, the cultural asset becomes increasingly human, more personal, closer to life and to young people, but also easier to deal with, to manipulate, more useful for school.

IV

Now all the preparations have been made to bring together the object and the child. The development of the relationship, the active encounters between the child and the object, comprise the process of instruction. It is a creative act, because it must always be re-created between teacher and student for each cultural asset. An act of this kind is in principle unrepeatable, which is why we must summon up the courage to step out onto uncertain ground, time after time. If we have the deepest objective substance of the object completely at our disposal, if we know of its educative substance *(Bildungsgehalt)*, if we know our students and understand their concealed striving for participation in cultural life, then we are free to commence the work of instruction without inhibitions, and the methodical progression of the lesson will be born of the teacher's vital relationship with the children and the object at the moment of confrontation. It is part of a teacher's experience that this kind of lesson is among the most successful. But the teacher does not always have the courage to step out into the unknown without having previously considered what methods to adopt. All too often, the creative moment fails. This is the point at which those considerations come into operation that make up actual *reflection of method*.

This comprises the anticipation of the encounters between the child and the object, as a theoretical trial run in the mind of the teacher before instruction itself begins.

How can the teacher plan such educative processes *(Bildungsprozesse)* in advance? The teacher's position at this juncture is similar to that of an intermediary who wishes two parties, each unknown to the other, to take an interest in each other. The intermediary, who is familiar with both parties, knows that they would have a great deal to say to each other. Like this intermediary, the teacher must try to establish the *natural points of contact* between the two, starting from the common ground that interests both sides. To this end it is necessary to think through the process of instruction radically, from the point of view of both the object and the child in their own peculiarity.

What forms of acquisition do the object and the child each suggest? That is the question, and there is no general, only a specific answer. In other words, a new answer must be found for each object, for each generation, for each child. The question can be most effectively dealt with by breaking it down into individual questions that, with reference to the object, could run as follows. Does the material lend itself to being experienced, recounted, performed, discussed, questioned, debated? Is it suitable for being looked at, observed, worked out, thought about as a group? Can it be tried out, experimented with, invented? Can it be designed by the students, demonstrated by the teacher, used by the group in exercises or games, through music or drama? Does it lend itself to individual or group work?

In endeavoring to answer these questions, one soon discovers that no arbitrary decisions can be made. Every object has its own peculiarities, its own logic in the way it is passed on, received, grasped, understood, and retained. However, as a result of the three stages of reflection that have preceded this consideration of method, the object will have become so transparent and plastic that it will itself reveal the method through which it is most accessible.

The other half of the question referred to the form of instruction suggested by the child. In attempting to answer this I must proceed from the capabilities for comprehension of a specific age group, with reference to such points as how the child or adolescent encounters the object in the natural course of their life? Has he or she dealt with the object in some way since the initial encounter? When did this first occur? Where does the object connect with the vital life interests of the child or adolescent? When and how does the object become a focus of astonishment, of wonder, of questioning? When does it become a problem? Where does the object contain interest for the child? What elements will fascinate most strongly? How can I use the elements of natural interest to arrange an intellectual experience of value? How can I maintain the momentary interest thus aroused and transform it into a real and lasting interest in the object? How can I introduce the object into the natural course of the child's life for the interest to be reinforced? How do I make the object part of the child's inner need, so that he or she will seek contact with it, even outside school?

But how do I find the points of contact from which to proceed? As far as a general response can be given at all, and in many cases only the individual case can decide, our answer is that the points of contact are to be found in the intellectual channels that were the original connection between human beings and the object. Reflection on method therefore requires a retrospective exploration of the object to reveal the genesis of its intellectualization, of its reference to the human world, in order to discover those points of contact likely to spark the vital interest of the children or adolescents and bring the object to life for them.

For if I resolve the object back into the aspects of its genesis (e.g., in referring lifeless old textbook contents to the actions of living people once again) and also try to allow it to be resurrected from human drives and interests, I re-create the primeval situation between human beings and the object that makes the cultural asset visible as a fruit of human longing and endeavor. I return the human being to the original situation in which the object appears as a help, an answer, an achievement, a piece of work—in short a cultural asset. Reflection on method has no other task than to exploit such thoughts in order to seek out the natural, dynamic, and fruitful points of contact between the child and the object. They are the fruitful elements of instruction from which a relationship spontaneously develops. In such reflection, everything depends on their discovery.

V

One more question remains. To what extent can the progress of a lesson or a unit be planned in advance? Do the points of contact ascertained by reflection on method impose a certain sequence to which I must or may keep? Can the structure of an instruction unit be planned ahead without inhibiting the creative freedom of the instruction process? May the teacher dispense with a plan if it promises success as the ripe fruit of preparatory thought? These are the questions.

Let us remind ourselves again of the situation before the teacher enters the classroom. To a large extent, it still resembles the situation of an explorer about to enter unknown territory, represented both by the child and by the object. The child repeatedly surprises in his or her behavior and remains unpredictable in his or her attitude to the object, whereas the object never completely surrenders its autonomy and often only reveals its innermost pitfalls for method *in actu*. Dispensing with a plan would, with regard to this situation, mean playing the explorer who penetrates an unknown continent without taking the necessary precautions. On the other hand, determination to follow a rigid plan would mean losing a degree of the flexibility that unforeseeable situations require. It all depends, therefore, on the elasticity and pliability of the plan. Potential changes must be built in. So let us now consider what can be established as unchangeable in the goal, the route, and the procedure.

Without doubt, I must know what I want. I must have a *goal*. The goal is the object. The school, the children or I, or we together have decided on it. One of the first unavoidable requirements is to know the goal and to have made it one's own. But what is this goal? Acquaintance with the object, knowledge of it, mastery of it, possession of it?

After our preparatory reflection on the matter, we should be in a position to say that the goal is independent thought or action appropriate to the object. More important than the memorization of the object is the possession of the ways of thinking and acting that are appropriate to the object. To have experienced oneself the process of understanding is more important than knowing the facts of the result, if for no other reason than because experienced understanding takes root more firmly than merely imparted knowledge. According to our pedagogical reflection, the goal is to achieve humane opinions and attitudes appropriate to the object. Appropriate thought must be accompanied by an appropriate attitude of mind. This must grow out of a loving interest in the object as a fruit of the intellectual, an interest to which the object gives rise during the instruction process, an interest that is aroused in the child. Loving interest is more than knowledge, even more than objective thought: It is the driving force of creative life itself that participates in the culture, giving and taking, and in its conscience knows itself to be morally responsible to the cultural asset.

According to our psychological reflection, the goal is the rooting of the object in the life interests of the individual and the opening up of hitherto concealed potential for understanding the object, the humanization of the cultural asset to the extent required by the individual capacity for understanding of a unique child, and the concretization of individual intellectual needs in order for objective intellectual substance to be comprehended.

We need such clarification and goal ascertainment for every object in order to become liberated from false goals, dictated by the "matter" and the "work load." The true goal that we must strive to attain in the face of all adversity frees us without making us aimless, secures us without paralyzing us. It is our pedagogical duty to ascertain this true goal before instruction commences and to identify with it personally.

What about the *route* we are going to take? The first task is to seek out the stops on the way to our destination or overall goal, to divide up our route into legs, each with its own goal. Can the stops be determined in advance? Let us contemplate the general direction! The important point is to establish a close connection between the child and the object that functions independently and fulfills itself in self-acting intellectual exchange. This connection can be achieved only via those points of contact between child and object with which we have familiarized ourselves as stimulating and fruitful elements in the reflection on method. They must represent the steps and stations on the way to the destination. They must follow upon each other like the scenes in an act, like the acts in a play. They are the intersections of understanding, the pedagogical fuel, the productive resistance to create sparks and bring to life. It is these I must always use as my points of navigation in teaching. Passing through them as stations in the process of instruction is as important as reaching the destination, because passing through them is itself part of the goal, of understanding the object. Therefore we must posses them, must keep them alive and in readiness. The necessity of the moment will decide how they are to be used. The sequence cannot be determined ahead, but depends on the cooperation of the children in moving, creating, wanting to be part of things.

How much of the *procedure* can we establish in advance? It depends not only on the characteristics and logic of the object, but also on the characteristics and logic of each stage in the course of instruction. The first stage could require an open discussion; the second could have the class gathering around a picture; the third might suggest focusing on a story, a report, a reading that divides the class into speakers and listeners; the fourth could initiate shared activity in the sense of a real communal effort; the fifth might require a craft to be demonstrated and tried out; the sixth could require intellectual or technical group work; the seventh individual work. Whether this change takes place at intervals of a quarter or half an hour, of days or weeks, the important point is solely that the procedure corresponds to the process of understanding, either in terms of the procedural conditions given by the object or in terms of the conditions of understanding on the part of the child. The art of preparing a dynamic procedure lies in developing the stages or stations into dynamic *pedagogical situations* that in themselves produce a gap in understanding with respect to the object, that project the children into the need or the joy of the cultural asset, transforming it into a question, a problem, a care, or a hope, in all events forcing them to the astonishment and wonder that is the very beginning of all intellectual life. Such pedagogical situations must be conceived and held in readiness, especially if a flexible procedure is desired, adequate to cope with the demands of the moment, the student's question, the dynamic process of instruction.

To conclude: Let us summarize from old and new standpoints. We must hold the *subject* at the ready, the cultural asset, the object. After all, this is to become the event itself in this lesson, is to be articulated, to speak for itself. So let us not forget this, the most important point. For too long school has omitted to deal directly with the object itself.

Let us have the *situation* ready in which the subject appears in the world, the situation that transformed and continues to transform the object into cultural asset, the pedagogical situation, which re-creates the same need or joy that opened up the object, made it comprehensible, and sparked a love of this object.

Let us keep the *comparison* at our fingertips, the "image," that is, everything that facilitates access to the subject matter, from documents to pictures to statistics. The comparison is the greatest aid when projecting the object onto the child's level of understanding. The comparison is conceived as a paradigm for the method of transforming the object into the child's or adolescent's manner of understanding.

Last but not least, let us keep *ourselves* in readiness. It is we who, acting in moral responsibility on the students' behalf, must return again and again to the task of attaining a proper understanding of the object in order to *exemplify* this endeavor to understand the world in intellectual terms.

Our main concern must be to prepare the ground for a true encounter between child and object. An encounter that leads the child to deal with the object. An encounter that enables the child to experience values in connection with the object and from there to develop love for it. An encounter that, on the part of the object, leads to a rebirth, to a refulfilling of its own essential substance. This latter affects the soul of the child, forming and educating, making the object come alive again in a new and original way as a reproductive force. But we must be honest and admit that we can plan only the approach to this encounter. The encounter itself is a matter of fortune.

ACKNOWLEDGMENTS

Based on Heinrich Roth, "Kunst der rechten Vorbereitung (1952)." In Heinrich Roth (1976), *Pädagogische Psychologie des Lehrens und Lernens* (Hanover: Schroedel), pp. 127–138. This translation is published with permission of Dagmar Friedrich, the copyright holder.

8

Didaktik Analysis as the Core of Preparation of Instruction

Wolfgang Klafki

Wolfgang Klafki was born in East Prussia (today part of Poland). After completing teacher preparation for primary and lower secondary schools in 1946–1948, he worked as a teacher at lower secondary schools. In 1952–1957 Klafki studied education, philosophy, and German studies at the universities of Göttingen and Bonn. His most influential university teachers in education were Theodor Litt and Erich Weniger, who were major representatives of the *Geisteswissenschaftenliche Pädagogik,* that is, human-science education.

After teaching at the teacher training college in Hanover, and later at the University of Münster, Klafki became Professor of Education at the University of Marburg in 1963, where he remained until his retirement in 1992.

Wolfgang Klafki was a member of several planning committees for educational policy and curriculum development. He was, for example, chair of the curriculum committee for lower secondary schools in North Rhine-Westphalia from 1967–1969, of the commission for the revision of curricula in Hesse from 1968–1971 and the state commissions for school change in Bremen (1991–1993) and North Rhine-Westphalia (1993–1995). Since 1965, Klafki has been one of the editors of the German journal *Zeitschrift für Pädagogik.*

His main fields of research are the history of education since the 18th century, the development of the educational system in Germany since 1945, the theory of Bildung, Didaktik and school organization and development, problems of a general theory of education, and the relations between *Geisteswissenschaftliche Pädagogik* and National Socialism.

Some of his major publications in the field of Didaktik are "Didaktische Analyse als Kern der Unterrichtsvorbereitung" [Didaktik Analysis as the Core of Preparation of Instruction] (1958), perhaps the most widely known and used paper from the classical Didaktik; this essay is presented in this chapter; *Studien zur Bildungstheorie und Didaktik* [Studies on Educational Theory and

Didaktik] (1963, 1975); *Geisteswissenschaftliche Pädagogik am Ausgang ihrer Epoche–Erich Weniger* [Human-Science Education at the End of Its Epoch–Erich Weniger] (1968), edited by W. Klafki together with I. Dahmer; *Neue Studien zur Bildungstheorie und Didaktik: Beiträge zur kritisch-konstruktiven Didaktik* [New Studies on Educational Theory and Didaktik: Contributions on Critical-Constructive Didaktik] (1985; Zum Verhältnis von Allgemeiner Didaktik und Fachdidaktik–Fünf Thesen [On the Relation between General Didaktik and Subject Didaktik–Five Theses]. In H. Meyer & H. Plöger (eds.), *Allgemeine Didaktik, Fachdidaktik, Fachunterricht* (1994); Kritisch-konstruktive Didaktik und Hermeneutik [Critical-Constructive Didaktik and Hermeneutics]. In P. Kansanen (ed.), *Diskussionen über einige pädagogische Fragen* (1995); Allgemeine Didaktik–Fach- und Bereichsdidaktiken–Schlüsselprobleme [General Didaktik–Subject and Domain Didaktiks–Core Problems]. In J. Keuffer & M. Meyer (eds.), *Didaktik und Kultureller Wandel* (1997); and Unterricht [Teaching]. In C. Wulf (ed.), *Vom Menschen: Handbuch Historischen Anthropologie* (1997).

In addition to the chapters in this book, he has also written in English "Characteristics of a critical-constructive Didaktik." In B. B. Gundem & S. Hopmann (eds.), *Didaktik and/or Curriculum: An International Dialogue* (New York: Peter Lang, 1998); and "Core problems of the modern world and the tasks of education: A vision for international education." In *Education: A Biennial Collection of Recent German Contributions in the Field of Educational Research*, Vol. 53 (Tübingen: Institut für Wissenschaftliche Zusammenarbeit, 1996).

—Jörg Biehl

The following chapter was first published in the journal Die Deutsche Schule *in 1958[1] and later appeared in several editions of collected papers on instructional preparation, as well as in my book* Studien zur Bildungstheorie und Didaktik *(1963). The concept I developed was used for about two decades in preservice teacher education at many universities and colleges in what was then West Germany and, particularly, in the second, school-based phase of initial training. It is still in use in places today.*

The concept drew on and developed theory of education (Bildungstheorie) *from the field of human-science pedagogy* (Geisteswissenschaftliche Pädagogik), *especially Didaktik, the theory of contents and curriculum* (Theorie der Bildungsinhalte und des Lehrplans), *as developed, in particular, by Erich Weniger. My formulation of the concept incorporated experience I gained as a teacher in primary and secondary modern schools and at the teachers college*

---

[1]Didaktische Analyse als Kern der Unterrichtsvorbereitung. *Die Deutsche Schule* (1958), pp. 450–471, and later in *Auswahl* (1962), a collection of essays edited by H. Roth and A. Blumenthal, Vol. 1, 14th edition 1977. Some of the changes I made to the essay in this version— especially in Section C—were influenced by W. Kramp, Hinweise zur Unterrichtsvorbereitung für Anfänger. *Die Deutsche Schule* (1962), pp. 78ff, and in the collection, *Auswahl*, mentioned earlier.

in Hanover from 1956, supervising student teachers on teaching practice in schools in different types of localities.

When I later came to develop the human-science theory of education (Geisteswissenschaftliche Bildungstheorie) *and Didaktik into a critical-constructive theory of education from the end of the 1960s onward, I also began to revise my concept of instructional preparation. This work led first to the essay* Probleme einer Neukonzeption der didaktischen Analyse *(1977) and then to the paper "Überlegungen zur Unterrichtsplanung im Sinne kritisch-konstruktiver Didaktik" (1980; reprinted in Adl-Amini & Künzli, 1980). The most recent version is contained in the essay "Zur Unterrichtsplanung im Sinne kritisch-konstruktiver Didaktik" in my* Neue Studien zur Bildungstheorie und Didaktik: Zeitgemäße Allgemeinbildung und kritisch-konstruktive Didaktik[2] *(1993).*

There is scope here to cite only the salient points that influenced the revision of my concept of instruction planning:

- *My earlier position was rooted in the human-science pedagogy* (Geisteswissenschaftliche Pädagogik) *of Erich Weniger, Theodor Litt, Herman Nohl, Eduard Spranger, and Wilhelm Flitner. My exploration of the basic ideas of the Frankfurt School of social philosophy (as propounded by Adorno, Horkheimer, and Habermas) as well as the dialogue with educational theorists working, like myself, on a critical revision of traditional German pedagogy led me, from the late 1960s onward, to evolve a draft for a "critical-constructive science of education" and, within this framework, a system of "critical-constructive Didaktik." In this context,* critical *is to be understood in the sense of "social criticism," which in terms of Didaktik implies constant reflection on the relations between school and instruction on the one hand (their goals, contents, forms of organization, and methods) and social conditions and processes on the other. "Constructive" continues to indicate an emphasis on practice, on "reform"—but more decisively than before it refers to a shaping of school and instruction in keeping with humane and democratic principles (self-determination, participation in decision making, solidarity; see chap. 5, this volume).*

- *A second element is the expansion of my previous, narrower concept of Didaktik (as theory of contents and curriculum,* Didaktik als Theorie der Bildungsinhalte und des Lehrplans). *I now use Didaktik generically for both the dimension of objectives and content and the dimension of methods, taking the preconditions given at both the personal and institutional level*

---

[2]W. Klafki, Zur Unterrichtsplanung im Sinne kritisch-konstruktiver Didaktik. In my *Neue Studien zur Bildungstheorie und Didaktik: Zeitgemäße Allgemeinbildung und kritisch-konstruktive Didaktik*; first edition (Weinheim: Beltz Verlag, 1985); considerably expanded for the second edition (Weinheim: Beltz Verlag, 1991); now in its fifth edition (Weinheim: Beltz Verlag, 1996).

into account. Now I emphasize the primacy of objectives against all other dimensions of instruction.

The most crucial stimulus for this expansion of my conception of Didaktik came from the criticisms and suggestions of the "Berlin School of Didaktik" (Heimann, Otto, Schulz) in the forms developed from 1972 onward, later integrated by Wolfgang Schulz and Gunter Otto into their "Hamburg Didaktik."

- In my current concept of instructional planning I stress, more emphatically than in the earlier essay, that teaching and learning must be understood as processes of interaction, that is, as processes in which relationships between people—between teachers and learners and between the learners themselves—play a central role. These processes must therefore be comprehended not only as processes of acquisition in which subject matter and problems are confronted, but also as social processes or processes of social learning.

This new emphasis on the relationship question was influenced in particular by the discussion of social learning, which has intensified in Germany since the 1970s, and the ideas of "communication-centered" or "Critical-communicative" Didaktik.

In presenting the older text "Didaktik Analysis as the Core of the Preparation of Instruction" for renewed discussion, this time in an abridged, English version, I see the justification in the fact that the central ideas of the earlier concept with its five basic questions have not been supplanted, but continue to be valid in an expanded, in places modified, and in a more differentiated form.

A. THE QUESTION[3]

I

Preparing lessons is one of those tasks of the teacher in which the basic pedagogical problems of the school converge. It is the place where the

---

[3]*Translator's notes:*

Bildungsgehalt: The substance of a content based on the content's history and current importance and use; limited by the curriculum, it is transformed by the interests and experiences vested in it by the teacher and the learner. As such the notion of substance is a holistic concept. In Klafki's model, the search for the substance is practically focused on the question of what educating *(bildend)* potential the content is reckoned to have (e.g., by curriculum authors, teachers) and how this potential can be realized. In this practical sense, the content of "substance" is close to Shulman's notion of "pedagogical content knowledge" (L. S. Shulman [1987], "Knowledge and Teaching: Foundations of the New Reform," *Harvard Educational Review, 57*[2], 1–22).

geistig: (Following the translation of Wilhelm Dilthey's [1989] *Introduction to the Human Sciences,* edited by R. A. Makkreel and F. Rodi [Princeton, NJ: Princeton University Press]) "human," of the "human world," with few exceptions.

interactive relationship between theory and practice fundamental to all education, the interplay between experience and reflection, must be concretized in the form of reflective decisions for planning instruction and learning. Good preparation for a lesson, for a sequence of lessons, or for an instructional unit is always a new, small-scale, and provisional construction as well as a synthesis of prior experience. If we make the "draft character" of good preparation clear enough to ourselves—for any planning of instruction can be only provisionally valid—then it is quite consistent to rate the instructional planning process highly, while at the same time recognizing that, in the end, each and every lesson holds in store a myriad unforeseeable possibilities and that the openness of teachers' minds to new situations, impulses, and the difficulties arising from the moment is a criterion of their pedagogical competence.

II

The principal purpose of instructional preparation can be summarized as follows: Preparation is intended as the design of one or several opportunities for children to make fruitful encounters with certain contents of education *(Bildungsinhalte)*.

But, even with this interpretation in view, there is a danger that the task will be understood primarily, or indeed exclusively, as a preliminary reflection about the "how" of the encounter to be engendered; in other words, preparation may be regarded first and foremost, or even wholly, as a question of *methods*. Usually the reflections of those who hold such a conception are dominated by a methodological principle (such as self-activity) or practice (such as learning in small groups), and the question is then how the material can be dealt with in keeping with this principle or this practice. (Basically, it is of no importance whether the principle of method or the form of instruction is a formal sequence [cf. Herbart: *Formalstufe*] or whether it is a matter of "hands-on activity," "self-activity," "classroom discussion," and so on.)

With respect to this misinterpretation, the specialist literature has repeatedly pointed out that the search for method must be the final, albeit necessary, step in good instructional preparation and is, in a manner of speaking, the crowning element. The working out of method is contrasted again and again with the first step of preparation, which is the preoccupation with the *subject matter* to be conveyed or acquired in the lessons. This throws up a crucial question that will, in the course of the argument, reveal itself as the core issue of the whole spectrum of preparation. What comprises "the matter"? What is the nature of this "lesson content"?

III

Let us proceed from the ordinary situation of teacher. (*Ordinary* refers here to the situation of a teacher who is not also a curriculum developer or educational theorist.) With this normal situation in mind, let us ask ourselves what kind of "matters" the teacher encounters as objects of preparation:

1. First, we can observe that the framework is, in the main, delineated by the curriculum or syllabus. This is no less applicable if the latter has assumed the desirable form of a set of guidelines that do not explicitly set out the individual items of subject matter but give basic issues or thematic areas, mostly with supporting examples, leaving the selection of suitable details up to the school or the teacher.

Our question as to the nature of the "objects" of preparation can now be brought more sharply into focus: What is the nature of the subject matter or topics of the curriculum?

2. This is not the place for a detailed critique of the different answers to this question that have been put forward, and that are still being offered today, either expressly or implicitly. They include, for example, the opinion that the specific nature of curriculum contents lies in their "scientificness," or that curriculum contents are cultural contents, more precisely the contents of the various authorities that are vehicles and sources of culture such as the church, the judicial system, science, art, commerce, or professional structures. The specifically pedagogical answer to that question would have to be, we feel, that the subject matter in the curriculum is characteristically seen by curriculum designers as *contents of education (Bildungsinhalte)*. This is, then, how the subject matter must be regarded, and validated as such, in the classroom.

A decision has thus been made long before our teacher begins to tackle the business of preparation. From among the wealth of the conceivable contents yielded by our civilization, certain contents or thematic areas have been selected as *contents of education (Bildungsinhalte)*. The teacher is not "unprejudiced" when approaching the curriculum contents. He or she is aware of the prior decision reflected in these contents—or at least should be aware of it. Now we can bring our question about the nature of the "matters" that the teacher engaged in preparation has first to deal with even more sharply into focus: The first step in preparation is the understanding of the *contents of education (Bildunginhalte)*. The teacher must reenact the pedagogical decision made by the curriculum designers and embedded in the curriculum contents, must reflect which considerations must have led to the inclusion of a particular item or a particular basic issue, that is, *why* these were selected as possible contents of education *(Bildungsinhalte)* that the practical work of instruction must bring back to life?

We believe that it would be demanding too much of teachers in terms of time and mental energy to expect them to "rationalize" about the contents in a prepedagogical context whenever they set out to prepare themselves for teaching. This would involve, for example, adopting the role of a scientist who sees the contents in question as a research exercise in a specific field. And we are of the opinion that this applies not only to teachers at primary, junior secondary, and vocational level, but also to those at senior secondary level! Admittedly, the teacher engaged in preparation must first concentrate on the "matter" at hand, on what is to be taught. *But this "matter" is from the very beginning an "object" seen through a pedagogical lens that a young person's mind is to "possess": It is, in short, content of education (Bildungsinhalt).* The task is to elucidate which aspects of the content contribute to Bildung, to explore what it contains that can or should comprise education, Bildung.

The term *analysis of subject matter (Sachanalyse)*, which in the relevant literature has become the common term for the first phase of instructional preparation, is not, therefore, particularly apt. Indeed, it could be misconstrued as referring to a prepedagogical, scientific analysis of the subject matter, making this the basis of instruction and thus losing sight of the specifically pedagogical nature of the task.

3. The "objectivity" demanded of the teacher in preparation requires a certain type of questioning. The teacher must adopt two positions, and must be able to assimilate both. He or she represents on the one hand the "layperson" the students will later become, and on the other hand the young people themselves and their individual potential. As a layperson, the teacher represents, for instance, the democratic citizen who is to be aware of his or her responsibility for our society and our state, the committed member of the religious community to which both teachers and students belong, or the "consumer" who should be able to choose critically and with taste from among the wide range of opportunities for experiencing and forming culture. And so the list could continue. In this perspective, teachers must be willing to be moved by the subject matter during preparation—honestly and seriously. They can fulfill their task of educating and instructing their children only if they *represent* the content that is to be acquired by education or instruction, if they themselves personify it and credibly reflect it. The poem the teacher is to present the next day, and which he or she will interpret with the children and render with the feeling it inspires, this poem must "enchant" anew the teacher herself, shake her up, delight her, affect her. The physics problems that will occupy the next few physics lessons must stimulate the teacher once again, like an unsolved puzzle, causing wonder, questioning, experimenting, advance hypothesizing, as a piece of reality with a bearing on and significance for the common person—for that is what we are all outside our own specialized field of work.

In the second position, as a representative of the young person, the teacher must view the capacity for understanding and questioning of the "educated layperson" *(gebildeter Laie)* from the perspective of the child or youth at a particular level, must re-create with vitality the particular questions, interests, and attitudes of the students, and explore them for their deeper educational potential *(Bildungsmöglichkeiten)*.

The "matter" the teacher is wrestling with in order to comprehend and exploit its educational substance *(Bildungsgehalt)* is a peculiarly dynamic complex. It is to be absorbed by and fill the young mind while, at the same time, pointing forward to future tasks and opportunities of a mature life.

4. If we adopt the term *Didaktik* as a subsumption of all mental effort directed at aspects of content, at the "what" of instruction and Bildung (as distinguished from the concentration of the "how," a topic of a theory of teaching and learning methods, i.e., *Methodik*), the first task of a teacher engaged in preparation can be termed *Didaktik analysis*. It is evident that we must first clarify our terms if we wish to get closer to the nature of Didaktik analysis. And although we are dealing here with a truly practical problem of schoolwork, we must not allow ourselves to shy from the "effort of terminology," from confrontation with the difficult, fundamental theoretical questions that the problem poses.

B. CONTENTS OF EDUCATION AND EDUCATIONAL SUBSTANCE *(BILDUNGSINHALT AND BILDUNGSGEHALT)*

1. A speaker who uses the term *contents of education (Bildungsinhalt)* tacitly acknowledges Bildung as a basic term of pedagogy. But it would be wrong to assume that everyone using the expression invests it with a clearly defined idea of what it comprises, inevitably infusing it, though perhaps implicitly, with their own metaphysically founded ideal or with ideals derived from their own worldviews. On the other hand, we believe that the term can be usefully employed if the controversial issues of ideals are set aside and a broad—not simply formal—understanding of Bildung is agreed on; as broad, for example, as that expressed by Litt (1963):

> When we refer to a person as educated *(gebildet)* . . . we mean at least that this person has succeeded in establishing a certain degree of *order* in the whole of his existence, in the wide variety of gifts, opportunities, drives, and achievements he incorporates, linking the one to the other in the appropriate relationship, guarding against overemphasis, but also against suppression of the particular. However, a person can never, never create order within himself, unless he has regulated his relations to the *world* in an appropriate manner. If we regard the one side by side with the other, we may use the term *Bildung*

for any state of mind of a person that puts him in a position to impose order on himself, as well as on his relations to the world. (p. 11)

Weniger, in his essay "Bildung und Persönlichkeit" (1958), put it more cautiously: Bildung remains "in essence in the forecourt of life. It only prepares for the decisions of life through which a person will become a 'personality'" (p. 138). With reference to Bildung as a result of the educational process, Weniger described it as "the state in which one can assume responsibility." An interpretation of the term, as recommended by the statements of Litt and Weniger, is adequate for our purposes as we now try to find a more precise definition of the terms "content of education" *(Bildungsinhalt)* and "substance of a content of education" *(Bildungsgehalt)*.

2. How does a content become a content of education? Otto Willmann (1957) in his *Didaktik als Bildungslehre,* gave the general answer that it is the *educational substance (Bildungsgehalt)* of the subject matter. He explained this statement as follows:

Within the whole of the contents to be acquired [we must distinguish between] the essential and the inessential, fruit and leaves, the interior and the exterior. As the learners process the matter, differences emerge . . . There are different degrees of internalization of what is presented: Some matter penetrates through to the roots of inner growth, the rest remains peripheral. From among the whole of an object of instruction, we distinguish its educational substance *(Bildungsgehalt)* and comprehend the latter as those elements of the former where the subject matter can begin to take root and be internalized, and on whose retention the value of the learning and the practicing essentially depends. . . . Teach in such a way that what is given is learned . . . and that its substance *(Bildungsgehalt)* can take effect. (p. 326)

Content of education is not, therefore, an externally given matter, but there is "rather an organic power contained in the content itself, which has a determining influence on the conceptions and thoughts during assimilation by the mind, bringing them into conformity with itself, and thus effecting internal organization" (Willmann, 1957, p. 324). In this interpretation, content of education appears, by virtue of its intrinsic substance *(Bildungsgehalt),* as something "wise," something vital, something invisible but objective that needs to be grasped if the matter is to be mastered. A system of Didaktik based on this view . . . explores the particular objects and items of subject matter in order to ascertain their structure and organization, their "ideal content" or the "wisdom" they contain, "their germinative forces and their productive drives" (Willmann, 1904, p. 59).

Willmann's concept of substance *(Bildungsgehalt)* and his interpretation as sketched out here represent a crucial discovery in the history of Didaktik. But in this most general form Willmann's definition does not yet give the elucidation necessary for our purposes. We must therefore press on and go beyond Willmann.

3. After Willmann, the terms *content of education, education substance (Bildungsgehalt),* and *educational value (Bildungswert)* were increasingly incorporated in the theory of education *(Bildungstheorie).* But Willmann's interpretation suggested the notion that objective contents per se, independent of the persons who assimilate them, have a certain substance or value contributing to education *(Bildungsgehalt, Bildungswert).* [Henceforth *substance* may be taken to refer to *Bildungsgehalt* where no other attribute is given: *translator's note*]. Until Kerschensteiner's *Theorie der Bildung* (1926), all attempts to explore the problems associated with the terms remained within the framework of this basic conviction. It was the proponents of human-science pedagogy *(Geisteswissenschaftliche Pädagogik)* who made the decisive move on to new ground.

Herman Nohl and Erich Weniger in particular saw, in contrast to the objectivism of Willmann and Kerschensteiner, that a double relativity constitutes the very essence of contents of education, in other words their substance or value. What constitutes content of education, or wherein its substance or value lies, can, first, be ascertained only with reference to the particular children and adolescents who are to be educated and, second, with a particular human, historical situation in mind, with its attendant past and the anticipated future.

The first point of relativity is emphasized when Nohl (1949) described the adjustment to the life of the student as "the pedagogical criterion":

> Whatever demands are made on the child by the objective culture and the social relationships, they must tolerate a transformation that proceeds from the questions: What is the sense of this requirement in the context of the child's life, for its development and the increase of his or her faculties? and What potential does the child have for coping with the demands? (p. 427)

This is a concrete interpretation of Martin Buber's (1953) thesis that conscious and volitional education is always "selection of the active world" (p. 23). Peter (1954) had the same sort of thing in mind when he said that "the object of teaching is dependent on the Didaktik aims of the teacher" (p. 72). "The concept of the object of instruction thus also contains an objective" (p. 75).

The second, historical relativity in what can be regarded as content of education, substance or value, was emphatically underlined by Weniger (1952). Reference to assets of education *(Bildungsgüter)* or contents of education means first that:

> The speaker has gained formative *(bildende)* impressions in contact with a substance of the human world, with a component and detail of culture, with

particular poetry, painting, music, constitutional doctrine, or with an historical or religious personality. He now possesses them, figuratively speaking, they now belong to him. The very fact that this is possible is the peculiarity of the human mind: An entity complete in itself, such as a sonata, an historical life, a poem, a cultural epoch . . . can be grasped and possessed by a person and yet remains unspent and independent. But for the person "educated" by this entity *(der durch dieses Gebilde Gebildete),* it has become his property; he has experienced the values concealed therein as educational values *(Bildungswerte) and possesses them.* Now he learns that others have also experienced the formative force *(bildende,* Kraft) of these contents, such as those with a similar educational career or interests, those with the same work and the same social class, in the same region or the same tribe. Thus we learn to term something an asset that is generally experienced by larger groups as formative *(bildend).* . . . (pp. 4–49)

But that is only one facet of the historical character of all contents of education. The other side becomes visible as soon as one recognizes that "historicity, not only looks backwards, but also points towards the future." It is an unreflected and by no means self-evident assumption

that something, that for a person speaking about substance has become an asset *(Bildungsgut)* in the course of his own experience of education *(Bildungserfahrung),* and what he experienced with his generation, must for future generations also become an asset, that is, will evoke the same experiences of education and must produce the same figure of an educated person *(gebildeter Mensch),* German, Christian. (Weniger, 1952, p. 49)

If we remain with the orientation to the life of the student as our pedagogical criterion, then we must agree with Weniger's (1952) hypothesis that:

Posing the problem of selecting and concentrating the contents of education means . . . reflecting on the existential concentration in which the human, historical world is given to us in our life context, *from the perspective of the tasks* that arise in our specific and individual situation. For a people, a group or the individual, as life progresses, particular challenges are always present. (p. 96)

This means, therefore, that everything that claims to be content of education must also have a significance for the future of those to be educated—the future for which education is supposed to equip the young people and that it must thus anticipate *(vorwegnehmen),* without being falsely premature and without narrowing the students' future scope for decision making.

4. Those contents of education, therefore, that present themselves to the teacher in the form of curriculum and the substance (or value) of which must be tracked down by "Didaktik analysis" must be comprehended as a

selection made in a particular human, historical situation and with specific groups of children in mind (according to environment, school types, grade level). Curriculum designers assume that these contents, once the children or adolescents have internalized and thus acquired them, will enable the young people to "produce a certain order" (Litt) in themselves and at the same time in their relation to the world, to "assume responsibility" (Weniger), to cope with the requirements, and take the free chances of life. The contents of teaching and learning will represent such order, or possibilities for such order, such responsibilities, inevitable requirements, and opportunities, and that means at the same time opening up the young people to systems of order (legal, social, moral, etc.), responsibilities (such as human welfare or politics), necessities (such as the mastery of cultural skills, a minimum of vital knowledge, etc.), and human opportunities (e.g., to enjoy and be active in leisure time, e.g., in the arts, in the choice of profession, etc.).

This form of opening up, of rendering the learners open to contents and values, can be achieved only by what we call contents of education because they have a particular characteristic: *They are always specific contents, are examples that represent a larger set of cultural contents.* A content of education must always make fundamental problems, fundamental relations, fundamental opportunities, general principles, laws, values, and methods understandable. Such elements that effect understanding of the general in or through the medium of the specific are conveyed in the term *educational substance (Bildungsgehalt).* Any specific content thus contains *general* substance.

The task of Didaktik analysis as the first and most important step in the preparation of lessons is, therefore, "to bring out the substance of the objects of learning" (Willmann, 1957, p. 460), to establish as the pedagogically crucial elements of the material those parts "on which its internalization [one could also say, its power to penetrate] depends or, inversely, in which the form of subjective Bildung becomes fulfilled and perfected" (Nohl, 1949, p. 144). In other words, Didaktik analysis is to indicate wherein the general substance of specific content of education lies. The substance almost always proves to be "a network of relations" (Peter, 1954, p. 72, cf. p. 77), a "nexus, a complex of connections, which is itself set in a wider . . . context" (Petzelt, 1947, p. 78).

C. DIDAKTIK ANALYSIS

I

Only after these preliminary fundamental reflections on the content of education and substance can the task of Didaktik analysis be more precisely defined. We make our general question more precise through the medium of five general questions that, together, should yield a definition of substance. It will be immediately clear that the answers to these questions can usually be obtained only from the specific situation, of the specific school class in question. Thus, our examples always remain distanced from the particular reality of school.

As the five basic questions, which we in turn break down into sections, are mutually dependent, the order in which they appear is not necessarily obligatory for Didaktik analysis in practice. Each question carries tacit overtones of the other four, and the answer to each individual question only becomes fully comprehensible in the light of all five answers.

What questions, therefore, should a teacher ask in the preliminary phase of instructional preparation, that is, Didaktik analysis, in view of the concrete topics/themes proposed by the curriculum or planned by the individual teacher?

I. What wider or general sense or reality does this content exemplify and open up to the learner? What basic phenomenon or fundamental principle, what law, criterion, problem, method, technique, or attitude can be grasped by dealing with this content as an "example"?

1. *What does the planned topic exemplify, represent, or typify?* The automobile engine stands for all gasoline engines, the cherry blossom for the basic biological phenomenon of blossom, a particular incident from the colonization of the eastern European regions by Germans for eastern European colonization in general, the painting theme "Hurrah, it's snowing!" for creative use of spray techniques in art, these specific arithmetic tasks from the field of banking, for the calculation of interest in general, and so on. The "exemplary" significance depends to a large extent on the teacher's goals. One and the same item of content can in some cases exemplify a variety of general subjects.

2. *Where can the knowledge to be gained from this topic be picked up on and used at a later date, either as a whole or as individual elements—insights, conceptions, conceptions of values, work methods, techniques?* When a child in the second grade learns to change small denomination money into larger denominations, the process will later reoccur as an "element" in understanding basic arithmetical operations in written form. The basic terms of, for example, history and science that the child learns at elementary school will later be applied in high school classes. . . .

II. What significance does the content in question, or the experience, knowledge, ability, or skill to be acquired through this topic already possess in the minds of the children in my class? What significance should it have from a pedagogical point of view?

It is crucial that this question should not be understood purely in terms of method. This is only its secondary sense. First and foremost it is a matter of whether the content in question, that is, the substance to be investigated in it, can and should be an element in the present education of the young people, that is, in their lives, in their conception of themselves and the world, in their areas of competence. Moreover, the term *Bildung* of the child or adolescent does not primarily mean "school" or "education" as a definable, special area of knowledge, ability, attitude, or behavior, but the world of the mind, the habits of the young person as a whole. Within this mental world, school should be understood as a place of clarification, purification, consolidation, expansion, stimulus. In this perspective, the foremost criterion of a school's efforts should be the query whether the activities can come alive and be effective *outside* the school's walls. Thus we ask what importance electricity, animals, foreign lands, music, crafts, stories, church, faith, religion, and so on have for the child *outside* school, and in what sense they could or should become significant.

To clarify: Has the planned topic already come up in questions occurring in class? Is the topic familiar to these children (to some? to all?) in their out-of-school experience? Does it play a vital role in their school or out-of-school life? Must the children first be acquainted with the questions from which this topic is to develop—perhaps by shattering certain conceptions they take for granted—or can the familiarity be presupposed? (bicycles, automobiles, fruit trees, the lives of knights, calculation of interest, letter writing, water cycle, trade union movement, multiplication and division of fractions by fractions, punctuation in direct speech). From which angles do the students already have access to the topic? Which angles are still unfamiliar? (In the case of the topic "local birds," e.g., the children might know birds as songbirds, as cherry and grain thieves, but they may not know of the economic benefits birds can have for humans.)

III. What constitutes the topic's significance for the children's future?

With this question we formulate more specifically the perspective of the layperson, mentioned earlier, which the teacher has to anticipate for the student.

To clarify: Does this content play a vital role in the intellectual life of the adolescents and adults the children will become, or is there justification to assume that it will, or should, play such a role? (e.g., coming to terms with our recent history, securing the foundations of our democracy, the problem of communism, the question of European unity, the double role of women, the organization of leisure, getting to grips with modern art, and so on). Is this content a genuine element of general education, *Allgemeinbildung*, of all-round, foundational Bildung in its positive sense, or does it preempt some sort of specialized education *(Spezialbildung)*, such as vocational training? If the answer to this is yes, then it should be rejected! Are the children already aware of the content's relevance to the future? Can it be made clear to them, or is it so difficult to understand that it cannot be explained to the children?

IV. How is the content structured (which has been placed in a specifically pedagogical perspective by Questions I, II, and III)?

It is vitally important to remember that the question about the structure of the content only can be properly asked, pedagogically, in the light of the first three basic questions. Detached from the perspective created by these questions, the structural question becomes a prepedagogical "subject analysis," that is, a theoretical-scientific question—at least by intention—that yields corresponding answers. The question about the structure of the content "electricity," for example, can be answered by key words such as "atomic theory," "electron current," "Ohm's Law," and so on. Responses of this kind can be educational *(bildend)* only if and when the question and comprehension level of the students matches them, as would be the case, for example, in the highest grades of general secondary education or in the final grades of particular vocational schools. A teacher wishing to deal with this topic in Grade 7 or 8, however, will be forced to conclude, after reflecting on the present meaning of this topic for his average students (i.e., from the point of view of what children in puberty can comprehend and how they regard the world), that the model constructs of atomic theory, the mathematical formulation of Ohm's Law, and so on, cannot (in general) be grasped in their inner meaning by these children, cannot be knowledge that contributes to Bildung. Any teacher, therefore, who believes the students must still be presented with these theoretical elements courts the danger of inducing misconceptions (such as confusion of the atomic model with reality) or mere rote learning that will play no functional role in the subsequent intellectual life of the young person in question (Ohm's Law). Physics at this level will have to be phenomenon oriented (Wagenschein). It will have to confine itself to those phenomena of electricity to which the students have ready access, either through their everyday experience or through simple experiments, and that interest them. This means that it will be first and foremost the practical effects and technical applications of electricity that create the framework within which electricity can be taught at this level.

With regard to these conditions, the basic question about the structure of a particular content can be broken down as follows:

1. *What are the individual elements of the content as a meaningful whole?* In the case of the gasoline engine, this would be, for example, (a) expansion

of gases on heating, (b) low ignition temperature of gasoline spark plug, (c) technical transmission of upward-and-downward motion into rotary motion (crankshaft), and (d) simple gear connections for transmitting the direction of mechanical movement.

2. *How are these individual elements related?* (a) Do they form a logically "obvious" series? (mostly in arithmetic and in mathematics, in the natural sciences). In this case, a certain order of logical steps must be adhered to. Or (b) do they form an interdependent structure, where all or some elements are interrelated, so that the order in which they have to be examined is not necessarily given by a unilinear "logic," but characterized by the reciprocal effects of some or several factors (such as the relationships of plants and animals in symbiotic systems, the geophysical factors essential to a particular landscape, geographical relations, etc.)?

3. *Is the content layered? Does it have different layers of meaning and significance?* In the case of a reading text, for example, either a complete text or an extract, this would involve, first, the layer of the narrated events and actions; second, the layer of inner experiences of the protagonists not expressly described; third, the (possible) symbolic meaning of the phenomena and relations ascertained in the first and second layers. To take another example, in geography, with the topic "Africa," it would involve the basic layer of knowledge about climatic and vegetation zones; then the layer of specialized and specific knowledge, including the anthropological, geographic, economic factors, and so on. In the case of a history topic, such as the 1917 Bolshevik Revolution in Russia, it would involve, first, the layer of essential historical facts; second, the layer of political ideology; third, the layer of fundamental historical, political, and sociological phenomena and basic concepts such as state, government, tsar/kaiser, class, revolution. . . . Can the layers be understood in relative independence of each other? or is knowledge of one layer a prerequisite for the understanding of another (as in our geography and history examples)?

4. *What is the wider context of this content? What must have preceded it?* The study of magnetism, for example, would need to precede the study of the electric motor.

5. *What peculiarities of the content will presumably make access to the subject difficult for the children?* Examples: In science topics, it is not only common sayings such as "the sun rises" that mislead the children, but also terms commonly used in instruction and even in science textbooks, such as "centrifugal force," "the *flow* of electric current," which either have caused or presumably will cause the children to make false analogies. The idea of electric current flowing, for instance, immediately evokes the conception of flowing water, which moves as a result of differences in altitude. (There is a so-called "illustration" that is still used, even in science textbooks today, where water is watched as it flows from one vessel into another placed at

a lower level. Even for primary science, this attempt at analogy is unsuitable or, more precisely, not isomorphic, inadequate, because it misrepresents the essence of electrical "current," which is a *circuit*. No phenomenon of electricity can be made comprehensible by means of that analogy with flowing water.)

In history instruction, the difficulty constantly reoccurs that the children project their notions, which are anchored in their present experience, onto previous periods of history, and thus make it harder to understand historical phenomena and processes.

6. *What is the body of knowledge that must be retained ("minimum knowledge") if the content determined by these questions is to be considered "acquired" as a "vital," "working" human possession?*

V. What are the special cases, phenomena, situations, experiments, persons, elements of aesthetic experience, and so forth, in terms of which the structure of the content in question can become interesting, stimulating, approachable, conceivable, or vivid for children of the stage of development of this class?

This final query of the five must be developed in three sections:

1. *What facts or states of affairs, phenomena, situations, experiments, controversies, and so forth—in other words, what experiences—are appropriate for exciting in the pupils' minds an interest in, and a positive attitude toward, developing questions oriented to deciphering the structure of the given problem?* It is this questioning that is to drive the course of the teaching–learning process.

Heinrich Roth (1983) formulated the problem as follows:

> How do I bring the object within the scope of the child's ability to question? How can I make it worthwhile for the child to ask questions? How do I transform it again into a question, an object that arose as an answer to a question? (pp. 123–124)

In reply he gave the following answer as a matter of principle:

> Child and object interlock when the child or adolescent can sense the object, the task, the cultural asset in the nearness of its processes of development, in its "original situation," from which it has become an "object," "task," "cultural asset." . . . By analyzing . . . the object in its genesis, I re-create the original human situation with respect to it and thus the vital interest from which it once stemmed. (p. 124)

Such a pedagogical "return to the original situation" strives to "retransform dead subject matter into the vital actions that engendered it: physical objects into inventions and discoveries, works into creations, plans into worries, treaties into decisions, solutions into tasks, phenomena into basic phenomena" (p. 124).

Copei (1963) gave us a good example involving a can of condensed milk. His students begin to ask questions directed at the effects of air pressure after observing, first, that the contents of a can of condensed milk cannot be poured out of one hole and, second, when two holes are punched, that the milk can be poured only if the can is held obliquely. The observation, in early spring, that children from a village on a hillside can still go sledding whereas their schoolfellows from a village down in the valley cannot be-cause all the snow has melted there, can induce questions directed at a basic issue of climate. The juxtaposition of different songs that the children perceive as "sad" and "gloomy" or "bright," "happy," or "light," and so on, can provoke questions that lead to a consciousness of the dominant sound character of major and minor keys.

2. *What pictures, hints, situations, observations, stories, experiments, models, and so on, are appropriate in helping the children to answer, as independently as possible, their questions directed at the essentials of the matter?* The answer here as a general principle can be summed up as "the model character of the elementary case" (Roth, 1964, p. 125) or "the fruitfulness of the elemen-tary" (cf. Spranger, 1954, pp. 87 ff.). For all contents that are themselves the product of a process of thoughtful development, the appropriate and ade-quate form of illustration is the "return to the original situation," a term that here is not primarily meant in an historical sense, but refers instead to the systematic origin. This is a principle with which we are familiar as a means of inducing a genuine process of questioning in the children and, at the same time, as the right way of adequate illustration.

After, for example, a story from before the time of steamships (e.g., about a becalmed vessel) has brought up the question of how the trade winds occur, the students can develop their answer using air movement in a heated room as a model. In the case of a question about German coloniza-tion of eastern Europe—prompted by the issue of German refugees after the Second World War—the teacher can present the material required to formu-late the answers by, for example, recounting a story in which the various motives are "symbolically concentrated" (*"symbolische Verdichtung:"* Heim-pel), made obvious by vividly characterized historical persons or groups. The theme "winter landscape" is appropriate to stimulate creative efforts in which the aesthetic quality of black-and-white color contrast and plane-line form contrast is strikingly illustrated.

3. *What situations and tasks are appropriate for helping the principle of content grasped by means of an example, of an elementary "case," become of real benefit to the students, helping to consolidate it by application and practice (immanent repetition)?*

Modern theories of language instruction justifiably demand "practice with a purpose" appropriate both to the subject and to the child. Once, for instance, the pattern of concessive clauses has been introduced using an appropriate example, the next step should be to seek situations in the life of the child where concessive clauses are required to verbalize the subject matter, and not, as is still so often the case, simply to set the task, "Write 10 sentences using *although*." A similar principle applies in arithmetic. And in science, for instance, the aim would be for the laws of radiation worked out with one or two examples to be discovered in other cases. Or the characteristics of an animal community could be first studied by using the example of bees, and improved with the students subsequently doing work of their own on ant communities.

D. PLANNING OF THE METHODICAL ARRANGEMENT OF TEACHING AND LEARNING

The second step of instructional planning, planning of teaching methods, can proceed only from Didaktik analysis. Methods planning is concerned with the "how" of teaching, more precisely with the questions "Which ways can lead to the fruitful encounter between the children and the content?" (the pedagogical significance and structure of which have been established by Didaktik analysis) and "What can follow for a fruitful encounter between the two to be achieved?" This interpretation of planning for methods clearly shows its dependence on Didaktik reflection.

The transition from Didaktik reflection to method planning has already been indicated several times in our sketch of Didaktik analysis (in the narrow sense of the term *Didaktik*): first, in the remarks on the introduction of initial questions and, second, in the reflections on the problems of illustration. Nevertheless, we consider it of utmost importance that these very problems—contrary to common belief—must be seen primarily as Didaktik issues (and not in the narrow sense), that is, as problems of content.

The depth of Didaktik analysis required as a first step in preparation will, of course, always depend on the chosen theme. This may be an instructional unit stretching over several months, but could equally be the topic for a week, or just for one lesson. Didaktik analysis is the foundation, not only for the introduction of a new theme, but for all teaching activity dedicated to this particular content. Thus, even the design of a practice or revision lesson—as such mainly a matter of method—depends on the results of Didaktik analysis. In the end, the only way of determining whether this or that form of practice or revision would be pedagogically right or wrong in a particular case is by ascertaining whether it is appropriate to the contents.

This is not the place for a detailed discussion of the second step for planning of methods of instruction. Suffice it to say that this phase of planning and preparation must, we feel, concentrate on four areas above all:

- The organization of instruction or learning into sections or phases or steps.
- The choice of forms of teaching, work, play, practice, and revision.
- The use of classroom aids (teaching and learning aids).
- The achievement of organizational prerequisites for instruction and learning.

Ideas about method will naturally occur to the classroom practitioner in the course of Didaktik analysis. Nonetheless, method planning, which is, after all, the outline of the lessons themselves, can really take place only after Didaktik analysis. This is an essential point, particularly because the outline of the questions as set out previously is by no means identical to the chronological order of the methodical steps. Thus the outlooks or applications that children can be shown on the basis of the ideas set out under Question III of the Didaktik analysis (relevance for the future) come, when method is under consideration, *after* the practical conclusions to be drawn from the considerations set out under Question V (exemplary cases, phenomena, etc. as "entries" to the processes of understanding structures). In short, the order of methodical steps obeys a different set of rules from those determining Didaktik reflection (in the narrower sense). The former is governed by practical considerations, whereas the order of Didaktik reflection follows theoretical-systematic norms.

ACKNOWLEDGMENTS

This abridgement and adaptation of "Didaktische Analyse als Kern der Unterrichtsvorbereitung" draws heavily on an initial translation of the paper prepared by Gillian Horton-Krüger. The adaptation incorporates the comments of Peter Menck of the University of Siegen and the corrections of Wolfgang Klafki on the translation. Support for both the translation and adaptation was provided by Institut für die Pädagogik der Naturwissenschaften (IPN) at the Christian-Albrechts Universität, Kiel, through its "Didaktik Meets Curriculum" group consisting of Kurt Riquarts, Roland Lauterbach, and Stefan Hopmann.

This translation was first published in the *Journal of Curriculum Studies* and with some revisions and corrections is reprinted by permission of the copyright holder, Taylor & Francis Ltd., London.

REFERENCES

Adl-Amini, B., & Künzli, R. (Eds.). (1980). *Didaktische Modelle und Unterrichtsplanung.* Munich: Juventa Verlag.
Buber, M. (1953). *Reden über Erziehung.* Heidelberg: L. Schneider.

Copei, F. (1963). *Der fruchtbare Moment im Bildungsprozess.* Heidelberg: Quelle & Meyer.

Kerschensteiner, G. (1926). *Theorie der Bildung.* Leipzig: B. G. Teubner.

Klafki, W. (1963). *Studien zur Bildungstheorie und Didaktik.* Weinheim: Beltz Verlag.

Klafki, W. (1977). *Probleme einer Neukonzeption der Didaktischen Analyse* (Schriftenreihe des pädagogischen Instituts der Landeshauptstadt Düsseldorf, Vol. 34). Düsseldorf: Pädagogisches Institut der Landeshauptstadt Düsseldorf.

Klafki, W. (1980). Zur Unterrichtsplanung im Sinne kritisch-konstruktiver Didaktik. In E. König, N. Schier, & U. Vohland (Eds.), *Diskussion Unterrichtsvorbereitung. Verfahren und Modelle* (pp. 13–44). Munich: W. Fink.

Klafki, W. (1996). Zur Unterrichtsplanung im Sinne kritisch-konstruktiver Didaktik. In W. Klafki *Neue Studien zur Bildungstheorie und Didaktik: Zeitgemäße Allgemeinbildung und kritisch-konstruktive Didaktik* (pp. 251–284). Weinheim: Beltz Verlag.

Litt, T. (1963). *Naturwissenschaft und Menschenbildung.* Heidelberg: Quelle & Meyer.

Nohl, H. (1949). *Die pädagogische Bewegung in Deutschland und ihre Theorie.* Frankfurt: G. Schulte-Bulmke.

Peter, R. (1954). *Grundlegender Unterricht.* Bad Heilbrunn: Klinkhardt.

Petzelt, A. (1947). *Grundzüge systematischer Pädagogik.* Stuttgart: Kohlhammer.

Roth, H. (1983). Die "originale Begegnung" als methodisches Prinzip. In H. Roth, *Pädagogische Psychologie des Lehrens und Lernens* (pp. 116–126). Hanover: Schroedel.

Spranger, E. (1954). Die Fruchtbarkeit des Elementaren. In E. Spranger, *Pädagogische Perspektiven* (pp. 87–92). Heidelberg: Quelle & Meyer.

Weniger, E. (1952). *Didaktik als Bildungslehre. Teil 1: Theorie der Bildungsinhalte und des Lehrplans.* Weinheim: Beltz Verlag.

Weniger, E. (1958). Bildung und Persönlichkeit. In E. Weniger, *Die Eigenständigkeit der Erziehung in Theorie und Praxis.* Weinheim: Beltz Verlag.

Willmann, O. (1904). *Aus Hörsaal und Schulstube. Gesammelte kleinere Schriften zur Erziehungs- und Unterrichtslehre* (2nd ed.). Freiburg im Bresgau: Herder.

Willmann, O. (1957). *Didaktik als Bildungslehre nach ihren Beziehungen zur Sozialforschung und zur Geschichte der Bildung.* Freiburg im Bresgau: Herder.

9

Teaching to Understand: On the Concept of the Exemplary in Teaching

Martin Wagenschein
Gillian Horton-Krüger (Trans.)

Martin Wagenschein (1896–1988) studied mathematics and physics in Gießen, completed his doctorate in physics in 1920, and his teacher certification examination in 1923. In 1924 he began work at Paul Geheeb's "Odenwaldschule," a comprehensive boarding school closely related to the German movement of reform pedagogy, where he taught until 1933. From 1933–1955, Wagenschein worked as a teacher in academic secondary schools. In addition, he taught physics and subject-Didaktik from 1947–1955 at a seminar for students in their second, practical phase of teacher education. He was appointed to a lectureship at the Technical University of Darmstadt in 1950, and became a professor at the University of Tübingen in 1956 where he taught teacher education until 1978. Martin Wagenschein died in 1988.

In addition to his work in teacher education, Wagenschein was actively involved in questions of school reform as a member of several commissions for the revision of curricula and school reform in the former Federal Republic of Germany.

Wagenschein's work focused on science Didaktik, the development of the principle of exemplary teaching, and the teaching method of genetic-Socratic discussion. He also advocated an orientation of school physics teaching on natural phenomena.

Wagenschein's publications include *Die pädagogische Dimension der Physik* [The Educational Dimension of Physics] (1962); *Ursprüngliches Denken und exaktes Verstehen* [Original Thinking and Exact Understanding], Vol. 1 (1965), Vol. 2 (1970); and *Verstehen lehren* [How to Teach Understanding] (1968).

—Jörg Biehl

"The exemplary as a medium for teaching"—this is the concept I endeavor to define in the following pages. Although the concept applies to all disciplines, many of my illustrations and examples are taken from physics, because this is the field I know best. First I define the exemplary by comparing and contrasting it with other related and unrelated approaches; then I address the following question: If we seek to educate *(bilden)*, in what sense can we regard an object, a theme, a problem within a subject area as "exemplary," and to what end?

I

I. The System of Knowing as a Course of Instruction

Let us begin with what we would do better to disassociate ourselves from if we do not want the school to degenerate into a mere apparatus for "getting through the subject matter," suffocating under the sheer mass of information. The older and more established a "subject," the more rigid its structure—I am thinking here of mathematics, for example, in contrast to the much younger field of "social studies"—and the more willingly we succumb to the temptation to run through from beginning to end, from the simple to the complex, without missing a single level in the so-called systematic course of instruction. Mathematics teaching, for example, starts out at a point somewhere near the axioms, whereas physics commences with basic skills, such as measuring, and basic concepts, usually of mechanics. The paths traced are linear—in the animal kingdom from single-celled organisms to human beings (or vice-versa), in history from the past to the present—and progress is made step by step. The essential point would appear to be: *Each individual theme appears as one small, cautious step on the way to more complex, more difficult topics as yet unknown to the learner.*

The justification for this approach is obvious: One thing builds on another, either logically or chronologically; there must be order; gaps will cause problems later; one can never know when a particular piece of knowledge will be needed. These justifications are "logical," but no more than that. They are not pedagogical. They pursue a vision of the complete subject. They do not see the child, but a scaled-down model of the finished human being, the adult, still limited in the faculty of understanding. But being a teacher means being conscious of the developing, the waking intellect. And being a subject teacher means at the same time being conscious of the developed and developing subject matter.

"First the simple, then the complex" of course has its legitimation. But it must not be the only valid principle. Its shortcoming is evident: The "simple" is often either not simple at all, or it is trivial. The more a learner reflects on the law of inertia, for example, the less credible it appears. A few lifetimes of research were necessary to discover it, and it is a great pity to find it served up with a scanty justification on page 3 of a beginners' physics book. Einstein (Einstein & Infeld, 1956) wrote of the law of inertia, "It is usually the first thing we learn by heart in physics at school, and one or two of us may remember it" (p. 12). The fact that certain "angles of parallels" are equal is credible, but all too credible. It is boring and "leads" nowhere; it simply "serves" a purpose.

A course of teaching of this kind brings no long-range motivation for the learner. It encourages only the anxious upward glance to the higher levels, as yet unknown, but already a burden (the fact that they are known to the teacher makes them no less of a burden). The student wonders what the teacher intends; the teacher begins by telling the students what the class is about to do.

A systematic course of this kind makes plenitude alluring—it wishes to supply it—with haste and lack of thoroughness as ever-present dangers. Thus an imposing pile of rubble is built up. In its very clinging to systematics, it buries systematics and obscures (see Fig. 9.1, No. I). It confuses systematics of subject matter with systematics of thought. This picture is deliberately exaggerated. The systematic course of teaching is hardly desired in such pure form today. But the fact that it still dominates is witnessed by our curricula, including the most recent.

Bildung is not a process of adding on. But where an additive matting of the subject matter "fabric" is wrong, a subtractive combing (see Fig. 9.1, No. II) cannot be right either, as the material will become threadbare and insubstantial, the result a thinned-out systematic course. No one would regard this knowing-a-little as a suitable alternative to knowing-a-lot. Yet many a recommendation to offer subject matter "in broad outlines" or "in overviews" is not far removed from such a proposition.

2. Creating Platforms

Principles for selection are required. There must be restriction to the "essential"—we consider what this could be in section II. Assuming for now that we already know what is essential, the first practicable form of the course would be as shown in III in Fig. 9.1. We need the courage to leave gaps, in other words to be thorough and to deal intensively with selected samples.

Instead of a uniform, superficial run-through of a catalogue of knowledge, step by step, we are allowed—indeed it is our duty—to stop in places, to dig deep, to put down roots. Some suggest the construction of "islands." But these would have to be linked by a conceptual underwater mountain range, for it is not decomposition of the subject that is required, but continuity, with exposed areas of higher density, intensification (Flitner, 1955), and concentration within the continuum. Or picture soundly anchored piers connected by overarching bridge sections that allow more rapid movement

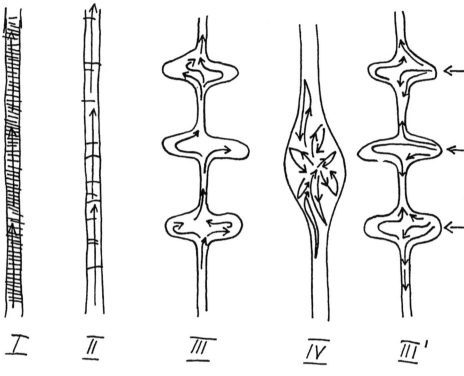

FIG. 9.1.

from one place to the next. The more substantial the concentration, the smoother the connections. Smooth, swift movement from one firmly grounded pier to another does not betoken lack of thoroughness. Other images can be used: that of the strawberry runner regularly putting down new shoots, extending and anchoring, or the glider gaining height on an up-current above one place and being thus enabled to glide swiftly forward until the next climb. I choose, to retain the idea of steps and levels, the image of *platforms* (such as those landings inside a tower where a climber may pause during the ascent). A misinterpretation of this image would be places to "rest" in order to "escape" from the "strict progress" of the systematic course. The image is flawed inasmuch as platforms in this sense are generally inhospitable, drafty places, whereas the areas of "concentration" should be inviting. The main point is that each platform of concentration also has the character of a step, but becomes a platform due to the efforts of concentration. The ascent of the tower then progresses from platform to platform, with connecting steps placed at wide intervals.

This procedure has often been termed *exemplary*. I consider it a very serviceable procedure, but would prefer to define exemplary more narrowly, as the following section shows.

3. The Exemplary Process

In search of the exemplary we must go beyond the image of steps and platforms. To anticipate: A platform of concentration at which we probe deeply into a subject or problem is not just a platform but a *mirror* of the whole. Words that are repeatedly used in this context include *substitutional, illustrative, representative, poignant, model, ideal, exemplary, paradigmatic.* The relation between individual and whole here is not that of the part, the step, the stage, the prestage. The individual is a focal point, admittedly only *one,* but one in which the whole is borne. In this sense, the individual does not accumulate, but bears and illuminates the whole; it does not lead away from the whole, but enlightens it. Through resonance it excites further, related knowledge (see Fig. 9.1, No. IV)

This is what Ernst Mach (1923) meant when he said the physicist "would be satisfied if every young man" (he forgets the young women) "could have experienced, as it were, a few mathematical or scientific discoveries and pursued them into their further consequences" (p. 344). Perhaps it is also what Lichtenberg's (1944) aphorism means when he said, "Something one has had to invent for oneself leaves a track in one's understanding that can be followed up at another opportunity" (p. 145), or indeed Confucius, who is supposed to have said he would dismiss the pupil who did not understand how to apply in the three other corners what he had learned in the first. This intent is clearest in the "Tübingen Resolution":[1] "Original phenomena of the intellectual world can become visible, through the example of a single object really grasped by the student." Commenting on this point, Hermann Heimpel (1951), himself a participant in the Tübingen discussions, said that "the general is contained within and traceable within the individual: *mundus in gutta*" (p. 7), and that it is possible "within the framework of a general view, to have a real encounter with the historical world in individual places and . . . to apply this to other areas" (p. 7). Another participant, Wilhelm

---

[1]In *Bildung und Erziehung,* 5 (1952), p. 58ff.; *Die Höhere Schule,* 4 (1951), pp. 6–7; *Die Pädagogische Provinz,* 1951, p. 623 ff. The resolution is discussed in Flitner (1954), pp. 125ff.

[Editors' note]: In 1951, representatives of German universities and teachers in academic Gymnasium came together in Tübingen for a conference on the "The University and the School." The participants' judgment that the *Lehrplan* for the Gymnasium prescribed excessive content coverage was the motivation for the meeting.

The conference passed four resolutions concerning schools, curricula, and teacher training. They demanded a reduction in the number of subjects taught in the Gymnasium, more freedom within the *Lehrplan,* and the opportunity for individual schools to choose to set their own emphases in the taught curriculum. Furthermore, they demanded improved cooperation between Gymnasiums and universities and a reform of teacher training—with a reduction of the number of required subjects and the introduction of practical courses for teacher students. These demands and suggested reforms were aimed at enhancing the quality of Bildung in the Gymnasium.

Weischedel (1955), spoke of the "presence of the whole in the individual" and the fact that "in an individual event something of the essence of history can flicker to life."

Exemplary contemplation is the opposite of specialization (Wagenschein, 1965). It does not seek to distinguish one from another, but to discover the whole in the individual. ("Impossible," would be the comment from those who only add up.)

To sharpen our definition: Radically exemplary mathematics teaching could, for example, confine itself to the observation of an ancient proof for the continuation of prime numbers (Wagenschein, 1965), and thus make something (not everything) of the character of mathematics visible (Menninger, 1954). The example is deliberately exaggerated and is not intended as a proposal. Yet I am convinced that a glance in this mirror alone, be it only deep enough, could reveal more of mathematics than many a student has grasped, including even successful examination candidates. (For more examples from physics and mathematics, see Wagenschein, 1965, chaps. 11, 18, 22, 41, 70.) In biology, Richard Goldschmidt (1927) showed us how the study of ascarids is sufficient to demonstrate the main points of biology. And Kerschensteiner (1928) wrote, "Forty years ago, Prof. Götte in Strasbourg . . . wrote an excellent little book in which five to ten animals were used to study and relate all essential phenomena, terms and laws in the field of zoology" (p. 116).

4. Spontaneity

So far I have centered deliberately on the object of learning. But we must have child and object in view simultaneously, which means that the exemplary found on platforms must also be exemplary to the subject of learning, must lead to concentration in the activity of the child. It must be penetrative and intense, entering deep into the matter at hand and into the soul of the learner.

The reflection must not only reflect the whole of the subject matter—in the most favorable case the whole of the intellectual world—it must also illuminate the whole of the learner (and not simply, e.g., the intelligence).

5. "Point of Entry"

In courses of teaching progressing in steps from one platform to the next (within the system), there is more than one "point of entry," meaning that it is not necessary to enter the tower of the subject at the base and make a vertical assent, in the sense of moving upward from the basic, rapidly ascending the steps, and lingering at the platforms. A point of entry leads directly onto a platform represented by a problem, avoiding the staircase offering "requisite basic knowledge." Entry thus immediately presents a relatively complex issue, challenging the spontaneity of the child (see Fig. 9.1, No. III′).

When teaching optics, for example, the usual line could be abandoned and the topic approached through the problem articulated by Kepler in 1604: Where do "sunshine circles" come from? It is a commonly known fact that when a shaft of sunlight shines through a hole or a crack, a circle appears on the opposite surface. Kepler pointed out that this phenomenon can be observed under gaps in roofs, opposite holes in stained-glass windows, indeed under any tree. It is, he said, a phenomenon that has fascinated and occupied scientists since ancient times, but for which he could still find no satisfactory explanation (Kepler, 1922).

III′ in my figure is intended to represent entry from "outside," with thought penetrating downward to the elements (here linear propagation) and upward to complicated issues.

A second point of entry repeats this procedure a little "higher up," perhaps using the phenomenon, described by Goethe, that a white stone against a dark background in clear water not only appears raised, but seems to have a colored edge, an appearance that is intensified the deeper the stone sinks. This would enable the complex of refraction and dispersion to be unfolded, with movement downward to reflection and upward to the spectrum (Picard, 1956).

From the point of entry, therefore, we move downward from a problem to the elementary, searching for the explanation we require. Selection becomes important: We no longer hoard information, but search out what we need. We proceed along the same lines as the original research. We are challenged by something strange to us, and we seek to reveal the simple facts within it.

A tried and tested point of entry to mechanics is the apparently harmless question, "Where does a stone fall that is held out of the window of a tower and dropped?" Seemingly trivial at first, the question soon takes on fascinating twists when the curvature of the earth and rotation come to mind. By the time the answer has been found, the law of inertia and the principle of independence have been revealed, as well as proof of the earth's rotation and—above all—the way in which a physicist thinks.

The greatest skill will be required in selecting an initial problem that is complex enough, but not too complex. And there should be no fanaticism over the procedure. It should be remembered that the basic principle "from the simple to the complex" also has its—restricted—validity.

6. Exemplary Learning as Experience

To return to the points I made in subsection 4: For the point of entry it may suffice if the problem is "interesting." But for the exemplary theme that—alone—is to reflect the whole, we demand greater spontaneity: The learner must grasp more profoundly and be affected more deeply. This would be the greatest contrast to the "getting-through-it" approach that threatens to dominate school today. The concept of "attention" needs reassessment (Wagenschein, 1965).

Max Picard (1956) found it characteristic of modern man "that there is no longer an encounter between himself and the object. It is no longer an event to behold an object: it is there before we have reached out for it, and it retreats before we have released it" (p. 79). According to Picard:

> [The objects] are arrived at indirectly, provisionally, approximately, noncommittally, i.e., they are not arrived at all, . . . they are delivered. Everything seems preempted. . . . All objects seem to be part of a monstrous apparatus for getting things done, with man at the point of delivery. . . . (p. 79)

And yet, Picard pointed out, "the purpose of an encounter is to devote time, and that means love, to the object at hand" (p. 79). All this seems to me to apply word for word to school. . . .

A purely organizational conclusion emerges immediately: Exemplary instruction cannot be reconciled to the piecemeal approach of the 45-minute period. It clamors for larger blocks, at least 2 hours on the same theme day after day. The theme can then engrave itself on the hearts of the students and teachers and the work there, day and night.

7. The Relationship Between the Exemplary and the Point of Entry

The concept of the point of entry has steps in view, the progression from platform to platform. The exemplary procedure—in its pure form—does not; it may restrict itself to a single problem radiating outward. It does not relate to steps, but like the point of entry, it does lead into the problem without preparation. (For this reason, a figure IV' would be superfluous.) A point of entry, on the other hand, can be exemplary (even if it anticipates step-by-step learning, just as a stove can work not only by air convection but also by radiation).

8. The Relationship Between the Exemplary and the Canon

Heimpel (1951) saw individual encounters within a general, overall view, and Flitner (1955) emphasized that history must first be recounted. The same applies to the sciences (and, at the right place and time, their history needs to be told). There are certain things we really need to know. Not how a radio works in detail or the "world age" theory of modern cosmogony, but what happens when water pipes freeze up, why electrical switches should not be used when there is a smell of gas, and a few more things besides. Not all of this will be utilitarian knowledge. For example: why the stem of a plant growing straight out of the water looks bent, although it is in fact not bent at all. We need to know how these things interconnect. Not only so that we are better able to remember them if we can make these interconnections, but because, as the physicist Tyndall (1867) once said, in the physical as in the moral world, the fact that things never stand in isolation inspires confidence in the world, and is thus an educative or formative *(bildend)* experience.

For the upper level of school, therefore, a canon of this type is the prerequisite for exemplary "deep drilling," boring down from the surface of the basic landscape laid out in earlier grades.

This does not mean to say that the basic landscape must still be laid out in the same old step-by-step routine, which would only shift the danger of overloading to the lower levels. And for the following reasons:

1. This canon need not be so full as we might at first think. In physics or biology, for example, restriction to phenomena (Wagenschein, 1953) and avoidance of premature and repeated mathematization and theorization would bring considerable relief (Spranger, 1952). Science teachers at the higher levels of secondary education, trained as they are in their subjects rather than in the history of human thought and in pedagogy, simply need to gain confidence to realize that this too is physics, this too is biology. Even the path to basic knowledge in astronomy can be greatly simplified without sacrificing stringency and insight (Wagenschein, 1955).

2. For the acquisition of this basic canon, the point of entry already exists, and even the exemplary is available. Platforms, even platforms that lend themselves to exemplary work, can be built early on in primary and lower secondary grades. But we need detailed reports of classroom experience to prove the point (Wagenschein, 1953, 1962).

II

1. After this attempt to define the exemplary in contrast with other modes of teaching, I now address exemplary teaching exclusively and ask: What are the exemplary themes in a subject and why are they exemplary? What does it mean to *illuminate the whole*?

Questions like these cannot be asked without a word of caution. The answers should not involve a universal "catalogue of exemplary matter." That would be the death of the process. Of course the choice of theme will not be insignificant. But the teacher must also be affected, and this varies individually. As Barthel (1956) pointed out, even the teacher must risk being unsure. Teachers and students are not only to act. They must be challenged in their security, if a problem is to be exemplary. We require not brief catalogues of exemplary themes, but wide-ranging reports on these individual activities, not for emulation, but for stimulation. We teachers must listen to each other as individuals, not obey a rigid program as functionaries. Perhaps we will not succeed in finding themes that lend themselves only to an exemplary (radiating) approach or only to a platform (gathering) approach. But it is not superfluous to know what we value in a theme.

2. Let us start with physics again. We have an essay by Spranger (1952) entitled "The Fruitfulness of the Elementary." The word *fruitful* points in the direction of our search. Here there is mention of the "pure case," that is, the case that is immediately comprehensible from the law of its composition, and that then gives the basic pattern for the wealth of real phenomena. For physics Spranger cited linear movement as the simplest and the parallelogram of forces. I would add the Newtonian laws of mechanics, particularly "force = mass × acceleration," the energy theorem, perhaps the principle of relativity, and so on. Kepler said the same when he reported he had been able to get to grips with a few laws of optics that appear insignificant, but that bear within them the germ from which the highest things will develop.

According to this, the elementary in this sense is always to be sought on the side of an object already covered by study, here therefore no longer in nature, but in nature as reduced by physics, an extracted general result that dominates the multiplicity of individual cases. Anyone who commands "force = mass × acceleration" can basically come to terms with mechanical situations through a process of integration.

The elementary is thus an important goal of physics teaching. It comprises the simple, which is not so simple after all, and for that reason cannot be presented at the commencement of teaching. For the expert it is the first tenet to apply; for the probing newcomer, it is the final discovery to be brought to light from the complex, peculiar phenomenon:

> The so-called pure case is recognized only through careful analysis of what is given in experience and through subsequent intellectual construction. This achievement is by no means at the beginning of knowledge, but is a result of complete command of the matter and of most mature thought. (Spranger, 1955, p. 98)

Teaching cannot begin with the elementary, but must steer toward it. From the point of entry it must descend to the elementary and uncover it. Command of the elementary theorems is command of key positions.

Necessary as it is to ensure, when selecting a problem, that its solution reveals the elementary, this is still not sufficient if our aim is to educate (*bilden*). For it is quite possible to imagine an eminently qualified physicist, or even a senior secondary student, who can apply "force = mass × acceleration" with confidence, but who could not be called educated *(gebildet)*.

If we understand the process of Bildung to be such that the learners as the subjects of this process must actively comprehend and absorb the object of learning and be themselves affected by it, a process leading to confrontation between the whole subject and the whole object, if we consider that we no longer comprehend physics as the study of how nature "really is" (Heisenberg, 1955; von Weisäcker, 1954), but as a way of understanding and as an aspect resulting from this that is based on specific regulations, a method with which nature allows us to interrogate her, then we acknowledge—as did Litt (1954)—that this method itself produces subject and object by restricting man to the role of "observer" insistent on logic (Münster & Picht, 1953) and nature to the basically measurable.

If we acknowledge all this, we cannot call any form of teaching educative *(bildend)* that does not constantly have this *triad* (Litt, 1954) of subject-method-object in sight—indeed, that does not make it the very substance of teaching. It is then no longer purely physics instruction, and in fact it cannot be that and that alone if it sets out to educate *(bilden)*. A physics teacher who is steeped only in physics, a physics teacher untouched by philosophy, is in no position to teach physics in the context of general education *(allgemeinbildung)*.

3. Heisenberg (1955) gave a biographical annotation to his school experience that aptly illustrates what is meant here. He wrote of his excitement upon discovering that mathematics in some way or other matches the pattern of our experience. "Usually," he said:

> school teaching lets the various landscapes of the intellectual world . . . pass by without our becoming properly at home in them. They are illuminated . . . to varying degrees, depending on the capabilities of the teacher, and the images remain a while in our memory or quickly fade. But in a few, rare cases, an object that has come into our view in this way suddenly begins to shine by itself . . . and the light it radiates fills an ever-increasing part of our thought, enlightens other objects, and at last becomes an important part of our own life. This is what happened to me when I realized that mathematics corresponds to what we experience. . . . (p. 39)

I am confident that what Heisenberg recounted reflects all the characteristics of the exemplary. Some elements of subject matter, which are not further described, became exemplary, but not elementary, which emerged more as a by-product and quite as a matter of course (e.g., $F = ma$). They became exemplary of the insight that certain natural processes may be expressed in mathematical terms. Perhaps we can call something like this the *fundamental*,[2] to distinguish it from the elementary (Wagenschein, 1962).

It does not resemble the elementary in physics, which enables the "observer" to solve a large number of individual problems, but is—a level deeper—something that causes man and his foundation and the matter and its foundation—and these are inseparable—to tremble. It shows man in a new light as one who can, under certain restrictive conditions, find mathematical laws of nature. And it shows nature as "submitting" to these laws, under the same conditions, acquiescing to the ceremonial of the experiment. Yet outside of these conditions, smiling enigmatically, nature remains untouched. Truly an "exciting" experience: the experience of Pythagoras and Kepler.

This experience is "exciting," not only interesting; and yet not everyone who can apply the Newtonian laws need notice it. We have to become deeply "at home" in a matter for it to reveal itself to us in this way. The experience itself begins to "glow" in contrast to the low background luminosity that is all the teacher can provide at the speed dictated. It begins to illuminate, and does so suddenly, like every decisive intellectual event that has been preceded by its due share of patient application. Plato reported how, after long, scientific study devoted to the object, it grew bright in the soul, like a light kindled by a jumping spark that from then on fed itself. It fills a larger space, not only in the subject, but in our thought, indeed, in the space of our lives.

Here, therefore, we have the rare and paramount instance of the whole of the intellectual world and the whole of the person affected by a fundamental experience of this kind. This is what sets a process of Bildung in motion.

The following general principle may be derived from this example:[3]

A certain problem (let us say Galileo's question how a ball rolls down a sloping board) can be exemplary of a fundamental experience (here the insight that certain natural processes can be expressed in mathematical terms). Experiences are fundamental if in them the common foundation of man and the matter (being confronted) are caused to tremble. Only then can we speak of an educative *(bildend)* experience. This experience is bound to deliver "elementary" insights as a by-product. Taking Galileo's experiment again, this would be, for instance, the law of inertia (as the ball runs back up a second board, Galileo slowly lowered the latter until it is horizontal, the plane to which his law of inertia is then restricted).

There are other fundamental experiences in physics . . . and it seems to me that it is these on which physics instruction depends if it is to be

---

[2] I owe the choice of this word to a helpful comment by Eduard Spranger.
[3] See chapter 16, this volume (editors' note).

educative *(bildend)*. I see no other way than the exemplary to achieve this goal. Not because time is too short to plow through everything the world has to offer in the way of knowledge, but because we have a great deal of time and because it would be pointless, and would neither school nor educate *(bilden)* successfully if this time were wasted with amassing knowledge. Exemplary teaching is no new emergency exit opened in resignation—it is a return to what teaching could only ever have been. . . .

6. The fundamental experiences in a subject, which can be obtained only through the medium of the exemplary, can be classed according to whether they upset or strengthen our sense of security. The sciences can do both: Rational comprehensibility of certain natural processes instills confidence; the demystification associated with this upsets it again. We can save a lot of what appears to be lost, although only to someone who misunderstands, by (a) observing closely, (b) keeping constant guard, from a methodological point of view, on scientific theory. It is then revealed that what appears to be loss, desolation, and fright appears so only because we have taken aspects of the world as "reality" and then added up the various (and contradictory) results, instead of recognizing them as various views of one and the same thing. We are then safe from seeing the living world as merely physical or chemical and the historical world as merely biological.

7. Perhaps there is in the biological, perhaps even in the physical, another, we could almost say a magical, entrance that also opens itself up in connection with one thing, and then stays open for all the things in this subject. It has, however, nothing to do with the method of the subject, nor is it a result. It happens once, associated with the auspiciousness of a moment, a name, a mood, a teacher. It can hardly be planned and thus approaches "encounter" in its true sense. It is often a revelation of the right view, a falling away of misunderstandings and prejudices, partly those that school has induced itself.

From biology I know the case of a girl who suddenly saw an entrance into a subject that had been blocked until that moment a teacher took her by the hand and showed her and her alone the flower nigella ("ragged lady") growing in the garden. The name and form not only told her all at once what this flower is: It became the girl's "key" to all other flowers.

From physics I know that the colored flash of a single drop of dew in the grass can spark an insight into what physics is, can show that the appearance is secondary, mediate, derived. This insight, shown in the right mood, can dissolve whole mountains of darkest misunderstanding into nothing.

Such experiences border on the question—which needs attention— whether there is in the teaching of language, in the experience of poetry and works of art, something comparable with the exemplary. Here too, maybe, a single entity may open up an original view, becoming not a mirror, not a transferable model, but a trigger, though quite how this could work needs to be elucidated. Perhaps we could call it "enchantment." . . .

8. What, then, is the exemplary? Is it perhaps the breakthrough of the principle of activity-centered learning to deeper, almost existential levels? Is it a training of regard for the fundamentals of a subject, focusing on what should be seen and what is overlooked within it? Is it the sobriety to see in the openings of physics, biology, history those elements that can jolt us out of our security—in order to preserve this very security by enlightening us about what we actually do in the subject and what it does to us? And is it about recognizing what cannot be preserved?

This would be a very different aim (although from time to time the subject matter would be the same) from allowing ourselves to be blinkered by a subject, something we must always guard against, and a very different aim from the mere amassing of matter.

No one knows how we will be living in this part of the world in 50 or 100 years from now. But I am certain that our descendants would shake their heads and smile in disbelief over a school system in which it was believed that anything could be achieved by amassing half-understood, but made absolute, knowledge. Earlier we lacked the "courage to leave gaps"—but this could be easily misunderstood; it should read courage to be thorough, courage to address the original.

We are evidently in search of something new to replace the idol of "completeness," broad-girthed and heavy in its immobility, in deference to which we are driven to hoard. To liberate ourselves, we seek to break through to the original sources. It is not the completeness of the final results we crave, *but the inexhaustibility of the original.*

ACKNOWLEDGMENTS

From Martin Wagenschein (1965), Zum Begriff des Exemplarischen Lehrens. In Martin Wagenschein, *Ursprüngliches Verstehen und exaktes Denken: Pädagogische Schriften I* (Stuttgart: Ernst Klett Verlag, 1965), pp. 297–316. For translation the original text has been abridged and contextualized. The paper was first published in *Zeitschrift für Pädagogik, 2*(3), 1956, 129–153. This translation is published with permission of the copyright holder, Beltz Verlag, Weinheim and Basel.

REFERENCES

[*Translator's note:* If a reference has a German title, it may be assumed that any direct quotations will have been translated by the translator of this text. References appended to the 1966 edition of the essay have been included here.]

Barthel, K. (1956). Über exemplarisches Lernen im Geschichtsunterricht. *Die Sammlung, 11*, 35–47.

Einstein, A., & Infeld, L. (1956). Die Evolution der Physik von Newton bis zur Quantentheorie. In *Rowohlts Deutsche Enzyklopädie* (Vol. 12). Hamburg: Rowohlt.

Flitner, W. (1954). *Grund- und Zeitfragen der Erziehung und Bildung*. Stuttgart: Ernst Klett Verlag.

Flitner, W. (1955). Der Kampf gegen die Stoffülle: Exemplarisches Lernen, Verdichtung und Auswahl. *Die Sammlung, 1955*, 556 ff.

Goldschmidt, R. B. (1927). *Einführung in die Wissenschaft vom Leben; oder Ascaris. Verständliche Wissenschaft* (Vol. 3). Berlin: Julius Springer.

Heimpel, H. (1951). Selbstkritik der Universität: Ein Wort zur Bildungsreform. *Deutsche Universitätszeitung, 4*(20), 5–7.

Heisenberg, W. (1955). Das Naturbild der heutigen Physik. In *Rowohlts Deutsche Enzyklopädie* (Vol. 8). Hamburg: Rowohlt.

Kepler, J. (1922). *J. Keplers grundlagen der geometrischen Optik (im Anschluss an die Optik des Witelo)* (F. Plehn, Trans.; M. von Rohr, Ed.). Ostwald's Klassiker der exakten Wissenschaften, Vol. 198. Leipzig: Akademische Verlagsgesellschaft.

Kerschensteiner, G. (1928). *Wesen und Wert des naturwissenschaftlichen Unterrichts* (3rd ed.). Leipzig and Berlin: Teubner.

Lichtenberg, G. C. (1944). *Aphorismen*. Reclam Universal-Bibliothek (Vols. 7569–7571). Leipzig: Reclams.

Litt, T. (1954). *Naturwissenschaft und Menschenbildung*. Heidelberg: Quelle & Meyer.

Mach, E. (1923). Über den relativen Bildungswert der philologischen und der mathematisch-naturwissenschaftlichen Unterrichtsfächer der Höheren Schulen [lecture, 1881]. In *Populärwissenschaftliche Vorlesungen* (pp. 313–355). Leipzig and Berlin: Teubner.

Menninger, K. (1954). *Mathematik in Deiner Welt*. Göttingen: Vandenhoeck & Ruprecht.

Münster, C., & Picht, G. (1953). *Naturwissenschaft und Bildung*. Würzburg: Werkbund Verlag.

Picard, M. (1956). Jenes Bild, das sich auf das Urbild bezieht. In E. Kern (Ed.), *Wegweiser in die Zeitwende* (pp. 79–80). Munich and Basel: Ernst Reinhardt Verlag.

Spranger, E. (1952). Die Fruchtbarkeit des Elementaren. In E. Spranger, *Pädagogische Perspektiven* (2nd ed., pp. 7–92). Heidelberg: Quelle & Meyer.

Spranger, E. (1955). *Der Eigengeist der Volksschule*. Heidelberg: Quelle & Meyer.

Tyndall, J. (1867). *Die Wärme, betrachtet als eine Art der Bewegung* (H. Helmholtz & C. Wiedman, Eds.). Braunschweig: Vieweg und Sohn.

von Weizsäcker, C. F. (1954). *Zum Weltbild der Physik*. Stuttgart: Hirzel.

Wagenschein, M. (1953). *Natur physikalisch gesehen*. Frankfurt a. M.: Verlag Moritz Diesterweg.

Wagenschein, M. (1955). *Die Erde unter den Sternen: Ein Weg zu den Sternen für jeden von uns*. Munich: R. Oldenbourg Verlag.

Wagenschein, M. (1962). *Die pädagogische Dimension der Physik*. Braunschweig: Georg Westermann Verlag.

Wagenschein, M. (1965). *Ursprüngliches Verstehen und exaktes Denken. Pädagogische Schriften*. Stuttgart: Ernst Klett Verlag.

Weischedel, W. (1955). Sinn und Widersinn der Wissenschaft. *Deutsche Universitätszeitung, 10*(18), 6–9.

10

Content: Still in Question

Peter Menck
Stefanie Pirags (Trans.)

Peter Menck studied theology, mathematics, physics, and education in Bonn and Vienna. He completed his doctorate at the University of Bonn and qualified for a university professorship at the University of Münster with a thesis on the theory of curriculum and instruction. He has been a professor of education at the University of Siegen since 1979; he teaches history of education, educational theory and research, and the history and theory of the curriculum and classroom instruction.

His major publications include *Unterrichtsanalyse und didaktische Konstruktion: Studien zu einer Theorie des Lehrplans und des Unterichts* [Analysis and Construction of Classroom Work: Studies Towards a Theory of Cuuriculum and Instruction] (1975); *Unterrichtsinhalt oder: Ein Versuch über die Konstruktion der Wirklichkeit im Unterricht* [Content of Instruction: An Essay on the Construction of Reality in Classroom] (1986); *Geschichte der Erziehung* [History of Education] (1993); and *Was ist Erziehung? Eine Einführung in die Erziehungswissenschaft* [Education: An Introduction] (1998).

—Jörg Biehl

Almost a quarter of a century ago, Horst Rumpf argued that the contents of instruction were not being questioned in Germany. What did he mean by this? Let us break his comment down into the following simple questions: What is "content of instruction"? What opportunities for pedagogical action become accessible to teachers when they perceive "instruction content" as more than something prescribed in the *Lehrplan* or syllabus that is to be transferred to the heads of the students? What can a particular content *signify* to students who deal with it in their classes? In the years that have passed since Rumpf published his criticism, no answers to these questions have been produced beyond those that were already available in the Didaktik in the early 1970s.

But it was not the answers from Didaktik that were the problem, rather their translation from the realm of philosophical reflection. And it was not, as might be expected, a problem of translation into the practice of instructional preparation—where in fact they were being successfully implemented despite all the criticism. No, the difficulty lay in finding the appropriate formulation to serve analysis and criticism of the teaching taking place every day, everywhere, under the guidance of such answers. In Germany the belief still predominates that teaching will run, by and large, as planned, provided that the planning is right. This, at least, is the situation reflected in the literature of subject-matter Didaktik *(Fachdidaktik)*, where models for "better" instruction continue to be produced whereas virtually nothing is to be learned about what is happening in classrooms.

In this chapter I outline my own synopsis of answers to my questions before applying them to the question of instruction content. In the concluding pages I use an example of a mathematics lesson in Grade 6 (12-year-old students) in an attempt to demonstrate how we could approach a definition and analysis of instruction content.

WHAT IS INSTRUCTIONAL CONTENT?

Instruction Content in Didaktik's Everyday Context

Instruction content (Unterrichtsinhalt) is an everyday term in the language of Didaktik. By "Didaktik" I mean the whole body of knowledge describing, in more or less lucid tenets, the structure of sense and purpose in school instruction, and how it may be shaped. I am thinking here of what we refer to as "models" and most of the "theories" of Didaktik as well as the many thoughts from which they have been distilled.

Throughout, we are presented with three components and their interlocking relationships:

- *First,* there is the *child,* young people as students, or rather the Me, the individual, the human self. Proceeding from particular individuals, the Didaktik tradition abstracts, though without quite acknowledging that the resulting abstract entity does not represent real young people. Sometimes "child" indicates attendant life worlds, relationships, everyday life.

- However, the abstraction is necessary because of the close association with the *second component,* namely *reality,* the world, or rather a natural and human world, particularly that of the sciences, something objective, general, and universal.
- In school and instruction, both sides are linked by the *third component,* the *teacher,* and the teacher's instructional arrangements.

There are many metaphors for those activities that help to bring together the general and the individual, the objective and the subjective—"reciprocating," "exchanging," "unifying," or "encountering"; the term *mediation* recalls philosophical discussion as well as everyday notions of the connection of both sides. The objective side is perceived as factual, as independently valid; the subjective side is perceived as spontaneous. It is these two factors that enable the teacher to function as a link. Sometimes the image of the "Didaktik triangle"(see Künzli, chap. 2, this volume) is used to illustrate this relationship, that is, students–subject matter–teacher. This much is agreed, regardless of the philosophy different parties may prefer or simply accept without evidence—though much is made of discussing the concepts and their meanings in exhaustive detail.

As a rule it is presumed, or in some theories explicitly argued, that the "instruction content" extends to the out-of-school relationship between students and reality. On the one hand, the objectifications processed in instruction refer to reality, to the world in which we live, to societal practice. On the other hand, the students have their own everyday life outside school, their present and their future life, their life world, which are all a part of societal practice. In this way, both sides are connected. In Didaktik, reflection runs along these lines when it is not only a question of planning or analyzing instruction itself, but also, or primarily, a question of pedagogical legitimation. The logic of subject matter is referred back to societal practice and thus linked to students' lives in society.

This summary is intended as an introduction, and at the same time as an indication that the concept of instruction content contains references to a complex nexus of relations, and can be adequately explained only if these relations are made clear. Moreover, the concept also contains an historical dimension. Historically defined forms of societal practice are preserved within instruction contents. The school "subjects," for instance, which I discuss later, reflect in their particular arrangement and divisions a body of knowledge about societal practice selected in certain and particular historical constellations. The nexus of complex relations for which the term instruction content stands has continued to undergo fundamental and revolutionary change. The "problem" of transmission, for example, is a modern achievement. In order for it to be recognized at all, let alone formulated and absorbed as standard knowledge within Didaktik, it was necessary for the divine order of the cosmos to be broken, or for its unquestioned validity to be challenged. Hitherto, knowledge had corresponded to the binding, un-challenged world order in that things, and the knowledge of things, were practically identical. The economic, social, theological aspects of that revo-lution in thought have not yet been properly and fruitfully explored in terms of a theory of instruction.

Definitions of Terms

Let me now approach the complexities I have mentioned and offer some definitions. For everyday purposes, the term instruction content is perfectly adequate, but for theorizing and reflection, particularly under a critical lens, integrative components are forgotten if there is no appropriate terminology. Reflection is then bound within the very framework that it seeks to address from a distance and in a critical perspective, namely the everyday practice of instruction. Unfortunately, we do not have a consistent set of terms, but the terms themselves are less important than the concepts they define, and in this respect we do have a wide consensus.

First of all, I have to cope with a lexical problem. There is no adequate English translation of the German word *Unterricht*. In German *Unterricht* means the teaching–learning working setting as a whole; it is thus more than what educational psychologists usually refer to as the "teaching–learning process." I prefer to describe *Unterricht* as everything that happens between, say, 10 and 10:45 a.m. within the four walls of a classroom, and I therefore use the term *classroom* in this chapter.

Subjects *(Fächer)* or *learning areas (Lernbereiche)* are the terms for the sections subject matter cuts from the factually related divisions of school-work.

Topic (Thema) defines a more or less delineated unit within a subject or an interdisciplinary unit that is defined by the *Lehrplan*. Thus we refer to the "topic" of a lesson, a series of lessons, or a course.

For everything put into words, pictures, or any other medium—related to the topic or not—I use the term *content of the classroom (Inhalt des Unter-richts)*, analogous to the "contents" of a trouser pocket or a handbag in everyday speech. One subdivision of these is the contents that are oriented to, provoked by, and produced in relation to the topic.

I use the term *outcome of classroom work (Unterrichtsergebnis)* to refer to everything that is produced, or is collated and recorded, as being valid in the course of instruction under the guidance of the topic in question. It therefore encompasses everything the students are later to have at their disposal. This requires a more detailed explanation.

Ever since the problem of instruction has existed, those responsible for transmission have been at pains not only to perform this task, but also to reassure themselves of the success of their endeavors. The dominant contemporary variant of this is "objectives-focused instruction": At the end of a lesson, a topic, or a course, students are to have at their disposal, in their heads, hearts, and hands, certain (cognitive, affective, and psycho-motor) guides for their lives that are deemed to be correct by those responsible for instruction. But as it is not possible to look inside the students' minds, behavior is taken as a reflection of these guides.

My definition of the outcome of classroom work does not include these considerations. In the classroom as a pedagogical situation, as an independent social reality, work results are produced—binding meanings, solutions to problems, or whatever one wishes to call the products. It is these work results produced in classroom, not what occurs in the minds of the students, that I term outcome of classroom work. Achievement corresponding to the learning objectives is an issue that must be left to learning theory. For the "content" in question, such achievement is only relevant inasmuch as the binding nature of classroom work is justified, and pedagogically legitimated, by anticipated "learning."

"Subjects" and "topics" refer to limited *sections of reality* outside school, to the practice of people who live and work in society. "Road safety education," for example, refers to traffic; "environmental education" to changes in the natural world brought about by human intervention and exploitation; "mathematics" to figures and calculation as a means of mastering structures and processes. This human societal practice is present in classroom *in symbolic form* within its subjects and topics: in the wording of science and myths, in the work of art and technology, and so on. To do *classroom work is to process symbolic representations of societal practice*. This can be simplified if we consider what can be done with symbols: *Work* here means *interpretation*. In the course of classroom work, symbolically coded references to societal practice are "interpreted" as that word is understood in hermeneutics. This not only encompasses the dominant form of text interpretation; Kerschensteiner's famous box for starlings, built to allow a pair to nest, can be seen as an interpretation of a cultivated environment made uninhabitable for starlings by human hands.

Content reflects the *classroom work*, including its by-products, as well as everything that does not belong to it in the strict sense of the topic. This work always aims at a product, which I term the outcome of classroom work. The product demands validity: the starlings' nesting box, the translation of a French prose, the faithful rendition of a Bach fugue, the solution of an arithmetic problem—they all demand *validity*. The product and the knowledge contained within can and should offer a guidance for the student at the end of a lesson and beyond.

This then is the *framework of terminology* into which the whole knowledge of Didaktik can be slotted: from curriculum theory *(Lehrplantheorie)* to subject-matter didactics *(Fachdidaktik)*, Didaktik analysis *(didaktische Analyse)*, and data on the life world of children. This framework is relatively narrow. It corresponds, metaphorically, to the classroom in the school building and does not define what makes up the content of classroom. For this we have to consider how classroom work is related to the environment of classroom. In the following I confine myself to topic-oriented content.

Production, Selection and Administration of Knowledge

The topics of the classroom do not refer straightforwardly and simply to societal practice. They are negotiated by interest groups in society, selected from the universe of knowledge at society's disposal, and stylized and combined to allow them to be used as classroom material. The interest in the success of education is not the only influence at work in this selection and stylization, but coexists with a desire of interest groups for the reproduction of social conditions as a whole. Under the title "educational politics" or "the political economy of the educational system" we find described what Erich Weniger (see chap. 6, this volume), in his theory of curriculum *(Lehrplantheorie)*, described as a "struggle to achieve a balance of forces in school and organized learning that corresponds to the relative positions of power held by the factors participating in school." Pierre Bourdieu and Jean-Claude Passeron's "theory of symbolic power" is an attempt to comprehend the specific function of school and school-based knowledge in the process of social reproduction: the prevalence and recall of meanings in accordance with the the the balance of power. The universe of knowledge is a problematic, a synoptic cipher for a multiplicity of bodies of knowledge produced in quite different contexts: in everyday life, in trade and industry, in factories, in the Church and, of course, in the sciences. The whole of this knowledge encapsulates human opportunities, both constructive and destructive, and preserves what makes humans human. In other words, knowledge refers to societal practice in all its variety and historicity. In this sense, the topics of classroom refer to sections of societal practice in its fullness and historical determination.

Knowledge, the precipitation of societal practice and human experience, continues to be collected, systematized, handed down, and administered, and "science" is the authority charged with this task. But it does not stand alone in this: Every grouping in society—associations, churches, families—collects and administers, which naturally means that a selection is made according to interests, and evaluation is defined by the administrators of knowledge. An example might illustrate the point:

> Instruction dealing with any of the topics in General Studies at primary level refers, for instance, to the life of people in their native region, to what could

be termed the social production of a focus of local patriotism. At the same time, the topic refers to those who produce the relevant knowledge: local cultural associations, the preservers of local flora and fauna, local history, expatriate organizations, the local press, and so on.

Vague comprehension of such relationships has repeatedly led various educationists to question the ideological overlays of "school knowledge." The call has been for all the "para-pedagogical" mechanisms of selection and tradition to be revealed in order to penetrate beyond school knowledge and to grasp unadulterated societal practice. Such expectations are, however, themselves ideologies borne of restricted pedagogical approaches and their perpetrators' overestimation of their own capabilities. Reality, call it societal practice or anything else, does not exist in unadulterated form. *Reality exists only in mediated form.* Educationists do not need to lament this fact: No one would be able to change it anyway. Instead, the concept of content of classroom must be made wide enough to encompass the processes of mediation.

To put it briefly: Before knowledge reaches school, it has gone through a multilayered process of production, tradition, and selection. Classroom work can be appropriately comprehended only if both the knowledge used to create it and the conditions of its genesis are analyzed.

The Classroom and World Images

Teaching should take into consideration students' experiences. This postulate encompasses instructional method's age-old rules for improving motivation and the achievement of learning. At the same time it expresses the expectation that school instruction must enable students to cope with their lives in the present and in the future. It is an attempt to relate classroom work to societal practice. It was hoped that the German branch of the to that point Anglo-Saxon curriculum field would, by providing knowledge of circumstances and the situations of students' future lives, yield frameworks for dealing with these circumstances and situations, which in turn would indicate content for young people's education. But this proved to be theoretically impossible—because life situations can, at best, be only roughly discerned and classified. And a more definite classification is—pedagogically—undesirable because it would mean restricting students to particular situations or classes of situations. The conception of the link between the students' life world and societal practice cannot be that a student's current, everyday life, identified with societal practice, provides the sole framework for the topics to be covered in the classroom. The connection must be interpreted in wider terms.

The practice of people living and working in society is, metaphorically speaking, the space in which individuals determine their own positions or are placed in particular positions. Classroom work guided by the topic thus refers to societal practice as *the framework given for the students by their scope for self-determination and the fact of (external) determination*. In other words, through classroom work students are to be enabled to acquire *for themselves* the opportunities that the humanity has tapped in the course of its history, to enhance themselves as human beings, to "form themselves," as Didaktik would traditionally put it. In this sense, the outcomes of classroom work may be understood as pieces of an image of the world *(Weltbild)* that students can acquire, as pieces of a framework within which they can take their bearings in their world, a framework that is wider in principle than that which their current life and any predictable future situation would offer.

We need to add something to the Didaktik tradition here. As a rule, Didaktik tends to regard only positive human achievements as being worthy of coverage in classrooms. This assumption is based on a selection that follows the interests of particular groups. I, however, use *achievement* neutrally and universally. The world in which the students must find their place is also characterized by inhumanity, be it interpreted according to a "dialectics of enlightenment" as an integrative factor of humanity or as a phase that has not yet been overcome in the progressive development of the human species. Positions within Didaktik called "critical" have worked on this factor of the content of classroom.

The Constitutive Rules—Discipline

The definitions I have been offering have suggested that more precise definitions of content are made within the classroom itself. The topic is initially nothing more than a heading, the only delineation being given by the subject. This applies, of course, to the classroom as a whole; it is not true for the individual participants, who already associate it with their own memories, experiences, and intentions. Classroom work then fills the topic with content, with everything that is put into words or otherwise occurs in its course. Finally it is ticked off and logged as a complete and valid outcome of classroom work. As we have seen, a clear distinction must be made between this and "learning outcomes," that is, whatever has been formed in the minds of the participants that can be recalled and assessed.

In its details classroom work follows rules that are in turn constitutive of the content. If we follow Basil Bernstein, these rules can be subsumed under the concept of *discipline*—of course the discipline of everyday "problems of discipline" is only a small section of this whole. The following points may contribute toward an explanation, though with no pretence to completeness:

- Topics are sorted, and thematically classified, according to subjects, or disciplines as we call them.

- They are dealt with in a disciplined manner, in a course vested with authority.
- They are covered outside the context of the participants' daily lives, and in a specific situation that—where necessary—must be maintained in the face of disruption.
- Everyday experiences voiced during classroom are included, if at all, only to the extent to which they can be, as it were, thematically channeled to fit the course.
- To facilitate the work, societal practice is transformed into a school world.

Since Reform Pedagogy *(Reformpädagogik)*, Didaktik has found fault with this separation of school and classroom from life, criticizing it for the alienation, for the loss of meaning to which the separation can only lead. However, the rules of the classroom are not suspended by pedagogically motivated accusations, and there is no reason for them to be suspended. A fixation on particular disruptions of discipline obscured the historical achievement that it is discipline that makes education possible; it is discipline that marks out the area in which education can take place and creates the order that, however problematic it may be, enables young people to interact in pedagogical situations, where confusion and disorientation would otherwise threaten. Disruptions of discipline cannot be resolved by the call to abolish discipline, but only by eliminating the causes of disruption.

"FORTY-EIGHT HALVES CAN'T PLAY BALL"— A MATH LESSON AS AN EXAMPLE

These general reflections can be illustrated by an example from mathematics teaching. A case study has the advantage of focusing on a particular lesson and a particular topic, though with the disadvantage that not all of the aspects touched on can be elucidated in as much detail as might be wished. But it should be adequate to demonstrate the idea.

I begin by introducing the lesson. In doing so, I am already moving within the framework marked out by my topic. The social climate of the classroom, or the teacher's communication techniques, need not interest us further. In what follows, the headings for each section provide a brief summary of the results of the classroom work; the passages that follow present the individual steps in the overall pattern of work. It should be noted that the time spent on the individual phases of classroom by no means correlates with the length of the respective sections, a point that also shows the emphasis of my report.

A Paraphrase of the Lesson—{ . . . } Is the Set
of Divisors of a Number x From N

1. *All possible ways of dividing 24 students into equal squads.* At the beginning of the lesson the teacher tells the students about "a small problem" in a physical education class: 24 students were to be divided up into squads, with the same number in each squad. The students in the class who know what a squad is first explain the term, then suggestions are made for solving the problem. The teacher picks up "Four groups, with six in each" and writes on the blackboard: "4 groups, with 6 students in each group," whereupon a student comments: "4 times 6." They continue with "8 groups of 3," "2 groups and times 12," "6 groups of 4," "24 groups" and "3 groups." The teacher encourages them to think of "all possibilities": "24 groups of 1 [person] is possible, even though it's something we wouldn't think of in a sports lesson. Still, we'll write it down, because it's conceivable." They continue: "Perhaps 3 groups of 8" and "12 groups of 2." The suggestion "48 groups with a half in each" is rejected, as is "1 group with 3 in each." Finally, "1 group of 24 players" is recorded and with it "all possibilities have been found." The correct answers are on the board in the same format as the first.

2. *"Task 1."* Working individually, the students complete Task 1 in their textbooks, which is analogous to the problem they have just dealt with. Beforehand, the teacher explains the required format for the solution. At the end the results are compared.

3. *The set of divisors of 24 and the definition of "divisor."* The teacher erases "a lot of what we were looking at earlier on in the lesson," but "the most important part remains," namely the number "24," as well as the other numbers, arranged in pairs. "What have all these numbers on the right to do with the one large number on the left, the 24?" Answers are forthcoming: "You just need to multiply them" and "Add them up or multiply them." The teacher picks up this one: "We could put lots of multiplication signs in here . . . and we always end up with 24." Then the teacher defines "the numbers 4, 8, 2, 6, 24, 3, 12, 1 . . . [as] the divisors of 24. So divisors of 24 are numbers . . . 24 can be divided by."

4. *The notation for divisors of 10 is $T(10) = \{1,2,5,10\}$.* Using the divisors of 10 as an example, the correct notation for sets of divisors is presented.

5. *Homework*

The Matter

In order to understand the content of this lesson, the most obvious first step is to examine the relevant science, that is, mathematics. From it we gain the following information:

An integer a *(i.e., a positive or negative number including zero) is called the divisor of an integer* b *if there is an integer* c *and it is true that* a × c = b.

It can also be said that *b* is related to *a* in the sense "is a divisor of." Therefore, "*a* is a divisor of *b*." It follows from the definition that each integer *b* has the divisors +1 and −1, as well as +*b* and −*b*, termed *trivial* divisors. Numbers that have only trivial divisors are known as *prime numbers*. The properties of the divisor relationship are of no further significance for our lesson. It remains to be mentioned only that there are conventions of notation, which were introduced in the lesson.

In the case of our lesson only the positive integers are taken into consideration: The divisor relationship is defined in *N*. Both multiplication ("times") and division ("24 can be divided by") are included. The interesting point is the method by which this is done.

Didaktik Preparation

We can proceed from a few observations about the lesson itself. First it can be noted that the divisors of 24, thanks to the practical model, the teacher's problem at the beginning, are implicitly given in advance. Other approaches would be feasible. The divisors could be given with the aim of arriving at the divisor relationship by induction. This was the approach taken in the parallel course—but more of that later. It is also noticeable that the relationship is not defined and then used to check divisibility of any numbers. We see by this that the teacher selects one of several conceivable and practicable possibilities.

The problem also ensures that discussion is restricted to *N*. This is most nicely apparent when a student suggests "48 groups with a half in each." In this case the teacher can point out that they could hardly play with halved students. On the other hand, this approach does involve the difficulty that the trivial divisors can be managed only with some stretching of the problem. After all, "squads" would not generally consist of a single person or the whole class.

The route taken from the problem to mathematics is also striking. The teacher pointed out that "the most important thing" remains. As this refers to the numbers, it would appear to devalue the problem. I feel that one can conclude from this step on the teacher's part that the problem is not a problem, but serves a purpose external to itself: the restriction to N and the design of the divisors. As the teacher said in an interview, it also serves to motivate, to commit students to the work set before them. In short, the problem serves to discipline in the widest sense of the term, as I outlined earlier.

Finally, it is conspicuous that, although the route taken to arrive at divisors proceeds—as in mathematics—via multiplication, it is then defined using division: "numbers 24 can be divided by," and without any remainder.

All this has in fact nothing to do with mathematics. On the contrary the simple mathematical facts, the definition of divisors, are restricted, concealed, then discovered, and finally shifted. If we want to find out why, neither mathematics nor the teacher's method will help us much further. If we wish to understand what it is we are observing, we must examine the context.

The Context

The textbook begins in almost exactly the same way as the teacher does: "There are 20 students in a class. The physical education teacher wants to form squads of equal numbers. What are the possibilities?" The four non-trivial solutions follow, then the question, "Can the teacher also form squads with 6 students in each? This is obviously impossible. . . . But the teacher could put all 20 students into one squad or leave each student to compete alone."

There are, however, a few differences. The book avoids the difficulties with the trivial divisors. The divisor relation is consistently defined through multiplication:

> If the 20 students are divided into 4 squads . . . , there are 5 students in each squad, because $5 \times 4 = 20$. The two divisors 5 and 4 are termed divisors of 20.

"Multiples" are thus given by "complementary" definition (as defined in the additional material in the textbook). In our example, on the other hand, "multiples" do not come until much later.

The relevant curriculum guidelines indicate the topic. The teaching and textbook are compatible with the guidelines, an almost banal point to make. But the guidelines do yield important additional information that refers to the organization of Grades 5 and 6, where our lesson took place:

> In Grade 6 the courses differ with respect to the standard of required achievement and the scope of the content, as well as with respect to the teaching methods. Whereas courses with lower achievement requirements focus on the mastery of arithmetical procedures and the development of strategies for solving concrete problems, the courses with higher achievement requirements progressively address the fundamentals of mathematics.

The students we are dealing with in our example belong to a course "with lower achievement requirements." On the basis of their previous performance they have been placed in a "C" set for mathematics (in a system of sets A and C) and the teaching is to be appropriate to this set. Let us now turn to the teacher, who said in the interview:

> Whereas the others [meaning the students in the C-set] have experienced practically nothing but failure in mathematics and can really, I believe, only be motivated if they are looking at something fairly entertaining, . . . something they can grasp, like forming squads in a sports lesson. . . .

And:

> Especially if the subject is rather abstract, not clearly structured, if reassurance such as "right," "good," "carry on like that" is not often forthcoming, the students make no progress at all.

Here we can see that the students are defined, just as the classroom situation, the interpretation of the topic, the work done on it, and its result are themselves determined in advance. The definition moves in what could be described as a practical circle: Students of low academic achievement need concrete instruction that is, they are not to be taught real mathematics. A number of observations become easier to understand if seen in this context, dominated as it is by school organization and guidelines.

We can underline these findings by comparing this lesson with a parallel lesson given by the same teacher in the A-set in the same grade. Here, too, the teacher begins with a mathematics-related situation. But the latter is already more abstract, more removed from reality:

> He reports he has found a jumbled assortment of numbers. He knows nothing about them apart from the fact that they come from two columns of a table. The task is to find out how these numbers could be ordered. The numbers are, as we soon discover, the divisors of 35 and 48. The students' suggestions include—as was to be expected—ordering the numbers in divisor groups. The teacher picks up this suggestion and asks about the principle of this ordering.

The different approaches the teacher takes in the presentation of the mathematical facts are nicely illustrated when students move outside N, something that happened in both lessons, a fortunate occurrence for the analyst!

> In the C-set John cries, to the delight of the whole class, "48 groups with a half in each." The teacher counters, "Well fine, but how can we split ourselves up into halves?" Gleefully the class volunteers suggestions: "Cut them in half," "You can have half portions, so why not?" The teacher appears to want to follow up these ideas, but John intervenes, "Look, one's pretty fat and one's really thin, so the thin one can be a half." Finally the teacher puts an end to the discussion, "You can't play ball if you are cut in half."

In the A-set George says, "But you can't divide 12 by 48," to which the teacher replies, "Not at the moment, no. Perhaps we'll be able to do it later. But for the time being that's correct."

In the second instance the question of fractions, though not actually discussed, is at least kept open. And, as in the relevant textbook and guidelines, divisors and fractions are explicitly linked. In the C-set, on the other hand, the discipline of keeping to the so-called concrete example blocks this route, although at least one of the students creates a conceivably simple link with fractions. Moreover, the teacher loses an opportunity to demonstrate a specific achievement of mathematics, which is—in simplified terms—its very capacity to reason in mathematical terms, to operate in detachment from concrete situations. Rubbing out also rubs out something of this achievement. Such a restriction only makes sense in connection with the teacher's expectations of the students: They are not expected to be receptive to such achievements.

Now we can understand what I termed the devaluation of the problem introduced at the beginning of the lesson. It is less a case of devaluing a practical problem, but more a case of there not being a practical problem at all. What does exist is a student-specific form of mathematics.

Authority and Autonomy

The next question to ask about the content of this lesson would be *how binding is the orientation given by classroom work in the—mathematical—world?* Behind this question is the problem I already mentioned, well known to school and curriculum theory *(Schul- und Lehrplantheorie),* of interest groups interested in reproduction and for that reason interested in school, the problem of the state as organizing factor, and of the relative autonomy of the education system. Here the focus is, in particular, on the teachers as those in whom the balance of power in society is expressed and who *at the same time* are interested in the students and their future lives. How does all this look in our lesson?

The topic and the sequence of steps are vested with the authority of the teacher: "There is a small problem I have to tell you about." Behind the teacher's "I" there appears to lurk, if we can take the teacher's word for it, an anonymous authority whom the teacher seems to represent and it would seem that the teacher has been instructed to report to. The correctness of the outcome of classroom work and the steps taken on the way there are first checked by the teacher. But the validity is not guaranteed by the teacher, nor by that anonymous authority. It is guaranteed by the mathematical matter itself, that is, by the logic of mathematics. The delegated authority analyzed generally in German curriculum theory *(Lehrplantheorie),* as well as the restricted scope for the pedagogical acquisition of the matter (the concept of "relative autonomy" of the education system) can thus be observed in fine detail here.

How much scope is there? In short, very little. And at no point does it open up a perspective outside the immediate confines of classroom, neither with regard to subsequent lessons and their topics (as at least the textbook and guidelines do), nor with regard to mathematical relations—not to mention mathematization and the social production of mathematics. But it is not, in truth, the scope that is restricted—this is not the pedagogical problem. Indeed, it is, as we have said, one of the achievements of classroom work in school that it restricts and thus makes ordering and orientation possible. The question is How does it do this? The point I wish to make clear is that it happens in this case without the achievement being recognizable as achievement, without the articulated knowledge being confirmed as achievement in its own right, without using what has been understood to open up the prospect of knowledge still to be attained.

It would be a mistake to make the teacher personally responsible for these restrictions. We can see that in this case the teacher was quite in keeping with the given conditions of educational policy and subject-matter Didaktik, in spite of individual variance. Why then, if everything is "understandable" in the sense of my methodical procedure, are we making such a complex analysis of what is in practice a matter of course as "content"? I should like to answer that question briefly, though without providing evidence in detail. There is individual variance, and it is not an arbitrary matter what decisions are made within a pedagogical intention. This brings me back to the question of the interest that guides such analyses.

CONCLUSION

The contents of everyday Didaktik, of the staff room, of the teacher education seminar dissolve into a web of relations. These can be described only by reconstructing them individually, an exercise that always has an objective and is always steered by interest. As I have said with express reference to the tradition of Didaktik, educationists are concerned for the *success of education*. What does this mean? Although a more comprehensive explanation would be appropriate here, no more than suggestions can be offered.

In several places I have mentioned that reflecting on the legitimation of classroom work has consequences for content. In principle a restriction of content to certain sections of societal practice, to certain life situations, would not be pedagogically legitimate; likewise, a restriction to certain bodies of knowledge would contradict the comprehensive concept of humanity that is preserved in the concept of Bildung as well as other concepts such as "responsibility" or "emancipation."

Herwig Blankertz, in his analysis of Weniger's *Lehrplantheorie,* articulated "the dialectical relationship between Bildung as participation in human tradition and Bildung as humaneness and maturity" as "legitimate grounds for a commitment" that represents the "humanity of man." There is no reason to keep a distance from Bildung in this sense. (But we must keep in mind that the humanity of humankind spans opportunities for destruction as well as production, barbarism as well as civilization.) Bildung in this sense is closely bound up with a Didaktik tradition that is highly interested in matter and content, and thus confers sense upon the classroom work. This, or an equivalent standard, must be incorporated into the concept of content, because classroom instruction would otherwise be understood as a social technique oriented to educational objectives, and not as a pedagogical situation.

Any educationist who does not pursue the multiple references made by content to its preconditions does not grasp this content in its specific quality as a medium for the Bildung of students; instead content becomes merely the sum of those pieces of knowledge that have been declared valid. This applies equally to those educationists developing on the tradition of Didaktik and to those analyzing classrooms. Any teacher who does not continually strive to pick up the references made by the "topic" has not grasped the latter as the children's own topic, and impedes them in the progress of their Bildung.

Unfortunately, such Didaktik exercises, of the kind that I have outlined here, hardly occur in our teacher education. I fear that the same can be said of inservice education, apart from the literature in subject-matter Didaktik: As a rule, tried and tested scenarios of instruction are passed on; the scene, the methodical arrangement is the topic; the content is taken as read, and may be questioned from the point of view of its scientific accuracy, but not in any other respect. All this is greatly to the detriment of the teachers and their opportunities for action, as I have endeavored to show.

ACKNOWLEDGMENTS

This chapter was published as "Unterrichtsinhalt—noch immer unbefragt?" In Deutscher Verein zur Förderung der Lehrerfortbildung und Lehrerweiterbildung (DVLFB) (1993), *Forum Lehrerfortbildung; Schwerpunktthema Lehrerwissen,* Vol. 24–25, pp. 137–167. I wish to thank Karl-Heinz Rebel, the editor of *Forum Lehrerfortbildung,* for his permission to publish the article in this English version.

REFERENCES

The following are the works cited in the text only. It is not an exhaustive list of the material on which I have drawn. My book *Unterrichtsinhalt, oder Ein Versuch über die Konstruktion der*

Wirklichkeit im Unterricht [Content or An Essay on the Pedagogical Construction of Reality in the Classroom], on which this chapter is based, contains a more complete bibliography.

Bernstein, B. (1977). *Beiträge zu einer Theorie des pädagogischen Prozesses.* Frankfurt: Suhrkamp.

Blankertz, H. (1968). Bildungsbegriff. In I. Dahmer & W. Klafki (Eds.), *Geisteswissenschaftliche Pädagogik am Ausgang ihrer Epoche: Erich Weniger* (pp. 103–113). Weinheim and Berlin: J. Beltz.

Bourdieu, P., & Passeron, J.-C. (1973). *Grundlagen einer Theorie der symbolischen Gewalt.* Frankfurt: Suhrkamp.

Klafki, W. (1985). *Neue Studien zur Bildungstheorie und Didaktik: Zeitgemäße Allgemeinbildung und kritisch-konstruktive Didaktik.* Weinheim and Basel: Beltz Verlag.

Menck, P. (1986). *Unterrichtsinhalt oder Ein Versuch über die Konstruktion der Wirklichkeit im Unterricht.* Frankfurt/Main: Peter Lang.

Rumpf, H. (1969). Sachneutrale Unterrichtsbeobachtung? Einige Fragen zu empirischen Forschungsansätzen. *Zeitschrift für Pädagogik, 15*(3), 293–314.

Weniger, E. (1982). *Didaktik als Bildungslehre, Teil 1: Theorie der Bildungsinhalte und des Lehrplans.* Weinheim: Beltz Verlag.

DIDAKTIK AS PRAXIS

11

Klafki's Model of Didaktik Analysis and Lesson Planning in Teacher Education

Stefan Hopmann

Stefan Hopmann is professor of comparative education at the Norwegian University of Science and Technology, Trondheim.

The most widely used model for Didaktik in Germany is Klafki's *Didaktik analysis* (see chap. 8, this volume). Klafki's step-by-step approach still prevails in German teacher education and can be used to illustrate the Didaktik perspective as it might be found in preservice teacher education. To illustrate how these steps are usually used in student work, I have chosen a lesson plan prepared by a student teacher working with eighth-graders in a *Hauptschule,* a lower secondary school, in a low-status neighborhood. The lesson plan is no masterpiece of Didaktik analysis, rather the opposite; however, it is quite typical of what German student teachers deliver during student teaching.

The lesson prepared by the student was meant to be the transition lesson leading the students from calculating percentage toward the calculation of interest rates, the calculating of what you have to pay when you borrow money or what you get by putting your money into a savings account. I set out Klafki's five steps of lesson planning and I comment on each one.

WHAT WIDER OR GENERAL CONTEXT OF SENSE OR SUBJECT DOES THIS CONTENT REPRESENT AND OPEN UP? WHAT BASIC PHENOMENON OR FUNDAMENTAL PRINCIPLE, WHAT LAW, CRITERION, PROBLEM, METHOD, TECHNIQUE, OR ATTITUDE CAN BE GRASPED BY MEANS OF EXAMPLES IN THE CONFRONTATION WITH IT?

Be aware of the starting point: In a way that is different from recent models of Didaktik analysis Klafki opts for the content (not frame factors, social functions, or the dynamics of classroom settings). For Klafki it is content that makes instruction, and often the meaning of content is not obvious, not given by its face value. But, instruction is not just conveying content, but it is—as Herbart put it—also education *by* content (see Künzli, chap. 2, this volume). Therefore, we have to look for the different impact and implications a piece of content may have: the substance of content, the *Bildungsgehalt.*

In theory, the aim of this step is to explain the *Bildungsgehalt* of a given content by a kind of hermeneutic interpretation. The teacher should activate any knowledge possibly related to this question. Practically, the analysis is usually much more abridged, concentrating on single features of the content. For example, my student teacher wrote in response this to this first question in Klafki's scheme for Didaktik analysis:

> Calculating percentage is itself a general content. It is, however, also an example of an equation with one unknown, as each of the three basic dimensions can be calculated with the help of the other two in the equation. The formulas for this calculation that exist parallel to this are a summary of the steps used in an equation with one unknown. Calculating interest is an expansion of calculating percentage, whereby the time factor is an additional dimension.

Within a "complete" Didaktik analysis, the content of instruction should be analyzed on three levels at least:

- Relating it to subject matter as a structure of knowledge.
- Relating it to subject matter as in use in everyday life.
- Relating it to subject matter as in use in the frame of schooling (its relations to other school subjects and its placement in the curriculum as a whole).

Using these three levels, it is quite clear that the student teacher addressed only one level: the subject matter as part of mathematical knowledge. Every attempt to relate the calculation of interest to everyday situations and/or to other fields of subject matter, like social science or language instruction, is missing. He sticks to pure math and misses the multiple meanings of the term *interest,* the social and political impact of interest, the practical importance of interest in everyday life, and so forth. This would have been no problem if the students were able to restrict themselves to pure math. But naturally they could not: Interest is much too interesting to be left to mathematicians alone.

WHAT SIGNIFICANCE DOES THE CONTENT IN QUESTION OR THE EXPERIENCE, KNOWLEDGE, ABILITY, OR SKILL TO BE ACQUIRED THROUGH THIS TOPIC ALREADY POSSESS IN THE INTELLECTUAL LIFE OF THE LEARNER? WHAT SIGNIFICANCE SHOULD IT HAVE, FROM A PEDAGOGICAL POINT OF VIEW?

This is a simple and a complicated question at the same time. Simple, because it should be the natural starting point of every lesson. If the teacher lacks a sense of *why* his or her students should become acquainted with what he or she is going to teach and if he or she does not know what they know in advance, why spend time on it? But it is also the most complicated issue. Schooling has to deal with a radical change in this respect: Until recently, school was a place where students met lots of things they had never seen before. The function of schooling was *"to open the student for a world"* (Klafki, chap. 8, this volume) not yet familiar. Today it is different, in industrialized countries at least. Students in a class do not have similar backgrounds. They come to school with lots of experience and information, gathered by chance or from educating institutions other than public schools (like newspapers and TV). The significance a content may have for the students may thus vary across a single class between none and dozens of different meanings, all of which can have an impact on the outcome of instruction. It is difficult to find items where the students share views and knowledge in advance.

So let's have a look what the student teacher said with respect to Klafki's second step:

> Calculating percentage—without going into calculating interest—is basically repetition for the students. In addition to this, a comparison with fractions ($\frac{1}{4}$ = 25%, etc.) is used to demonstrate percentages. Calculating percentages should represent a further means of comparing sizes, in addition to the direct comparison of absolute numbers. Being able to calculate percentages outside the classroom is also important. We are confronted with it, for example, in connection with investing money, figuring out salary, inflation, etc. In the students' world of experience, at best, they see how money in a savings account

increases. The theoretical confrontation with statistics, e.g., in the news ("8% unemployment"), also plays a further, subordinate role. Finally, it is surely necessary to be able to compare amounts with one another that refer to differing basic values (Company A employed 3 trainees earlier, Company B 12; Company A now has 4 trainees, Company B 23).

The lesson plan begins at the first of the three levels, the placing of percentage within the structures of subject matter as developed to that point. Not being a mathematician, I refrain from saying anything about the strategic place of equations inside mathematical knowledge; but the step from fractions to equations is much more complicated than it is indicated here.

Following this, the student teacher added a few remarks concerning the function of percentage arguments in everyday life. It is the perspective of an adult that dominates his view, not the one of young people at the age of 14. All but one example are taken from areas eighth-graders normally know nothing about. Conventional eighth-graders do not calculate inflation (at best they are angry because of rising prices), let alone invest money. They will barely know that interest rates define how much interest is added each year in their saving account—if they have a bank account and manage it themselves. Other examples eighth-graders might be familiar with, like the places on top-20 music charts or the use of percentage functions in computer games, are not mentioned. If one were to take items from where the students are aware of the social reality of percentages and interest rates, for example, the comparative numbers of refugees and immigrants (much less than they would expect) has been a very hot issue in Germany, or—on a more personal level—the interest rates charged by mail-order distributors, there is a whole world of calculations.

Even if one concedes that percentages, let alone of interest rates, are not an everyday content in the life of teenagers, one could think about where they might have met percentage or rates before, especially in relation to the third level of Didaktik analysis, with respect to other subject matter and the curriculum as a whole. And, indeed, there are several places where both are included in the curriculum of the seventh and of the eighth grade: in geography, when talking about the structures of agriculture and the growth of industry; in chemistry and physics, when introducing characteristics of different materials; in civic education, when talking about elections; and so on. And the student teacher does not mention the most important application of percentages in German schools: the calculation of grades which, from the very beginning of school—and especially in math teaching—are often legitimated by counting the percentage of correct answers.

The trouble is not that the analysis is incomplete; if we take into account how difficult and complicated it is to trace the social history of a piece of content, it will always be incomplete. Instead, the problem is that this student teacher's analysis lacks an understanding of *who* is going to be instructed. It would not sound much different for students at other stages or in another part of the town. Focused on his narrow view, the student teacher is neither able to enlarge the understanding of the students nor able to recognize where his instruction might be hampered by already-given knowledge.

Other models of Didaktik discuss students in a separate section of the analysis, dealing with learning histories and classroom settings. Klafki keeps the issue focused on content. There is no content that is completely new. As we can learn from Herbart, *the substance of a content, the Bildungsgehalt, is what you get when placing it between the interests and experiences already at hand.* Even inside a pure subject-matter approach this is obvious: The impressive research on story-telling mathematics and on the construction of subject matter inside mathematics have both indicated that even instruction that seems to be concentrated on pure math operates with underlying conceptions that are by no means purely mathematical but, rather, are a mixture of previous instruction and lots of intervening experience from different fields. When talking about fractions, students don't always operate mathematically, but on the basis of the fractions they see in real life: How can I secure my share? How much would my little sister get? and so on. Even adults reconstruct mathematical knowledge by reframing it within everyday experience. Therefore, it is no solution to keep the contents pure. Instead a teacher has to become aware of what might frame students' understanding and, if possible, to reframe it with respect to their previous cognition.

The third question deals with both the problems of framing and of reframing, but within a perspective of *legitimation*. The answer gives an idea why we are right to ask a learner to learn the content the way we teach it.

WHERE IS THE SIGNIFICANCE OF THE TOPIC FOR THE FUTURE?

This is the classical question of curriculum making. It is no surprise that reasonable answers to this question will never be far from what conventional curriculum analysis would suggest. One of the most important German curriculum theories, Saul Robinsohn's (1992) model of curriculum of 1969, asked explicitly for an analysis of those future situations that might affect the student as an adult, and for which he or she should be prepared. Naturally, an analysis done by a student teacher cannot deliver an elaborated result of research. It can only indicate situations and their impact:

> Knowledge about how to calculate percentages enables the students to, for example, explain the amount of interest they get for their savings accounts, i.e., to judge the fundamental differences in paying interest. The banks, how-

ever, currently offer such complicated investment schemes that an advantageous selection is no longer guaranteed. The distorted presentation of numbers, statistics, etc., e.g., in the media, makes it almost impossible to make an objective judgment without increased knowledge of the subject. The purpose of this lesson content is, however, understandable.

Once again the scope is limited. Curiously enough, this time it focuses on what interest rates may mean in the future life of the students as young people. Other issues that would affect problems of future adults are not even mentioned. However, the analysis does recognize the fact that even a complete introduction of the calculation of interest will necessarily fail to prepare the students for all the tricks banks may use. One should not underestimate the importance of this idea; young teachers generally tend to overvalue the impact of the information given by school instruction.

But the last sentence of the answer, saying that the purpose of the lesson content "is understandable," is confusing. What does he mean by saying the purpose is understandable? That the students have an idea about why *he* is teaching this—or an idea about why *this* is to be taught—or an idea about why it might be useful to listen? The problem once again is that the central aspects are missing. First of all—and surprisingly—there is nothing said about equations in general, or the problems of applied equations particularly, in the process of math learning. If I am correct in analyzing the syllabus, this is the first time that students have to deal with the fact that one and the same mathematical operation can have different names and—to put it emphatically—*ideologies,* depending on use. Dealing with the first question, the student teacher himself observes that equations might be something of general importance inside mathematical knowledge. However, he does not elaborate on what might occur at later stages of math instruction as a result of dealing with this subject matter in a specific context now.

What is equally lacking is a word about the prominence of applied equations in the future curriculum as a whole: in science, geography, civic education, computer instruction, and technology, where applied equations play a significant role. In this respect it would also be important to work in the direction of a clear understanding of what is the mathematical core and what are the conditions of application.

This awareness should also affect the answers concerning the fourth question.

HOW ARE THE CONTENTS STRUCTURED?

This fourth step is at the core of the concept of a Didaktik analysis. It reminds us that the steps of an analysis are not the steps or contents of instruction, but go far beyond the preparation or evaluation of instruction. To give an impression of the items that could be involved, let me summarize the six questions Klafki says are enclosed by the analytical task:

- What are the individual elements of the content as a contextual whole?
- How are these individual elements related?
- Is the content layered? Does it have layers of meaning and significance?
- What is the wider context of this content? What must have preceded it?
- What peculiarities of the content will presumably make access to the subject difficult?
- What is the body of knowledge that must be retained ("minimum knowledge") if the content determined by these questions is to be considered acquired?

What did my student write in his plan?

The basic equation for calculating percentages is:

$$\frac{P}{p'} = \frac{B}{100} \quad \text{or} \quad \frac{P}{B} = \frac{p'}{100}$$

where P is the percent value, p' the percentage, and B the basic value. Using the basic equation, two known values enable us to calculate the one unknown. The equation can be calculated according to each of the variables. The result is three different equations that the students are familiar with yet do not use due to the increased abstraction. In addition it has been determined that 1% of the basic value is equal to $B/100$. This connection is familiar to the students. One problem the students have is the fact that for calculating percentages they are not based on 1% of the basic value but rather on one elementary unit. The minimum amount of knowledge necessary is evidenced by the practical use of the method for solving the problem.

We get math—and nothing else! The layers of content, the fact that the subject matter is embedded in multiple worlds with multiple meanings are completely lost. Even that which he elaborated earlier—the everyday connotation of the calculation of interests in savings accounts—is not mentioned. The shortcomings in terms of math are obvious. At least, a complete table of equations and errors, which might occur in the course of instruction, would have been helpful. However, except for short descriptions of two formulas, we get no idea of what the content is about. Anyone who is used to working with 14-year-old students will know that even the writing of the formula itself is by no means an easy task. Therefore, the minimum amount of knowledge is not evidenced by the practical use of the method. Students may be able to produce correct results without understanding what they are doing. A very common complaint of students in math is that they know what they are expected to do, but do not understand why. This is justified when confronted with this kind of short-sighted math.

WHAT PARTICULAR CASES, PHENOMENA, SITUATIONS, EXPERIMENTS, PEOPLE, EVENTS, FORMAL ELEMENTS CAN BE USED TO MAKE THE CONTENTS IN QUESTION INTERESTING, WORTH ASKING QUESTIONS ABOUT, ACCESSIBLE, COMPREHENSIBLE?

In Klafki's model this last question leads directly to the problems of how to present the content, how to treat it, how to assess progress, and how to assess impact. The core of the fifth question is what is termed *Anschaulichkeit* in German pedagogy. As developed in different approaches, like those of Pestalozzi and Immanuel Kant, it is almost impossible to translate the meaning of *Anschauung*. It includes epistemological basics (e.g., that insight comes from seeing something) as well as debatable Didaktik implications (as, e.g., that showing something makes it more accessible than explaining it by words alone). Moreover, *Anschauung* is something transitory. It is not attached to something you may show. Whether or not something enhances *Anschauung* depends on the spectators and the circumstances more than on the item itself. The "fruitful moment in instruction"—as Friedrich Copei called it—very often comes from surprising examples, which make something that was hitherto complicated strikingly clear. Suddenly you know what it's all about! But it is almost always impossible to use these surprising metaphors of subject matter a second time or to reproduce the results. *Anschauung* is the centerpiece of a good teacher's pedagogical content knowledge. It is what makes the difference.

My student teacher was also looking for this kind of fruitful moment. Going back to a dispute between his class and a parallel one on which class was better at sports, he created an example that was designed to help his students to understand the practical advantages of calculus:

An example: After the national sports competition the students in two classes have to compare the absolute number of certificates awarded to the number of students. The opportunity to select the ratios in such a way that the class with the fewer number of certificates is the more successful one presents itself in order to clearly show the students the difference in comparison. The fact that having only absolute numbers does not always lead to a usable comparison should be self-evident to the students. But the development of the ability to calculate percentages can hardly be expected. Applications of how to calculate percentages can be found in sufficient amounts in everyday life, as for example the already mentioned calculation of interest for savings.

At first, I was pleased that, finally, the analysis indicated that we were talking about a specific group of students, not just about anyone who might be subject to math instruction. But it did not surprise me that this turn was delayed until the very last question. Faced by the problems of *Anschaulichkeit*, even true believers in pure math turn toward everyday life. They are well aware of the fact that *Anschaulichkeit* is nothing people normally associate with math and they want to prove that this might be otherwise.

In my view, however, this inconsistency, substituting *Anschauung* for everyday life, creates many problems in math instruction. If math is not *anschaulich* at the level of math itself, how could it be *anschaulich* at any other level? Thus, the last question indicates one of the most important features of Didaktik analysis: It is never enough to hand one of the three levels over to one or two steps of analysis; *on each level all questions and each question at all levels have to be involved* to get a systematic understanding of what a content is about. More sequential models of analysis that compartmentalize the levels and questions in subsequent steps and viewpoints, like Hilbert Meyer's (1980) popular model, do not do this. A well-done analysis focused on content is more likely to force real consequences.

Didaktik analysis provides nothing that a good teacher would not be aware of. And many aspects and results stemming from the various fields of psychology and curriculum research are not considered in a Didaktik analysis. But what does a Didaktik analysis offer?

1. Whereas experienced teachers may be able to fulfill the requirements of good instruction by simply following their experience and the implicit understanding built on this experience, student teachers have to have a tool to organize their encounters with content.

2. Compared to conventional curriculum theory, this kind of analysis makes it easier to hold the line between theoretical frames and practical discourse. Both perspectives are constantly integrated by focusing analysis on the scope of teaching and the analysis of teaching on the scope of the content involved.

3. On a more theoretical level, this kind of analysis allows for a fruitful combination of epistemological analysis, cognitive psychology, research on teaching, and research on subject matter, by integrating these by way of a *shared* perspective on content.

4. Even if one agrees that instruction is not about content itself, but about more sophisticated things like the learning of learning, the fact remains that all instruction is organized around content, or, to be more exact, around arguments about what happens if a teacher and students meet a certain

content. Systems with centralized curriculum development, like those found in the German states, need a language to communicate and evaluate arguments about instruction that is accessible to administrators, teachers, students, and parents. Didaktik has elaborated this kind of language and has an instructive history of experience with its use.

5. Finally, this kind of analysis is open to almost any access point that might be reasonably applied to instructional settings. Even if it is not always necessary for experienced teachers, it is helpful in making researchers aware of the complexity involved in a given lesson or in an analysis of the impact of instruction.

REFERENCES

Meyer, H. L. (1980). *Leitfaden zur Unterrichtsvorbereitung.* Königstein i. Ts.: Scriptor.
Robinsohn, S. B. (1992). A conceptual model of curriculum development. In S. B. Robinsohn, *Comparative education: A basic approach* (H. Robinsohn, Ed.; pp. 125–144). Jerusalem: The Magnes Press.

12

Levels of Classroom Preparation

Gotthilf Gerhard Hiller
Gillian Horton-Krüger (Trans.)

Gotthilf Gerhard Hiller is a professor of special education at the Pädagogische Hochschule in Ludwigsburg/Reutlingen. His publications include *Konstruktive Didaktik* [Constructive Didaktik] (1973) and *Plädoyer für eine Archäeologie des Lehrens und Lernen* [Pleading for an Archeology of the Forms of Teaching and Learning] (1994).

THE PROBLEM

Preparation for instruction focuses on the preparation of individual lessons. This is a fact, no matter what the theorists might wish. Preparing for instruction normally means shaping individual lessons or a series of lessons, instructional units, as we call them. Proof of this can be found in the relevant literature: Klafki's (1965) Didaktik analysis concludes with such examples; Heimann, Otto, and Schulz's (1965) *Unterricht: Analyse und Planung* [Instruction: Analysis and Planning] is comprised to a large extent of "lesson charts"—I have used them myself (see Hiller 1970); and even Meyer's (1981) concept aims at "lesson plans."[1] That this approach is taken for granted may be disturbing, but it is not without explanation, because syllabi apply to

---

[1]The same can be said of most of the more recent publications on the subject, including Gebauer (1977), Messer, Schneider, and Spiering (1977), Moser (1978), and Walter and Edelmann (1979).

school subjects. These subjects are mainly taught, or were taught until recently, using the format of a lesson *(Lektion)*, and the straightjacket of school organization imposes the primitive routine of 45-minute periods. Given these facts, the institutions that train teachers can evidently do no more than react. Following the dictates of tradition, the introduction to school practice, and thus the introduction to instructional preparation, presents the teacher's future career as an endless chain of plannable 45-minute appearances. The chain simply breaks off when the teacher retires. During training the sole emphasis is on the optimization of the beginners' stage-management abilities, adapted as appropriate to suit Didaktik tastes.

The consequences are obvious: Didaktik theories are reduced to rules and criteria for planning individual lessons. Didaktik models are debased to lesson models. And, conversely, the 45-minute period becomes the arena within which Didaktik theories have to prove themselves: "The multiperspective approach is quite interesting. How about showing the staff a multiperspective lesson!" This questionable attitude—that Didaktik theories and models serve chiefly to improve individual lessons, or at best instructional units—results in a peculiar punctuation of instruction, at the same time giving it a dramatic character all of its own. The styling of individual periods—as a rule for lessons—produces what is known as the "double start": the first start for motivation (carrying the class through the next 40 minutes) and the second start when work begins in earnest. The teacher is obliged to produce clearly articulated targets, declaimed within the first few minutes. Under the pressures of the "valid form" of the individual lesson, so-called "introductory lessons" are the main component in training. The traditions of exercise and practice are given no room to develop, for who is prepared, metaphorically speaking, to eat up a dish someone else has already picked at? In Didaktik terms this would mean practicing a topic another teacher has introduced, and this, of course, would give no scope to show what capable teachers we are! The concentration of Didaktik thought on the preparation of individual lessons leads, not least, to a self-inflicted loss of meaning in instructional activities. And it falls to the students themselves to integrate the total sum of the day's, the week's instruction; they must work out how to interrelate, how to knit together, the many strands with which they are confronted over the months and years.

The problem can be more closely defined if it is seen as the result of a dubious "division of Didaktik labor." On the one hand there are the syllabi, which most of the people who have to teach them have no influence on. Then there is the school architecture, with its concrete, glass, and wood, its fittings and props, which often determines what is possible and what not. A plethora of legal requirements pertaining to the organization of instruction narrow the teachers' scope even further, and then—as Luhmann (1971) showed—there are the complex processes of public communication that bring certain themes to our general attention, usually with a specific emphasis, and block out others. Given all this, it is doubtful whether teachers actually have the degree of influence on content and target decisions that Didaktik models have wished us to believe occurs. The education industry has in recent years been publishing more handbooks for teachers, which evidently sell better if they are presented as series of well-designed lesson crib sheets, increasingly forcing teachers out of their role as instructional designers and claiming them as engineers for learning processes, schooled in communication psychology and motivation theory. Instructional preparation remains a marginal issue for the practitioner. Maintaining teachers as members of a Didaktik "subculture," these publications draw on traditional forms of teaching without elucidating them, without making them accessible to teachers for reflection and independent use. To put it bluntly: If we continue to accept that Didaktik issues can only be taken seriously and discussed by the majority of teachers inasmuch as they relate to the organizational framework of the individual period, we need not be surprised that instructional preparation—reduced to the production of lesson plans—concerns novice and student teachers only during a course of training that demands and assesses products of this kind. It is then of little wonder that serious doubts about the necessity and desirability of so-called general Didaktik models for instructional preparation are voiced.

In the following I explore which instruments—instead of general models for stylizing individual lessons simply as means to an end—we must teach prospective teachers to develop and (re)use in order to regain more planning competence at the grass roots of the profession. This will be impossible without sensitivity to traditions in the Didaktik design of instruction, without a scientific processing of the Didaktik subculture.

THREE LEVELS OF INSTRUCTIONAL PREPARATION

My proposal is that teacher education and everyday school practice should concentrate in future on the following three levels of instructional preparation:

- The first level concerns the conception of school time as an orchestrated whole, based on the development of a "score" *(Schulzeitpartitur)* representing this whole. In physical terms this would be a detailed chart of subjects, topics, and approaches spread over, say, a school year. In effect, this would be a recultivation of the traditional German *Stoffverteilungsplan,* the precursor of the modern curriculum structure (cf. Bernstein, 1971; Frey & Isenegger, 1975).
- The second level concerns the search for models or patterns for directing teaching and learning, developed over the years within the

traditions of Didaktik and still in use today, in some cases unchanged, in others modified. We need to redefine their worth for the present.

- Finally, a third level of instructional preparation concerns the stylization, the development, even the creation of new elementary forms of teaching, of Didaktik miniatures.

In the next sections I discuss each of these levels in more detail, concluding with a few remarks on their interrelationship.

SCORES: SCHOOL TIME AS AN ORCHESTRATED WHOLE

In the past, the instrument for the pedagogical design of school time was the *Stoffverteilungsplan* (literally, the subject-matter distribution plan), in which the teacher listed the topics and objectives and the teaching and learning processes envisaged for a given school year. Today, however, at least so it would seem, it serves no practical purpose: At primary schools and *Hauptschulen*[2] many teachers copy from each other year after year, a tiresome administrative task. What is the point of wishing to connect medium- or long-term theme-related teaching and learning processes in such a way that an overall design of the time to be spent at school is apparent to all parties? Our own experience tells us that any number of contingencies could arise to damage such a fragile construct. What more could such a plan ever achieve than the perennial disappointment of all concerned?

In *Gymnasien* and increasingly in *Realschulen,* available school time is divided into 10 to 15 parallel subject channels with no institutionalized connections between them. Teachers' associations, the education industry, and school bureaucracy usually come to some agreement over the topics to be "covered," the aims to be pursued, the sequence to be followed, the pace to be observed, and the form in which "testing" is to take place. These are the forces shaping each school subject. To this extent, the subjects—removed from any context of educational or pedagogical legitimation—have become an arbitrary framework of distribution with no justification in terms of educational theory, within which blocks of content are allotted time and teachers. The Gymnasium and the Realschule have thus surrendered any claim to providing a coherent introduction to the cultural tradition of our society and, thus, adequately preparing young people for their future within this society, enabling them to decide whether to adopt and perpetuate existing conditions and processes or whether to effect change.

---

[2]The German secondary school system is still largely tripartite, separating students according to academic ability: *Hauptschule*—terminating at Grade 9; *Realschule*—terminating at Grade 10; and *Gymnasium*—terminating at Grade 13.

Few schools recognize this form of socialization as one of their tasks, although there are comprehensive schools, experimental schools, or other alternative types of school where staff do their best to put it into practice.[3] It is well known that such projects exert considerable fascination on all those interested in educational policy or involved in institutions within the educational system. Yet no catalytic affect to speak of can be noted within the public education system, particularly in the area that interests us here, that is, the development of instruction as a coordinated entity in the medium and long term (as a composite structure of interrelated teaching and learning processes). This is reflected, for example, in teacher education: At no point can teachers adequately learn how to plan in phases, interlinking teaching and learning units synchronously and diachronously in an explainable and pedagogically justifiable relationship. This means that there can be no competent planning of the wider contexts of teaching and learning.

If we were prepared to return to the orchestrated planning of school time, to compose the appropriate scores, this could mean rediscovering an issue that has been all but forgotten: the development of curriculum structures at the grass-roots level—by the teachers themselves. We would no longer need to take refuge in the metaphysical construct of the school subject, but could take up the challenge to exploit the wealth of available material and produce an attractive composition likely to satisfy the socialization demands of society on schools, in a manner that is accountable and no longer merely coincidental or dictated by tradition.

Let us now take a closer look at the elements from which such a composition could be made.

The pedagogical purpose within the overtly dramatic structure of a *project* is for young people to experience, through examples, that conditions can be influenced, even changed, and how this can be done. Students can discover the obstacles that need to be considered, the pressures that can occur, the pace at which one can be compelled to work, the inescapable situations where decisions have to be made and action taken, the successes that can be achieved, and the defeats that must be accepted. They can see something of the ambiguous and relative nature of achievements and of the difficulties arising from them, and may realize that there are no conclusive, unequivocal paradigms for interpreting and assessing the results of one's own work.

---

[3]Compare in particular the University of Bielefeld's documentation of its school projects *Laborschule/Oberstufenkolleg* in the series Sonderpublikation der Schriftenreihe der Schulprojekete Laborschule, Oberstufen-Kolleg (Stuttgart: Klett, 1973).

For reports of the Glocksee pilot project, compare Autorenkollektiv "Glocksee": Schulversuch Glocksee. In *Ästhetik und Kommunikation* (Vol. 6/7, 1975/1976; Vol. 22/23, pp. 23–149). Compare also Rist and Schneider (1977).

It is in keeping with the school's socialization commitment for society to be represented as formed, and as such formable, possibly even in need of change. Consequently, the enablement of young people to contribute to shaping their social context critically and responsibly is one of the most important tasks of school. However, as our general education system can only transmit the experience of exerting influence in principle and can only lay the foundations for the young people's own subsequent contribution, it is wrong to say that our schools should set up projects aiming to effect change in as many areas of society as possible where change would be necessary. School should assess its reformatory or even revolutionary potential soberly: Exaggerated hopes or fears are as pointless as contemptuous or resigned pessimism. More important than parallel activities in a plethora of minor school projects is the experience of participation in processes changing conditions and people. A few powerful examples should be provided to stimulate and encourage the young people to join in the work of action groups and institutions outside school. School should aim to achieve this through as few projects as possible, in other words to effect the "delivery" of its clientele to "State, Church, and Science" (cf. Schleiermacher, 1966) in as short a period of school time as possible.

The pedagogical purpose of *lessons,* utilizing texts of all kinds, is to enable young people to recognize that an appropriate medium—specific forms of access, specific methods—is required to make the conditions and entities comprising our reality visible in constellations that interest us. The lesson in its epic form is a teaching and learning vehicle with two characteristic facets: Through lessons students can discover and compose the forms of knowledge and action, the methods and processes for (re)constructing reality and—vice versa—can learn how to reapply data and facts, information and opinions, objects, and instruments to methods and processes stemming from specific interests and positions. Free of any immediate pressure to act, epistemological elementary instruction as an introduction to major forms of knowledge about things, processes, and the self should succeed, enabling the students to comprehend reality in multiperspectival terms, which means they would neither surrender themselves unthinkingly to an opinion nor take refuge in arguments simply to escape commitment when faced with justified demands.[4] What was said of projects also applies here: In schools within the general education system, a small number of appropriately chosen themes will suffice for the students to gain awareness of the constitution of knowledge and action. Of course, some time will be needed before students are equipped for active—analytical or constructive—participation in

---

[4]With regard to *lectio,* compare Paulsen (1919). On multiperspective instruction see the publications of the CIEL working group in Reutlingen (CIEL-Arbeitsgruppe Reutlingen, 1974, especially Giel, 1975).

such processes. Nevertheless, each school should ensure that this type of instruction is kept to the required minimum. As soon as the students have acquired elementary abilities of this kind, there is theoretically no reason to keep them within the artificial confines of institutionalized schooling.

Play and practice should be offered to young people and stylized as forms of self-design, as life activities with a merit of their own. With conscious reference to Schleiermacher's (1966) arguments, play and practice should not be seen as mere motivational embellishment, nor devalued to minor stepping stones on the way to more important ends. Take, for example, the highly sophisticated systems of practice through play developed in east Asian cultures to maintain and promote physical, mental and spiritual faculties throughout life. Anyone who takes the trouble to examine one of these systems more closely, including the experience others have had within it (cf. Herrigel 1968; see also Bollnow, 1978), will grasp that play and practice is an unmistakably independent, indispensable form of teaching and learning.

General education should offer play and practice as an exemplary form of self-cultivation. Children and adolescents should have these opportunities as students. Again, there is no need to offer too much for too long and thus hold young people back from the opportunities on offer outside school.

It is no doubt appropriate that school should cultivate a further form of teaching, namely the transmission of utilitarian knowledge in linear *training programs,* providing young people, in their role as students, with examples of how specific qualifications can be obtained in the shortest possible time. But such training programs cannot fill up the majority of the time students are required to spend in general education. For this there are specialists in relevant institutions, who generally train their clientele more intensively, and more effectively, than schools can. Once again, school should concentrate on a few programs of general usefulness and emphasize their function as demonstration.

It is from these four elements—projects, lessons, play and practice, and training programs—that the school score is to be composed. Some time will also be needed to come to an agreement, for example, about the structure of this Didaktik frame and the reciprocal expectations and opportunities for action that occur within it. It is a time for constructive criticism, for discussing learning processes as they have been perceived so far, and for reporting and assessing results.

Scores as described here are specific cooperation plans for a staff of teachers, a foundation for longer term forms of cooperation between teachers and students. Presented as a succinct wall chart for the classroom, they serve as a guide for everyone involved in the teaching and learning process and provide easy access to information on what has been covered, what is "on" at the moment, and what is planned. If a score is condensed into an information leaflet for parents, indicating what the students will be occupied with, and when, it serves as a guide for parents to anticipate how their own interests, skills, and experience will allow them to give their children constructive support.

Anyone setting out to write such school scores will encounter a large number of Didaktik problems that have always been coped with in practice, but rarely mentioned in theory. Presumably, such patterns of time organization follow patterns of school economics shaped by long tradition and differing from culture to culture. In all events, the criteria for what occurs simultaneously in the course of a day or a week within the available instructional time, and at what speed the topics and requirements change, can only be indirectly tied to extracurricular frames of reference. School time is organized in accordance with *intra*curricular rules that, as we have said, have scarcely been explored in theory. It is high time new studies were undertaken to chart the organization of school time at other periods in history and adequate modern theories of composition developed to create new forms of organization, functioning rather like composition theories in painting and music.

The example that I use to illustrate my argument here can only document how far the preparatory work for the development of school scores has progressed. Nevertheless, the construct, insufficiently supported as it is in both theoretical and empirical terms, can by its very provisional nature serve as a productive matrix for further reflection.[5]

The basic scheme of the score is simple. The first column (see Fig. 12.1) gives the number of school periods to be taught per subject in the class in question, according to the appropriate timetable. These figures are transposed into "subject lines" of differing lengths. The following columns each represent one school week. The "ideal" school year comprises four self-contained blocks of instruction: approximately 10 weeks from the beginning of the year after the summer vacation until the autumn vacation; approximately 7 weeks between the autumn and Christmas vacations; approximately 11 weeks between the Christmas and Easter vacations; approximately 10 weeks from Easter to the end of the school year in summer. This adds up to a total of approximately 38 weeks of instruction.

In the second line of the figure, the numbers 1 to 14 represent the dates of a few events in the cultural calendar (2–5: the four Sundays in Advent; 6: the beginning of the winter sales, etc.). Regardless of our personal attitude to these events, we need to be aware that the time scale of instruction interweaves in many ways with other objective and subjective rhythms of time organization.

---

[5]This is confirmed by a series of trial compositions produced by student teachers under my guidance during the winter semester 1978/1979 at the Pädagogische Hochschule in Reutlingen.

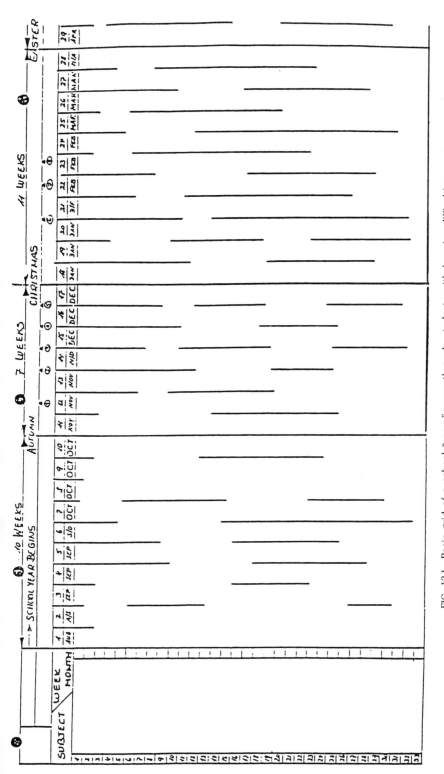

FIG. 12.1. Basic grid of a school "score": seventh-grade students with learning difficulties, following the timetable for the Länder of North Rhine-Westphalia.

215

The basic structure encompasses all available school periods. Within these limits, instruction that is attractive to all concerned must be designed. When school scores of this kind are being developed, a number of formal principles apply:

1. With reference to federal and state guidelines and curricula and with regard for local agreements, the plan for a specific grade must be coordinated with the plans for the other grades, in particular for the grades immediately below and above.

2. It is advisable to plan no more than 70% of the available time in detail. Particularly toward the end of each term, about a week should be set aside as a "flexibility zone," providing scope to adapt and follow up as required (taking interests, strengths, weaknesses, etc., into consideration).

3. Activities affecting more than one class or grade (fêtes, field trips, etc.) and activities with external involvement (from Outward Bound centers, employers offering work-experience placements, churches, school camps, etc.) need to be fixed in advance and time allocated for preparation and evaluation.

4. Time should be set aside for discussing, explaining, and revising planning decisions, for sounding out the students' interests, and for involving students and parents as responsible, active participants in the design of instructional phases.

5. Particular sequences that are to be regularly repeated should be ascertained in advance. As a rule this will apply to forms of teaching in the play and practice category, but could also include regular lessons on a chosen theme.

6. Projects should be planned with the cultural calendar in mind and, conversely, "seasonal" projects should be scheduled for the appropriate times of the year.

7. If specific knowledge will be required at a specific date (for internal/external examinations, etc.), training periods must be timetabled accordingly.

8. In the free portions of the score, interdisciplinary lesson sequences should be given priority.[6]

School scores of this kind, it should be emphasized, are *not* a set of directions to be followed blindly. They are intended as an instrument around which renewed discussion of the organization of school time can take place, enabling all concerned, students and teachers alike, to recomprehend school time as a whole as a purposeful entity. This is a process that would start at the level of groups of teaching staff. In a wider context, the scores

---

[6]On interdisciplinary studies, compare, in particular, Hiller-Ketterer and Scholze (1979).

can provide a basis for discussion of what would constitute a justifiable limitation of the time spent in general education. If the teachers' planning responsibility is reduced to the preparation of individual lessons or instructional units, the planning loses its frame of reference. General models from Didaktik for the preparation of single school periods cannot compensate for this loss. It is well known that they are temporary surrogates for most new teachers, but even more worrying is the presumption that when teachers are no longer obliged to produce this type of lesson plan, they have little interest in even qualitatively quite different forms of planning. Initial trials undertaken with students on postgraduate teaching courses to recultivate medium-term planning skills (for coordinated or "fully orchestrated" phases of a school year) have revealed that teachers felt this approach considerably eased the burden of their day-to-day planning. And not only that! Teaching at a mainstream school, it was found, can again become more of a way of life. The teachers were no longer simply getting lessons over with. When reading newspapers and magazines, for example, they began to notice material with a challenge for their teaching, even if there was nothing specific to be made of it for the classroom at that time. In a team, we began to collect such spectacular "objects" from the print media and compiled slides for future use. This is not a strictly required exercise, but most useful nevertheless. It produces a form of nonspecific, highly stimulating instruction preparation, and gradually an attractive Didaktik archive is built up.

PATTERNS OF TEACHING

Given the requirement that school scores should be developed from projects, lessons, play and practice, and training programs, the question now is how these forms of teaching can themselves be composed. Existing general Didaktik models, used or misused as a guide to the production of lesson plans, offer no answers. On the contrary, analyses of students' lesson plans for their final (teacher certification) examinations over several years (see Schaible, 1974) confirm that the candidates are quite adept in their "preliminary reflection" at utilizing current arguments from the Didaktik discussions as apologies for their ideas. However, the lesson plans following these preliminary remarks are so true to the traditions of a teaching subculture that the preliminary reflections using Didaktik models would seem to be interchangeable. In other words, if we look at the lesson plans produced over the last 25 years and, in each case, separate the plan itself from all the reasoning, explanation, and justification in which it is embedded, the arguments can mostly be dated relatively easily, but not the lesson plan. In search of design possibilities specific to teaching forms, therefore, we must work on the traditions of school rhetoric manifest in the lesson plans.[7] The composition forms arising over the years deserve our renewed interest, the patterns of pedagogical "stage management" that have to a greater or lesser degree lost their original functions and acquired new ones, but at least have remained in a more or less clearly recognizable form. In these patterns, forms of stylization are prefigured, which we generally describe, unfortunately only formally, as interdependence. A task for studies of Didaktik speech and action would be to explore systematically and pragmatically which patterns grew up against which background and when, and how and why they were transformed. Studies need to examine which new creations revolutionized the order of school teaching and learning, which counterreforms became possible and how, and which restorations yielded which results. By sympathetic observation and by analysis of instructional plans and records, the present stock of such forms of teaching could be recorded and carefully reconstructed, drawing on the available documents. Then it could be checked—possibly by means of "faithful" reimplementation of old forms of instruction—whether they could be brought up to date and applied to modern conditions and modern needs, and if so how.

What use is express reference to existing patterns of teaching developed throughout history in connection with instructional preparation? One thing at least should be clear by now: The social situation of instruction should not have to be presented as an interdependent nexus of formal structural elements with teachers free and able to decide how to combine them. Would it not be better to introduce the teacher (as planner) to the wealth of teaching patterns developed over centuries, and to their specific claims, in order to enable those who are to prepare instruction today, and for the next 30 years, to achieve a reflective handling of these traditions, to tinker intelligently with familiar and new Didaktik forms and objects? A teacher educated in this way would have to decide for and against patterns of teaching, just as any theater director must choose how a play is to be performed. The teachers, even if they wanted to experiment with completely new forms, could then perceive themselves as part of a craft tradition, working creatively toward socialization.

ELEMENTARY DIDAKTIK FORMS

Particularly since teacher training became the province of academics, the theoretical representation of elementary forms of Didaktik action—as well as their practice—has become an increasingly difficult field. Where is the university or college in Germany today where student teachers can acquire

---

[7]I owe this argument to Giel, who expressly demanded the development of a Didaktik topic. See Giel (1976).

the knowledge and skills of their "craft"? Where can they learn, for example, how to make wall charts, how to compile worksheets, how to design written texts, how to deal with students' comments, how to prepare Didaktik objects appropriately for use in class, how to arrange individual pieces of information to create a whole that is easy to remember, and how to define and explain concepts and terms? Such things cannot be organized in the simple learning-theory models of microteaching. To recultivate these skills we need specific play-and-practice courses at our faculties of teacher education in which general Didaktik can be exemplified in the form of Didaktik miniatures.

Using appropriate examples, it could be shown, for instance, what can be made of our knowledge that the type of blackboard common in German schools is fashioned in the tradition of the Gothic altarpiece, with its fixed central section and hinged side sections. What relationships can be forged between the individual sections of the board? What can an open or closed board display? How can the side sections be productively used if the students are to be introduced, say, to dialectical figures of thought? Other stimulating ideas can be developed for the use of colored chalk or colored ink on overhead transparencies. Would it be helpful, for example, to draw on ancient conventions of color symbolism and develop a system of color use for texts to be processed or produced during instruction?

Instructional preparation at this level proves itself as the skill both to perceive and to compose Didaktik processes as structured, formable, and yet open processes, a skill that is developed and restructured through practice and play that can never be acquired as a prefabricated entity.

LINKING THE THREE LEVELS

My argument so far could lead to either of the following conclusions:

1. Instructional preparation under the spell of general Didaktik models, conceived of as a freely suspended context of decisions able to serve any aim of socialization policy, remains for students and young teachers an enforced ritual that they abandon as soon as possible. If, on the other hand, the medium-term and long-term design of school time (Level 1) could be successfully represented and made teachable as work comparable with that of a stage director, as a vitally necessary scientific and creative occupation dealing productively with the traditions of teaching (Level 2), and drawing on elementary Didaktik forms with the support of both reflection and action (Level 3), then we would be justified in hoping for a new upswing in Didaktik. Teachers would gain a new self-image, could be seriously committed to their role as teachers (and not just as motivation engineers, learning-target executives, and pedagogical therapists).

2. It has become fashionable to make arbitrary demands on our general education system, following the dictates of current educational policy, without considering whether schools have the wherewithal to meet so many, varied, and at times contradictory and unreasonable demands. Schools themselves over the past 20 years have rarely rebutted any such demands with, for instance, Didaktik or pedagogical arguments. A possible explanation is the fact that general Didaktik models of instructional preparation, the supposed core of Didaktik theory elaboration, are in danger, internally and externally, of ascribing too little significance to traditional forms of instructional activity in Didaktik decision making. For the limits to the efficiency of instructional planning to be defined, constant testing would be required to ascertain whether school has either the experience of forms of teaching or potential recourse to such forms in order to educate *(bilden)* as desired or prescribed with a view to adequate success. In this context it would then have to be asked how adaptable these teaching patterns are, that is, how and with what effects certain elementary Didaktik forms can be integrated into such patterns. Which teaching concepts and individual measures damage or even destroy the inward character of instruction? Questions such as these are important, irrespective of whether the instruction is designed by a teacher, a student, or a group of students.

Until now these questions have been obscured. It is little wonder that in the *terra incognita* of "Didaktik subculture" not only many reform projects but also countless preparation efforts have been unable to overcome the solid mass of teaching tradition. Systematic research into this gray zone is therefore a pressing need.

ACKNOWLEDGMENTS

Based on Gotthilf Gerhard Hiller (1991), "Ebenen der Unterrichtsvorbereitung." In Bijan Adl-Amini and Rudolf Künzli (Eds.), *Didaktische Modelle und Unterrichtsplanung* (3rd ed., pp. 119–141). Munich and Weinheim: Juventa Verlag. This translation is published with the permisison of the copyright holder, Juventa Verlag, Weinheim.

REFERENCES

Bernstein, B. (1971). Klassifikation und Vermittlungsrahmen im schulischen Lernprozess. *Zeitschrift für Pädagogik, 17,* 145–173.
Bollnow, O. F. (1978). *Vom Geist des Übens: Eine Rückbesinnung auf elementare didaktische Erfahrung.* Freiburg im Breisgau: Herder.

CIEL-Arbeitsgruppe Reutlingen. (1974). *Stücke zu einem mehrperspektivischen Unterricht.* Stuttgart: Klett.

Frey, K., & Isenegger, U. (1975). Anordnung von Bildungsinhalten und Aufbau der Curriculumstruktur. In W. Potthoff (Ed.), *Schulpädagogik* (pp. 77–83). Freiburg: Herder.

Gebauer, M. (1977). *Praxis der Unterrichtsvorbereitung: Ein Studienbuch.* Stuttgart: Klett-Cotta.

Giel, K. (1975). Vorbemerkungen zu einer Theorie des Elementarunterrichts. In K. Giel, G. G. Hiller, & H. Krämer (Eds.), *Stücke zu einem mehrperspektivischen Unterricht: Bd. 2. Aufsätze zur Konzeption* (pp. 8–181). Stuttgart: Klett.

Giel, K. (1976). *Allgemeine Pädagogik.* Freiburg im Bresgau: Herder.

Heimann, P., Otto, G., & Schulz, W. (1965). *Unterricht: Analyse und Planung.* Hanover: Schroedel Schulbuchverlag.

Herrigel, E. (1968). *Zen in der Kunst des Bogenschiessens.* Weilheim: O. W. Barth.

Hiller, G. G. (1970). *Konstruktive Didaktik: Empirische Beiträge zur Definition von Unterrichtszielen durch Lehrformen und Unterrichtsmodelle.* Stuttgart: Polyfoto Dr. Vogt KG.

Hiller-Ketterer, I., & Scholze, O. (1979). Fächerübergreifender Unterricht als didaktisches Prinzip. In K. Wöhler (Ed.), *Didaktische Prinzipien: Begründung und praktische Bedeutung* (pp. 85–110). München: Ehrenwirth.

Klafki, W. (1965). *Studien zur Bildungstheorie und Didaktik.* Weinheim: Beltz.

Luhmann, N. (1971). Öffentliche Meinung. In N. Luhmann, *Politische Planung: Aufsätze zur Soziologie von Politik und Verwaltung.* Opladen: Westdeutscher Verlag.

Messer, A., Schneider, J., & Spiering, T. (1977). *Planungsaufgabe Unterricht* (Workshop Schulpädagogik 10). Ravensburg: O. Meier.

Meyer, H. (1981). *Leitfaden zur Unterrichtsvorbereitung.* Königstein/Ts.: Scriptor.

Moser, H. (1978). *Didaktisches Planen und Handeln: Eine praxisbezogene Einführung.* Munich: Kösel.

Paulsen, F. (1919). *Geschichte des gelehrten Unterrichts auf den deutschen Schulen und Universitäten vom Ausgang des Mittelalters bis zur Gegenwart mit besonderer Rücksicht auf den klassischen Unterricht* (R. Lehmann, Ed.; Vol. 1). Leipzig: Verlag von Veit.

Rist, G., & Schneider, P. (1977). *Die Hibernia-Schule: Von der Lehrwerkstatt zur Gesamtschule: Eine Waldorfschule integriert berufliches und allgemeines Lernen.* Reinbek: Rowohlt.

Schaible, H. (1974). *Unterrichtskonzeptionen im Heimatkundeunterricht der Sonderschule für Lernbehinderte im Spiegel von Unterrichtsentwürfen.* Unpublished master's thesis, Tübingen Universität.

Schleiermacher, F. (1966). *Pädagogische Schriften* (2nd ed.). (E. Weniger, Ed., 2 vols.). Düsseldorf: Kupper.

Walter, H., & Edelmann, I. (1979). *Pragmatische Unterrichtsplanung.* Braunschweig: Westermann.

13

Oral and Written Communication for Promoting Mathematical Understanding: Teaching Examples From Grade 3

Christiane Senn-Fennell

Christiane Senn-Fennell graduated from the Free University of Berlin and is an elementary school teacher in western Germany. This chapter, which was translated by the author, is a revision and adaptation of the thesis she completed for her Second State [Teacher Certification] Examination in Berlin. As she notes herein, the structure of the practical part of her thesis and, therefore, this chapter, was determined "according to an unwritten law that generations of German student teachers have followed in their Second State Examination thesis."

THEORY PART: CONTENT ANALYSIS

What wider or general sense or reality does the foreseen theme exemplify and open up to the learner? What basic phenomenon or fundamental principle, what law, criterion, problem, method, technique, or attitude can be grasped by dealing with the theme?

On the 10th of November 1619 René Descartes, a 23-year-old Frenchman, had a vision of a *mirabilis scientiae,* a wonderful science, the rationalization of the world by means of measuring, counting, and quantitative analysis. In the 20th century this dream has become reality, and the so-called *mathematization* of the world has gone far. Physics, astrophysics, and chemistry are purely mathematical in their theoretical parts; biology, medicine, and ecology, as well as sociology and psychology, have gained a mathematical base.

More and more the world is being dominated by technology and mathematics. The technical languages of the sciences invade all areas of everyday life. Although all mathematical communication has to use standard language, it is often overlooked that the language of everyday life is full of mathematical terms and concepts. In these times, a general understanding of "language" requires the understanding of basic mathematical language. Many things can be understood only if one knows the "language of space, of number, of measurement, of logic"—with their mathematical terms. In Western society, technology and progress are regarded as identical and are highly valued. It is taken as a sign of quality for a statement or a theory when it can be expressed in the language of mathematics.

This faith has gone so far that mathematics has become a rhetorical medium—a way of "intended misleading" (see Ellerton & Clements, 1991). On the one hand, information in mathematical form is parsimonious, easy to read, and easy to understand. On the other hand, its effect must be acknowledged: Numbers and dates provoke not only insights but also feelings and prejudices. Values are being transmitted. The media use the idea of mathematics as "objective, clear, unequivocal, value-free, and unquestionable" in their information politics. Mathematics becomes a "rhetorical mathematics." Just as the increasing influence of technology and mathematics on our surroundings is reason enough for the unchanged importance of teaching mathematics at school, language, mathematics, and Western culture are connected with each other. Technology, natural science, and mathematics are basic elements of this world. The teaching of mathematics as an abstract discipline can no longer be the only task of our schools. One aim of teaching mathematics has to be the active and passive *understanding* of mathematical language in order to help children understand how the world functions and to shed light on the rhetoric I mentioned previously. The teaching of mathematics becomes a kind of "teaching of a foreign language," the language Mathematics (see Garlichs & Hagstedt, 1991; Pimm, 1987).

What significance does the theme in question have from a pedagogical point of view? What constitutes the significance for the children's future? What is the wider context?

Mathematics as a Language

Die Mathematiker sind eine Art Franzosen. Spricht man zu ihnen, so übersetzen sie alles in ihre eigene Sprache und so wird es alsobald etwas ganz anderes.
—Goethe

Mathematicians are a kind of Frenchmen. Whenever you say anything or talk to them, they translate it into their own language, and right away it is completely different.

Mathematical Technical Language

A technical language is characterized by a specific vocabulary used with standard syntax.

Historical Development. Over the years, the mathematical language has developed into today's form. A specific character of mathematical language is the mix of standard language and symbols. During the history of mathematics this mixture has not always been taken for granted. One point of view was that mathematical language could be expressed only in symbols. (Leibniz's idea of creating a universal symbolic language is probably based on this.) Such a language would allow all human thoughts to be expressed unequivocally, unmistakably, and perfectly clearly. All controversy would be solved by calculation only. As the French mathematician Condillac commented at the end of the 18th century, "Mathematics is a well-treated science, its language is algebra" (Laborde, 1981, p. 6).

Another opinion was offered in England: There symbols were looked on as short and perfect expressions of terms from standard language. The translation of Euclid's *Elements* caused a dispute: Should it be translated—as in the original version—without using any symbols? Would it be acceptable to find suitable symbols in order to develop a shorter version and, therefore, a new representation of its content (see Laborde, 1981)? The first of these points of view reduces mathematics to mechanical calculation only. The second does not acknowledge the influence of symbols on the development of mathematics. Because of the range of mathematical applications, a mixed use of symbols and standard language cannot be avoided. This requires changing the lexicon and syntax of the standard language.

Characteristics

The mathematical (technical) language is used to represent mathematical results, theorems, or proofs and to do mathematical operations. It is characterized by its own sign system, which contains many symbols. Various classes of symbols have to be distinguished (see Pimm, 1987):

- *Logograms* are signs that have been specially invented to express whole concepts. Some represent complete words: + for "and," @ for "at," $ for "dollar"; 0–9 and % are others. Some letters have been stylized as well and lost their literal meaning (the integral sign, $\int$).
- *Pictograms* are stylized icons that remain close to their original meaning. They are found mainly in geometry as images of objects that can easily be recognized. They are also called "motivated symbols."
- *Alphabetic symbols* and *punctuation* are used as symbols as well.

In addition, *order* and *structural relations* allow only a restricted number of changes (the algebra laws!).

In order for a symbol to be effective, and to function, it may not be altered, and it must not occur with more than one meaning.[1] But the mathematical technical language is also ambiguous. Several signs for numbers and notations for operations exist parallel to each other, and, as well, there are different algorithms for addition and different notations. An American billion is a German milliarde, a trillion a billiarde. In Germany division is symbolized by ":," in the United States by "÷" or "/." In addition to symbols, the mathematical language often employs words from standard language and gives them a new or limited meaning, for example, *degree, face, product, power.*[2] The use of the passive voice and the creation of substantive nouns are commonplace. "We" as a kind of general subject is often used.[3]

Effects

In order to communicate about mathematics, a standardized use of symbols and clear definitions of terminology are necessary. The representation of, and teaching about, mathematics using a highly formalized language reduced to its basics conceals the informal stages during the development of a theory, the incomplete statements that emerged in the course of the search for *the* perfect term.

The "perfect" language of mathematics sometimes causes a kind of symbol shock or a comprehension block. Usually the difficulties are said to lie within the science itself and not in its representation in the technical language. In the math classroom, the mathematical language as described earlier often appears in the teacher's explanations and, even more so, in the texts and workbooks. But the structure of this technical language has developed its own, specific character, although it is based on the standard language. Because of this, it has to be asked whether this character of mathematical language should be considered in methods, and the content, of mathematics teaching. However, to this point this aspect of math as a foreign language has been ignored or denied.

Communication Rituals in the Math Classroom

> The feeling entertained by many that they can think or even reason without language is an illusion.
>
> —Sapir

---

[1]This might explain the very conservative use of mathematical symbols.
[2]See also the discussion of comprehension problems.
[3]See a very interesting article by Pimm (1984).

Discourse: Thought and Language. Sapir's student, Benjamin Whorf (1956), concluded that thought is conditioned by language to such an extent that, once mental structures are fixed in one language, they cannot accommodate the structures necessary for thought in another language (see Ellerton & Clements, 1989). Vygotsky (1986) took this further in a slightly modified way: Thought and language are separate in early childhood, but influence each other at a later stage. The purpose of language is to solve problems. It allows for conscious thinking. Vygotsky said that concepts can enter the cognitive structure of an individual only when they can be expressed verbally.

Many psycholinguists have shown that the formulation of a written or spoken language can be achieved only when the objects to be described are made abstract. A certain distance from these objects has also to be created. In other words, the activity of formulating stimulates abstraction, distance, and decentralization: *Language controls or regulates human thought and action.* For the math classroom, this means that students can understand mathematical concepts only if they can express them in their own words. But it also means that talking and communicating within the classroom can significantly help understanding the content.[4]

Comprehension Problems in the Math Classroom

The teaching of mathematics is confronted with the contradiction that, on one hand, language is needed to explain things and, on the other hand, language is *the* problem in comprehending mathematical concepts. One source of these problems lies within the lexicons and syntaxes of the standard and technical language. This plays an important role within geometry. Especially here, the technical language often uses standard words in a different, a wider, or a more limited form than in the standard language. As a result, misunderstanding occurs between teachers and pupils. Fully absorbed by the geometrical context, the teacher often can no longer see the original meaning in the standard language.

For example, in German the following can be distinguished:

- A term has a vague meaning in standard language and the geometrical term can be abstracted from it only with difficulty, for example, *Ecke* (i.e., corner; in mathematics, angle). The same can be said about *Seite* ("page" [of a book] or "side" [of a house]; in mathematics, line segment or side [of a triangle]). Children may think of the page of a book and, therefore, a flat area, but not the "side" of a triangle!

---

[4]It is very well known that you only really understand something if you are able to explain it to someone else, that is, to verbalize it.

- Sometimes a word has a wider or a more limited meaning in geometry, for example, quadrangle, square, rectangle.
- The construction of sentences can be very peculiar, for example, *die Gerade* (the straight) instead of *die gerade Linie* (the straight line). Verbs are also used in ways that are different from their original meaning: *einen Kreis schlagen* (to beat a circle, i.e., to draw a circle with a compass) or *das Lot fällen* (to fell [in the sense of chop down] a perpendicular," i.e., to draw the perpendicular), and so on.
- The teacher and pupils talk in different contexts. The teacher has a mathematical point of view; the pupils are thinking of objects from their surroundings (see Maier, 1983; Pimm, 1987).

Verbal Activities in the Math Classroom

However independent a science might be, to teach it to others a standard language is required—as well as verbal interaction and communication. In terms of verbal activities, *speaking, listening, writing,* and *reading* have to be distinguished. In the traditional math classroom, these activities are divided between teacher and pupils as follows:[5]

1. *Speaking:* (a) *teacher:* exposition, questions to control understanding, instructions concerning organization, question-developing talk (teacher-guided inquiry), exam questions, instructions concerning disciplinary actions; (b) *pupil:* questions to teacher, answers to teacher's questions, informal talks between pupils, short answers to test questions.
2. *Listening:* As in #1, the other is listening.
3. *Writing:* (a) *teacher:* on blackboard (standard language), verbal remarks when correcting; (b) *pupil:* copying of items on blackboard (mainly formal language), making notes when teacher is explaining; informal activities (letters, crib note), homework.
4. *Reading:* (a) *teacher:* reading aloud a sentence to remember, individual reading of notes for lessons, reading pupils' written work; (b) *pupil:* reading in the schoolbook, problems.

Written activities traditionally take up a considerable time in the math classroom. It is obvious how little standard language is used during these verbal activities. Furthermore, the communication is usually single-tracked, or to the teacher only. If standard language is used, it is to give instructions or to organize things.

---

[5]These phenomena were intensely analyzed by Del Campo and Clements (1987).

The so-called word problems are one field of math that is said to be linked to reality and, therefore, represented in standard language.[6] In this case pupils have to translate from an everyday context into the mathematical context, with its formulas. The pupils always presume that the problem makes sense—an examination of so-called "captain-problems" demonstrated this (see Baruk, 1989). The pupils believe that numbers provide a link between the objects that do not go together without numbers, that is, sheep and the captain's age. The technical language of mathematics is consequently regarded as a linguistic phenomenon, although the pupils have to do a double translation when solving word problems. They must move the problem from an everyday life context into an appropriate mathematical context. Having solved this, they then have to translate the solution back into the original context. This second translation (the answer) is very often left out or forgotten (see Hughes, 1986).

Children know that word problems are nothing more than a vehicle to make them solve operations. The numbers are merely signals, intended to make them react. Where the standard language does have a meaning, it is ignored or not understood. The pupils experience mathematical language as a string that follows its own laws and view the standard language as nothing but wrapping.

Communication in the Math Classroom

There is a sense in which, in our culture, teaching is talking.

—Michael Stubbs

In Germany, teacher talk and question-developing talk are probably the most frequent forms of communication in the math classroom. But, according to Brousseau (1986), a real communicative situation is as follows:

Two partners A and B are needed (A or B can also be a group of individuals; B can also be a machine). B has to fulfill a task, but does not have enough information to do so. A has this information, but does not want to complete the task himself. In order to enable B to solve this problem, A has to communicate the necessary information in form of a message (oral or written). B's success depends on the quality of the information.

In this situation language functions in a "message oriented" way (see Brown, 1982; Pimm, 1987). In message-oriented speech, the speaker has a goal and wants to express/pass on information in order to change a listener's state of knowledge. It is of great importance that the listener understands correctly

---

[6]Their "real" connection with reality cannot be discussed here. But see Winter (1985) and Baruk (1989).

(see Laborde, 1990). In the math classroom, this form of speech is found when the teacher is talking to the pupils.

As opposed to message-oriented speech, Brown (1982) talked about *listener-oriented speech*. In listener-oriented speech, a slow mode of speech, with many pauses, is typical; the speech is broken into chunks. Only one thing is said about a referent at any one time. The relationship between the chunks is rarely marked syntactically. The *listener* is expected to know the context.

In the classroom, listener-oriented speech is usually seen as pupils address the teacher. The explanation for the role of this kind of speech might be that the pupils do not have to explain anything the teacher does not already know.[7] Message-oriented speech is much more difficult than listener-oriented speech in that it requires precise expressions and a complicated syntax. *The mathematical technical language is message oriented, but such a language is not part of everyday life.*

In order to understand further patterns of communication in the math classroom, I investigated two transcripts of lessons. In general these transcripts indicate little verbal interaction between the pupils themselves (particularly about mathematics). Much of the interaction is led by the teacher talking and questioning.

The first example is a classic (and very typical) text, part of Plato's dialogue to Meno (see Pimm, 1987):

Socrates: Tell me, boy, do you know that a figure like this is a square?

Boy: I do.

Socrates: And you know that a square figure has these four lines equal?

Boy: Certainly.

Socrates: And these lines that I have drawn through the middle of the square are also equal?

Boy: Yes.

Socrates: And don't you agree that such a figure might also be bigger or smaller?

Boy: Certainly.

In this manner the dialogue continues over several more pages. There is a specific term, *Mäeutik,* for Plato's technique, the method of insight by asking questions in a dialogue. This method has become the model for question-developing teacher–pupil talk (teacher-guided inquiry). Maybe because of its classic background it is sacrosanct. The teacher's domination and control over language is obvious. The only thing the pupil can do is agree or give a *one*-word answer; nothing else is necessary or wanted.

---

[7]See also the transcript of the math lesson described later.

This also becomes quite clear in the transcript from 1987 (see Pimm, 1987). The pupils also mainly give one-word answers to the teacher's questions. The teacher's agreement is mainly expressed as a repetition of the word itself (teacher echo!) put into a complete sentence, or in a different formulation of the same contents. Then the teacher's monologue continues as if this exchange, this interruption, had not happened at all. At this stage the reader of the manuscript is reminded of a play (maybe by Harold Pinter or Samuel Beckett?), as Pimm (1987) stated correctly. Every once in a while the teacher is given a word from the prompter (pupil) during his performance! Of course this kind of asking does have the advantage that the teacher is always in control of the dialogue. It is a teacher talk—which is sometimes interrupted to find out whether the pupils understand. The danger of the whole thing developing into a "guess-what-is-the-particular-word-in-my-mind" is high (see also Pimm, 1987).

This is an artificial communicative situation in that the teacher is asking the questions, although she is not the one who either wants to know or learn something new. She already knows the answer, as the pupils well know. Motivation to communicate cannot be expected from the pupils. As a whole, two-track communication rarely happens in the math classroom. If it does, it takes place between teacher and pupil, but not between the pupils themselves.

Who Is "We" in Mathematics? "We," which I mentioned earlier, deserves special attention. In the math classroom it can hardly be interpreted as "an agonized cry for group identity in the face of an uncomprehending world" (Pimm, 1984, p. 40).

It is quite obvious how ambiguously *we* is used in the transcript presented next—by the teacher as well as by the pupils. If it were the standard use of the personal pronoun in the plural form, then the usage was simply wrong. Therefore, it must have a pragmatic function. When the teacher says: "So what do *we* do then? *We* go to the . . . ," the teacher actually means "That's the way we do it here and no other way." In other words, *we* represents a convention, which is perfectly well understood by the students. The teacher's domination is expressed in an indirect way. It would seem that the pupils have equal rights to talk, but they know and understand very well what is really meant. *We* is a convention used to express what has to be done here and now! Although *all* of the pupils might be drawing a triangle without a ruler, the teacher can say "*We* are drawing with a ruler!"

Another message underlying *we* is the one of uniformity and adaptation to the group. In the math classroom we all do it the same way; there is only one way and one solution. Beyond this there lies a certain view of math and of teaching.

Transcript of a Lesson

Problem: 26 – 17 = □ (10-year-old pupils, Grade 4)

Teacher (T): Can you get out your workbook please, I want to do some of those take-aways with you now . . . Don't disturb . . . people please. Now, we got up to these two, didn't we.

Pupil (P): Yes.

T: Right, can you remember? OK, you . . . you start it off and tell me what you are doing.

P: Put one there.

T: No. Lets start from the very beginning. Six take away seven. Can you do it?

P: No.

T: No. Why can't you do it?

P: 'Cause it's . . . a bigger number on the bottom.

T: Alright. Because six is smaller than seven. Alright? So what do we do then? We go to the . . .

P: The . . . the units.

T: No. What column's that? The ten's column. Right. And what do we do there?

P: We cross that one out . . . and then we put one there.

T: We take a . . .

P: Er . . . er . . . er . . .

T: We take a . . . What do we take from the ten's column? We take a ten, don't we. One ten. All right, take one ten from the ten's column.

P: Put one there.

T: Yes, you've got one left there. And where do you put the ten you've taken?

P: There.

T: You put them in the unit's column, right. How many units have you got?

P: Twenty-six.

T: No. Put your ten in the unit's column. No. No. Come on, you go to the unit's column and you take a ten.[8] Where do you put the ten? We put it in the . . . unit's column, don't we. Like we did there, and there, and there, and there. Now how many units have you got there in the unit's column now?

---

[8]See Pimm (1987). As a matter of fact, the teacher's statement is wrong. The tens can be taken only from the tens' column and not from the units' column. Whether this is to be looked at as a slip of the tongue or whether the teacher is already as confused as the pupil cannot be decided here. The whole explanation of the teacher is incorrect, as in subtraction the tens are being added.

P: Sixteen.

T: Do you know where they came from?

P: Tens . . . and six.

T: Yes . . . How many units in a ten? How many units in a ten?

P: Sixteen.

T: No. (To another child) Can you pass me a ten block, and ten singles as well? . . . And ten single units please. No, go and get me ten single units as well.

P: (Another pupil, almost inaudible) . . . chocolate.

T: Pardon?

P: (Same pupil) . . . Shall I tidy it up?

T: No! Get on with your sums. We tidy up at the end, don't we.

Steps to Improvement in the Sense of Mathematics Teaching

In his play *La leçon,* the French playwright Eugène Ionesco (1954) described the characteristics of a typical lesson. The communication between teacher and pupil causes the professor to kill his girl student. Ionesco wanted to show that it is impossible for human beings to have meaningful communication. But at the same time, the play can also be interpreted as saying that a successful lesson can take place only on the basis of meaningful communication. Communicative problems in the math classroom might be caused by lack of abilities and capabilities on the pupils' side. However, as shown earlier, such difficulties are far more connected to mistakes in the technical run of communication and to lack of motivation.

"Mathematics and language" was a popular subject in the didactics of the 1970s and 1980s. Austin and Howson's and Ellerton's projects from the 1970s must be mentioned. And the Nuffield Mathematics Project in England showed a special interest in language and doing. The materials provided, for example, the *Green Set* (1969) and *Red Set* (1970), are good examples of this.

Later there was a change of direction, to a focus on teaching itself. In the late 1970s, the IOWO materials developed at the University of Utrecht were tried out in the Netherlands with Hans Freudenthal as director of the project supervisor (*Five Years IOWO,* 1976). In addition to the independent discoveries made by the pupils themselves, the IOWO curriculum concentrated on their individual verbal expression. Carraher, Lave, McBride, and Pimm have to be mentioned as well. Most of the research was done in England, the United States, and Australia. Apart from the work of Bauersfeld, interest in this question in Germany has increased only recently. (Much of the research in this area deals with second-language acquisition and the learning of mathematics in a foreign language. This is an aspect that has to be neglected in this chapter.)

In the 1980s, interaction *between* pupils was of main interest (Uyemura-Stevenson, Pirie and Schwarzenberger, Laborde). One direction—writing in the math classroom—has been very strong in Australia and some research has been done on it within the BLIPS-Project (see Ellerton & Clements, 1991). Recently there has been, once again, a new move toward reformation within mathematical Didaktik. One important representative is the French Freinet pedagogue, Paul Le Bohec, with his theory about mathematical creations. For him the pupils' language and the writing of texts in mathematics play a key role.[9] He shared his opinion with the Swiss researchers Gallin and Ruf. They examined learning strategies that "prove the sufficiency of standard language to represent technical contents without any problems" (Garlichs & Hagstedt, 1991, p. 103). For the teaching of mathematics, they concluded that: "In communication with individual pupils it is not the technical language which gives the base for teaching, but the pupils' individual languages. Now it is the teacher who has to try to understand, and no longer the pupil" (p. 103). This demands a lot from the teacher!

At the same time, this approach totally denies the importance of symbols for mathematics as a science. Modern Didaktik of mathematics starts off from a child-adequate, gradual approach to a moderate bilingualism (standard and technical language); the teacher has to lead pupils through these two languages and help them translate them, like an interpreter (see also Garlichs & Hagstedt, 1991). On one hand, the different use of *terms* in standard and technical language has to be taught, with clear distinctions made. But, most of all, *communication* in the math classroom has to be reinforced and increased. More communication is simply not enough. Pupils' message-oriented speech has to be increased; true motives for communication have to be created—and they must be really motivating for the pupils. The speech has to refer to a task or a goal. The pupils have to know and to understand *why* they have to speak. Grevsmühl and Storbeck (1989) pointed out that there are many occasions for this, for example, at the beginning of a lesson as a kind of verbal repetition of the contents of the previous lesson, during the lesson to find out about the actual knowledge of the pupils, and at the end of a lesson to repeat or summarize the most important issues of the lesson.

Del Campo and Clements (1987; see also Ellerton & Clements, 1991) found that receptive modes of communication dominate the teaching of mathematics. To increase pupils' expressive language use, they suggested *speaking* instead of *listening* as the spoken language mode. (Grevsmühl & Storbeck's, 1989, suggestion could be of use here as well as pupil talks and

---

[9]His *Le texte libre mathématique* will be published soon.

message-oriented speech.) For the written mode, they suggested *writing* instead of *reading.*[10] For the pictorial mode, Del Campo and Clements demanded more *drawing* instead of interpreting pictures and diagrams; for the active mode, more *performing* than interpreting other's activities. Other suggestions for the communicative math classroom include free construction at material stations and the documentation of these constructions. All four of the verbal modes are included in such work as well as message-oriented speech. The message game is similar. The pupils have to describe objects or mathematical contents to each other, orally or in writing.

The ability to communicate includes knowledge of how language is used in different social contexts. Communication is the exchange of information and of contents. In both communication-oriented language teaching and communication-oriented mathematics teaching, the pupils who are supposed to talk to each other have to *want* to express some contents. Therefore, private experiences and interests, emotional relations to numbers and calculations, and so on, always have to be included in the communication. The contents of communication should never fall a victim to formalism.[11]

The examples mentioned previously are very motivating for communication, especially interaction between pupils themselves. (This is of social importance as well.) In the following part of this chapter, I describe my attempts to test these ideas in the math classroom.

PRACTICAL PART: PEDAGOGICAL CONTENT ANALYSIS AND DIDAKTIK ANALYSIS[12]

Subject of the Unit

This is not a standard unit with the lessons built on each other but, rather, it is a collection of single lessons with different contents (mainly geometry).

---

[10]Le Bohac's idea of a learning diary, which pupils keeps like a travel diary, might be interesting here. Pupils document their progress in learning and make clear to their teacher how they have dealt with a problem. The production of their own math book, where they note vocabularies and sentences, seems helpful. To increase interaction between pupils, the writing of letters makes sense. The children describe objects that the "pen friend" has to draw or build to each other. A letter to a sick classmate to "teach" missed material is a perfect real writing situation. See Garlichs and Hagstedt (1991).

[11]How close numbers and emotions are linked for children is shown by their way of explaining their favorite numbers: house number, age of their mother or a friend, date of birth, and so on.

[12]The "practical" section of this chapter is structured according to an unwritten law that generations of German student teachers have followed in their Second State Examination thesis. Some terms were difficult to translate into English and might therefore seem strange.

From a Didaktik point of view the main purpose of these lessons is to improve oral and written communication in the primary math classroom.

Analysis of Conditions

In Class 3c, there are 10 girls and 14 boys. I have been teaching this group in math and social science for 5 hours a week since August 1992. Originally, the children were from two different groups that had been brought together. For the first few months, the origins of the class were quite noticeable in the behavior of some of the boys, but now it is difficult to tell who belonged to which class.

In general the children are highly motivated. One boy is mentally absent quite a lot of the time. He often forgets his books and does not perform well in any subject. Three girls and two boys have exceptional skills in verbal expression. Two of these girls have had moderate success in arithmetic, but in geometry they show great interest and insight. The other three perform well in all fields of mathematics.

According to the principal, all of the other children are more or less "average" in German literacy. Some have great problems with spelling. Four pupils grew up bilingual, but in each case German is the dominant language.

At the beginning of the school year, the children still had great difficulties working in small groups and in solving problems on their own. Now they are more and more capable of doing this. According to Piaget, 7- to 11-year-old children (children in Grade 3 belong to this group) are in the so-called "stage of concrete operations." They are capable of thinking in a quite abstract way, but they are still in need of concrete materials as aids for orientation. Although such a generalized view has to be handled carefully, in its basic structure it does apply to the pupils of Class 3c. They are still very childlike and need to play a lot. They have a strong urge to physical activity and to verbal exchange with their neighbors. Therefore they have a need for communication.

This stage of development also means that the pupils still need to visualize concrete materials to help them express their thoughts verbally. They have to duplicate their verbalized thoughts by doing. However, some boys and girls in this class are already very capable of thinking in an abstract way, without the aid of any concrete materials.

Reasons[13]

> *Reasons for the "subject": What does the planned topic exemplify, represent, or typify? Where can the knowledge to be gained be picked up and utilized— insights, conceptions, work methods, techniques?*

---
[13]The general relevance of the theme is based on the earlier theoretical discussion.

Together with the other subjects taught in primary level, math is part of the children's development and education. Mathematics "form[s] competence and behavior. On this basis the pupil can experience the applicability of mathematics in real-life situations" (Senatsverwaltung für Schule, Berufsbildung und Sport, 1988, p. 1).

School also has a general educational purpose: to educate the children to be responsible and, therefore, critical beings. However, responsibility is possible in this world only with an active and a passive communicative competence in all fields of life. And, as the fields of life are more and more mathematized, mathematics has to be considered in a special way over and above the requirement of "each subject to develop speech and verbal competence" (Senatsverwaltung für Schule, Berufsbildung und Sport, 1989, pp. 1, 9). "Speech acts, name things from your surroundings exactly, ask for things you did not understand, express spatial and time relations verbally," and talk to partners are themes from the curriculum for German literacy. In math they are of interdisciplinary importance.

Reasons for the themes: What situations and tasks are appropriate for helping the principle grasped to become a real benefit to the pupils?

For Didaktik reasons, I decided against a unit with a single subject-matter focus. I am sure some such models could have been developed on, for example, symmetry, but they would not have been exemplary and would make transfer to other areas difficult for the pupils. They would have connected an increase in communication with *this* subject matter only. A general change can happen only gradually, a process that takes more than seven to nine lessons.

The role, importance, and difficulties of problem solving have been written about extensively. The children of Class 3c are already familiar with writing their own problems. Therefore the communicative situations have been chosen mainly from geometry. Language and doing can easily be combined in this field.

Conceptualization Underlying the "Unit"

Long-Term Goal: Improvement of Mathematical Understanding. Following my theoretical outline, I set the goal of improving the communicative situation in Class 3c in order to achieve a better understanding of math on a long-term base.

Main Goal: Practice Message-Oriented Speech. The improvement of communicative competence is a long-term process. The main goal was the pupils' understanding that there are two languages in mathematics, "my math" and "other people's math." Communication is possible only after consideration of the other's math. In order to reach this goal, the pupils have to practice message-oriented speech. There is also a social factor in that the pupils must try to understand other ways of thinking and, therefore, to understand the others themselves. In addition, at least some mathematical technical language and terminology and special characteristics have to be understood.

Subgoals. The pupils should:

- Be able to describe geometrical objects and patterns clearly and unequivocally.
- Practice putting themselves into someone else's perspective.
- Practice oral instructions.
- Practice written instructions.
- Practice drawing instructions.
- Practice listening carefully.
- Be able to follow an instruction (by doing, in writing or drawing).
- Understand the importance of an instruction being unambiguous.
- Recognize mathematical terminology as a help for clear and short explanations.

Didaktik Analysis—Some Notes

The possibility of changing verbal activities in the math classroom, and the Didaktik basis for this change, have already been discussed. This discussion does not need to be repeated here.

For the sequential order of the lessons, I thought it would make sense, first, to increase and practice oral communication and then move to written forms. The lessons all had a similar pattern and consisted of three main phases:

- The teacher gave, showed, or read instructions or other documentation in a group discussion in order to give the pupils an *orientation.* Consciousness of the *problem* needed to be awakened by this discussion so that the pupils approached the task with understanding.
- Afterwards, in all lessons, there was time for constructing, building, or calculating. All this activity was always combined with intense communication among the pupils themselves. The *interaction* was oral or written.
- At the end there was always a time for the pupils to talk together. They *verbalized* their problems and experiences and, therefore, digested what had happened and what they had been doing.

In the writing phases there was no emphasis on spelling as long as the text could be read and understood. Working in pairs guaranteed intensive exchange and active participation of all pupils.

I had the possibility of working with small groups. Because an increase in communication also means an increase in noise (which can be a problem in a group with 24 children), this was a great advantage. It was important to create a base that makes verbal activities an essential part of the math classroom. Attitudes toward mathematics should be changed by such a verbal emphasis; the seeming lack of ambiguity and sacrosanctity of math is to be thrown into doubt. Communication and strategies to solve problems had priority over mathematical contents.

Documentation and Analysis of Selected Lessons

Individual phases of three of the lessons in my unit are examined in the following discussion. I have selected one oral and one written lesson as well as one lesson that left the children space for their own decisions. These lessons showed communication with a special partner as well as with an unknown group of partners. The essential communicative phases are described and analyzed. It does not seem necessary to document here the whole lesson, in every detail and with every Didaktik decision. The content of each acquisition phase is briefly explained to make it easier to understand the analysis. For the last lesson, all of the previous lessons offered a kind of orientation.

Theme of the Lesson: Instruction to Build a Tower of Building Blocks (Lesson No. 3)

Intentions of the Lesson

Long-Term Goal.   The pupils will improve their oral communicative competence (speaking and listening).

Goal of the Lesson.   The pupils will be able to give their partners clear oral instructions for rebuilding a tower they have built.

Acquisition Phase.   The children worked in pairs and sat behind each other at their tables. The partner sitting in the back built a tower out of blocks. This partner described it to the other partner, who then had to rebuild it with his or her own blocks.

Didaktik Analysis—Some Notes.   The material itself was very motivating for the pupils. They used only cubic blocks of the same size to limit the difficulties with the instructions. One pupil in every pair described his or her tower to a partner. Each partner could hear, without being able to see the tower itself. The speaker had the object in direct view and could visually verify the instructions being given. The speaker could change or simplify the construction when the tower was too hard to describe. The seating arrangement also obviated the confusion of *left* and *right/front* and *back* that would have occurred if the partners faced each other. Working in pairs allowed for intense verbal exchange. Each pupil could speak, and many pupils could speak at the same time without this being a nuisance. The partners' proximity did not make it necessary to speak loudly.

Comparison of the objects was direct as the original was behind the rebuilder. It was important that the plan for the tower not be given by the teacher and that the towers be constructed by individual pupils. The teacher was no longer the manager who decided right or wrong. The pupils themselves could and must control, help, and advise each other.

Analysis of the Lesson. The pupils started with lots of enthusiasm. The material and instruction had the intended motivating effect. In comparing their objects, they noticed where they had to be more clear and precise. They improved each time. At first they built very complicated towers, later easier ones as they realized how hard their complicated constructions were to describe clearly. They used the opportunity of self-differentiation. This showed how closely doing and thinking were still linked in these children.

In their description of the towers, many pupils used comparisons with real objects (stairs, pyramids), but then they developed other strategies for description. They counted the number of blocks used or went step by step. Some pupils constructed their own towers while describing them. The parallel run of building and speaking did help them to verbalize their actions. This also highlighted the necessity of material to structure their thoughts.

Communication on math contents was intense. After the first trials the rebuilder was usually accused of having built it "wrong"; there then was a dispute over what was said and what was inferred. The pupils saw the difference between *my math* and the *other's math*. I was surprised by the children's strong wish to get it right. At first I was asked for help a few times, but most of the pupils came to realize that this time the teacher could not really help. (See Figs. 13.1 and 13.2.)

Theme of the Lesson: Letter With Description of a Pattern (Lesson No. 6)

Intentions of the Lesson

Long-Term Goal. The pupils will improve their competence in written communication.

Die roten und blauen und die grünen
bedeuten sie übernander sind

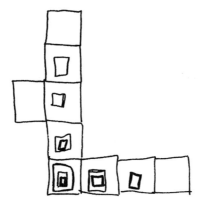

The red and the blue mean they are on top of each other.

FIG. 13.1. Tanja's solution.

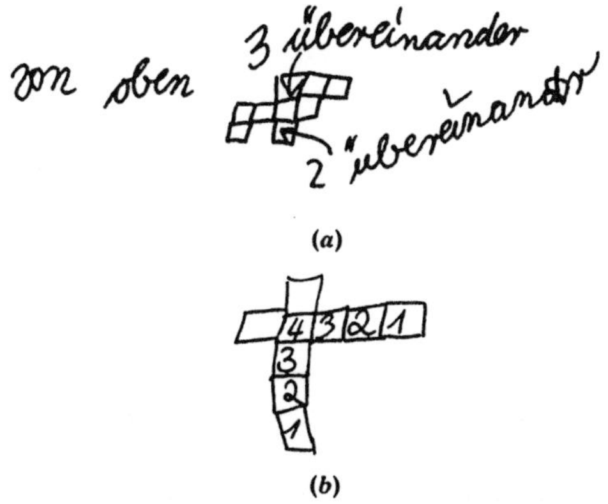

von oben
3 übereinander
2 übereinander
(a)
4 3 2 1
3
2
1
(b)

From above, 3 on top, 2 on top of each other.

FIG. 13.2. (a) Maxi's instruction and (b) Maxi's short version.

Goal of the Lesson. The pupils will be able to describe a particular pattern to a pen friend.

Acquisition Phase. Two pupils write a letter to each other. In this letter they describe a pattern they had been given by the teacher. After reading the letter, the reader had to be able to draw what it described.

Didaktik Analysis—Some Notes. In this lesson the pupils described, for the first time, a pattern in writing. A letter was regarded as very motivating: They knew who they were addressing it to and they could look forward to getting a letter themselves. This helped with communication through a medium (letter) and provided them with the motivation to engage with this time-consuming activity. All this letter writing was a real writing occasion.

For reasons of differentiation, the teacher had to decide who was to work together. For the same reasons, I distributed seven different patterns at different levels. In order to make it easier to describe the patterns, they consisted of only basic geometrical shapes (some were colored) that were all known to the children. It would have been possible for the children to invent their own patterns, but this would have made the process of writing even more time-consuming and difficult. For these reasons, I decided against such invention at this stage. The lesson had to be very well organized in the distribution of the material. The pupils had the whole of the lesson after the organization phase to design and write their letters and envelopes individually.

Analysis (I) of the Lesson. The pupils took the task of writing their letter very seriously and concentrated on the receiver of the letter when designing it. Some were not happy about their partner and at first refused to write at all. However, after a while, they joined into the others' enthusiasm. A few children worried about their spelling and asked me many questions; they nearly changed the problem, even though I kept telling them that the spelling was not that important. In the end, all the letters could be read without any problems. In this one lesson, I could sense the children's great satisfaction with the idea that someone was writing especially to them; the letter writing was even more motivating than I had thought it would be!

Analysis (II) of the Lesson. A second lesson followed. All the letters were distributed, the patterns were drawn and compared, and problems were discussed.

The partners were very proud when their results were correct. In such cases, assuming that the task was complete, they did not discuss it any further. (When the children regarded the problem as solved and finished with, there would not be any mathematical communication.) In other cases, as the children tried to resolve misunderstandings, the partners quoted from their letters to justify their solutions. In doing so, they recognized that the written instructions offered a documentation that did not exist with the oral instructions of the tower problem. In a few cases, there were actual mistakes in the instructions: One child wrote "triangle" instead of "rectangle." Another partner did not read the letter to the end.

One pupil summed it all up perfectly: "You have to write carefully, but you also have to read it carefully." Another pupil said, "Well, I always explain it to myself this way, but Phil cannot understand it like that. I have to explain it in a different way, more general and more with words from math." These remarks support the conclusion that the pupils had gradually started to understand the difference between *my math* and *your math*.

Communication on the math content was quite intense and motivation was high. However, there were problems with time organization: Some pupils wrote very slowly. After the letter writing, one pupil said that he had faxed his letter to his pen friend who was sick at home. The latter faxed back his answer pattern, a possibility from technology that, although it does not (so far) belong to everyday life, should not be ignored (see Figs. 13.3 and 13.4).

Theme of the Lesson: Instructions for Self-Constructed Geometrical Objects and Patterns (Lesson No. 8)

Intentions of the Lesson

Long-Term Goal. The pupils will improve their communicative competence in all modes.

Goal of the Lesson. The pupils will be able to describe a geometrical object/pattern they invented clearly and comprehensibly to their classmates.

Acquisition Phase. At four different tables, the pupils worked with various materials (building blocks, logic blocks, etc.). They had the choice of where they wanted to work and which materials they wanted to use. There was only one condition: They had to document their objects on the cards on the table. They had to prepare this documentation in such a way that their classmates could rebuild their object.

Didaktik Analysis—Some Notes. This lesson also had the goal of increasing verbal interaction between pupils (in pairs or groups) and improving communication through a medium (here written instructions). During the acquisition phase, the pupils deepened and practiced the experiences they had already had with oral and written instructions. Once again, the motivation lay in the material itself as well as in the freedom of choice around the object, the form of its documentation, and the social form they worked within. To avoid additional difficulties, I chose materials they already knew from other situations and were used to. They did not have to feel

Liebe Laura

waagerecht senkrecht

Du sollst 4 Kästchen waagerecht in einer Reihe malen. Links setzt du noch einen Kasten drauf Nach dem 2. linken Kästchen malst du noch einen unter dem 2. linken. Beim zweiten rechten Kasten tust du noch zwei Kästchen nach oben senkrecht Den ersten von den 4 Kästchen von links malst du rot danach blau grün und wieder blau. Über dem grünen Kasten ~~grün~~ blauen und grünen Neben dem roten ist ein blauer Kasten unter dem blauen ein grüner Kasten Über dem roten noch ein blauer.

Viel Spaß

Deine Janina (Nini)

Dear Laura

You have to draw 4 squares horizontally in a line. To the left you have to put another square on top. After the 2nd square you have to draw another one under the 2nd left one. On the 2nd from the left you must put two more squares on top vertical. The first of the 4 squares on the left you have to color in red after that blue then green then blue again.

Above the green square a blue one and a green one. Next to the red one a blue square under the blue square a green square. Above the red one is another blue one.

Have fun and many greetings.

Yours, Janina (Nina)

FIG. 13.3. Janina's letter.

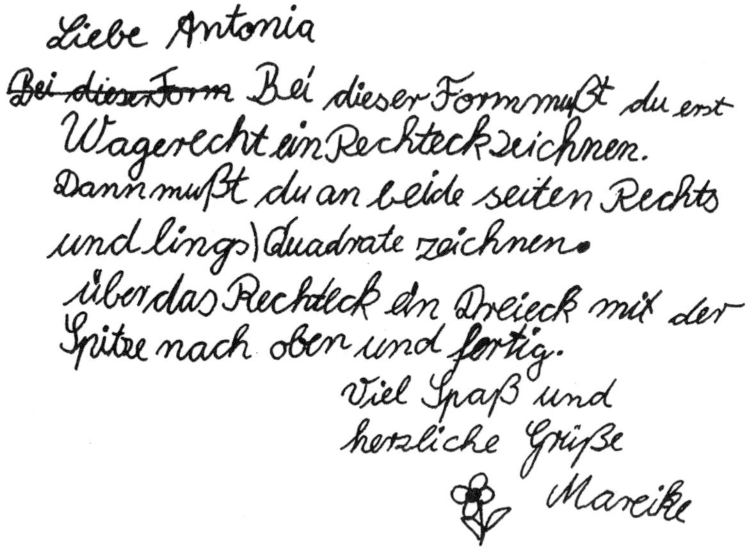
Liebe Antonia
~~Bei dieser Form~~ Bei dieser Form mußt du erst
Wagerecht ein Rechteck zeichnen.
Dann mußt du an beide seiten Rechts
und lings) Quadrate zeichnen.
über das Rechteck ein Dreieck mit der
Spitze nach oben und fertig.
Viel Spaß und
herzliche Grüße
Mareike

Dear Antonia

With this shape you first have to draw a rectangle horizontal. Then you have to draw a square on both sides (right and left) above the rectangle a triangle with the top upwards and finished. Have fun and many greetings.

Yours Mareike

FIG. 13.4. Mareike's letter.

insecure due to the strangeness of the material. The various possibilities were limited to three to avoid the choice itself becoming the theme of the lesson. In order to give direction to the children within this freedom, they were restricted to going to one other table once they had documented their object.

After making their object, the children destroyed it and only the documentation (drawing or text) remained. This documentation replaced the original and, therefore, had to be extremely precise, clear, and effective. But these are the characteristics of mathematical language itself.

The pupils differentiated themselves in various ways. They chose the social form and the material, depending on their preferences. When they realized that an object was too difficult to describe, they made it simpler. As the pupils worked with the materials, they thought about how to capture its structures in a drawing or text in a way that it was clear to their classmates. Doing, thinking, and language were undoubtedly linked here. They could profit from their previous experiences: They knew where, and how, their earlier partners had had difficulties and where they had had some themselves.

Analysis (II) of the Lesson. Even more than the material itself, the freedom this lesson offered was a great motivation. The pupils were very busy building, and they showed a lot of fantasy. It was interesting that they mainly chose to work by themselves when constructing. However, they had made earlier agreements with friends: "You try mine and I'll try yours."

In the case of many of the boys, I noticed that they started off with a big project, used nearly all the building blocks on the table, but then reduced the scale of their construction drastically when faced with the problems of documenting it. Maybe the temptation of the material was so strong that it made them forget their experiences from previous lessons. Other children chose the simplest solution of drawing a pattern, or even tracing the outer lines. But then they built more difficult objects and described them in writing. The pupils did not always choose the easiest way, but they also showed self-direction—without the teacher's pressure.

The atmosphere in the classroom was very relaxed and calm. The exchange between the pupils was very intense. I was rarely asked for help. Originally I had planned the lesson to have two phases (a documentation phase and a rebuilding phase), but this turned out to be unrealistic. The children started to rebuild when they were ready, and sometimes even went back to the documentation phase to try out different materials. No time was wasted with waiting at the tables.

Evaluation

> *Mathematik müßte so allgemein gemacht werden wie die Muttersprache: wir müßten lernen, in ihr zu leben, wahrzunehmen, zu denken, zu kommunizieren. . . . Wir müßten die Mathematik . . . entzaubern.*
>
> —Hentig (1972)

> *Mathematics should be made as general as the mother tongue: we should learn to live in it, perceive in it, think in it, communicate in it . . . we should de-mystify math.*

The suggestions found in the literature discussed in the theoretical part of this chapter proved realizable and meaningful in the lessons described previously. But real "success" can show only on a long-term basis, and is not measurable in the common sense of the word. Here I can only describe my observations and offer some conclusions based on the children's work.

All the lessons had a very relaxed and calm atmosphere. I had plenty of opportunity to observe and recognize, and then attend to individual problems.[14] The pupils did have communicative contact in different modes. They documented objects and patterns, both in writing and orally, for their classmates and practiced message-oriented speech. They documented their solutions in words, in words and symbols, or in drawings. The appropriateness of the documentation, that is, its readability, was evaluated in comparison and discussion with their partners.

However, there were situations where no mathematical communication took place. The main reason for this was that some tasks could be solved without communication. Some pupils also found a specific task to be too difficult and, therefore, they had a learning block. There were social problems as well, for example, when two children could not stand each other and did not want to work together.

The class discussion that took place at the end of each lesson proved very important. It gave a general meaning to all the observations, discoveries, difficulties, and questions. It also provided transfer between individual efforts to find symbols and the technical conventions. In these discussions the pupils gave each other hints and advice, and talked about the strategies they had developed.

The statements of some pupils seemed to show that a change of mind as well as some insight into the structures of mathematical language and the nature of mathematics had started to take place:

You have to say everything. I am not inside your head. . . .

You have to say it the way it is and not how you think it is. . . .

I do not understand what you mean. You have to say it in such a way that I can mean it that way as well. . . .

If you explain that, then you have to talk more in general, more like a mathematician. When I use these math words then everyone knows them and understands them, for example, rectangle. . . .

---

[14]A gender-specific observation was so obvious that it should be mentioned. The boys were very quick with oral formulations, but these were often neither precise nor well reflected. The girls worked far more slowly, but more precisely and exactly. The same can be said about the written phases: In general the girls worked far more accurately and decorated their documentation. In reading/decoding/listening they kept precisely to the instructions and laid/built/drew in the ways that were spelled out. From the beginning, the boys argued, asked questions, or even questioned the whole plan.

In this chapter I cannot evaluate these differences in behavior or explore their consequences for teaching. But there seem to be parallels in what was observed here to descriptions in studies on "girls and mathematics." See Srocke (1989) where a detailed listing of further literature on this subject can be found.

With these statements the pupils show that they have become aware—maybe unconsciously—that there is a difference between "*my understanding*" and "*other's understanding*" of mathematics, that, just as in everyday life, there are two languages in mathematics, and that in explanations and descriptions the *other's mathematics* has always to be included to make things clear and unambiguous.

In addition to these statements, quoted from memory, a few written and visual examples are presented. Tanja used a graphic representation as solution (see Fig. 13.1). She even invented her own symbols (colors), which she explained in words. This is a very mathematical way of doing it that anyone can understand.

Maxi (see Fig. 13.2a) used words and symbols as well. He used the words to explain his symbols and, therefore, his individual symbol convention. He also gave a hint of perspective, "from above."

In Maxi's second attempt (see Fig. 13.2b), he assumed his symbol convention was understood and used nothing but symbols (numbers). He gained a very short and brief representation with the necessary minimum of information. He used a typical mathematical approach—making conventions and applying them subsequently.

Janina (see Fig. 13.3) explained mainly in words, using the medium of the letter. She described very precisely, step by step: First she explained the shapes, then the colors; in her legend she also explained the technical terms (horizontal and vertical) she used in the text. She put herself into Laura's role and tried, by this information, to minimize difficulties and misunderstandings.

Mareike (see Fig. 13.4) wrote very exactly in words only. She gave very precise positions to exclude misunderstandings ("on both sides," "left and right"). She was aware of the fact that in the language of everyday life there is usually only a right side and a left side, whereas in the technical language of math there are also upper and lower sides (e.g., of rectangles).

All these examples show that the pupils were very much aware of the fact that they were drawing or writing for a communication partner who needed all the information available and that they had, therefore, to use message-oriented speech. They tried to put themselves into their partner's position and, to avoid misunderstandings, they showed sensitivity to their partner's potential problems. This suggests that the pupils did realize that the use of mathematical technical language is a help to clear and precise expression. But they showed that they were also aware of potential difficulties and, to prevent problems, they explained their technical terms. Symbols or logograms, as aids for clear representation, were also used. In other words, the children did use technical mathematical language within the limitations of their knowledge and understanding. Because of this fact, and as a result of the observations made during the oral communicative phases (which unfortunately could not be documented within the limited frame of this thesis), the main goals outlined earlier can be said to have been "fulfilled/reached." Communicative competence around math content has been improved. The children learned to distinguish two parts of the mathematical language: *my math* and *other people's math*.

The pupils realized the meaning, use, and necessity and, therefore, the essence of message-oriented speech. They even managed to use message-oriented speech in their own oral and written communications. They showed understanding of the essence of mathematics and its characteristics, *efficiency* and *clarity*. They have come some way in the improvement of their mathematical competence.

The children were very eager to learn during this unit. They stressed several times how much fun they had in these lessons and also mentioned this in their final letters to the teacher. We can conclude that many children changed their attitude toward mathematics in a positive way—which should have an impact on their mathematical competence. But whether the long-term goal of enhanced competence was reached cannot be decided here; but the beginning shown here does allow a positive hope. I can only express my wish/aim to continue teaching in this way and to try out further ideas, for example, learning diaries, stories, invention of mathematical games, and so on.[15]

ACKNOWLEDGMENT

This chapter was first published in the *Journal of Curriculum Studies* and is reprinted by permission of the copyright holder, Taylor & Francis Ltd., London.

REFERENCES

Baruk, S. (1989). *Wie alt ist der Kapitän? Über den Irrtum in der Mathematik.* Basel: Birkhäuser.

Brousseau, G. (1986). Fondements et methodes de la didactique des mathématiques. *Recherches en Didactique des Mathématiques, 7*(2), 33–115 .

Brown, G. (1982). The spoken language. In R. Carter (Ed.), *Linguistics and the teacher* (pp. 75–87). London: Routledge & Kegan Paul.

---

[15]When there are children in the classroom who speak German as a foreign language, the problems are different. In that case, nonverbal communication has to be considered—although this is already present in a hidden way in the pictorial representations (drawings). But this is message-oriented speech. A and B contact each other, but independent in time and language. Therefore a new dimension arises.

Del Campo, G., & Clements, M. A. (1987, July). *Children hearing, watching, reading, writing, talking, drawing, imagining, acting out, practising and creating mathematics.* Paper presented at the Tenth Annual Conference of the Mathematics Education Research Group of Australasia, Townsville, Australia.

Ellerton, N. F., & Clements, M. A. (1991). *Mathematics in language: A review of language factors in mathematics learning.* Geelong, Australia: Deakin University.

Five Years IOWO (1976). *On Freudenthal's retirement. IOWO snapshots.* Reprinted from *Educational Studies in Mathematics, 3*(7).

Garlichs, A., & Hagstedt, H. (1991). Mathematik als erste Fremdsprache? In H. Postel, A. Kirsch, & W. Blum (Eds.), *Mathematik lehren und lernen: Festschrift für Heinz Griesel* (pp. 102–112). Hanover: Schroedel, Schulbuchverlag.

Grevsmühl, U., & Storbeck, C. (1989). Kommunikation im Mathematikunterricht: Hindern wir unsere Schüler am Sprechen? *Die Grundschule, 12,* 11–13.

Hughes, M. (1986). *Children and number: Difficulties in learning mathematics.* Oxford, England: Blackwell.

Ionesco, E. (1954). La leçon. In E. Ionesco, *Theatre I* (pp. 57–93). Paris: Gallimard.

Laborde, C. (1981). Besondere Aspekte der Kommunikation im Mathematikunterricht. *Osnabrücker Schriften zur Mathematik: Reihe P: Preprints* (No. 35). Osnabrück: Universität Osnabrück, Fachbereich Mathematik.

Laborde, C. (1990). Language and mathematics. In P. Nesher & J. Kilpatrick (Eds.), *Mathematics and cognition: A research synthesis by the International Group for the Psychology of Mathematics Education* (pp. 53–69). Cambridge, England: Cambridge University Press.

Maier, H. (1983). Zum Problem der Sprache im Mathematikunterricht. *Beiträge zum Mathematikunterricht, 1983: Vorträge auf der 17. Bundestagung für Didaktik der Mathematik* (pp. 30–39). Hanover: Schroedel.

Nuffield Mathematics Project. (1969). *Problems—Green set.* New York: Wiley.

Nuffield Mathematics Project. (1970). *Problems—Red set.* New York: Wiley.

Pimm, D. (1984). Who is "we"? *Mathematics Teaching, 107,* 39–42.

Pimm, D. (1987). *Speaking mathematically: Communication in mathematics classrooms.* London: Routledge & Kegan Paul.

Senatsverwaltung für Schule, Berufsbildung und Sport. (1988). *Vorläufiger Rahmenplan für Unterricht und Erziehung in der Berliner Schule: Grundschule Klasse 1 bis 6: Fach Mathematik.* Berlin: Senatsdrucksache.

Senatsverwaltung für Schule, Berufsbildung und Sport. (1989). *Vorläufiger Rahmenplan für Unterricht und Erziehung in der Berliner Schule: Grundschule Klasse 1 bis 6: Fach Deutsch.* Berlin: Senatsdrucksache.

Srocke, B. (1989). *Mädchen und Mathematik: historisch-systematische Untersuchung der unterschiedlichen Bedingungen des Mathematiklernens von Mädchen und Jungen* (E. C. Wittman, Ed.). Wiesbaden: Deutscher Universitäts Verlag.

Vygotsky, L. S. (1962). *Thought and language.* Cambridge MA: MIT Press.

Whorf, B. (1964). *Language, thought and reality.* Cambridge, MA: MIT Press.

Winter, H. (1985). *Sachrechnen in der Grundschule: Problematik des Sachrechnens: Funktionen des Rechnens: Unterrichtsprojekte.* Bielefeld: Cornelsen.

14

Reflecting as a Didaktik Construction: Speaking About Mathematics in the Mathematics Classroom

Michael Neubrand

Michael Neubrand is a professor of the Didaktik of mathematics at the Bildungs-wissenschaftliche Hochschule Flensburg, Flensburg (Germany).

A key issue in modern mathematics teaching at all levels of schooling is captured by Lacampagne's (1993) assertion that "Mathematical discussion should be a daily part of classroom activity!" (p. 7). However, this demand produces a number of basic questions that raise very fundamental considerations for *Didaktik der Mathematik,* the Didaktik of mathematics, with its focus on hermeneutic approaches, epistemological embedding, and structuralist thinking. There are questions about:

- *The content of the discourse:* What is possible when we try to reflect on mathematics in the classroom? What are the most appropriate ways of speaking about mathematics? Do we have a broad range of possibilities for such reflection and discourse?

- *The personal interests and capabilities of the students:* What are they able to do? What are they able to capture? What can be transformed into simpler questions without losing its authenticity—and how can this problem be dealt with (see Kirsch, chap. 15, this volume)?

- *The overall structure of the lessons:* What setting is appropriate for such discourse? Are there methods to facilitate it? What is the role of the teacher in such discourse?

The examples of classroom "speaking" we consider later show that even in lower level classes, say Grades 7, 8, or 9, there are many appropriate opportunities for addressing real questions that reflect these issues: We *can* ask How does mathematics proceed? What is mathematics all about? Are there specific ways of problem solving in mathematics? How should one behave when working mathematically? and so forth. In a sense, our argument responds to some of the observations by Schoenfeld (1988) that show that the failure of mathematics teaching is often caused by perspectives that lose the inner sense of the mathematics being treated in the classroom.

In the German tradition of Didaktik thinking, we emphasize a more general content for discussion in the classroom when compared to, for example, Lampert's (1988) description of American classroom discourse, which is more oriented toward discussions on and about problems. There is, however, some similarity with the recent article of Cobb, Boufi, McClain, and Whitenack (1997)—but also a different focus: We do not seek to make assertions about the individual or about the social processes in the classroom. We focus on the potential for reflective discourses of particular elementary subjects. Cobb et al. pointed out, as we do, that awareness by the teacher of the reflective potential of a task is a condition for initiating "shifts in the discourse" (p. 269) toward collective reflection.

It is just such an awareness we try to foster by Didaktik analyses and constructions. Our approach picks up Steiner's (1987) prescription for a "reflection-oriented teaching" which, in turn, addresses the core questions of Didaktik; that is, what is or could be the meaning, the sense, and the context of the topic to be taught? However, this prescription is often not realized in classrooms, despite the concrete possibilities that are there for teachers. Maybe this failure highlights the fact that a teacher's preparation has to be more mindful of the inherent potential of a topic rather than immediately looking for smooth access (cf. Senn-Fennell, chap. 13, and Hopmann, chap. 11, both this volume).

I argue in this chapter that learning and reflecting are the two sides of one coin. However, the two apparent contradictions in this combination of learning and reflecting must be addressed immediately. On the one hand, there is a tension between learning and reflecting, which may be hidden by the word *and*. Does this *and* mean that one first learns, then reflects? Or is it possible to learn *and* reflect? We suggest—and this is explored later in greater detail—that reflection is inherent in every learning process and vice versa; that is, reflections without a sound basis of learned and available knowledge will be empty. On the other hand, there is a second problem: Is it possible to *teach* a student to reflect? In a strict sense, it is, of course, impossible. Reflecting is always a very personal task of the learner herself; that is, it is her own responsibility. But teachers can provide *opportunities* and the *stimulation* for reflection. We give examples for realizing this later in this chapter.

This chapter, therefore, explores a twofold tension: the tension between learning and reflecting and their mutual influences, and the tension between a reflection-oriented learning process and the teachers' various tasks in the class. We can indicate these tensions in a diagram:

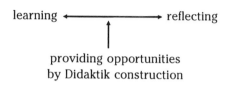

learning ⟷ reflecting

providing opportunities
by Didaktik construction

The structure of this chapter is as follows: In the first part, reasons are given for why reflection is indispensable for the learning process. In this part various aspects of the concept of reflection are described; we proceed from general reasons to reasons decisively dependent on the content. In the second part, we concentrate on the concept of reflection in the mathematics classroom. Reflection-oriented teaching and learning can be realized as "speaking about mathematics" at several levels. The third part is devoted to a collection of examples, stemming from the areas of geometry and arithmetic. The examples are drawn from German syllabi and from experience in teacher education. It should be possible for the reader to transfer them to other classroom situations. The topics are classical in the sense that they belong to the core curriculum in mathematics. Some concluding remarks try to connect the ideas about reflections with other topics in mathematical Didaktik.

THE NECESSITY OF REFLECTION DURING THE LEARNING PROCESS

Although no one might doubt the necessity for reflection in any learning process, it seems worthwhile considering the various justifications for its importance. The most important are:

Reasons From Cognitive Psychology. Simple models for learning are not applicable to the learning of complex materials and, as a result, modern cognitive psychology, with its more active model of learning, is in favor today. To learn means to actively construct as dense a cognitive network of knowledge as possible. This knowledge is organized and represented in several relatively closed units, and is internally structured by a variety of relations and connections. These units must be connected with each another. Then, all these connections have to be controlled. This is the task of metacognition.

Learning is a complex task and a highly personal endeavor. Reflection is, therefore, necessary in two ways: It controls, first, the complexity of an individual's learning, and, second, it ensures that communication can take place between several learners and/or the teacher about the subjects to be learned: From such reflection the learner is aware of the *meaning* of the subjects learned. Furthermore, reflection not only has the function of monitoring thought backwards, but also the inherent property that it is helpful in moving the learning process forward.

Reasons From Pedagogy. Learning and understanding also have affective aspects. Understanding results in pleasure and inner satisfaction. It is part of the educational task to also elaborate and cultivate these affective aspects. Aeschbacher (1986) drew the following consequences from such insights: In order to foster self-guided learning, it is important for the learner to get to know about understanding itself. Aeschbacher stated that "metacognitive feeling" (p. 64), that is, the affective aspect of understanding, the feeling or sense that one has understood, may often be confused. Thus, it has to be cultivated—and reflecting should, therefore, take the form of cognitive self-experience.

The educational task is to construct, as explicitly as possible, opportunities for such self-experiences. This is not possible without also considering the social context in which learning takes place. Self-experiences are difficult to imagine in strongly teacher-guided instruction, and even more so in the absence of a teacher as a guide into the material. They may be possible only in an atmosphere that encourages students to learn on their own, and to speak freely about their experiences.

In these two paragraphs I have used the word *reflection* with a twofold meaning. Reflection refers to both the inner and outer connections of the subject itself *and* awareness of how far one's own thinking about *this* subject has proceeded. These aspects are, of course, not independent.

Reasons From the Needs of Bildung. In Germany, there is currently a broad discussion about what schools should contribute to the Bildung of students (see Heymann, 1996), especially in an age of growing specialization, rapidly growing availability of scientific media of all kinds, and the changing demands of the vocational sector. *General* education under this perspective has the task, as, for example, von Hentig (1996) pointed out, to bridge the gap between specialist knowledge and that which is appropriate for a general orientation toward the world. In this perspective, reflection has its place as a means of introducing scientific thinking.

Thus reflection should be seen not only as a content-free cognitive control mechanism, but also as bound to a specific domain, to reflection on scientific work and ways of thinking. The mere facts on the surface are not the focal point; the concern is for the ways "facts" might be acquired, how they might be evaluated, the connections between them, the methods used to create *these* facts as facts, and the extent to which these methods were those of the scientific community.

In comparison with the more psychologically oriented conceptions, we now concentrate on the specific ideas underlying the scientific method. This concentration may be justified, if we consider—from a Didaktik perspective—learning in the context of schools, and not content-free learning, as psychologists often do.

Reasons From Epistemology. Steiner (1987) described the various connections and relations between the learning and teaching of mathematics on the one hand, and philosophical positions and epistemological theories related to mathematics on the other hand. Seeking to evaluate the basic philosophies of mathematics from a decisively educational perspective, he concluded that philosophies that relate to and respect the dynamics of the development of mathematics knowledge are to be preferred in teaching contexts: "Such philosophies of mathematics should become an ingredient of a form of reflective mathematics teaching and learning, and contribute to the development of an adequate meta-knowledge, not only for teachers but also for students" (p. 11).

Thus the term *reflective mathematics teaching* implies a specific kind of reflection. Reflection is now related to the *qualities* of mathematics knowledge, the *processes* that lead to the acquisition of mathematics knowledge, the characteristic issues of working mathematically, and so on. In this context one also has to emphasize my earlier observation about reflection in the psychological sense: Reflection is not restricted to the control function; *it has productive power in the whole learning process.*

REFLECTING AS SPEAKING ABOUT MATHEMATICS

Reflections in mathematics learning should be concentrated on issues in the development of mathematical knowledge. This may take place in the concrete classroom situation as "speaking about mathematics." However, to realize this in classroom situations, we have to describe the range of the possibilities in greater detail. Different levels of speaking about mathematics are possible and, as a result, speaking about mathematics can mean:

- Speaking about mathematical subjects and problems themselves, for example, about the correctness of a proof, about the adequacy of the formulation of a definition, about logical dependencies, and so on. We may call this *the level of the mathematician.*

- Speaking about specific mathematical ways of working, their value and meaning, for example, about heuristic techniques in problem solving; about the various modes of concept formation in mathematics; about specific mathematics methods like systematization, classification, or abstraction; about schemes and techniques of proof; and so forth (see, e.g., Polya, 1945; de Villiers, 1990). We may call this *the level of the deliberately working mathematician*.
- Speaking about mathematics as a whole with critical distance, for example, about the roles of applications and their relation to mathematics concepts, about proofs as a characteristic issue in mathematics, and so on (see, e.g., Freudenthal, 1983; Hanna & Jahnke, 1993). We may call this *the level of the philosopher of mathematics*.
- Speaking about mathematics from an epistemological perspective, for example, about the characteristic distinctions between mathematics and other sciences, about the nature and the origin of mathematical knowledge, and so on (see, e.g., P. J. Davis & Hersh, 1980; Hadamard 1945; Lakatos, 1976). We may call this *the level of the epistemologist.*

We see the ideas of reflection described earlier across all of these levels. Thus, meta-cognition is included in the various aspects of heuristic thinking and also in the experiences that a learner has had with applications. Reflection, in the sense of general education, may be found at the levels of the philosopher of mathematics and the epistemologist. Speaking about the ideas behind the mathematical content itself is a kind of reflective learning and teaching found at every level. But one should not take the categories I have used to summarize the four levels too literally: Even when a student is not a philosopher in the academic sense, he or she may ask questions— and give preliminary answers to him or herself—that belong to the levels of the philosopher. Even though the teacher cannot expect students to express themselves like epistemologists, they may be faced with questions of a very general kind; for example, What is it that we know when we do mathematics? The key problem for the teacher is to be open and aware of the existence of the various levels of thinking about, reflecting upon, and speaking about mathematics—even in seemingly simple topics. Such a Didaktik awareness should consciously guide the teacher's construction of the lessons.

We may ask, however, whether the more personal and subjective moments of learning and reflecting are included in the four levels. This is not a problem: Speaking about the conditions of doing mathematics can easily (and indeed should) include some very subjective issues. We may discuss, for example, how, in mathematics, it is necessary to be *patient* when searching for the solution of a problem (first level), to be *careful* when giving a proof (second or third level), to be *skeptical* when reading a text (third or fourth level), to be *self-critical* when making a proposal (second or third level), to be *courageous* when trying out an insecure step (first or second level), or to find the right *balance* between distant behavior and personal engagement when working on long-term topics (all levels), and so forth.

So, speaking about mathematics implicates many aspects of reflection. And speaking about mathematics is, in concrete cases, realizable in the classroom if we respect the fact that reflection can take place on the variety of levels we sketched previously. Reflection, therefore, need not be restricted to the philosophical levels in the narrow sense. The second and the third stage of our levels play an especially important role in the use of reflection with students. At these levels, the teacher can adjust reflection to the state of knowledge and capability of the students. This also opens opportunities to introduce—by conscious Didaktik constructions—more advanced problems, at least as questions worth thinking about. Furthermore, at these two middle levels, reflection is close to the subjects taught at school.

However, one should repeat the earlier warning. Speaking about mathematics in the sense of reflection is the task of each and every learner. Teachers do, however, have an important function. They have to stimulate, to initiate such discussions, and they have to present their subjects in a way that opens the minds to questions, to looking at backgrounds, to asking for the sense, and so on—by adequate design of the lesson. And, clearly, the social context of speaking about mathematics is of decisive importance, although hard to describe. This is the problem in any example: They can be seen only as hints to possibilities, ideas, impulses—and "proofs" of the fruitfulness of Didaktik thinking.

SOME EXAMPLES

The Systematization of Quadrilaterals

In elementary geometry, consideration of the relations among the different types of quadrilaterals, that is, squares, rectangles, rhombi (diamonds), parallelograms, trapezoids, kites, and so on, is part of the core of most syllabi. But, unfortunately, discussion of these topics is usually about the efficiency of the one or another teaching approach, for example, if one should systematize according to the geometric transformations or according to the number of pieces that one needs for a geometrical construction. *But efficiency is not a good criterion if one aims to stimulate reflection, nor is it the appropriate way to think about the sense of the topics.*

The topic of quadrilaterals offers many useful opportunities to initiate reflection about the various modes of systematization in mathematics, and about some aspects of concept formation in mathematics. Thus, speaking about mathematics at the second and even the third level is inherent in the topic, and makes it more than just another systematization to be learned.

If we first start with the best-known quadrilaterals we mentioned earlier, we have the diagram seen in Fig. 14.1 (to more general cases = upward; to more special cases = downward). We use easily understood icons to indicate the various types of quads.

This diagram is not very well balanced. The types of quads that seem to be comparable, like rectangles (four equal angles) and rhombi (four equal sides), should be placed in the system with equal values. In the diagram, however, rhombi are special cases of two types, rectangles only of one. The diagram would be in better equilibrium if at the place "?" we filled it with the equilateral (symmetric) trapezoid. But then, if we draw only the type of the diagram, it apparently shows a gap, and again does not look fully balanced.

At this point, one can initiate a discussion about the typical concern of mathematicians to systematize in a balanced way. Balance in a systematization is not by clarity alone, or even aesthetics, but is also indicated by the respective content, as we already observed in the rectangle-rhombi case. Therefore, the need to fill the gap arises by itself—and not just as an imposed task.

Filling a gap in a systematization is an important general, and typical, procedure used by working mathematicians. Often concepts are designed to fit what was previously only a partly existing system, as with the gap in Fig. 14.2. But "speaking about this systematization" opens a way to point to a further characteristic of mathematics. Such generalizing and gap-filling concepts need not be unique; in our case the two types of "skew" kites seen

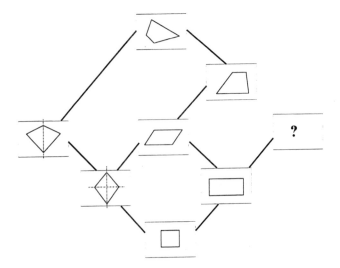

FIG. 14.1. Preliminary systematization of quadrilaterals.

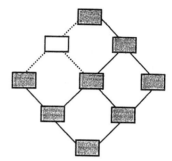

FIG. 14.2.   A non-balanced system.

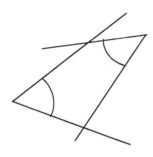
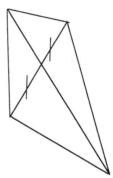

FIG. 14.3.   Two types of "skew" kites.

in Fig. 14.3 both fill the gap equally well. These are quadrilaterals, characterized either by one pair of opposite equal angles or by one diagonal halved by the other. Here speaking about mathematics starts with attempts at proofs or refutations of theorems that are not yet well known, and continues later with establishing the respective theorems. Thus, in our case, to justify the correctness of the diagram, one has to prove that any "skew kite"—of whatever type—which is also a trapezoid, must necessarily be a parallelogram. Mathematics thus appears as a dynamic approach to a certain content and not a dogmatic science, as often is believed.

We gradually shifted the focus of the reflection from the working mathematician to the epistemological level. On this level, speaking about mathematics points out that, contrary to a widely held opinion about mathematics, there is no need to establish uniqueness in these cases of filling the gap. Only an evaluation derived from even more general considerations (e.g., a certain duality between angles and sides, or a reference to invariants under certain transformations) can generate arguments for one or the other solution. Thus, speaking about such problems contributes to a more adequate picture of mathematics: It is not "the science with the always-unique results."

A mathematics appears in which arguments count, creativity is appreciated, and so on—not commonly shared views in typical mathematics classrooms.

Other patterns of concept formation and systematization in mathematics can be discovered when working with quadrilaterals (see Neubrand, 1981). The approach is always to formulate conjectures that are to be proven or refuted until a clear picture of the whole situation emerges. Only then can a closed theory be established, the result of a dynamic process guided by the formulation of adequate concepts. This process should be the subject of further reflection on the formation and the use of concepts in mathematics.

The example of the systematization of quadrilaterals, as simple as it is, offers a number of opportunities to reflect upon mathematics. And in this context mathematics is a dynamic, process-oriented, human-created science.

The Theorem of Inscribed Angles

As Fig. 14.4 shows, the theorem of inscribed angles states that angles over the same chord of a circle are all equal (or supplementary in the respective cases): angle AXB = angle AYB. The easy and, unfortunately, the common approach to this topic is to construct a straightforward unit that results in an "efficient" proof of this well-known theorem. But if teaching is constructed to only reach a theorem efficiently, it fails in the task of transmitting an adequate picture of *doing mathematics,* and ignores the Didaktik question of the *meaning* of the theorem for the students (cf. Schoenfeld, 1988). These possibilities emerge only if reflection on how theorems in general emerge in mathematics is included in the unit. The inscribed angles theorem serves as a paradigm in this respect, if we can work out some typical situations for reflection in the process of dealing with a theorem in the classroom. I suggest some of these situations:

1. *A theorem originates from different contexts and needs.* One such situation is embedded in the task of finding the location of a ship by measuring

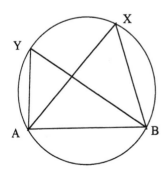

FIG. 14.4. The theorem of inscribed angles.

two angles to known points, like lighthouses or towers. Another very different context may be formal analogy: We know the locus of the points with *equal distances* to two points A and B, so we can also ask—behaving as a curious and formal-thinking mathematician would—for the locus of the vertices of *equal angles* with the legs through the two given points. Shifting focus once more, the last question may also take the form of a concrete geometric experiment: A template of the constant angle is moved along two nails indicating the two points A and B. In the same way, a computer experiment is possible: Allow the students to drag a point X across the screen and simultaneously measure the angle AXB to the two fixed points A and B. In both experiments: How does X need to move in order to keep the angle constant? And vice versa: Why is it that around a circle the angles remain equal? A classical experiment is the use of a geoboard with nails along a circular line: Fix two points and stretch an elastic ribbon from the other nails to the fixed points and observe the angles.

All of these experiment are intended to give a background for the phenomena that appear when keeping angles constant. If these observations are subjected to reflection, a picture of mathematics may result. Mathematics is aimed at logical orientations in a complex field of observation, connections, and relations—whether from the outer world or from within mathematics. "Orientation" has a typical and much more precise meaning in mathematics than in other scientific fields: It has the tool of proof.

2. *A theorem should be proven from different assumptions.* If we take seriously the idea of mathematics as an orientation-providing discipline, different proofs for a theorem, and not only one, are needed: Being authentic means being multirelational. During our discussion of the proofs, we first observe that every proof has to rely on the idea of "being constant." Thus, the most widespread proof in textbooks using the decomposition around the center M of the circle of the isosceles triangle ABC relies on "being constant" as being equal to a constant quantity while X itself is changing (see Fig. 14.5: Angle AXB is half of the angle AMB). A geoboard experiment yields another proof via the property that the opposite angles in an inscribed quadrilateral supplement to 180° (see also Fig. 14.5): If one keeps the Y-part of the quadrilateral AXBY fixed and moves the X-part, then the angle at X could not have changed its size, because it always supplements the angle AYB to 180°. "Being constant" now only means "does not vary," but no concrete comparison bounded to the original configuration "circle and segment AB" can be given because the location of Y is arbitrary.

The approaches mentioned in Item 1 are not accidental, but lead directly to the kernel of the theorem in Item 2. Appropriate Didaktik construction by the teacher considers these possible ties when choosing the contexts to start from. And, again, this observation offers opportunities for speaking about mathematics. Applications from both inside as well outside mathe-

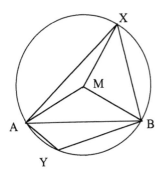

FIG. 14.5. Ideas for proof of the theorems of inscribed angles.

matics serve as valuable heuristic tools and provide a basis for understanding and appreciating the theorem (Hanna & Jahnke, 1993).

3. *A theorem should be worked through; it has to be applied and recognized in various situations.* This phase of dealing with a theorem in the geometry classroom should never be drill-and-practice; it can be very productive! Knowledge about the theorem should be embedded in a dense network of other observations. It is the central task of Didaktik construction to identify appropriate questions for working through this phase. For this purpose, in the case of the inscribed angle theorem, the following question—answers left to the reader—may serve as an example: *When the angle AXB is known, determine the angles 1, 2, 3 in Fig. 14.6, and any other angles you find remarkable.* This is an open-ended task, aimed at seeing the theorem under different perspectives, that should stimulate discussions about how hard it may be to recognize a well-known theorem under different configurations. This also a characteristic form of productive thinking in mathematics: seeing connections where they did not exist earlier.

4. *A theorem is to be used as a tool in further investigations.* At the conclusion of the process of becoming familiar with a theorem, the particular theorem we are addressing must be the focus. This is the basic condition for being

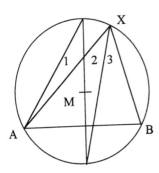

FIG. 14.6. A working-through example.

successful with more complicated applications of that theorem. But we may speak about our theorem at this stage in the unit by posing the questions Why is it necessary to formulate a certain insight explicitly as a theorem? Why do we give a theorem a particular name?

One answer to these questions may be in the fact that it is only with simple, and in themselves closed, "modules" or easily applicable "procedures" that one can effectively move to longer chains of inferences. This can also be illustrated in the case of the inscribed angle theorem by, for example, solving the following problem: *Construct (with ruler and compass) a triangle where one angle and the radii of both the inscribed and the circumscribed circle are known.* The reader should carefully monitor that using only the inscribed angle theorem as a closed "module" as a tool ensures the solution. Otherwise, one will be stuck because too many details block thinking. This kind of modular thinking is surely one of the most striking characteristics of working mathematically—and, thus, a good topic to speak about (see Neubrand, 1990 for further discussions).

On the Number of Divisors of a Whole Number

Let us consider one further example from arithmetic. This example also gives insight in what working mathematically is. Here the emphasis is more on the working aspects and less on ideas of mathematics as a whole.

This example comes from experiences in preservice teacher education. It demonstrates the possibility of stimulating reflection through an appropriate construction on the chalkboard or in the textbook. The arrangement suggested here should foster both learning the subject itself and considering the processes by which the development of the subject proceeds. I call this special arrangement the "two-column method."

The subject dealt with in the following is the problem of determining the number of divisors of a given number N, using the decomposition of numbers into products of prime numbers. The text was developed in the two columns on the chalkboard. It should be read by jumping between the two columns.

The subject itself	*Reflection: What do we think? How do we think? What ideas lead to the next step?*
How many divisors does a whole number N have?	*Transformation* of the problem from the given general and abstract formulation into a problem that one can handle more easily. Essentially, transforming it into a call for the *action* of counting.

How can one *count* the divisors?

How can one *depict* the divisors?

What facilitates counting? → pictures! structured *patterns!*

Let's try an *example for orientation.* But remember: We are not interested in the example itself. The example should reveal the structure of the general case:

Example as a *paradigm.*

Example: N = 175 = $5^2 \times 7$

The divisors of N = 175 are shown in the list:

1,5,7,25,35,175

Ordering the list by lexigraphic order:

$5^0 7^0, 5^0 7^1, 5^1 7^0, 5^1 7^1, 5^2 7^0, 0^2 7^1$

The pairs of divisor exponents:

(0,0),(0,1),(1,0),(1,1),(2,0),(2,1)

The list is not suitable for counting because one cannot recognize a general pattern.

We *observe* that only the exponents are important.

There is a well-known method to represent pairs: the x-y coordinate system

Now, we *recognize a "structure"/"pattern":* the rectangle. Therefore, one can count by the rectangle-rule length × width.

exponents
of 7

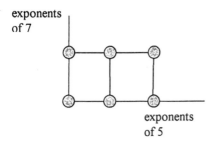

exponents
of 5

FIG. 14.7. Exponents of the divisors.

There are $3 \times 2 = 6$ divisors of a = 175

Theorem:
If $N = p^r \cdot q^s$ then N has
$(r + 1) \times (s + 1)$ divisors.

Analysis: Where do the factors 2 and 3 come from? → one has to draw a rectangle with the outer vertex at (r,s) if $N = pr \cdot q^s$ is given. So far, we have considered only a special case (two prime divisors). Now, *generalize* these ideas!

We stop at this point. It should be clear how the problem is to be continued: Next, one considers cuboids, then the cuboid-rule of multiplication in "higher" dimensions (cf. Neubrand & Möller, 1992).

With the two-column notation, the attempt is made to stimulate students to think about the various problem-solving methods used here and elsewhere. Even in this short piece of mathematics, we have encountered several fundamental problem-solving activities, that is, searching for a pattern, using expert knowledge, and so on. Awareness of these processes is a goal of the National Council of Teachers of Mathematics (NCTM) *Standards* (see Lacampagne, 1993); our two-column method is a means to realize this goal. One additional important aspect often met in mathematics and problem solving is the conscious use of different "languages," in this case arithmetic and geometric representation, including the respective translation processes. This should lead to the insight that mathematics does not consist only of syntax, but that the languages used in mathematics should have rich semantics. One task of the teacher then is to foster explicitly some translation activities with the students.

FINAL REMARKS

The reflection approach is not only a theoretical concept. The examples show several concrete means of realizing reflection in the classroom. These means form the basis for the Didaktik preparation of the teacher. We encountered the progressive formulation of a systematization when given the appropriate starting points: in the case of the quadrilateral, the explicit differentiation of the phases of dealing with mathematical theorems—which can remind the teacher not to omit important steps in the presentation. In the arithmetic example, the two-column method is a stimulus for discussion.

But to this point, we have said almost nothing about individual processes of learning in the classroom under the perspective of reflection. Reflection, stimulated by speaking about mathematics in the classroom, provides a basis from which students' own understanding comes into the agenda of the classroom. Aeschbacher (1986) referred to four essential types of models under which that process of "comprehension of one's own understanding via reflection" may be seen. These models are:

- Understanding as the (visual or not) grasping of connections, as, for example, Gestalt psychology has elaborated.
- Understanding as flexibility in applying knowledge to various situations.
- Understanding as the integration of intuitive and formal aspects of the subject, as was pointed out by Skemp (1979).
- Understanding as the elaboration of common structures and general patterns.

Our examples relate to all three models. The exercises suggested for working through the inscribed angles theorem may, for example, be used to increase flexibility in applying this theorem (Aeschbacher's second model). The idea of visually recognizing the inscribed angle (Aeschbacher's first model) is also in this example. The arithmetic example shows the elaboration of a "pattern" (Aeschbacher's fourth model). Aeschbacher's third model may also be found in several examples; for example, the problem-solving approach of the arithmetic example appeals to some very intuitive general techniques. The quads example may be interpreted as the search for pattern in a more general sense.

By including reflection in the mathematics classroom, one not only broadens and deepens mathematics knowledge, but also gives valuable impulses to Bildung, general education. Being conscious of mathematics, both in the technical and in the epistemological sense, as well as on one's own understanding, is the central goal of Didaktik thinking.

REFERENCES

Aeschbacher, U. (1986). *Unterrichtsziel: Verstehen—über die psychischen Prozesse beim Denken, Lernen und Verstehen.* Stuttgart: Klett.

Cobb, P., Boufi, A., McClain, K., & Whitenack, J. (1997). Reflective discourse and collective reflection. *Journal for Research in Mathematics Education, 28*(3), 258–277.

Davis, P. J., & Hersh, R. (1980). *The mathematics experience.* Boston, MA: Birkhäuser.

de Villiers, M. D. (1990). The role and function of proof in mathematics. *Pythagoras, 24*(1), 17–24.

Freudenthal, H. (1983). *Didactical phenomenology of mathematical structures.* Dordrecht, Netherlands: Reidel.

Hadamard, J. (1945). *The psychology of invention in the mathematical field.* Princeton, NJ: Princeton University Press.

Hanna, G., & Jahnke, H. N. (1993). Proof and application. *Educational Studies in Mathematics, 24*(4), 421–438.

Heymann, H. W. (1996). *Allgemeinbildung und Mathematik.* Weinheim: Beltz.

Lacampagne, C. B. (1993). *State of the art: Transforming ideas for teaching and learning mathematics.* Washington, DC: U.S. Department of Education.

Lakatos, I. (1976). *Proofs and refutations.* Cambridge, England: Cambridge University Press.

Lampert, M. (1988). When the problem is not the question and the solution is not the answer: Mathematical knowing and teaching. *American Educational Research Journal, 27*(1), 29–63.

Neubrand, M. (1981). Das "Haus der Vierecke"—Aspekte beim Finden mathematischer Begriffe. *Journal für Mathematik-Didaktik, 2*(1), 3–50.

Neubrand, M. (1990). Mathematische Aktivitäten rund um den Umfangswinkelsatz. *Didaktik der Mathematik, 18*(4), 271–289.

Neubrand, M., & Möller, M. (1992). *Einführung in die Arithmetik.* Hildesheim: Franzbecker.

Polya, G. (1945). *How to solve it.* Princeton, NJ: Princeton University Press.

Schoenfeld, A. (1988). When good teaching leads to bad results: The disasters of "well taught" mathematics courses. *Educational Psychologist, 23*(2), 145–166.

Sierpinska, A. (1996). *Understanding in mathematics* London: Falmer.

Skemp, R. (1979). Goals of learning and qualities of understanding. *Mathematics Teaching, 88*(2), 44–49.

Steiner, H. G. (1987). Philosophical and epistemological aspects of mathematics and their interaction with theory and practice in mathematics education. *For the Learning of Mathematics, 7*(1), 7–13.

von Hentig, H. (1996). *Bildung.* Munich: Hanser.

15

Aspects of Simplification in Mathematics Teaching

Arnold Kirsch
John Scherk (Trans.)

Arnold Kirsch was a Professor of Didaktik of Mathematics at the University of Kassel.

INTRODUCTION: SIMPLIFICATION AS A WAY OF MAKING ACCESSIBLE

In discussion about the curriculum, the main problem is *choosing* and *justifying* the content. Everyone expects the teacher to "simplify" and "elementarize." In what follows I consider *simplification* as the process of making accessible. I do not touch on simplification in the sense of "pruning" (cf. Griesel, 1974; Rumpf, 1971) or "stepping down to a lower level."

Simplification in the aforementioned sense has been discussed at length in the pedagogic-psychological literature, for example, as "restructuring" *(Umstrukturieren)*. However, in practice it takes place without much further thought. Becker (1974) made a study of "elementarization" in a specifically mathematical context, and I use this as a starting point.[1]

The term simplification is commonplace: This should not lead one to believe that, in a concrete situation, there is necessarily agreement as to whether the matter at hand has been simplified or not. A mathematician

---

[1] I am grateful to many colleagues for discussions and suggestions, in particular to Mrs. E. Schildkamp-Kundiger and Messrs. B. Artmann, G. Becker, W. Blum, H. Meißner, and S. Seyfferth.

talks of "simplifying" a proof if he or she can eliminate extraneous concepts and machinery—which often means that the arguments become more refined and less obvious, and thus *more difficult* for the student. Or else the didactician tries to make equations "easier" to understand by explaining the concepts *term, variable, expression*—which the classroom teacher may see as *complicating* the matter. The author of a pedagogical best-seller recently "simplified" the concept of a null sequence of positive numbers by defining it as a monotone decreasing sequence ("every number is smaller than the preceding one"; Vester, 1975, p. 169), which is simply *false*.[2]

Who is to decide whether something has really been made easier to understand? One would like to leave this to the judgment of *teachers;* yet they often find something difficult only because it is new to them. What about the *pupil*? But how is she to judge whether what she has been taught is the real thing—whether something essential hasn't been "removed from her way," and thus withheld from her.

These questions illustrate the methodological difficulties in developing general and sufficiently precise concepts in a science of mathematics education. I do not try to give a general theory of simplification that aims at being widely acceptable. I use simplification, in the sense of making accessible, as a *guiding line* along which to organize some Didaktik developments, and in order to report on some concrete suggestions. To do this I classify certain *specifically mathematical aspects of making accessible*. Perhaps they can be seen as part of more general questions in learning theory, but I do not think they can be inferred from the latter.

The first aspect is:

MAKING ACCESSIBLE BY CONCENTRATION ON THE MATHEMATICAL HEART OF THE MATTER

This aspect corresponds to the view that mathematics in its most mature form, that is, *mathematics in the narrowest sense of the word,* stripped of all its genetic elements and connections with reality, is the simplest mathematics.[3] Working out the central concepts, generalizing, and emphasizing the fundamental structures is a way of making mathematics more accessible.

This corresponds to certain approaches in learning theory (cf. also Lenné, 1969). In his "principle of progressive differentiation," Ausubel and Robinson (1969) suggested that one should first present the general, inclu-

---

[2]The (old) dichotomy of simplification-falsification is discussed in Rumpf (1971) and, especially with reference to mathematics teaching, in Wittmann (1974).

[3]This was the point of view taken by Pringsheim in his controversy with Felix Klein, cf. *Jahresberichte der DMV*, 1898, pp. 73–83.

sive ideas of a discipline, as they called them. These should make access to special problems easier by playing a "subsuming role." Here one may also think of Dienes' well-known deep-end principle.

As a first example of this, take the approach to *word problems in primary school,* which uses letters as variables before numerical computation. Freudenthal (1974b) reported recently on the suggestions and experience of Davydov and his school in the USSR in this direction. Abstraction and generality are supposed to be achieved here directly rather than from a large number of special cases, and so make access to concrete problems easier.

On the other hand, it is possible to make a concept more difficult by refusing to take a sufficiently general point of view. I had a chance to observe this recently in a class of 15-year-olds. A full hour was used to explain the invariance of parallelism under shear mappings; the proof was split up into many cases requiring special geometrical arguments that even ran over into homework experiences. If one had thought back to the *heart of the matter* here—that a shear is a line-preserving permutation of the plane—then the question would have become clear immediately.

And no one will deny that *Fermat's little theorem* can only really be understood and appreciated in its abstract group-theoretic form. But the following observation makes one pause and think. Repeated efforts to lead student teachers to the group concept via permutation groups[4] found little resonance: They objected that it was "much easier" to begin straight away with "real" groups.

In vector geometry in schools, one still finds the fossil expressions "colinear" and "coplanar," the introduction of which creates many difficulties, especially with the zero vector. These ideas become much better accessible if *linear dependence,* which is what one is aiming for, is introduced immediately. A suitable definition might be: "Vectors are linearly dependent if at least one of them can be written as a linear combination of the others."[5] It is not the notion itself that is difficult for pupils, but the definition that mathematicians usually give in order to simplify the deductions that follow it.

Here one sees that making accessible is not the same as simplifying the deductive structure. In school mathematics, which I am restricting myself to here, *it is the understanding* of the meaning of important concepts and the ability to manipulate them with understanding that counts. For this it is not enough to establish deductive interrelations (cf. Freudenthal, 1973; Spanier, 1970).

---

[4]With the permutation groups, it is natural first to consider the inversion of permutations, and then to look for the identity element so that one can compose permutations; with abstract groups one must first introduce the identity and then inverse elements.

[5]It is natural at first not to explain linear dependence for one vector. This follows later as an extension (not a revision!) of the given definition.

There is no doubt that a proper choice of definitions and axioms makes an area of mathematics much more accessible; but a simplification of the deductive structure cannot be the only criterion of choice here.[6] Above and beyond internal mathematical considerations, the didactician and teacher must show imagination, and take into account the pupils' background knowledge. He or she must be *sensitive to alternatives* just where a mathematician would see no difference. (E.g., are vectors as classes of arrows "the same as translations" or not?)

The following examples illustrate what I would call a (structural) simplification by *putting the cart before the horse,*[7] which serves only to make access more difficult:

- "Defining" the product of natural numbers via the Cartesian product of sets.
- "Defining" the sum of fractions as $\dfrac{a}{b} + \dfrac{c}{d} = \dfrac{ad+bc}{bd}$.[8]
- "Defining" a square as a quadrilateral with four axes of symmetry.
- "Defining" a rotation as a product of reflections.
- "Defining" a plane in three-dimensional space via a linear equation.
- "Defining" a convex function via the first or even the second derivative.
- "Defining" the area of a trapezoid with curved sides using an integral (defined via primitive functions).
- "Defining" the logarithm as the integral of $\dfrac{1}{x}$.
- "Defining" the sine and cosine as solutions of a system of functional equations.

Here, and in many similar situations, one uses properties as definitions that can and must be explained if the essence of the concept is to become clear.[9] From a scientific point of view, this is of course legitimate; I do not want to make a value judgment, but only pinpoint a possible complication in the learning process. Of course, what the essence of a concept is may be hard to decide. But it is by no means merely a matter of taste.

Thus the phenomenon of putting the cart before the horse illustrates a *specifically mathematical problem* in making something accessible: Structural simplification can make access more difficult.

The next aspect is in a sense complementary to the proceeding one.

---

[6]Fischer (1976) also emphasized this.

[7]This is related to what Freudenthal (1973) called "anti-Didaktik inversion" (p. 100).

[8]Interpret the fractions as lengths, say. The given equation then follows from the properties of a domain of quantities (cf. Kirsch, 1970).

[9]This is true for many axioms that have been suggested for Didaktik reasons.

MAKING ACCESSIBLE BY INCLUDING THE "SURROUNDINGS" OF MATHEMATICS

One has always tried to make mathematics more accessible to pupils by introducing mathematical objects in a less abrupt fashion and by taking a *broader view of mathematics*—which includes the origin of concepts and their relations to reality. This approach is also supported by arguments from learning theory, in particular those concerned with the problem of motivation. It is supported by methodological experience as well.

A controversial example from primary school mathematics is the introduction of powers. Instead of attacking the heart of the matter (iterated multiplication) immediately, some masters of method try to make the concept easier by talking about iterated "bundling" of real objects, and thus to relate it to the surroundings of mathematics.[10]

A particularly important example where the origins of an idea have been exploited is Dienes' treatment of *groups*. He was able to make the group concept accessible even to younger pupils by distinguishing between "states" and "operators" and, in particular, by using Cayley graphs (thus going back to the prehistory of group theory).[11]

What lies behind this, from the mathematician's point of view, is a *"duplication" of the group structure*, in the sense expressed in Cayley's theorem. At this level, a group is a sharply transitive group of operators acting on a set of states. This avoids many difficulties: Operators appear as concrete objects, and one "knows" an operator as soon as *one* initial state and the corresponding target state are known (!). But just here arises the danger that pupils (and teachers) will not reach mathematical maturity.

Such a duplication of the group structure also lies at the base of the traditional *arithmetic of fractions*. Unlike group theory, this is a substantially meaningful topic[12] for the majority of pupils. In treating the multiplicative group **Q**+, one differentiates between "concrete" numbers and "pure" numbers, or in the current terminology, quantities and operators. Exhaustive analyses, especially by Griesel, have cleared up this area and have succeeded in justifying several traditional methods of presentation. The importance of the concept of a "domain of quantities" for teaching, which is

---

[10]Originally I talked of the "premathematical area" here. But Semadeni (Warsaw) kindly pointed out to me that the notion of "premathematics" has been used since 1973 with a well-defined meaning (see Z. Semadeni, 1973, "The Concept of Pre-Mathematics as a Theoretical Background for Primary Mathematics Teaching," *Institute of Mathematics, Polish Academy of Sciences*), so I have avoided this term.

[11]Of course, what concerned Dienes may not be making the group concept accessible, but rather the more general goal of stimulating the cognitive development of younger pupils.

[12]Kahle (1976) discussed "substantially meaningful—suitable for more general goals" as alternative criteria in selecting teaching material.

oriented toward genetic development and applications, has also been recognized (see, e.g., Griesel, 1970; Kirsch, 1969, 1970; Steiner, 1969).

As a result, the operator method in the arithmetic of fractions, originally proposed by Braunfeld, Dilley, and Rucker (1967) and Pickert (1968), has been steadily developed[13] and is widely used today. One gives increasing weight thereby to decimal fractions and the fact that these, considered as operators, can be realized directly with hand calculators.

Critics of current mathematics teaching see an unnecessary *complication* in the distinction between states and operators. It is indeed true that the distinction has been "overworked." The main problem has turned out to be that background analyses meant for the teacher have often been mistaken for proposed classroom material. Here is an example of "making implicit content explicit," which Thom (1973) criticized. Notice by the way that many mathematicians introduce the same complication (duplication of the basis group structure) at a higher level when they treat affine spaces parallel to vector spaces—despite Dieudonné's (1962) categorical condemnation of any such concession to genetic aspects.

The set of states of a Cayley graph, domains of quantities, and affine spaces are outlying objects in relation to the central concepts of mathematics. They are added to mathematics (in the strict sense) to make it more accessible. Another example of this, which seems to me to typify the efforts of mathematical Didaktik in Germany to take into account the surroundings of mathematics, is the use of metaconcepts in introducing the *language of algebra,* that is, in teaching how to cope with variables.

After this approach had first been clarified, particularly by Steiner (1961) and Wäsche (1961), there followed a period where it was taught with an exaggerated perfectionism that led to dismaying complexities. One is now beginning to find a mean and to reap the fruits of experience (see Volrath, 1974). There is no doubt that this area has become more accessible thanks to its having been demystified. The number of pupils has been reduced whose helplessness in the face of "statements" like $a - b$ impeded their mathematical progress. In return, one must accept a certain complexity caused by the use of such metaconcepts.

How does this fit in with our first aspect? All experience indicates that *complexity does not usually bother pupils and teachers as much as does excessive abstractness.* This too is a specifically mathematical observation about simplification that probably cannot be deduced from general learning theory.

The aspect just discussed can be put under the label, *enrichment* (cf. Becker, 1974). The next one, on the other hand, is a form of *reducing the content* (cf. Becker, 1974). However, what concerns me here is not a systematic theory, but rather certain aspects that I consider especially important

---

[13]Compare *Der Mathematikunterricht,* Vol. 2, 1970, and 1975, Vol. 1.

in the present state of mathematics teaching. The following aspect is formulated deliberately in a positive way (not as a reduction).

MAKING ACCESSIBLE BY RECOGNIZING AND ACTIVATING PREEXISTING KNOWLEDGE

In emphasizing this aspect, we are setting ourselves against the widespread tendency to develop mathematics *ab ovo,* from the egg, or to go right back to the beginning and start without assuming anything. This tendency can be found not only with systematizing mathematicians (when, e.g., they tell their students to forget what they learned in school), but also in genetically oriented didacticians like Wittenberg (1963), and even in the primary school methodologist when she ignores children's previous experience with numbers.[14]

We, on the other hand, want to see pupils encouraged to make use of preexisting knowledge, and also knowledge from outside of mathematics. This approach takes into account realities like "Sesame Street," and saves time and effort on the part of the teacher. Above all, we want to avoid the frustration that can be caused by denigrating what pupils already know.

Learning theory also encourages a linking-up to existing knowledge. In particular, it belongs, according to Ausubel and Robinson (1969), to the conditions for "meaningful learning." At the same time, it is in accordance with Didaktik principles like Wittmann's (1974) integration principle, or with the genetic principle more generally (cf. Wittmann, 1975).

Here is an example: One should recognize and utilize the pupil's knowledge of the *division algorithm* when explaining periodicity in decimal fractions or when introducing nested intervals. Because of the student's experience with this algorithm, she will see that the repetition in the calculation in the shaded part of Fig. 15.1 corresponds to a repetition in the decimal expansion. This insight will only be made hazy if one tries to explain the algorithm, or to translate everything into "mathematical" language. And the student will immediately see that the inequalities on the right hold. But she would not understand a formal proof of them using the theorem on division with remainder.

One should also accept that the familiar notion of a decimal fraction as a sequence of digits[15] is a perfectly good basis for introducing the real numbers. One doesn't have to begin with a precise *definition of a negative.*

---

[14]This holds particularly for the teacher in the fifth school year who tries to "explain" the natural numbers via one-to-one correspondence between sets; cf. Kirsch, 1973.

[15]Here is a striking (though artificial) example of how fruitful the naïve idea of "infinite decimal fractions" can be:

Claim: There exists an injective probability measure P on the power set of $\mathbf{N}$ (as sample space).

Proof: for $A \subset \mathbf{N}$, let $P(A) = 9 \cdot 0.z_1 z_2 z_3 \ldots$ where $z_i = 1$ if $i \in A$, $z_i = 0$ otherwise.

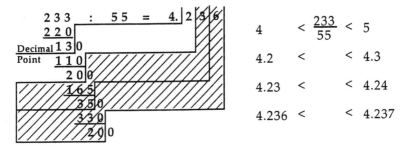

FIG. 15.1. Represenation of the diverse algorithm as an example for explaining periodicity in decimal fractions.

In analysis too, this naïve idea of a sequence is sufficient for a long time. Defining sequences as mappings with domain **N** too early in fact inhibits the development of a creative understanding of what a sequence is and makes it impossible to operate freely with subsequences. Fortunately one "forgets" this definition soon: for example, when one explains monotony (already defined for functions) in the form $a_1 \leq a_2 \leq a_3 \leq \ldots$

Pupils' experience with the *decimal representation* of natural numbers makes possible a proof of the insolvability of the equation $\left(\frac{m}{n}\right)^2 = 2$ ($m, n \in$ **N**), which experience shows to be particularly accessible to them: One simply compares the last digits in the expansions of m^2 and $2n^2$.

Children's acquaintance with finite sequences as *words* can also be built upon in elementary combinatorics (cf. Kirsch, 1975). One can already explain to younger pupils what a word with eight letters in a given alphabet of n letters is. What they have learned in spelling enables them to recognize when two words are the same and when they are different. In this way, they understand immediately that there are precisely n^8 such words. And they can apply this in real situations by using the words as "code words" (to describe escape routes, e.g.). For such purposes it is superfluous and indeed harmful to define a "word," something children are familiar with, as a mapping, a concept that in early stages isn't even available. This doesn't mean that we are for a return to the misleading language of combinatorics as it was traditionally taught. We are simply arguing for the recognition of what pupils have already learned where it can be made use of.

In the classroom situation, this requires that *the teacher can judge* what knowledge of the pupils can be built upon. It is too much to expect a general consensus on this. By no means do we wish to exclude that this already existent knowledge be later questioned or deepened. In fact it *should* later be delved into and made dispensable, step by step. But one shouldn't throw it out straightaway. This should be kept in mind especially in the following examples.

Pupils have considerable experience that can be made use of in elementary geometry.[16] In particular, I am thinking of their familiarity with the existence and properties of the elementary measures of length, angle, and area. This familiarity comes from outside the mathematics class, even from outside of school, which we may regard as a particularly fortunate situation.

In the classroom today, one doesn't insist on developing elementary geometry completely rigorously (cf. Holland, 1972), and usually makes use of these measures without saying anything. But even at a more demanding level, the use of these measures as undefined basic concepts can lead to a desirable simplification. This was originally brought out by Birkhoff and Beatley (1959). In recent years it has been further developed and put successfully into practice in several courses (see DIFF Studienbrief III, 1974; Holland, 1974).

By the way, one is carrying the recognition of existing knowledge even further if one bases elementary geometry on vector spaces like Dieudonné. For this means that one assumes, *de facto,* previous knowledge of the similarity theorems. This does not seem justified, either in classroom teaching or in the instruction of student teachers.

What we are concerned about becomes especially clear if you think of how trigonometric functions are sometimes introduced: It is a waste of time and only frustrates pupils if one turns down their existing knowledge of angle or of arc length. It is quite possible to build on this knowledge even in teacher training programs. An independent development of the trigonometric functions is on the whole necessary only as background knowledge for teaching the final school years, and here it is necessary.

In the same way, it is legitimate in school mathematics to make use of the formula for the area of a sector (in terms of arc length) in order to prove $\lim_{a \to o} \frac{\sin x}{x} = 1$ (cf. Laugwitz, 1973). The basic inequality $x < \tan x$ $(0 < x < \frac{\pi}{2})$ then follows by comparing the corresponding areas (see Fig. 15.2).[17]

On the other hand, it is not justifiable to obtain the inequality by simply comparing the arc with the tangent segment, without any arguing, as is commonly done. Here lies the dividing line between legitimate simplification and a falsification that does not get past critical pupils.

The *area* of plane figures is a concept where intuition is particularly reliable. It seldom leads to false conclusions (unlike one's intuitive idea of arc length, where zig-zag lines can already cause difficulties). The demonstration that there are unmeasurable figures in the plane is refined and nonconstructive. Imagine what it means for a pupil if her notion of area is

---

[16]Like Dieudonné, we understand this as "a kind of physics of space," though not as a purely experimental discipline the way he did.

[17]Freund (1960) also proved the inequality $\sin x > x - \frac{x^3}{6}$ by considerations of area.

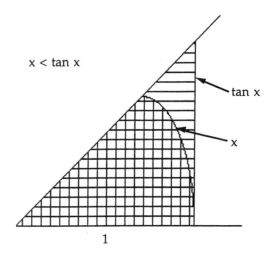

FIG. 15.2. Visual representation of the base inequality $x < \tan x$ $(0 < x < \pi/2)$.

questioned: The formula for the area of a triangle no longer appears as a theorem one can prove, but rather as a definition (another example of putting the cart before the horse). And Hippocrates' discovery about the "little moons" is degraded to a hypothetical statement.

Intuitive ideas of area can even be used as a foundation for the concept of integral (cf. Kirsch, 1976a). This is useful for pupils in courses with a minimum of mathematics, who at present tend to have no contact at all with integrals. We simply define (following Artin[18]) the integral of a function as the area under its graph (taken positively above the x-axis and negatively below). Then we can devote ourselves straightaway to the central problem of calculating integrals.[19] We thus avoid questions of definitions and existence proofs, which cause insurmountable difficulties for weaker pupils and which they forget later anyway. With this geometric definition, one can also *prove* the fundamental theorem of calculus; one doesn't have to degrade it to a definition as in the approach via primitive functions.

In the proof that all primitive functions (of a function defined on an interval) differ from one another by a constant, one should accept that the pupils know from experience that $f' = 0$ implies f constant. This knowledge can come from watching a speedometer, given a little imagination. What is important, first of all, is that they can make the little step from this statement to that about all primitive functions, and understand its meaning. Only then is it justified in Didaktik terms and thus desirable to examine its plausibility, and to provide a proof.

---

[18]A freshman honors course in calculus and analytic geometry, Princeton University, 1957.
[19]Blum (1975) pointed out that this is really the main problem for beginners.

In this connection, let us formulate a general *principle for constructing courses*: One should construct them so that things one has assumed that the pupils are familiar with can be isolated and examined more closely later, or even removed altogether, without the whole structure collapsing. This principle is an example of how to sensibly isolate difficulties, and is also in accord with Bruner's (1960) spiral principle.

An illustration of this occurs in what is called in Germany *mapping geometry (Abbildungsgeometrie)* (see, e.g., Breidenbach in Drenckhahn, 1958). Analyses have shown that "mapping proofs," when carried out in detail, are usually more difficult than the traditional proofs using congruence theorems. But they don't fall to pieces if part of the proof is removed and replaced by what pupils know about congruences—knowledge that actually comes from outside of mathematics lessons, from their everyday experience of rigid bodies.

Some topics that up to now have been quite inaccessible to school mathematics can be made so by recognizing existing knowledge and, indeed, by *cultivating* it. An impressive example of this is the fundamental theorem of algebra. In a Didaktik analysis, Steiner (1964) showed how to make the well-known topological proof accessible for the classroom. Making the topological elements in the proof precise would by no means give the simplest proof of the theorem. The simplification here arises because one can isolate them in the way explained previously.

How does this aspect of recognizing preexisting knowledge fit in with the tendency, widespread today, to introduce concepts *axiomatically* when it is too laborious to define or construct them rigorously? One need only think of the axiomatic definitions of area, of the real numbers, or of the exponential function.[20] This is not "exactly what we mean." Here too one should develop a certain sensitivity to differences, even if at first glance the two are the same. For example, recognizing preexisting knowledge of order properties in geometry does not mean that one makes explicit axioms out of them, but rather that one doesn't even talk about them (cf. Kirsch, 1972).

In general, I would like to emphasize that, if introducing a concept axiomatically simply formulates explicitly what one can reasonably assume is known to the pupils, then it corresponds to what we have in mind. (To be more precise, the axiomatic formulation is a higher form of what we have in mind.) But if it is a case of putting the cart before the horse, if the axioms come out of the blue, then it is not at all what we intend.

If we view the recognition of preexisting knowledge as a *reduction in content,* then it is nonetheless a relatively slight reduction. One is only doing without explanations for which there is no need anyway. A teacher often

---

[20]Incidentally, in all these cases it is a question of categorical system of axioms, where the real importance of the axiomatic method does not yet become clear.

has to undertake much *more extensive reduction,* even to assume results that are by no means known to her pupils.[21] But I do not want to discuss this problem here. Instead, I would like to turn to an aspect that perhaps can also be seen as a form of reduction, although this does not necessarily mean sacrificing any mathematical substance.

MAKING ACCESSIBLE BY CHANGING THE MODE OF REPRESENTATION

One has always tried to make mathematical concepts more accessible by illustration, more generally by changing the mode of representation (cf. Becker, 1974). Following Bruner (Bruner, Oliver, & Greenfield, 1966), one differentiates nowadays between *enactive* representation, *iconic* representation, and representation by *symbolic means* (through language as well as symbols in the narrower sense). In Didaktik principles like the "prefiguration principle," one encourages the use of the presymbolic modes (see, e.g., Wittmann, 1974).

We cannot develop a theory, or even the phenomenology, of the ways of representing mathematical ideas here.[22] This is a problem that the psychologist is not in a position to solve, and that doesn't interest the mathematician. So it falls to the specialist in Didaktik. Bruner's E-I-S scheme must be modified or refined before it can be applied to mathematics. One can't simply fit the usual ways of representing mathematical concepts into this scheme. (How, e.g., is one to categorize the representation of structural algebraic concepts through models inside of mathematics?)

In what follows, I recall only briefly how one can represent mathematical ideas enactively or iconically to make them more accessible.

First of all, an example of *enactive representation:* We explain the rule for divisibility by 9 on a primitive abacus. Let the given number n be represented by n beads in the one's column. We perform the following *action* as often as possible: "Take 10 beads, place 1 in the column to the left and set the other 9 aside." The beads remaining on the abacus give the decimal representation of the number n. The number of beads remaining is the sum of the digits in the decimal representation. Now we have put aside groups of 9 beads each time, so the number n is "just as well" divisible by 9 as the sum of its digits is.

There is no doubt that the essential point has been adequately presented here, and it has been made accessible to pupils for whom the rule might

---

[21] It is common in all the sciences to assume results in this fashion, especially from other disciplines. In mathematics, too, it has its place, and pupils should get a taste of it (cf. Lenné, 1969).

[22] Kirsch (1977) is a first try at this.

otherwise only be a recipe. Translating the argument into a more sophisticated form is by comparison of secondary importance.

It should be part of the professional expertise of the teacher to know such possibilities for representing ideas and how to employ them fruitfully. This is not always easy: The transition to the enactive level has its pitfalls. As is well known, representing permutations by "games" with real objects can lead to considerable complications (see Freudenthal, 1973; Kirsch, 1977; Pickert, 1975).

I would now like to make two remarks on *iconic representations*. The first concerns arrow diagrams, which have become widespread thanks to the efforts of Papy. Apparently, some pupils can only understand concepts like "injective" or "surjective" (regardless of whether one already uses these terms or not) via arrow diagrams, in other words in the form "in no point do two or more arrows end" or "in every point at least one arrow ends." One asks oneself whether it is adequate to understand concepts in this form. The answer is "yes," if one then argues with them at this level in a sound way. This is the case, for example, when one proves, using arrow diagrams, that if the mapping $g{\circ}f$ is injective then so is f, or if $g{\circ}f$ is surjective, then so is g.

The next remark concerns the representation of a finite algebraic system via composition tables. That these representations are two-dimensional is definitely an iconic feature. Experience in the classroom has shown the following: Concepts like the regularity of a composition (cancellation rule) or deductions such as "regularity implies that every equation $ax = b$ is solvable (in the finite case)" become accessible to many pupils only when they are interpreted in an imagined table; that is, "In every row and in every column each element occurs only once, so it must occur at least once."

In one class I taught, pupils were led (independently) through their work with tables to make the conjecture: "Every proper subgroup of a finite group G has at most half as many elements as G."[23] (Lagrange's theorem was not known to them.) And the pupils could give good reasons why this should be so. Thus they worked creatively at a lower level of representation. This is doubtless better than their being largely passive at a higher level.

The same holds for the many possible gradations in *verbal and symbolic representations*. For example, when one can see, in teaching proportions, how a suitable verbal explanation (see Kirsch, 1969)[24] of the basic equality enables pupils at all levels to work with them on their own, whereas symbolic formulations are largely lost on them.

There are new results in this direction on the functional equation of the exponential function. Engel (1971) reported that when they discuss real

---

[23]This statement and its explanation using the table hold true already for (finite) groupoids instead of groups.

[24]Fischer (1976) emphasized the importance of verbal explanations.

growth processes, pupils suggest formulations like "equal lengths of time always give the same growth factor." This form of the equation can be used to deduce nontrivial consequences and applications that become accessible in this way to large groups of pupils.

An example (from Kirsch, 1976a): Let us follow a growth process on the scale of a slide rule. Equal factors mean moving equal lengths along the scale. So to equal lengths of time correspond steps of equal length on the scale. In other words, we travel at a constant speed along the scale. Now pupils can make logarithmic graph paper themselves, simply by marking off the slide rule scale on the left- and right-hand sides of the paper and connecting the corresponding points.

Thus anyone who has ever drawn a timetable graph will see: exponential growth appears on logarithmic paper as a straight line (see Fig. 15.3). In this way—and by using enactive and iconic modes as well—one makes an important aid in practical mathematics understandable for all pupils. Teachers have assured me that this is "too easy" for advanced pupils. However, at present the majority of pupils do not become acquainted with logarithmic graph paper, nor do they even acquire the capacity to learn about it on their own.

I cannot go into questions of symbolic representation in the more restricted sense here. Let me say only that one can make mathematics accessible using different modes of representation. Here "anything goes," be it

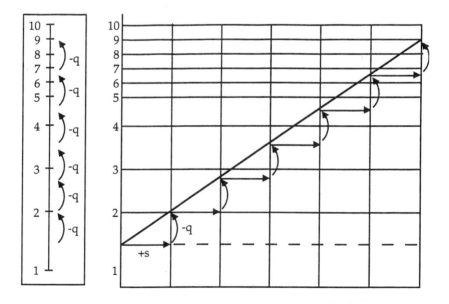

FIG. 15.3. Drawing showing how the use of logarithmic paper makes exponential growth appear as a straight line.

"abus de language" or comics, as used by Braunfeld. I have experienced how Braunfeld had to defend himself against the accusation that this wasn't mathematics. However, "it is not justified," as Fischer (1976) said, "not to call something mathematics simply because it is communicated in a different jargon." Doubtless many simple mathematical ideas remain inaccessible at present to our pupils only because they are presented in a formulation or symbolism that brings difficulties having nothing to do with the mathematical essence.

By emphasizing the validity of the more "primitive" modes of representation, we may seem to be neglecting the question of *intermodal transfer:* Bauersfeld (1972) in particular pointed out how important this is.

Naturally we should exercise pupils in the various modes and especially in the various levels of language. Freudenthal (1974a) illustrated this in a particularly impressive example. Nonetheless, we can do perfectly good mathematics already at the simplest level, and open doors for our pupils without misleading them, or falsifying anything. Perhaps a better formulation of our fourth aspect would be: making accessible by *beginning* at the appropriate level of representation.

CONCLUDING REMARKS

I must finish here. Doubtless I have left out important aspects of making mathematics accessible, such as through illuminating examples. These are certainly of great importance for learning mathematics.[25] But I haven't tried to cover the whole question anyway.

I wish to especially stress that all the ideas sketched here are only aids to make access easier for the learner; they cannot spare the pupil the basic act of understanding. Not every pupil manages this in every case.

Long experience seems to me to suggest that mathematical induction is a "counterexample" in this sense. It has driven teachers to remarkable efforts and stimulated impressive Didaktik creativity, beginning on the enactive level with falling dominoes. But so far there doesn't seem to be any widespread success in teaching it (see Leppig, 1976).

In closing, a word about the *method* in this chapter. The aspects sketched are meant mainly to be a means of organizing some experience and thoughts on teaching mathematics, rather than the objects in their own right of theoretical studies. Nevertheless, perhaps they can serve to organize, to set standards for, or even to stimulate Didaktik researches.

---

[25]Griesel (1971–1973) showed how important it is, particularly in primary school, to continuously provide examples.

ACKNOWLEDGMENTS

This chapter was first published (in a limited circulation edition) in the *Proceedings of the Third International Congress on Mathematical Education*, Hermann Athen and Heinz Kunle, Eds. (Karlsruhe, 1976), pp. 98–120. This article is reprinted here with the permission of Professor Heinz Kunle and Arnold Kirsch. John Scherk, the translator, is a professor of mathematics at the University of Toronto, Canada.

REFERENCES

Ausubel, D. P., & Robinson, F. G. (1969). *School learning.* New York: Holt, Rinehart & Winston.

Bauersfeld, H. (1972). Einige Bemerkungen zum "Frankfurter Projekt" und zum "alef"–Programm. In *Materialien für den Mathematikunterricht in der Grundschule.* Beiträge zur Reform der Grundschule (Vol. 13, pp. 237–245). Frankfurt a. M.: Arbeitskreis Grundschule.

Becker, G. (1974). Möglichkeiten und Probleme des Elementarisierens im mathematischen Unterricht. *Die Schulwarte, 10/11,* 10–19.

Birkhoff, G. D., & Beatley, R. (1959). *Basic geometry.* New York: Chelsea.

Blum, W. (1975). Ein Grundkurs in Analysis. *Didaktik der Mathematik, 3*(3), 163–184.

Braunfeld, P., Dilley, C., & Rucker, W. (1967). A new UICSM approach to fractions for the junior high school. *Mathematics Teacher, 60*(3), 215–221.

Bruner, J. S. (1960). *The process of education.* Cambridge, MA: Harvard University Press.

Bruner, J. S., Oliver, R. R., & Greenfield, P. M. (1966). *Studies in cognitive growth* New York: Wiley.

Deutsches Institut für Fernstudien (DIFF). (Ed.). (1974). *Grundkurs Mathematik III: Geometrie und Lineare Algebra, III.1.1: Elementargeometrie* (Part 1). Tübingen: Author.

Dieudonné, J. (1962). Moderne Mathematik und Unterricht auf der Höheren Schule. *Mathematische-physikalische Semesterberichte zur Pflege des Zusammenhangs von Schule und Universität, 8,* 166–178.

Drenckhahn, F. (Ed.). (1958). *Der mathematische Unterricht für die sechs–bis fünfzehnjährige Jugend in der Bundesrepublik Deutschland: Auf Veranlassung des deutschen Unterausschusses der Internationalen Mathematischen Unterrichts-Kommission.* Göttingen: Vanderhoeck & Ruprecht.

Engel, A. (1971). Anwendungen der Analysis zur Konstruktion mathematischer Modelle. *Der Mathematikunterricht, 17*(3), 5–56.

Fischer, R. (1976). Fundamentale Ideen bei den reellen Funktionen. *Zentralblatt für Didaktik der Mathematik, 8,* 185–192.

Freudenthal, H. (1973). *Mathematik als pädagogische Aufgabe.* Stuttgart: Klett.

Freudenthal, H. (1974a). Kennst Du Deinen Vater? *Der Mathematikunterricht, 20*(5), 5–18.

Freudenthal, H. (1974b). Soviet research on teaching algebra at the lower grades of the elementary school. *Educational Studies in Mathematics, 5*(4), 391–412.

Freund, H. (1960). Die Gewinnung von Steigungswerten durch analytisch-geometrische Betrachtungen. *Der Mathematikunterricht, 6*(2), 22–51.

Griesel, H. (1970). Der wissenschaftliche Hintergrund der Bruchrechnung. *Der Mathematikunterricht, 16*(2), 5–29.

Griesel, H. (1971–1973). *Die Neue Mathematik für Lehrer und Studenten* (2 Vols.). Hanover: Schroedel.

Griesel, H. (1974). Überlegungen zur Didaktik der Mathematik als Wissenschaft. *Zentralblatt für Didaktik der Mathematik, 6,* 115–119.

Holland, G. (1972). Vorschläge zur Entwicklung eines Curriculums für den Geometrieunterricht in der Sekundarstufe I. In *Beiträge zum Mathematikunterricht, 1972: Vorträge auf der 6. Bundestagung für Didaktik der Mathematik* (Part 1, pp. 103–118). Hanover: Schroedel.

Holland, G. (1974). *Geometrie für Lehrer and Studenten* (Vol. 1). Hanover: Schroedel.

Kahle, D. (1976). Gesichtspunkte zur Stoffauswahl und zur Lernziel-Problematik. In *Beiträge zum Mathematikunterricht, 1976: Vorträge auf der 10. Bundestagung für Didaktik der Mathematik* (pp. 103–106). Hanover: Schroedel.

Kirsch, A. (1969). An analysis of commercial arithmetic. *Educational Studies in Mathematics, 1,* 300–311.

Kirsch, A. (1970). *Elementare Zahlen- und Größenbereiche: Eine didaktisch orientierte Begründung der Zahlen und ihrer Anwendbarkeit.* Göttingen: Vanderhoeck & Ruprecht.

Kirsch, A. (1972). Ein didaktisch orientiertes Axiomensystem der Elementargeometrie. *Der mathematische und naturwissenschaftliche Unterricht, 25,* 139–145.

Kirsch, A. (1973). Eindeutige Zuordnungen im 5. Schuljahr: In Begründung des Zahlbegriffs oder Förderung der Kombinationsfähigkeit? In *Beiträge zum Mathematikunterricht, 1973: Vorträge auf der 7. Bundestagung für Didaktik der Mathematik* (pp. 143–149). Hanover: Schroedel.

Kirsch, A. (1975). Eine moderne und einprägsame Fassung der kombinatorischen Grundaufgaben. *Didaktik der Mathematik, 1*(2), 113–130.

Kirsch, A. (1976a). Eine "intellektuell ehrliche" Einführung des Integralbegriffs in Grundkursen. *Didaktik der Mathematik, 4*(2), 87–105.

Kirsch, A. (1976b). Vorschläge zur Behandlung von Wachstumsprozessen und Exponentialfunktionen im Mittelstufenunterricht. *Didaktik der Mathematik, 4*(4), 257–284.

Kirsch, A. (1977). Über die "inaktive" Repräsentation von Abbildungen, insbesondere Permutationen. *Didaktik der Mathematik, 5,* 169–194.

Laugwitz, D. (1973). Ist Differentialrechnung ohne Grenzwertbegriff möglich? *Mathematische-Physikalische Semesterberichte, 20,* 189–201.

Lenné, H. (1969). *Analyse der Mathematikdidaktik in Deutschland.* Stuttgart: Klett.

Leppig, M. (1976). Leistungen von Studienbewerbern hinsichtlich des Beweisprinzips "vollständige Induktion." In *Beiträge zum Mathematikunterricht, 1976: Vorträge auf der 10. Bundestagung für Didaktik der Mathematik* (pp. 120–124). Hanover: Schroedel.

Pickert, G. (1968). Die Bruchrechnung als Operieren mit Abbildungen. *Mathematische-physikalische Semesterberichte zur Pflege des Zusammenhangs von Schule und Universität, 15,* 32–47.

Pickert, G. (1975). *Mathematik für weiterführende Schulen: Fachwissenschaftliche Grundlagen, Lehrerbegleitheft W.* In B. Andelfinger (Ed.), *Mathematik für weiterführende Schulen.* Freiburg: Herder.

Rumpf, H. (1971). Probleme der didaktischen Vereinfachung. In H. Rumpf, *Schulwissen: Probleme der Analyse von Unterrichtsinhalten* (pp. 68–82). Göttingen: Vandenhoeck & Ruprecht.

Spanier, E. (1970). The undergraduate program in mathematics. *American Mathematics Monthly, 77,* 752–755.

Steiner, H.-G. (1961). Logische Probleme im Mathematikunterricht: Die Gleichungslehre. *Mathematische-physikalische Semesterberichte zur Pflege des Zusammenhangs von Schule und Universität, 7,* 178–207.

Steiner, H.-G. (1964). Elementare Beweise zum Fundamentalsatz der Algebra. *Der Mathematikunterricht, 10*(2), 60–93.

Steiner, H.-G. (1969). Magnitudes and rational numbers: A didactical analysis. *Educational Studies in Mathematics, 2*(2/3), 371–392.

Thom, R. (1973). Modern mathematics: Does it exist? In A. G. Howson (Ed.), *Developments in mathematical education: Proceedings of the Second International Congress on Mathematical Education* (pp. 194–209). Cambridge, England: Cambridge University Press.

Vester, F. (1975). *Denken, Lernen, Vergessen: Was geht in unserem Kopf vor, wie lernt das Gehirn, und wann läßt es uns im Stich?* Stuttgart: Deutsche Verlags-Anstalt.

Vollrath, H.-J. (1974). *Didaktik der Algebra.* Stuttgart: Klett.

Wäsche, H. (1961). Logische Probleme der Lehre von den Gleichungen und Ungleichungen. *Der Mathematikunterricht, 7*(1), 7–37.

Wittenberg, A. I. (1963). *Bildung and Mathematik: Mathematik als exemplarisches Gymnasialfach.* Stuttgart: Klett.

Wittmann, E. (1974). *Grundfragen des Mathematikunterrichts.* Braunschweig: Vieweg.

Wittmann, E. (1975). Zur Rolle von Prinzipien in der Mathematikdidaktik. *Beiträge zum Mathematikunterricht, 1975: Vorträge auf der 9. Bundestagung für Didaktik der Mathematik* (pp. 226–235). Hanover: Schroedel.

16

The Law of Free Fall as an "Exemplary Theme" for the Mathematicizability of Certain Natural Processes

Martin Wagenschein
Klaus G. Witz (Trans.)

Martin Wagenschein (1896–1988) was a professor at the University of Tübingen. For an extended biography, see p. 161, chapter 9, this volume.

> *There is no certainty in science where mathematics cannot be applied.*
> —Leonardo[1]

> *I found it extraordinarily peculiar and exciting that mathematics somehow fits with the objects of our experience.*
> —Werner Heisenberg[2]

One of the fundamental experiences that physics instruction wants to transmit is that "mathematics fits to the things of experience."

At first one has the impression that this precise goal of "functional relationship" is *not* being neglected, certainly not in *Gymnasien:* There is almost no physics lesson, especially no demonstration lesson, where one doesn't measure and where one doesn't walk the path from observation through a series of measurements to the mathematical function.

Nevertheless one has the following experience: 25 students at a college of education, among them some practicing teachers, all of them Gymnasium graduates, recall nothing at all about the law of free fall in the course of an informal discussion about teaching (not an examination).

---

[1]Clark (1969, p. 63).
[2]Heisenberg was talking of his experiences in school. See Heisenberg (1956, p. 39).

Finally there comes, hesitantly, the formula fragment "$(1/2)gt^2$." But how are you going to tell this to the kids, "in English"? That would be too difficult, too advanced for them, because of the "squared."

It is clear that this kind of thing should not happen. This "$(1/2)gt^2$" is a false flower, a paper flower. When one is not able to express a condensed, "scientific" fact also in simple English, one does not really possess it (at least in the area of elementary physics). Of course this simple form "was there" at some point. But it was there too fleetingly.

In the works of Galileo, the discoverer of the law of free fall, we look for such a formula in vain. He expressed it only simply—just like the Greeks who, of course, could only express their mathematical insights in the manner of the people, so to speak. They did not yet know the ingenious language of formulas, which admits so easily of abuse (this was certainly a lucky thing for young people who wanted to learn mathematics). In Galileo it says this:

One sees therefore, . . . that . . . the segments [i.e., distances] traversed in equal time intervals are proportional to the uneven numbers one, three, five . . . ,

which of course says nothing more and nothing less than that [famous] formula $s = (1/2)gt^2$, for

if one looks at the total distance covered, then in double the time the fourfold distance is traversed, in triple the time the ninefold distance, and in general the distances traversed are proportional to the squares of the times.

And, in this form "1, 3, 5, 7 . . ." every child who has reached the age of boy- or girlhood understands it.

But if one has finally brought the college students to this point and asks, "Aren't you wondering why, *precisely,* the uneven whole numbers appear here?"—No, most of them are not wondering about anything any more! Sometimes they even say "That has to be that way!"—And why does it have to?—"Because it's a natural law!"

I suspect that such failures in our instruction simply derive from the fact that teachers in *Gymnasien,* with the (of course correct) idea of really driving home the so-very-fundamental mathematicizability of certain natural processes, do so again and again, in almost every lesson, and for that reason always hurriedly, that is, in 45 minutes.

But even without psychology, one cannot possibly believe that a thousand fleeting impressions, one after the other, replace a single deep impression. That would be thinking mechanistically, following the connotation of the inadequate word *impression.* But a thousand dalliances are not worth one real love! It may well be that in these thousand dalliances everything works logically and is exact every time. But we cannot make visible what is physically fundamental when we are satisfied with artificially fabricating the peripheral state that in school we call "attention" and when we address only the logical functions of the child. (That we always have to address these logical functions in some form does not mean that we have to worry *only* about them. Isn't that logical?) Experience of the fundamental is always something that concerns the whole human being, that makes him or her humble and serious, even in physics.

But how could one achieve this? without an "emotional" talking it up (of the kind some readers might fear), and, as always, in an atmosphere of the strictest focus on subject matter: solely through time—the time we let the class have. Lesson plans, as they have been up till now, never actually leave us time. Don't we always have to "go on," continue, finish up? And the success?—In the curricula, in at least the upper levels of the Gymnasium, we need guaranteed freedom for the teachers to choose and form the material.

Let us then have the courage sometimes, occasionally—for example, in the case of the law of free fall—to spend not 45 minutes but several weeks on a topic, and perhaps—it is only a proposal—to try it in something like the following way. (What follows has for the most part been classroom tested; to a lesser extent it is proposal.)

Presupposition: Within some particular and living problem context (which is not included in the following discussion), the students are warmed up for the idea of finding out "how" a ball runs down an inclined table. "How?"—that means how it increases its speed. "Faster and faster"—that is not enough for us. *In what way* faster and faster?

It is good if the teacher has read Galileo (because I only got to do that when I was 50 years old, I am the more convinced that every physics teacher should read him during preservice training):

On a linear track, or shall we say on a wooden board of 12 cubits in length (12 cubits = 6.7 meters), with a width of half a cubit and 3 inches thickness, there was dug along the length of the board a groove a little bit more than 1 inch wide. This groove was drawn very straight, and in order to have the surface inside the groove very smooth there was pasted inside a very smooth and clear parchment; in this groove one lets run a very hard, completely round and smoothly polished brass ball. After the board has been set up, the board is lifted on one side, now one cubit, then two cubits high, then one let the ball fall through the canal. . . .

This first-ever experimental arrangement in physics is obviously a very solid piece of carpentry! And although, today, we wouldn't want to use a board 6.7 meters long, like Galileo, we should start in a somewhat similar way. Not right away with a precision instrument we've bought. Only someone who is first inexact understands exactness.

In measuring time we should, without any qualms, first try to get along with the simplest and the most natural methods. It is true that our technologized kids will, without hesitation, bare their watches with one flick of their wrists. But they will also follow with pleasure the proposal of the teacher to at first remain sort of completely "natural." Just the way the genius Galileo had to do it—because he, of course, lived before Huygens and also didn't know about the pendulum clock, not to mention the wristwatch and the electric stopwatch. Didn't he do this first-ever physical experiment in the history of the world without any of that? (Of course, he could have used a simple thread-and-ball pendulum that has to be pushed constantly with the hand; he was familiar with that. But, as appears shortly, he proceeded immediately to weighing, presumably because it seemed to him more precise. Riccioni, who repeated the experiments soon after Galileo's death, used a fast pendulum, 1.15 in. = 2.8 cm. long [cf. Piel (1954–1955)].)

It seems that Galileo at first used his pulse beat as a clock. He wrote at some point in his report:

> . . . and we found no differences whatsoever, not even a difference of 1/10th of a single pulse beat.

So now, today, one of the students, with his right hand on his left arm, beats his foot in time to his pulse beats; and another one runs, chalk in hand, beside the ball rolling down the board and, each time she hears a beat, puts a chalk mark at the place on the board where the ball is flashing by. This is, of course, very imprecise, particularly if one thinks it is possible that Galileo (who was of course colicky) got excited during the experiment, possibly over the experiment itself. (For him it was, of course, not a purely logical matter. He was very deeply moved by it.)

Of course, if one now measures the distances from one chalk mark to the next, they won't come out 1, 3, 5, 7, . . . , but perhaps something like 1, 3.4, 4.8—or something like that. One will want, therefore, to increase the precision of this "clock." And the kids will surely want to do that also right away.

But the teacher can't immediately do everything that they say. It will be easy to slow them down a little by proposing, "Good, in a little while. But before we do that, assume that we had to depend on this crude way of measuring, that we had to stay with it, would there then be no way of finagling this inexactness?" Perhaps he can say, "[Is there no way to] balance or cancel it out?" Probably they will hit on something like: "Repeat the experiment!" Will the results be the same? If not, then it is not exact. Actually this is a very peculiar proposal. It would be interesting to see how they justify it, because at this point things are already being thought of very causally. It's a matter of "an accident," of "errors," of "influences," which don't have anything to do with the principle. Actually, who determines what "has to do with the principle"? Are we perhaps making prior assumptions? Are we making rules? Apparently.

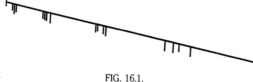

FIG. 16.1.

After four experiments (let us assume, always with the same observers) the board with the chalk marks perhaps looks like Fig. 16.1. Are they wondering why the clumps of marks spread out as one goes farther down the board? Why is that?

And how do we measure the distances? From clump to clump? Which one of the chalk marks should be used? Presumably the students will want to estimate the "center of gravity" of the clump "by feel," and choose. That is again a peculiar aspect about which one can start to reflect. (It is certainly not necessary to become more precise about that. It is important to notice that here one starts on one's own, completely spontaneously, to make one or another choice.)

One could also use different observers. And ask oneself whether one can mix different observers within the same series of measurements. But, anyway, by now they are becoming impatient: The observer, his pulse at least, has to go no matter what. That is too "subjective," "personal," unreliable!

Perhaps they now think of a metronome. Its tick-tock is better than a pulse beat. It has nothing human about it. The picture of the clumps on the board is already looking better. Perhaps like Fig. 16.2. It is true there are still clumps of marks, but they're shrinking! (Why are they shrinking?) In any case, the centers of gravity of the clumps can now be measured more easily. Presumably the experiment still does not yield 1, 3, 5, 7, . . . because, in this kind of estimating, the human being is still involved. Maybe one could calculate the center of gravity? Calculating always gives an impression of exactness! One can think about that in class. Then it becomes apparent that, before calculating, one has to measure the position of the individual marks in a clump with a ruler. Measure it exactly? New reflection about the fact that such a chalk mark will, of course, always have a certain thickness and, by the way, so also will the marks on the ruler. Here's a limit that can't be crossed.

So let us improve the other thing that can still be improved. All kinds of proposals might come. By the way, Galileo had no metronome. And of

FIG. 16.2.

course, the pulse beat was not good enough for him. Presumably no student will think of his ingenious idea of weighing the elapsed time:

> In order to measure the time we set up a bucket full of water, at the bottom of which there was fixed a narrow channel, from which there squirted a fine beam of water that during each observed time of falling was caught in a small cup. The water that was collected in this way was weighed on a very precise scale; from the differences between the weights we got the ratios of the weights and the ratios of the times.

One should go ahead and do this without any qualms. Ramsauer (1953), who repeated the classic experiments in physics in the style of their periods, wrote: "I have repeated the measurements and I was amazed at the precision that could be achieved with such a water clock" (p. 3).

Meanwhile the kids will have found out long ago that there is also somewhere else where the "human being" has to be taken out of the experimental arrangement: the place where she makes the chalk marks. And now one can put them on the track of the idea of whether the ball (which, of course, can easily become a car running on a track) . . . whether perhaps the car itself might carry the clock, and whether this clock could then make the time marks by itself while rolling down the track.

One may propose a drip bottle fixed to the bottom of the car, or a pendulum (of the kind that was once available from teaching supplies companies) that would, on the down part of each swing, break with its tip a small wall of sand that had been piled up on a slat underneath and parallel to the track. Or better still: When the pendulum is transformed into a swinging hourglass, in other words into a paper cone with a tiny hole at the bottom, that would paint a beautifully swinging line on a slat underneath the track that one can afterwards measure to one's heart's content. (Many questions arise there: whether, as the pendulum slows down, it still chops up time into equal pieces? One has to check that!) There are still inexact results in spite of all the machinery.

So it becomes more and more comfortable. Magnets to start the car, an electric stopwatch, then sparks, automatically controlled by the stopwatch, that arc between the car and a soot-covered measuring slat underneath it making needle-sharp points—and what else? The experiment is now fully automatic. The "human being" only needs to push the start button and afterwards measure the results that the car has laid out. (But one shouldn't forget that she has thought the whole thing out to begin with.)

Result? When does it really become "exact"? Obviously never. So never exactly 1, 3, 5, 7, . . . ? Is the business with the whole numbers wrong? No, it's right. But only in the following sense, and that is amazing enough: The numbers 1, 3, 5, 7, as they stand in their bare exactness, never appear in this fashion. But the more and more exactly we proceed (and what that means has now, of course, become clear), the more the little clumps of measurements shrink, the closer the distances between their centers of gravity approach the series 1, 3, 5, 7, . . . Admittedly this has to be said by the teacher. For he cannot perform the much more precise measurements needed in a school—for example, those in which everything happens in a vacuum, without air resistance. But after walking with their teacher so thoroughly through the first part of the way, the students will believe him completely.

And when at this point one asks them whether they're astonished that, in this experiment and in this sense (of a limiting case), the odd whole numbers emerge from nature, then they will probably say "Yes." Because nature must never do what we want. What would we want to do if nature aimed at the numbers 1, 3.12, 4.98 in this free-fall experiment? Then we would learn *that* in the schools and then *that* would be the "law of free fall." Incidentally, even then there would be still enough cause for amazement: namely, that the same numbers always emerged, even if they were not whole numbers.

But we have to be doubly amazed at the way nature actually expresses herself in the law of free fall. Not only do the same numbers come out all the time, but whenever we repeat the experiment, the same *natural numbers* come out all the time. The *simplicity* is the most astonishing thing. That's more than we can expect. That's a mysterious "coming to meet us" [by nature]. That's the miracle of "mathematicizability," and [here] even with whole numbers.

Of course this "coming to meet us" is not a spontaneous one. Nature doesn't "come" out of her own volition. *We* have to take the first step. We propose to her the natural numbers, of course in the simplest series 1, 3, 5, 7 time units. She did not necessarily have to oblige this procedure. But she does. The wonder is scarcely diminished. And it now becomes clear that a certain ritual has to be initiated and kept by us (which includes the repeatability, the independence from the observer, the closed system).

So modern physics is therefore not needed.[3] This elementary experiment has already made that clear: Physics does not describe how nature "is," but how nature answers. And there are cases where following the ritual yields nothing; it remains fruitless. The ritual is always applicable. We can surround a human being wrestling with a decision with physical apparatus that registers his impulses, and in fact it will register something. But there is nothing repeatable, nothing simple, nothing essential.

It is strange, from this point of view, to come back to him again, to Galileo. For in his case the experiment did not proceed at all in the way it did for

---

[3]Compare Litt (1956).

us this time. It was nowhere near as precise, and there wasn't so much reflecting about things.

But, with the total innocence of the first discoverer, he was convinced from the very beginning, at least he hoped and expected, that nature is mathematicizable, and in a simple way:

> Finally we were led by the hand so-to-speak, by the attentive observation of the ordinary happenings and of the order in nature in all its arrangements, in the execution of which she habitually utilizes the simplest and easiest means: for I think nobody will believe, that swimming and flying can be accomplished more simply and more easily than through those means that fish and birds utilize with natural instinct. When I therefore notice that a rock falling from rest from great height acquires more and more new increments in speed, why should I not believe that such increments come about in the very simplest manner that is plausible to everyone?

And for that reason he forewent completely even telling us about the values that he had measured. So we are amazed that, "Galileo still does not know what today is the experimenter's duty, namely the exact description of all experimental details, like the diameter of the ball, the angle of the groove [in the board], as well as the reporting of all numerical experimental results and a critique of all sources of error."[4] He repeated, but did not compute any means; rather he found his hypothesis only always confirmed anew. He was, so it seems to us today, not so conscientious as we have to be even with the kids. And still, that we owe to him too; he was such a genius to show us the beginning so that today, when we are at the end of the beginning, we can also be conscientious. So we find in his writing the following:

> Then one let the ball run through the canal and recorded the time it took to cover the whole distance. We *frequently* repeated . . . and found no differences at all, not even of 1/10th of one pulse beat. Then we let the ball run only through 1/4 of the distance and found *always exactly* the same time as before . . . *with perhaps 100 repetitions* we always found that the distances traversed were proportional to the squares of the times: and this was true for every inclination of the board on which the ball ran down . . . , and that is to say with such precision, that the numerous observations *never noticeably* differed from each other. (Emphases added)

ACKNOWLEDGMENTS

Translation of Martin Wagenschein (1995), "Das Fallgesetz als ein für die Mathematisierbarkeit gewisser natürlicher Abläufe 'exemplarisches Thema.'"

---

[4]Ramsauer (1953, p. 3). Incidentally, Galileo did specify the inclination of the board: the 12-cubit-long board is raised "now one, now two cubits high." The corresponding angles are roughly 4° 50′ and 9° 30′.

In Martin Wagenschein, *Naturphänomene sehen und verstehen: Genetische Lehrgänge*, Hans Christoph Berg, Ed. (Stuttgart and Dresden: Ernst Klett Verlag für Wissen und Bildung), pp. 202–208. This chapter was originally published in *Zeitschrift für die Höhere Schule*, 1957, Nos. 2/3, pp. 67–72. This chapter is reprinted here with the permission of the copyright holder Ernst Klett Verlag GmbH, Stuttgart.

Translator's note: In his discussion of Galileo's experiment, Wagenschein quotes from Galileo Galilei (1891), *Unterredungen und mathematische Demonstrationen über zwei neue Wissenszweige, die Mechanik und die Fallgesetze betreffend: dritter und vierter Tag* (A. von Oettingen, Ed. and Trans.). Oswalds Klassiker der exakten Wissenschaften, Vol. 24 (Leipzig: Verlag von Wilhelm Engelmann). Stillman Drake (Galileo Galilei *Two New Sciences: Including Centers of Gravity and Force of Percussion*, Stillman Drake, Trans. [Madison: University of Wisconsin Press, 1974]) noted that, like all early translations, von Oettingen's translation presented Galileo's thought "without due consideration of the nature of earlier physics and its special terminology" (p. xvii). Drake's interpretation of the relevant passages is found on pages 169–70 of his translation. In this chapter we have translated Wagenschein's Galileo.

REFERENCES

Clark, K. (1969). *Leonardo da Vinci in Selbstzeugnissen und Bilddokumenten* (Rowohlts Monographien 153). Reinbeck bei Hamburg: Rowohlt.

Heisenberg, W. (1956). *Das Naturbild der heutigen Physik* (Rowohlts deutsche Enzyklopädie: Sachgebiet: Physik 8). Hamburg: Rowohlt.

Litt, T. (1956). Philosophische Anthropologie und moderne Physik. *Studium Generale: Zeitschrift für interdisziplinäre Studien, 9*(7), 351–363.

Piel, C. (1954–1955). Die ältesten Versuche über den freien Fall. *Der mathematische und naturwissenschaftliche Unterricht (MNU), 7,* 300.

Ramsauer, C. (1953). *Grundversuche der Physik in historischer Darstellung.* Berlin: Springer.

17

Open Experimenting: A Framework for Structuring Science Teaching and Learning

Peter Reinhold

Peter Reinhold is a professor of the Didaktik of physics at the Universität Gesamthochschule-Paderborn and an associate of the Institut für die Pädagogik der Naturwissenschaften, Kiel. He is author of *Offenes Experimentieren und Physiklernen* (Kiel: Institut für die Pädagogik der Naturwissenschaften, 1996).

THE ROLE OF THE EXPERIMENT IN SCIENCE TEACHING

Since the end of the last century, the fundamental place of the experiment in science education has been generally unchallenged, at least in its role as a basic method of teaching content. But although this conviction is part of every book, and every course, on science teaching, teaching practices are often different. Faced with organizational problems and time pressures, with lack of materials, and the problems of handling equipment, teachers use talk-and-chalk more often than the approaches advocated by theorists of science teaching.

But, in the early 1980s, the role of the experiment in science teaching became controversial in the thinking of science educators. Questions about the effectiveness and goals of the school experiment emerged (Hodson, 1988, 1992; Hofstein & Lunetta, 1982; Tamir, 1990) and a radical reshaping and restructuring of the role of the experiment in science classrooms was called for.[1] But asking for a reshaping and restructuring of the role of the experiment in science teaching involves much more than issues of method—which reduces experimenting to an effective means of instruction. *There are more fundamental issues to be asked.* What do we conceive the general aim of teaching science to be and how might the experiment contributes to that aim? What might the school experiment contribute to Bildung?

In the traditions of German Didaktik (Litt, 1963; Wagenschein, 1976) all teaching has to initiate, and offer a structure for, formative *(bildend)* development on the part of the learner. From this perspective two questions follow:

- What is the specific contribution of teaching science to formative development, or Bildung? or, as Wagenschein (1965: see also chap. 9, this volume) put it, what are "exemplary" themes in science that the learner should encounter and experience?
- How might a framework of answers to such questions change the role of the experiment in teaching science?

These questions are, of course, intimately related. Thus, in his *Naturwissenschaft und Menschenbildung*, Litt argued that the specific contribution of the natural sciences to Bildung is their method; and Wagenschein (1965; see also chap. 9, this volume) referred to Litt when he outlined his concept of Bildung:

> If we understand the process of Bildung to be such that the learners, as subjects of this process, must actively comprehend and absorb the object of learning and be affected by it—a process leading to confrontation between the whole subject and the whole object—and if we consider that we no longer comprehend physics as the study of how nature "really is," but as a way of understanding and, as an aspect resulting from this . . . , a method by which nature allows us to interrogate her, then we acknowledge—as did Litt—that this method itself *produces* subject and object, by restricting man to the role of an "observer" insistent on logic and on nature as the basically measurable.
>
> If we acknowledge all this, we cannot call any form of teaching educative *(bildend,* i.e., formative) that does not constantly have this "triad" of subject-method-object in sight, indeed that does not make it the very substance of teaching.

---

[1] I should note that, with a few exceptions (see Muckenfuß, 1979; Raufuß, 1989), this controversy has not found its way to Germany. Why this important issue is not being raised in Germany is an open question. It may be that the traditional rhetoric justifying experiments conceals the issue; it may be that the complexity of the issue is the problem; or it may be that a fundamental and a generally accepted commitment to teaching and learning science by experiment is missing.

Just as the natural sciences can be conceived as a process whereby we interact with nature in a specific, methodologically founded way *and* as a body of knowledge describing and explaining nature, the experiment can be seen as having two aspects. It is an instructional setting to teach content knowledge, *and* it is a means for teaching experimenting itself. Learning to plan and perform an experiment, to analyze results, and to reflect on methodological problems—thereby experiencing the method—defines the educational or formative *(bildend)* role of the experiment in science education. *The experiment itself must be a topic in the science curriculum.*

In other words, a Didaktik of experimenting encompasses more than just methodological or instructional questions. It involves a discussion of all the functions of the experiment in the teaching and learning process as well as a search to relate them in order to form a consistent and educational *(bildend)* approach. *Open experimenting* is one way of thinking about how to plan for teaching and learning that aims in this direction.

Functions of the Experiment in Science Teaching

In the literature of science education, the experiment is given many roles (see Table 17.1). As a way of teaching content knowledge, experiments are considered to be starting points for forming and deriving scientific concepts. From an educational viewpoint, the experiment is seen as a way of offering experience of self-activity, independence, and precise and critical thinking. From a psychological perspective, experimenting is said to be important for motivation and the development of problem-solving skills. Process approaches to science teaching emphasize a methodological and epistemological function of experimenting. Finally, experiments have a practical function: They are a means by which students become familiar with equipment, measuring devices, and procedures.

But, when compared to these proclaimed functions of the experiment, teaching practice and its outcomes looks very different (see Table 17.1). Thus, the effectiveness, relevance, and acceptance of lab work, and instruction based on experiments, is strongly questioned by research on students' conceptions (Pfundt & Duit, 1994), interests (Häussler, 1987), and problem solving (Garett, 1986), to name but a few areas. Everyday thinking is *not* transformed by lab activities (Reif & Larkin, 1991) and scientific concepts are *not* acquired from experiments in a way that allows students to operate with them in problem-solving tasks. Furthermore, students often hold distorted views on scientific methods and epistemological issues as a result of their experiences in school labs (Hodson, 1985). Students follow lab instructions like cookery recipes: They gather and record data without a clear sense of purposes and procedures. Labs make few cognitive demands and provide a context that precludes methodological and epistemological reflections on the process of experimenting.

TABLE 17.1

The Experiment in the Teaching–Learning Process

Content-Related Function	Problems
• teaching content of physics • teaching the structure of the discipline • teaching concepts, laws, principles, theories • extending or supporting theoretical lessons • relating theoretical and empirical knowledge • verifying facts and principles already taught	• students' preconceptions are not sufficiently transformed • students have problems with conceptual change • concepts, laws, and principles are (only) memorized • students have difficulties in applying the knowledge taught
Practical Function	Problems
• developing manipulative skills • giving experience with standard techniques • encouraging accurate observation and description • taking notes • performing and representing measurements • becoming able to comprehend and carry out instructions	• problems related to planning, performing, and interpreting experiments • hands on-minds off • following lab instruction like recipes • students mostly have no idea of the (epistemological) purpose when performing an experiment (results are known in advance)

Methodological Function	Problems
• developing scientific methods • gaining epistemological knowledge about scientific process • teaching issues from philosophy, sociology, and history of science	• no adequate or realistic views of scientific methods • students' methodical conceptions are not useful for gaining knowledge • distorted views of the development of scientific theories • problematic view on epistemological issues like scientific truth, objectivity • highly developed equipment obstructs methodological insights

Psychological Function	Problems
• making phenomena more real through experience • helping to remember facts and principles • supporting problem solving • arousing and maintaining interest • supporting motivation	• declining motivation in the course of the instructional process • declining interests • low problem-solving ability • problem-solving methods are context related

Pedagogical or Educational Function	Problems
• promoting a logical, reasoning method of thought • developing the ability to cooperate and to communicate • fostering self-reliance • promoting a critical attitude • promoting student action • promoting a reflective practice	• general cognitive skills are conceived to be context related • perfect equipment, prescribed instructions, and known results obstruct self-activity • no methodological reflection on experimenting

To address these problems, many approaches have been suggested (Carey, Evans, Honda, & Unger, 1989; Hodson, 1992; Lock, 1990; Millar, 1987; Niedderer, 1987; Padilla, 1991; Roth, 1994; St. John, 1980). However, a review of these suggestions shows that each one focuses on only a few of the functions outlined earlier (and sometimes in ways that contradict others). *And, not surprisingly, none of the suggestions address the formative (bildend) development of the learner.* In other words, an integrated Didaktik of the science experiment is missing.

How should learners experiment so that they acquire both a knowledge of, for example, physics content and adequate methodological and epistemological knowledge about physics such that (a) they are able to apply and use their knowledge in new contexts, (b) they are motivated to understand (Wagenschein, 1965: see also chap. 9, this volume), and (c) they experience formative *(bildend)* development? These are the central questions in my exploration of open experimenting (Reinhold, 1996).

Open Experimenting

The term *open* invites two lines of observation and speculation about classroom experiments. Thus, experiments are normally open-ended. The results are not known in advance. But although this holds for research experiments, it is not the case for experiments in science classrooms. When students perform a classroom experiment, they usually know the correct answers—from theory. They receive high grades if the investigation secures the "right" data. Whether they relate their results to the problems under investigation is of minor importance. The methodological function of experimenting is hardly considered.

Second, can students "mess about" in an open-ended way as they experiment, without any guidance from the teacher? This question suggests the open experiments or open-ended experiments as described in, for example, the Nuffield Curriculum. Students should be given "some chance in a rich experimental field to discover rules in the profusion of natural phenomena" (*Nuffield Physics Teachers Guide I*, 1966, p. 184). "Make a spring, and hang things on it, and find out how it stretches. Here is some copper wire that you can wind on a pencil to make a spring" (*Nuffield Physics Teachers Guide I*, 1966, p. 43). But this is neither a realistic description of the scientific process nor productive for the students.

Abstracting and developing rules or laws without help is a demand that is too complex for many, if not most, students. To be sure, learning is a process that students have to do for themselves. Learning is active and constructive; based on what they already know it is learners themselves who form the *meaning* of new information as they process it. But, in contrast to the radical constructivist position that denies any pedagogic intention, I believe that a learning process necessarily needs to be guided by the teacher. What is needed is an ample support, support that challenges and fosters students so that they expand their knowledge *self-actively*. The problem is how to balance self-activity and ample support in the classroom setting.

Open experimenting seeks this balance. The teacher starts off with an open-ended and challenging experimental situation. Students are given the opportunity to develop and carry out experiments themselves—addressing questions that they themselves have formulated in order to explain the experimental situation. Perturbations in the students' cognitive processes occurring in the course of their activities force them to reflect, *by themselves,* on their conceptions and the procedures they apply in order to proceed with the investigation of the phenomenon. This reflection on their own activities is essential: It is, when supported by the teacher, the starting point for the development and expansion of conceptual, methodological, and epistemological knowledge *and* an important contribution to formative *(bildend)* development.

Theoretical Framework and Research Method

A theoretical framework for planning and performing open experimenting, together with an experimental example, was developed in the first step of the Didaktik project described here.[2] This framework was then tested in a semester-long seminar (2 hours a week) on physics teaching in which the participating student teachers engaged in open experimenting. The seminar was recorded on video. A case study of the teaching and learning process in the seminar followed. Based on the case study, the theoretical framework was modified and expanded. A second semester-long case study followed, using a different experimental example but almost the same group of students. This iterative process was repeated for two more semesters.

From this process, a specific structure, involving an elementary concept of the experimental method and a constructivist teaching–learning method based on *productive perturbations,* was established. The structure for planning open experimenting balanced learners' self-activity and ample support by the instructional setting (see also Engeström, 1987; Lawson, Abraham, & Renner, 1989; Schön, 1987; Scott, Asoko, & Driver, 1992). In this chapter, I describe this structure on two levels. First, starting with an example, I tell the story of a group of second- and third-year student teachers of physics

---

[2]Guided by a theoretical framework based on activity theory (Engeström, 1987; Leont'ev, 1978), constructivism (von Glasersfeld, 1989), and the concept of *System-Bildung* (Walgenbach, 1990; Wolze, 1989).

investigating a phenomenon I presented. Second, I reflect on that teaching–learning process from a theoretical point of view, both to elucidate my perspective and to offer a rationale for the structural elements in planning open experimenting.

THE OPTICAL DICE PHENOMENON

A slide projector with a vertical slit placed in front of it forms a linear light source that produces divergent light. If a square diaphragm is placed in the beam, we would expect a two-dimensional pattern of umbra and penumbra on a screen. Surprisingly, we see a three-dimensional dice on the screen. On a closer look, we also observe that the edges of the dice are more intensively emphasized as bright lines. How does this happen? (See Fig. 17.1.)

A Situation in Need of Explanation

Open experimenting starts with the demonstration of a phenomenon that generates a situation in need of explanation by students. The demonstration involves certain moments of surprise: Why do we see a three-dimensional dice on the screen? Where do the bright lines come from? These phenomena

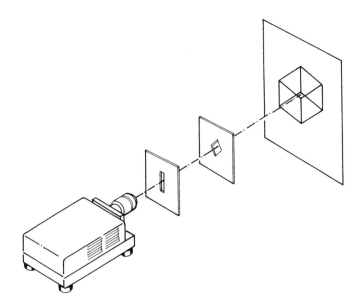

FIG. 17.1.   Experimental setting to demonstrate the optical dice phenomenon.

did not easily fit into the students' prior experience; they could not explain it within their available cognitive system. For some students a cognitive conflict arose: Shadows—they argued—are normally two-dimensional. Why does this specific formation of shadows look like a three-dimensional dice? Answering these questions and removing the cognitive conflicts can form a motif that leads students to investigate the phenomenon more thoroughly.

Trying and Speculating

If the teacher does not intervene, a phase of trying and speculating on the part of the students follows. First assumptions are put forward, ad hoc hypotheses are suggested, and attempts are made to confirm these assumptions and hypotheses. Turning or tipping the diaphragm, or varying the distance between the vertical slit and the diaphragm, changes the form but not the plasticity of the figure on the screen. However, if the slit in front of the projector is shortened to almost a pinhole, the dice shrinks to a two-dimensional square. The linear light source can be imagined as an array of infinitely many point sources, each one producing a light square on the dark screen. Thus the observed formation of shadows can be conceived as a superposition of infinitesimally shifted squares. Thus far, our description is based on geometrical optics. But where do the bright lines come from? Are they due to diffraction, or are they "only" an optical illusion? (See Fig. 17.2.)

During this phase of trying and speculating, the students gather experience. Their questions become more specific as they activate available knowledge. In this process of "reflection-in-action" (Schön, 1987), the students create an object-to-be-investigated and discuss their conceptual representation of that object. The process is open, without any interventions from

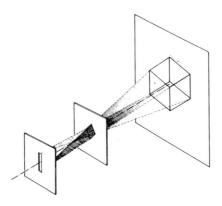

FIG. 17.2. Course of principal rays for the dice phenomenon.

the teacher who should insist only that the students document all their ideas and detailed observations. This openness is an important requirement: The students must develop their concrete aims, which relate to what *they* have established as *their* object of investigation.

Reflecting on the Formed Systems

Over time, trying and speculating becomes less and less productive. No new or more specific hypotheses and no further experiments are suggested. But the complexity and variety that has been generated require systemization. The teacher can induce such a change in perspective, with the related reflection, by asking the students to conceive the phenomenon as a system. This implies, on the one hand, questions about the elements, relevant properties, and the relationship between the elements within such a system and, on the other hand, a new problem for the students: What should be the essential feature, or underlying conception, when forming such a system? Stimulated by such a productive perturbation, the students try to apply available knowledge in order to develop an adequate conceptual representation and description of the system. Compared to the phase of trying and speculating, a higher level of abstraction and understanding is stimulated. Finally, reflecting on the formed systems leads to a research program that contains more specific hypotheses when compared to the speculations at the beginning of the investigation.

What about the observer? Is the observer an essential element of the system? If one tries to keep the observer out of the system, as experimental methods normally require, then the bright lines should exist independent of an observer; that is, they could be measured by some device.

Experimenting in Normal Science

Open experimenting can be compared to Kuhn's (1970) "normal science." The students systematically experiment within a framework based on their own description of the phenomenon. By means of a simple device, for example, a photomultiplier, the change of intensity along different paths across the shadows on the screen can be measured. The result fits into the description based on geometrical optics. Maxima of intensity due to the bright lines that an observer perceives, however, are not detectable. Was the measuring device not sensitive enough? Or, do the bright lines not exist? Are they an optical illusion, a construction of our perception system? If not, we had to question the explanation. However, if we stick to that explanation, we are forced to extend a system based on geometrical optics: *The observer, or at least the perception system, has to be included in our system.*

Reflecting on the Formation of a System

In an experiment, for reasons of objectivity, we normally try to keep the observer out of the investigated system. But the investigation of the dice phenomenon leads almost unavoidably to a methodological problem that induces another productive perturbation. And there is a further problem: Are the experiments and considerations developed to this point sufficient to be sure that the bright lines are, in principle, not measurable?

How students think about this issue, how they argue, depends on their methodological and epistemological conceptions around experimenting. These conceptions become, almost unavoidably, a point at issue. The students must reflect on them, to transform or expand them, in order to proceed in their investigation directed toward an explanation of the phenomenon.

Toward a Theory of the Phenomenon

The explanation of the dice phenomenon leads to physiological optics. There the bright lines are called *Mach bands* (Mach, 1865, 1866a, 1866b, 1906). They are the result of a so-called simultaneous contrast based on an interaction of neighboring retinal elements. When light affects a particular retinal element, the affection reduces the sensitivity of neighboring retinal elements. Therefore, the neighboring elements transmit a signal of a lower intensity of light to the brain than they actually receive. Thus, perceiving a bright surface element on a dark background, the edges of the surface appear to be brighter than the surface itself.

THEORETICAL FOUNDATION OF OPEN EXPERIMENTING

My example involves the structure seen in Fig. 17.3. I now discuss the structure of open experimenting from a theoretical framework in order to elaborate and ground its structural elements. My framework is a conception of Didaktik based on activity theory *(Tätigkeitstheorie)*. I start with an introduction of the concept of *complementarity* that is essential for this framework.

The Concept of Complementarity

We all know that a winning soccer team needs more than 11 good players: The whole is more than the sum of the parts. But, how can we define the relation between terms like *part* and *whole,* or *element* and *system?* Any definitions of these terms are mutually related, the one depending on the other. To form an idea of the whole (the team) we need a conception of its parts (the players) and vice versa. A conception of the function, or structure, of a system that is related to its context requires us to decide which things

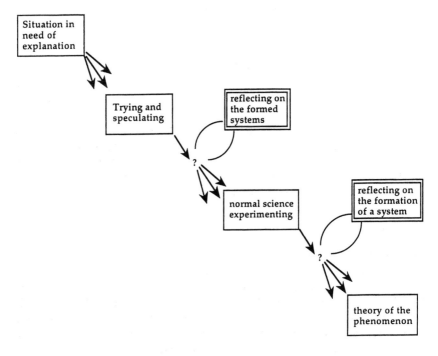

FIG. 17.3. The structure of open experimenting.

or individuals should be conceived of as elements of the system and which not. Such issues raise the general question of how concepts or entities like "system" and "element" are related. How can we describe the structure of their relationship?

The concept of complementarity, as suggested by Wolze (1989), refers, on the one hand, to Bohr (1964–1966) and his interpretation of quantum mechanics and, on the other hand, takes up Hegel's dialectic concept of thesis and antithesis. A complementary relation can be characterized in the following ways:

- Complementary terms are not contradictory to one another; they are not the negation of each other.
- Complementary opposites are not isolated aspects.
- Complementary opposites are not polar opposites with a continuous "more" or "less" existing between them.
- Complementary opposites mutually determine each other.

Following Bohr, these features are interdisciplinary. Starting from the problem of a consistent interpretation of quantum mechanics, Bohr extended his concept of complementarity to philosophy. For him complementarity represents a universal structure of human experience—like the relation between cognition and emotion, thought and will, love and justice. Hegel emphasized that it is the mutual determination of complementary opposites that forms their unity.

The Complementarity of Knowledge and Activity

As I have already noted, my Didaktik is based on activity theory *(Tätigkeitstheorie)* (Fichtner, 1985; Reinhold, 1988, 1996; Walgenbach, 1990; Wolze, 1989).[3] Activity is a category that relates and mediates a subject (a person) and its object (a material thing to work on, like a stone that is molded by a sculptor, or an idea, like a theory, that is expanded by a scientist). In other words, subject and object interact. The subject constructs and determines its object and vice versa; that is, the object can be seen as the counterprocess to the subject's cognitive or material activity. Litt and Wagenschein had this notion in mind when they discussed the triad of subject-method-object.

For learning or cognition, that is, for our context, a central issue in activity theory is the mutual dependence of knowledge and activity. Just as in a developmental phase and a developmental process (i.e., a seed and a growing plant), knowledge and activity are complementarily related: They are two sides of the same coin. We know, for example, that students' learning is determined by preconceptions. Or, if we think about the development of scientific theories from a Kuhnian perspective, it is the disciplinary matrix, or the paradigm, that guides scientists in their research—and, vice versa, these research activities constitute the disciplinary matrix.

For a scientist, knowledge must have a specific quality. She works within a particular paradigm and tries to develop and expand what she knows. For this, knowledge must be effective, meaning that it has to be an efficient means for its own development and expansion. There is no other knowledge available for the scientist. Thus, in addition to conceptual knowledge, "knowledge" also has to include methodological and epistemological knowledge to become functional in the scientist's cognitive activity. If we add norms, that is, the societal aspect of knowledge and paradigmatic examples, then we have what Kuhn called a "disciplinary matrix."[4]

---

[3]This approach is rooted in cultural-historical activity theory (Engeström, 1987; Leont'ev, 1978; Wertsch, 1981), in philosophy of science (Kuhn, 1970; Lakatos, 1976; Sneed, 1971; Stegmüller, 1970–1973; Wittgenstein, 1967), and German Pädagogik (Diesterweg, 1956; Litt, 1963).

[4]For instance, to acquire Ohm's law, some theoretical preknowledge about electric current and voltage is essential. But knowledge about experimental methods and epistemological knowledge (what the nature of laws in physics is about) is also necessary. It is obvious that these levels of knowledge are interrelated. This interrelation is expressed in paradigmatic examples.

In order to emphasize that scientific knowledge encompasses different interrelated levels, we conceive of knowledge as *systemic*. Knowledge and knowledge about knowledge, that is theoretical and metatheoretical knowledge, are related to one another within so-called cognitive systems *(Erkenntnissysteme)*. These cognitive systems are an efficient means for cognitive activities only when seen as a whole, in a similar way to a disciplinary matrix, and, again, they can be acquired by a learner only as a whole. In other words, *an activity-theoretical approach to Didaktik describes the learning process as a development of cognitive systems through the expansion of the learners' cognitive activities.*

But, referring back to our example of Ohm's law (see Footnote 4), a fundamental question arises: Where does the necessary metatheoretical knowledge within a cognitive system come from? Surely, it results from a generalization of earlier cognitive processes. But, if theoretical and metatheoretical knowledge are mutually dependent, we have, from a logical point of view, a circular argument. Faced with such a predicament, activity theory assumes that conceptual, methodological, and epistemological knowledge expand simultaneously. We call this the "problem of expanding cognitive systems." It implies a shift from formal logic to dialectics, to thinking in complementary categories, like state and process, part and whole, or invariance and change. As a consequence, the learning process has to always address *all* levels of knowledge. If one, for example, the methodological level, is neglected when deriving science concepts from a few prepared examples, inadequate conceptions of experimental methods may follow.

If we shift from an epistemological to a learning-psychological perspective the problem of expanding cognitive systems is similar to what Bereiter (1985, pp. 204–205) called the "learning paradox." He asked "How can a structure generate another structure more complex than itself?" Theoretically, the problem is "how can the development of complex mental structures be accounted for by mechanisms that are not themselves highly intelligent or richly endowed with knowledge?" In other words, how is progress toward higher levels of complexity possible without there "already being some ladder or rope to climb on."

Open experimenting attempts to address the problem of expanding cognitive systems. The approach aims at a development of cognitive systems *as a whole*. While investigating the phenomenon the teacher presents, students implicitly develop and expand knowledge at all levels of their cognitive systems: explaining the phenomenon, designing and performing real experiments, and thinking about the justification of knowledge when interpreting their experiments and data. However, the structure of open experimenting is arranged in such a way that different levels of knowledge are explicitly invoked, and considered, at different points in the process.

Activity and Reflection

Another issue in an activity-theoretical approach to Didaktik centers on the relation of activity and reflection. Activity theory conceives an activity as a conscious process. When, for example, a certain cognitive activity cannot be realized by means of the related cognitive system, that is, when a perturbation occurs, an *orienting activity* starts. Reflecting on the previous activity and its constraints, the acting person develops ideas about restructuring and re-forming that activity. The activity refers to itself; it is a self-referential system. By means of such reflection, knowledge about the activity is abstracted, modified, or expanded.

This was an important assumption for the conceptualization of open experimenting—and for when I was looking for suitable experimental examples. Thus, my first approach consisted of two steps: activity and reflection. However, this approach, offering the students metatheoretical knowledge to reflect on their experimenting, failed. As the case study of my first seminar suggests, the offered knowledge was artificial to the students; they could not relate it to their experience. As a result, I decided to wait for situations when the students' own activity faced them with problems that needed to be addressed. As illustrated in the discussion of my second seminar, this occurred twice:

- When trying and speculating was becoming unproductive, and a change in perspective was induced by asking the students to reflect on the phenomenon in terms of a system.
- When the students met methodological problems because of their conceptions of experimentation.

In terms of activity theory, both phases are orienting activities in the course of the students' investigation of the phenomenon.

Activity and Motif

Activity is a structured process determined by a *motif (Motiv)*. In the terms of activity theory, a motif is the object or useful result of an activity that satisfies the underlying need of the activity. A motif also encompasses the emotional assessment of the activity. Leont'ev (1978) distinguished personal sense *(persönlicher Sinn)*, that is, the individual meaning of an activity for a particular person, and an objective or societal meaning *(objektive Bedeutung)*. (In an examination, e.g., the personal sense may be approval, but the objective meaning is regulating selection.) It is, therefore, essential that a learning process establishes not only objective meaning (in the sense that knowledge about induction is essential for understanding electrodynamics) but also personal meaning; the students must experience this knowledge as situated and useful, as "situated cognition" (Hennessy, 1993).

Open experimenting addresses this problem by the arrangement of its starting point. The demonstration of the experimental phenomenon must place students in a challenging situation, a situation that is in need of explanation when viewed from *their* cognitive systems. Wagenschein (1965; see also chap. 9, this volume) called this the "point of entry," challenging and "exciting" the child's "spontaneity." The point of entry has to affect the child by offering a "fundamental experience"—it must support the development of personal sense *and* form a motif that drives the investigation of the phenomenon.

In his activity theory Leont'ev (1978) suggested a hierarchy consisting of three system levels: the level of the *overall activity* regulated by motifs, the level of *constituent actions* regulated and determined by goals—in a system-theoretical description these are the elements of the activity, and the level of *operations regulated and determined by conditions*. These three levels are not stable or fixed; rather, activity is to conceived as "continuously proceeding transformations" between the levels.

For open experimenting, the problem is how motifs, and goals, develop and how this process can be supported. At this point Leont'ev's psychological activity theory, as I understand it, is not very precise. However, this problem was taken up by Engeström (1987, p. 295): In his discussion of "learning by expanding" he explored the means for "expansive transitions" to "envision and project the evolving object and motif of the new activity" during a voyage through the "proximal zone of development" (Vygotsky, 1978). Engeström suggested the use of *springboards* to support the development of motifs:

> The springboard is a facilitative image, technique, or socio-conversational constellation (or a combination of these) misplaced or transplanted from some previous context into a new, expansively transitional activity context during an acute conflict of a double-bind character. The springboard has typically only a temporary or situational function in the solution of the double-bind. (p. 287)

In open experimenting, the presentation of a situation in need of explanation can be seen as such a springboard. The structural element "trying and speculating" then establishes and stabilizes motif and goals. Schön (1987) called this process "reflection-in-action":

> Surprise leads to reflection within an action-present. Reflection is, at least in some measure, conscious although it need not occur in the medium of words. We consider both the unexpected event and the knowing-in-action that led up

to it, asking ourselves, as it were, "What is this?" and, at the same time, "How have I been thinking about it?" Our thought turns back on the surprising phenomenon and, at the same time, back on itself.

Reflection-in-action has a critical function, questioning the assumption structure of knowing-in-action. We think critically about the thinking that got us into this fix or this opportunity; and we may, in the process, restructure strategies of action, understandings of phenomena, or ways of framing problems. . . .

Reflection gives rise to an on-the-spot experiment. We think up and try out new actions intended to explore the newly observed phenomena, test our tentative understandings of them, or affirm the moves we have invented to change things for the better. . . . On-the-spot experimentation may work, again in the sense of yielding intended results, or it may produce surprises that call for further reflection and experiment. (p. 28)

Here Schön described a fluctuation between knowing-in-action and reflection. In terms of activity theory, this fluctuation is a shifting between activity and orienting activity. When "coached" (Schön, 1987, p. 296), it supports the learner in developing specific goals for an investigation. Another "springboard" (Engeström, 1987, p. 287) appears when, at the conclusion of a phase of "trying and speculating," the "system question" is raised to induce cognitive activity on a more general level.

Self-Activity *(Selbsttätigkeit)* and Guidance

Learning could be conceived as pure self-activity, as in Bruner's (1961) "discovery learning" or, as in Dewey's (1933) project method, learning by doing. We also have Ausubel's (1968) meaningful verbal learning in which knowledge is presented to the learner following the disciplinary structure of science. From my point of view, both of these approaches involve idealizations of the teaching and learning process. Self-activity, on the one hand, requires stimulation from the learner's environment, that is, from teachers, classmates, material, and so forth, and, on the other hand, learners have to construct the meaning of offered information by themselves—as constructivism states. Self-activity and guidance should not be conceived as opposites; they are two sides of the same coin. In terms of activity theory, a complementary unity of "self-development" *(Selbstentwicklung)* and "being-developed" *(Entwickeltwerden)* is assumed as a main characteristic of every process of development.

Nevertheless, in some situations the teacher will have to introduce science concepts to students, and the question is how to manage this when the idea of self-activity is being taken seriously. Some approaches (e.g., Driver, 1989; Lawson et al., 1989; Scott et al., 1992) suggest that students should compare the results of their own cognitive activities with scientific concepts introduced by the teacher. But then we are confronted with the learners' alternative frameworks. The students subsume the new information under their existing frameworks, using these frameworks as the means of processing. In addition, they have no basis for a comparison—inasmuch as comparison involves higher order concepts. In other words, the problem of self-activity and guidance reappears on the level of concept formation. Conceptual change modeling (Hewson & Hewson, 1992) or analogical reasoning (Brown & Clement, 1989) are faced with the same problem.

My approach to this problem starts with the assumption that orientations and constraints on concept formation should enable *and require* the processes of abstraction that are involved. The need or necessity for deriving a new concept should be the outcome of the learner's cognitive activity. But guidance by the teacher is needed. Therefore, an additional assumption is that, using the terms of constructivism, consensual domains exist as a result of previous interaction between teacher and students. These interactions ensure that the information offered by the teacher is understood by the learner. This involves, in contrast to a radical constructivist view, that learners are—with respect to information—only *relatively* closed systems. There is an irreducible field of tension—one that science education has to face—between external pedagogic intention and internal formation on the part of the learner.

Constructivist approaches, even a radical constructivist view such as that of von Glasersfeld (1989), emphasize the importance of external perturbations for the development of the student or person. *These perturbations should not be productive by chance.* Intentionally induced, they offer guidance which challenges and supports self-activity. In this sense they are productive perturbations, "producing" a productive self-activity, and thus relating self-activity and guidance.

Open experimenting is structured in such a way that productive perturbations occur during the whole process, at the level of expanding the cognitive system as well as at the level of motif and goal development. For example, at the very beginning of open experimenting, there are productive perturbations when a surprising and interesting phenomenon is presented; and, later, when the teacher suggests seeing a set of phenomena as a system and asks students to determine the elements of this system, both a new way of thinking and a higher level of abstraction are offered to the students—and their self-activity is challenged. The students have to ask themselves how they want to see the phenomenon as a system.

System-Formation (System-Bildung)

I have introduced the terms *systems* and *system* into this discussion several times. I described how the students form systems and reflect on that process. This brings us to a fundamental goal of open experimenting. Taking the self-activity of the learner seriously implies a conception of *open goals* that leaves the development of the concrete targets to students themselves. Considering *Bildung*, it is obviously necessary that students form skills, attitudes, behavior, or values. However, to arrive at new ideas for a better future of humankind and nature, we must go beyond such goals: Our students must develop creative or heuristic activities that can serve to transform or transcend the present stage of humankind's relation to nature. From our point of view, the most developed conceptualization of such an activity in our present society seems to be *system formation*.[5] Such system formation (referring to education) is more than an ability to solve problems within given or limited systems; it also involves a creative and heuristic activity that transcends and expands given systems in such a way that new systems emerge.

Open experimenting seeks to foster system formation as it guides students to form systems *self-actively*. It aims at giving students the capability to manage complexity and to analyze problems.

Experimental Method

Within the terms of activity theory, experimenting can be conceived as a cognitive activity *(Erkenntnistätigkeit)* that mediates between the subject (e.g., scientist) and the object on which he or she works. Following the concept of system formation, this activity entails forming systems. Reframing this within the framework of open experimenting, I suggest distinguishing the formation of *material systems* (*gegenständliches System*, i.e., building apparatus and equipment to show a phenomenon or to confirm a hypothesis) and *theoretical systems*. Both processes are mutually related: They interact and are directed toward one another (Batens & van Bendegem, 1988; Parthey & Wahl, 1966; Tetens, 1987; cf. also Hanson, 1972).

Forming the *material system* starts with a phenomenon within a situation that is in need of explanation. This process is directed at producing singular empirical statements or theoretically anticipated events. While reproducing, varying, and sifting out the essential thing, a "pure" phenomenon is prepared and preserved to provide a basis for generalization and theory. Forming the *theoretical system* aims at a systematic description of such pure phenomena, their explanation, and a prediction of possible behavior and future change. This includes, for example, forming and modifying hypotheses and cognitive goals, transforming statements into mathematical terms, and interpreting the results within existing cognitive systems.

---

[5]Here the German term *(System-Bildung)* has a double meaning. It refers to education *(Bildung)* and to the activity of forming systems *(Systemebilden)*. System formation (Walgenbach, 1990) is conceived to be guided by theory (a conscious activity), integrating (forming coherence), and productive (changing societal practice by materializing possible systems).

The interaction of material and theoretical systems can be characterized by complementarities—like the theoretical and the empirical, or knowledge-development and substantiation. The first relation reflects the understanding that, on the one hand, any empirical assertion is theory-laden whereas, on the other hand, every theory has to have an empirical basis. The second relation takes up the epistemological distinction between the context of *discovery* and the context of *justification*. Traditionally, philosophies of science discuss only the justification of established hypotheses whereas the development of hypotheses is excluded as a problem of psychology. However, as Nickles (1980) argued, both topics should be addressed by philosophers of science. An approach that extends this additive view was suggested by the Russian activity theorist Lektorskij (1984). He argued for a complementary relation between development and substantiation. On the one hand, to develop knowledge presupposes general and justified developmental means that could only be substantiated and expanded while developing knowledge; on the other hand, justifying developed knowledge implies structuring it to construct idealizations and to change assumptions. This, of course, leads to a development and expansion of that knowledge from which the reflection started (cf. Steiner, 1989).

This conception of experimenting is another springboard in the process of open experimenting. It is part of the structural element *reflecting on the formation of a system* when students reflect on their experimenting. The students investigating the optical dice phenomenon, for example, were faced with the problem of whether their experiments and analyses were adequate to be certain that the bright lines are not measurable. In the seminar we discussed this issue based on the complementarities mentioned earlier.

Integrating the Functions of Experimenting

I began this chapter with the assertion that the structure of planing open experimenting, with its elements of a situation in need of explanation, trying and speculating, reflecting on the formed systems, normal science experimenting, and reflecting on the formation of a system, integrates the functions of the experiment as it is traditionally understood in science education. To highlight the claim that these functions are constituent elements of the structure as a whole, and not just separate aspects focused on at different times, I take up the concept of productive perturbation once again. Productive perturbations run like a thread through open experimenting. They are the central to its structural elements.

Thus, seen in terms of *pedagogy,* productive perturbations facilitate the formation of the self in interaction with others and nature that is Bildung: They aim at a support of students' *self*-formation. Seen in terms of the *psychology of learning,* they entail a cognitive conflict. This conflict enables the emergence of motifs and goals. But such conflict has to occur *within* the learners' preconceptions: A problem within the structure of the discipline does not necessarily provide such a conflict. In terms of *methodology,* productive perturbations involve learners becoming aware of their knowledge and of the procedures that are available to extend that knowledge, and that they reflect on the adequacy of the application of those procedures. And seen in terms of learning, *content-knowledge* productive perturbations are based on a need for explanation, which involves forming and testing hypotheses by the learner. However, this does *not* mean the teacher answering questions students have never raised.

In other words, what we have called here productive perturbations encompass the pedagogical, learning-psychological, methodological, and content-related aspects of the experiment. Once we see the idea of productive perturbations as the central element, open experimenting integrates the functions traditionally ascribed to the experiment.

CONSEQUENCES

What do we learn from open experimenting as a structure for planing and teaching physics? There are direct and less direct consequences. First, open experimenting is not an alternative to traditional science instruction: *It is a desirable complement.* It is an opportunity for learners to experiment—to acquire both concrete knowledge of science content and firm methodological and epistemological knowledge about science—so that they are able to apply and use their knowledge in new contexts. They are motivated to understand (Wagenschein, 1965: see also chap. 9, this volume) and this implies formative *(bildend)* development. Open experimenting both elaborates Wagenschein's concept of *exemplary teaching* and extends the range of teaching approaches that focus on the specific functions of the experiment.

To be sure, transferring this approach to secondary schools would need different examples than the optical dice phenomenon—which was appropriate for student teachers at a university level. In general, the structural elements of open experimenting can be interpreted as a guide for constructing suitable examples. Thus, such examples must generate a situation in need of explanation that is related to the learners' cognitive system. They must enable students to form different material and theoretical systems. This involves simple apparatus so that students can design their own experiments *and* phenomena that are puzzling at every level of investigation. In addition, the parameters of any investigation should not be obvious when the phenomenon is demonstrated.

We can also conceive the structural elements of open experimenting as a method for planning science teaching in general. The structure suggests

an orientation to the development of cognitive systems, to motif development, and to a paradigm of experimenting. It offers a guideline for planning
not only students' lab work but also teaching based on teacher experiments.
In this way, open experimenting becomes a program reconciling course
work and project method—and could make science teaching more interesting, efficient, and relevant.

REFERENCES

Ausubel, D. P. (1968). *Educational psychology: A cognitive view.* New York: Holt, Rinehart & Winston.
Batens, D., & van Bendegem, J. P. (1988). *Theory and experiment: Recent insights and new per-
spectives on their relation.* Dordrecht, Netherlands: Reidel.
Bereiter, C. (1985). Toward a solution of the learning paradox. *Review of Educational Research,
55*(2), 201–226.
Bohr, N. (1964–1966). *Atomphysik und menschliche Erkenntnis.* Braunschweig: Vieweg.
Brown, D. E., & Clement, J. (1989). Overcoming misconception via analogical reasoning: Abstract
transfer versus explanatory model construction. *Instructional Science, 18*(4), 237–261.
Bruner, J. (1961). The act of discovery. *Havard Educational Review, 31*(1), 21–32.
Carey, S., Evans, R., Honda, M., & Unger, C. (1989). "An experiment is when you try it and see
if it works": A study of junior high school students' understanding of the construction of
scientific knowledge [Special issue]. *International Journal of Science Education, 11*, 514–529.
Dewey, J. (1933). *How we think.* Boston: Heath.
Diesterweg, F. A. W. (1956). *Sämtliche Werke* (H. Deiters, H. Ahrbeck, R. Alt, G. Mundorf, & L.
Regener, Eds.). Berlin: Volk und Wissen.
Driver, R. (1989). Changing conceptions. In P. Adey (Ed.), *Adolescent development and school
science* (pp. 79–103). London: Falmer Press.
Engeström, Y. (1987). *Learning by expanding: An activity-theoretical approach to developmental
research.* Helsinki: Orienta-Konsultit Oy.
Fichtner, B. (1985). Learning and learning activity. In E. Bol, J. P. P. Haenen, & M. Wolters (Eds.),
Education for cognitive development (pp. 47–62). The Hague, Netherlands: SVO/SOO.
Garrett, R. M. (1986). Problem-solving in science education. *Studies in Science Education, 13*,
70–95.
Hanson, N. R. (1972). *Observation and explanation: A guide to philosophy of science.* London: Allen
& Unwin.
Häussler, P. (1987). Measuring students interest in physics: Design and results of a cross-sectional
study in the Federal Republic of Germany. *International Journal of Science Education, 9*(1),
79–92.
Hennessy, S. (1993). Situated cognition and cognitive apprenticeship: Implications for classroom
learning. *Studies in Science Education, 22*, 1–41.
Hewson, P. W., & Hewson, G. A'B. (1992). The status of students' conceptions. In R. Duit, F.
Goldberg, & H. Niedderer (Eds.). *Research in physics learning: Theoretical issues and empirical
studies* (pp. 59–73). Kiel, Germany: Institut für die Pädagogik der Naturwissenschaften.
Hodson, D. (1985). Philosophy of science, sciences and science education. *Studies in Science
Education, 12*, 25–57.
Hodson, D. (1988). Experiments in science and science teaching. *Educational Philosophy and
Theory, 20*(2), 53–66.
Hodson, D. (1992). Redefining and reorienting practical work in school science. *School Science
Review, 73*(264), 65–78.

Hofstein, A., & Lunetta, V. N. (1982). The role of the laboratory in science teaching: Neglected aspects of research. *Review of Educational Research, 52*(2), 201–217.

Kuhn, T. S. (1970). *The structure of scientific revolutions.* Chicago: University of Chicago Press.

Lakatos, I. (1976). *Proofs and refutations.* Cambridge, England: Cambridge University Press.

Lawson, A. E., Abraham, M. R., & Renner, J. W. (1989). *A theory of instruction: Using the learning cycle to teach science concepts and thinking skills* (NARST Monograph No. 1). Cincinnati, OH: University of Cincinnati, Department of Science Education.

Lektorskij, W. A. (1984). *Subject, object, cognition.* Moscow: Progress.

Leont'ev, A. N. (1978). *Activity, consciousness, and personality.* Englewood Cliffs, NJ: Prentice-Hall.

Litt, T. (1963). *Naturwissenschaft und Menschenbildung.* Heidelberg: Quelle und Meyer.

Lock, R. (1990). Open-ended, problem-solving investigations: What do we mean and how can we use them? *School Science Review, 71*(March), 63–72.

Mach, E. (1865). Über die Wirkung der räumlichen Vertheilung des Lichtreizes auf die Netzhaut. *Sitzungsberichte der kaiserlichen Akademie der Wissenschaften: mathematisch-naturwissenschaftliche Klasse, 52,* 303–322.

Mach, E. (1866a). Über den physiologischen Effect räumlich vertheilter Lichtreize. *Sitzungsberichte der kaiserlichen Akademie der Wissenschaften: mathematisch-naturwissenschaftliche Klasse, 54,* 131–144.

Mach, E. (1866b). Über die physiologische Wirkung räumlich vertheilter Lichtreize (dritte und vierte Abhandlung). *Sitzungsberichte der kaiserlichen Akademie der Wissenschaften: mathematisch-naturwissenschaftliche Klasse, 54, 55,* 393–408, 11–19.

Mach, E. (1906). Über den Einfluß räumlich und zeitlich variierender Lichtreize auf die Gesichtswahrnehmung. *Sitzungsberichte der kaiserlichen Akademie der Wissenschaften: mathematisch-naturwissenschaftliche Klasse, 115,* 633–648.

Millar, R. (1987). Towards a role for experiment in the science teaching laboratory. *Studies in Science Education, 14,* 109–118.

Muckenfuß, H. (1979). Kritische Bemerkungen zur etablierten Form des Schulexperiments aus psychologischer und methodologischer Sicht. *Physica Didactica, 6,* 61–79.

Nickles, T. (1980). Introductory essay: scientific discovery and the future of philosophy of science. In T. Nickles (Ed.), *Scientific discovery, logic, and rationality* (pp. 1–59). Dordrecht, Netherlands: Reidel.

Niedderer, H. (1987). A teaching strategy based on students' alternative frameworks: Theoretical concept and examples. In J. D. Novak (Ed.), *Proceedings of the 2nd International Seminar in Misconceptions and Education Strategies in Science and Mathematics* (Vol. 2, pp. 360–367). Ithaca NY: Cornell University, Department of Education.

Nuffield Physics Teachers Guide (Vol. I). (1966). London: Penguin.

Padilla, M. J. (1991). Science activities, process skills, and thinking. In S. M. Glynn, H. Yeany, & B. K. Britton (Eds.), *The psychology of learning science* (pp. 310–329). Hillsdale, NJ: Lawrence Erlbaum Associates.

Parthey, H., & Wahl, D. (1966). *Die experimentelle Methode in Natur- und Geisteswissenschaften.* Berlin: VEB Deutscher Verlag der Wissenschaften.

Pfundt, H., & Duit, R. (1994). *Bibliography for students' alternative frameworks and science education.* Kiel, Germany: Institut für die Pädagogik der Naturwissenschaften.

Raufuß, D. (1989). *Die physikalisch-naturwissenschaftliche Denkweise: Zur Vermittlung durch Schule, Hochschule und Medien.* Cologne, Germany: Aulis Verlag Deubner.

Reif, F., & Larkin, J. H. (1991). Cognition in scientific and everyday domains: Comparison and learning implications. *Journal of Research in Science Teaching, 28*(9), 733–760.

Reinhold, P. J. (1988). *Systembildenlernen am Beispiel von Carnots Wärmemaschine.* Kiel, Germany: Institut für die Pädagogik der Naturwissenschaften.

Reinhold, P. J. (1996). *Offenes Experimentieren und Physiklernen.* Kiel, Germany: Institut für die Pädagogik der Naturwissenschaften.

Roth, W. M. (1994). Experimenting in a constructivist high school physics laboratory. *Journal of Research in Science Teaching, 31*(2), 197–223.

St. John, M. (1980). Thinking like a physicist in the laboratory. *Physics Teacher, 18*(6), 436–443.

Schön, D. (1987). *Educating the reflective practitioner.* San Francisco: Jossey-Bass.

Scott, P. H., Asoko, H. M., & Driver, R. H. (1992). Teaching for conceptual change: A review of strategies. In R. Duit, F. Goldberg, & H. Niedderer (Eds.), *Research in physics learning: Theoretical issues and empirical studies* (pp. 310–329). Kiel, Germany: Institut für die Pädagogik der Naturwissenschaften.

Sneed, J. P. (1971). *The logical structure of mathematical physics.* Dordrecht, Netherlands: Reidel.

Stegmüller, W. (1970–1973). *Probleme und Resultate der Wissenschaftstheorie und Analytischen Philosophie: Vol. 2. Erster und zweiter Halbband.* New York: Springer.

Steiner, H.-G. (1989). The nature of theoretical concepts in physics and mathematics: Implications for the fragility of knowledge in the educational context. In S. Vinner (Ed.), *Proceedings of the 2nd Jerusalem Convention on Education: Science and Mathematics Education: Interaction Between Theory and Practice* (pp. 387–396). Jerusalem: Convention on Education.

Tamir, P. (1990). Overcoming misconceptions related to the concepts underlying the science processes. In J. Coolahan (Ed.), *Teacher Education in the Nineties: Toward a New Coherence* (Vol. 2, pp. 363–378, Proceedings of the 15th Annual Conference of the Association for Teacher Education in Europe). Limerick, Ireland: Mary Immaculate College of Education.

Tetens, H. (1987). *Experimentelle Erfahrung: Eine wissenschaftliche Studie über die Rolle des Experiments in der Begriffs- und Theoriebildung der Physik.* Hamburg, Germany: Felix Meiner.

von Glasersfeld, E. (1989). Cognition, construction of knowledge and teaching. *Synthese, 80*(1), 121–140.

Vygotsky, L. S. (1978). *The development of higher psychological processes.* Cambridge, MA: Harvard University Press.

Wagenschein, M. (1965). Zum Begriff des Exemplarischen Lehrens. In M. Wagenschein, *Ursprüngliches Verstehen und exaktes Denken: Pädogogische Schriften (Vol. 1).* Stuttgart, Germany: Ernst Klett.

Wagenschein, M. (1976). *Die Pädagogische Dimension der Physik.* Braunschweig, Germany: Westermann.

Walgenbach, W. (1990, May). *Self-system formation through interdisciplinary system formation with flowing matter.* Paper presented at the 2nd International Congress for Research on Activity Theory, Lahti, Finland.

Wertsch, J. V. (Ed.). (1981). *The concept of activity in Soviet psychology.* Armonk, NY: M. E. Sharpe.

Wittgenstein, L. (1967). *Philosophische Untersuchungen.* Frankfurt: Suhrkamp.

Wolze, W. (1989). *Zur Entwicklung naturwissenschaftlicher Erkenntnissysteme im Lernprozeß.* Wiesbaden, Germany: Deutscher Universitäts Verlag.

18

Klafki's Didaktik Analysis as a Conceptual Framework for Research on Teaching

Sigrun Gudmundsdottir
Anne Reinertsen
Nils P. Nordtømme

Sigrun Gudmundsdottir is a professor in the Department of Education at the Norwegian University of Science and Technology, Trondheim, Norway.

Anne Reinertsen is vice-principal of Heimdal High School, Trondheim.

Nils Nordtømme is a teacher of history and English as a foreign language at Gerhard Schønings High School, Trondheim.

One of the most important roles theories and theoretical concepts play in educational research is to enable researchers to define practical units of analysis and thus "visualize"—often for the first time—events in, for example, the familiar world of classrooms. Hence, there are very few things within research and teaching that are as practical as a good theory. Klafki's (see chap. 8, this volume) analysis of the five questions lying at the core of lesson planning and Shulman's (1987) model of "pedagogical reasoning and action" are examples of such theoretical, but immensely practical, constructs. These models emerged because Wolfgang Klafki and Lee Shulman were working theoretically with concrete and practical issues. And both arrived at solutions which, in many ways, parallel theoretical constructs, which enable us to see the world of classrooms and teaching in special, practical ways. Shulman and his associates arrived at the concept of "pedagogical content knowledge" through grounded theorizing (see Wilson & Gudmundsdottir, 1987, for a description of the process). Klafki theorized toward the five questions he identified as lying at the core of Bildung-centered lesson planning as he worked in teacher education.

Shulman's notion of pedagogical content knowledge has inspired a small army of researchers on teaching and teacher education to embark on extensive analyses of classroom processes, and of the process of learning to teach a subject matter. This effort is consistent, of course, with the strong empirical tradition that characterizes the Anglo-Saxon educational research community. The German (and, to a lesser extent, the Scandinavian) educational research tradition is more philosophical and textual than empirical and, although Klafki's framework continues to be widely used in German teacher education (see Hopmann, chap. 11, this volume, and Senn-Fennell, chap. 13, this volume; see also Jank & Meyer, 1991; Prichard, 1992), it was not used as a theoretical foundation for empirical research until Reinertsen, Nordtømme, Eidsvik, Weidemann, and Gudmundsdottir (1996) study of three Norwegian history teachers. One of the informants, "Per," is used in this chapter as an illustration of the methods and analyses. We do not present here a detailed and comprehensive analysis of Per's pedagogical content knowledge; rather we offer a brief and focused glimpse into his repertoire of ways of thinking about and teaching one specific topic to a specific group of Norwegian teenagers.

Researchers' questions invariably become a part of the informants' answers along with various cultural imprints. This gives rise to somewhat different expressions of basically the same phenomena, *Fachdidaktik* and pedagogical content knowledge. *Fachdidaktik,* or subject-matter Didaktiks with their subject-grounded rationales, has its roots in the classical German Didaktik tradition. Shulman's pedagogical content knowledge emerges from an empirical tradition and from educational scholarship inspired by Joseph Schwab (1961/1978) and John Dewey. Each construct has strong elements of the context and culture from which it emerged, elements that shape it and infuse it with meaning. Thus, aspects of Shulman's notion of pedagogical content knowledge simply "appear" when excellent experienced teachers are asked to talk about their teaching and are observed. "Pedagogical content knowledge" emerges in different clothing in interviews based on Klafki's questions because more time is spent exploring textual issues rather than the practical, pedagogical implication of the basic ideas. Klafki's questions aim at systematically exploring the educational potential of the content. Shulman was also concerned with this, but he was also focused on how the potential can be transformed into representations appropriate for a given group of students.

DIDAKTIK

Didaktik here is considered as the theory of the process that enhances the essential pedagogical elements of a given content, similar to Schwab's notion of "curriculum potential" (see Ben-Peretz, 1974). *Bildungstheoretische Didaktik,* the tradition reflected in Klafki's work, is the oldest and most important trend within the modern Didaktik tradition. Gundem (1980; 1983/1991) identified and described four characteristics of this tradition. The first of these characteristics is the *primacy of practice:* The starting point for educational discourse is not the laboratory or the armchair, but practice. The second characteristic is also related to practice: *Concept and theory development must be grounded in practice.* In terms of research, this means that concepts and theoretical models are grounded in empirical (practice) data. The third characteristic is "a basic notion of *historicity* taking into account the past, present, and the future." The fourth and last characteristic of *bildungstheoretische Didaktik* is its strong *hermeneutic and interpretative stance* on research and scholarship. Didaktik analysis is not research based; but as Klafki's five questions are applied as a research instrument, a teacher's understanding of the "organic power" embedded in content itself can be explored and an understanding of how the content's "germinative forces" and "productive drives" can be exposed.

Klafki's questions start, as Shulman's model does, with the content to be taught. Specifically, Klafki asked, What is the nature of the "stuff" lessons are made of? He formulated a five-step set of questions that explore answers to this fundamental question addressing *the contemporary and future meaning of the content for the students, its structure and exemplary value, and its pedagogical representations for a given group of students.*[1] The questions represent three levels of the analysis of the content of teaching:

- Relating the teaching content to the subject matter as it appears in daily life (now and in the future).
- Relating the teaching content to the structure of knowledge.
- Relating the teaching content to the larger frame of schooling.

Klafki recommended that student teachers, explicitly, and experienced teachers, implicitly, engage in answering such questions while preparing to teach. He pointed out that such preparation is not a technical issue, but rather an interpretative issue, a kind of *pedagogical interpretation* (McEwan, 1987). Klafki's five questions (see chap. 8, this volume) are as follows:

1. *Contemporary meaning:* What significance does the content in question or experience, knowledge, ability, or skill to be acquired through this topic

---

[1] In Germany and the Scandinavian countries content is, to a certain degree, mandated in the *Länder* (state) or the national curricula. However, much is left to the discretion of the teacher. The curriculum guidelines leave the pedagogical interpretation open, and no authority can "instruct" teachers as to how to interpret the mandated content: As long as they have "covered" the mandated topics, they are following the letter of the law. In this way, all topics become an open "text," with multiple possible meanings and multiple "potentials" to be explored and transformed into different representations. Experienced teachers take full advantage of this opportunity to exercise the interpretative authority invested in them (Gudmundsdottir, 1988, 1990a, 1990b, 1991; Gudmundsdottir, Reinertsen, & Nordtømme, 1997; Reinertsen, Nordtømme, Eidsvik, Weidemann, & Gudmundsdottir, 1996).

already have in the minds of the children in my class? What significance should it have from a pedagogical point of view?

2. *Future meaning:* What constitutes the topic's significance for the children's future?

3. *Content structure:* How are the contents structured (which have been placed in a specifically pedagogical perspective by questions 1, 2, and 4)?

4. *Exemplary value:* What wider or general sense or reality is exemplified and revealed to the learner by the contents? What basic phenomenon or principle, what law, criterion, problem, method, technique, or attitude can be grasped by dealing with these contents as "examples"?

5. *Pedagogical representations of the ideas:* What particular cases, phenomena, situations, experiments, people, events can be used to make the content in question interesting, worth asking questions about, accessible, comprehensible, "conceivable" for the children at their level and grade?

In Klafki's approach to Didaktik analysis, a pedagogical interpretation of a text has to focus on *why* that particular content has been chosen out of all possible cultural artifacts to become an object for schooling. The aim of the analysis is to reenact the rationale that led someone at some time to arrive at the decision that "this" small range of cultural artifacts and ideas have more power than others to awaken young minds to life, to offer intellectual tools that students can use now and later to develop morally and intellectually. When systematically applied in lesson planning in teacher education, such Didaktik analysis can be highly elaborated, a kind of "literary essay" or *explication de texte* (see Senn-Fennel, chap. 13, this volume; see also Prichard, 1992). When Didaktik analysis is used as a research instrument, teachers are invited to systematically tell about what they have done, and why: A kind of unwritten "text," one that has taken many years to compose, is offered in response to the five questions. Unlike student teachers, who plan to the smallest detail, such teachers are concerned with the "big picture," making their story general rather than specific and detailed. Experienced teachers appear able to step back as they look at their topics and ask the fundamental questions Klafki proposed without dwelling too long on details. In the classroom, they seem to reactivate "scripts" (or operations) that enable them to effortlessly put their ideas into classroom practice (Gudmundsdottir, 1988; Reinertsen et al., 1996).

TEACHING THE NORWEGIAN CONSTITUTION: A BRIEF DIDAKTIK ANALYSIS

It is an impossible task to describe the knowledge base of an experienced teacher in a subject that has been an essential part of his life for 25 years.

We nevertheless endeavor to offer a brief glimpse into the rich knowledge that Per works within in each teaching day.

Per is one of three informants in Reinertsen's study of how three history teachers in a Norwegian high school teach a required topic in history. As part of the fieldwork, the three teachers were interviewed for 6 hours about their professional background and the curriculum, and observed and video-taped over five periods. These periods and the video recordings of them were used as background for an additional five interviews about what happened in the classroom (for a total interview time of 11 hours). None of Reinertsen's collaborating teachers had been prepared as part of their teacher education to use Klafki's specific approach to Didaktik analysis.

Per cuts an impressive figure in the classroom. Nobody disrupts the quiet concentration, even if Per's strategies for maintaining discipline are invisible. For his own part, he considers his prime disciplinary strategy to be to interest and engage his students in the study of history, not as something for their high school years but for the rest of their lives. There is never a dull moment during Per's classes, and an outsider does not need to observe Per's classroom for long to discover why history is fascinating. Per is a past master of the narrative art, so that he can easily recapture his class if interest is on the wane. Moreover, he uses class conversations and peer- or small-group work where appropriate.

Per has been teaching for 23 years. He majored in history, writing a master's thesis about the radicalization of the labor movement in Norway during the First World War. The main focus in his thesis was on the political processes, more specifically the backdrop of contemporary social conditions. His supervisor during the politically active 1960s was Professor Edvard Bull, one of the "great" historians in Norway. Per mentions Bull as one of the major influences on his selection of the topic he finally settled on for his thesis and 20 years later Per's pedagogical content knowledge still reflects his influence.

The topic of the study is Per's teaching of the Norwegian constitution, "Eidsvoll 1814." (Eidsvoll is the name of a large country estate north of Oslo and is now a town with the same name.) Since the late Middle Ages, Norway had been a colony of Denmark but, in the spring of 1814, inspired by the peace treaty concluding the Napoleonic wars, the French Revolution, and the American constitution, a group of intellectuals, clergy, civil servants, wealthy farmers, and Christian Fredrik, the Danish crown prince, met at the Eidsvoll manor. There they discussed politics and freedom, and wrote a Norwegian constitution based on the American model.

This constitution is an important topic in all Norwegian history classes dealing with this period, and a required topic in grade school. May 17, the day the constitution was signed in 1814, is Norway's National Day, celebrated each year with children's parades, banners, and flags. Eidsvoll 1814 is also an important topic for historians in Norway, with each new generation offering a reinterpretation of the event.

When Per began his teaching career, history was more or less exclusively political history. Later, and as a result of the influence of Bull, social history came to be considered important. More recently, economic history has come into vogue. These three historical interpretations, that is, political, social, and economic, determine which topics or themes Per selects for teaching, and he gives his themes concrete expression in single events or persons that his students will take an interest in. Per has learned that it is easier to make students interested in events or particular persons, but that it is essential that these should represent important historical themes or topics. This general approach to history establishes the underpinning for all his pedagogical interpretation of the texts used for teaching.[2]

In teaching Eidsvoll 1814 and the Norwegian constitution, Per creates a narrative that he "tells" through class discussion, small-group work, and some lecturing. This narrative weaves together single events and persons with larger themes that are tinted with one or more of the types of history (political, economic, or social) that Per's conception of history includes. The narrative does not exclusively describe; it also explains. In this way the events of 1814 not only become the history of when farmers and public officials met at a manor at Eidsvoll during the month of May, they also become an open text holding as many interpretative options as a good novel.

Question 1: "Contemporary Meaning?"

Per splits his examination of Eidsvoll into five themes, spending about one class period on each: (a) the general background in Europe prior to 1814,

---

[2]Per's general approach to the teaching of history relies on his students doing their homework. At the beginning of the fall he establishes what he calls the "ground rules": He does not teach unless students have done their homework. He structures the work for them by giving them a detailed plan for the whole semester, including homework assignments, tests, and essays, all with fixed dates. Also, at the beginning of each fall, he reestablishes his reputation as someone who is strict, particularly about homework.

In another study, Gudmunsdottir (in press) observed Per in early September. He had been doing his usual questioning of the students at the beginning of the period, to see if they had done their homework. About halfway through he decided that this was not good enough and said in a low stern voice: "I can't do anything if you haven't done your homework." He turned around and walked briskly out of the door. The class was shocked; the observer was stunned, not just that he had walked out, but that all the "heads" in the class turned to the textbook and read quietly until the bell rang. Afterwards, Per told Gudmundsdottir that, with each class, he looks for an excuse to do "this kind of thing" early on in the fall semester, "because it will be a long time until they arrive again at school without having done their homework" and his reputation as a "strict teacher who checks if students have done their homework" is maintained for yet another school year.

(b) the peace treaty of Kiel and the reactions this awoke, (c) the assembly at Eidsvoll and the figure of Christian Fredrik, (d) the accomplishments at Eidsvoll, and (e) the new Swedish/Norwegian union. As these themes have so many similar aspects, there is some overlapping at the start and conclusion of each class.

Per's familiarity with his students has influenced this organization of the topic Eidsvoll 1814 into themes, and their concretization. According to Per, students generally lack knowledge background because they have not explored world history prior to reading Norwegian history. This background restricts his choices. Usually Norwegian students of the age of his students know four things about the events at Eidsvoll: (a) that Norway was a Danish colony, (b) that some men met at Eidsvoll and signed the constitution (an event they celebrated each year), (c) that Norway ended up in union with Sweden, and (d) that the kings (in Scandinavia) were no longer absolute monarchs. Based on their 10 years' experience as participants in the children's parade every May 17, their preconception of the event is romantic and idealized, and they have no conception of the underlying historical processes.

Per tries to address these preconceptions by "telling" his students, through the various activities he organizes in the classroom, that Eidsvoll 1814 was merely one episode in a larger context, a short story in a longer narrative. However, Eidsvoll remains far ago, and experience has shown him that it is easier to motivate students for modern history than for older history. Nevertheless, there are many issues in the topic that do lend themselves to illustrating the development of democracy and universal suffrage in a small nation.

Per tries to emphasize, not just through his coverage of Eidsvoll 1814, but in all his history teaching, a sense of belonging to a culture and community, and of identity and citizen rights. His students are old enough to vote and he is concerned that they should be active participants in the democratic process. But his goals for this unit are modest:[3] that the students should form opinions about (a) the development from absolute monarchy to democracy, (b) national independence and the constitution, (c) the fact

---

[3]The typical Norwegian high school student is silent in class, preferring to be spoon-fed by the teacher, who imparts information in formal lectures that students diligently write down in their notebooks, to regurgitate on the exam. Per feels this sad state of affairs is his greatest challenge as a teacher. He has developed pedagogical strategies such as diverse questioning strategies, small-group work, and dialogue with the whole class to activate the students. The small groups work with questions that can only be inferred from the text and, through the class dialogue, Per attempts to get the students to join in reasoning out ideas and seeing historical relationships that go beyond the textbook.

many people were involved in the process (although restricted to the upper classes), and (d) the complex issue of nationalism.

Question 2: "Future Meaning?"

Eidsvoll 1814 has significance for Per's students' futures in that it can play a role in shaping their values. It is important that they appreciate the democratic process and the way compromise works to enhance or limit that process, particularly in view of the fact that Norway is a small country that lives under the shadow of big and powerful neighbors who have organized themselves into an even bigger union. Although Norway is not formally a member of the European Union (EU), it belongs to many of the EU's institutions. Norwegian membership in the EU has been voted down in two national referendums, but this issue is likely to resurface in the students' lifetime.

Question 3: "Content Structure?"

Per structures the content in a way that explores what actually happened and puts this into a larger context. In the third period, when Per covers Eidsvoll 1814, he asks about concrete events, for example, What happened? Where? When? and Who was involved? Thereafter he attempts to put this in a larger historical context: Thus, the topic examined in one period concerns the role of Christian Fredrik, the Danish crown prince, in the events at Eidsvoll Manor. The details of what he did at Eidsvoll are significant in that various historians have interpreted his role differently. Some claim that he was genuinely interested in Norway becoming an independent country, even though he was the king-designate and in the position of possibly ruling Denmark and Norway. Other historians see him playing a game of deception, with the ultimate goal of bringing Norway back into the union with Denmark. Using primary sources such as diary entries and contemporary accounts, Per asks his students to list all of Christian Fredrik's activities during the hectic months in the spring of 1814, and then to reflect on what they mean in a larger context: "What signs/indications can you find that Christian Fredrik was on the side of the Norwegian people? What signs/indications can you find that Christian Fredrik actually intended to bring Norway back into the union with Denmark?" During the discussion of a video recording of this episode, he explains:

> The objective was to elicit two things from the material. Firstly, the purely factual history which happened; let us call this times, dates, etc., which at least on the surface are irrefutable. Secondly, how this [factual history] is used? how this is placed in a context? how the material is interpreted? to, let us say, pull out the larger issues.

Per has structured his material to fit his own perceptions of history and his ideas of the background of students. He does so all the time, using concrete events that are, to use his own word, "irrefutable"and then placing these events in a larger context. This he then interprets so that the events take on a larger and more important meaning—so that what happened in 1814 is no longer a local affair, with a small group of peasants and civil servants meeting at Eidsvoll farm in the spring of 1814 to debate independence for the nation. He creates a comprehensive and dramatic narrative that reveals causal relationships among historical events in Europe long before 1814. He tells a story about emerging democracy in a small country in Northern Europe, making 1814 a stage in this development.

Question 4: "Exemplary Value?"

Eidsvoll 1814 is, according to Per, only a small step in history and a direct result of the Enlightenment and the American constitution. Therefore, he does not want to spend "too much time on it" (he covers the topic in six periods). But there are three important issues that can be specifically exemplified through his coverage of the topic.

First, Eidsvoll can be used to exemplify how international conflicts can influence countries, even those that are not directly involved. It is also an excellent illustration of how external forces can influence ordinary people's lives. Thus, there is a wealth of primary sources and poems to illustrate how the English naval blockade affected all citizens. This blockade caused the only famine recorded in Norway since the early Middle Ages. There was a shortage of wheat because it had to be imported, and people mixed all sort of things into the flour they used to bake bread to make it go further: bark, moss, sawdust, and seaweed.[4] This experience has lived a long time in the collective memory of the nation. In an interview Per discussed a well-known poem by Henrik Ibsen about Terje Wigen, a poor fisherman-farmer from a small village on the south coast who, during this blockade, rowed in his small boat over the open sea to Denmark to buy wheat for his starving family. Like so many who tried to do the same, he was captured by the British as he returned. This poem, more than most cultural artifacts, captures the feeling of the nation during hardship, be it famine, war, or both. According to Per, this poem should be used with great care because it can raise strong nationalistic feelings.[5]

---

[4]Today one can buy at the bakery "bark bread," evoking the image of Terje Vigen in his small boat on the open sea.

[5]It is traditionally Norwegian seamen who have dared the blockages of a foreign naval power during wars.

The second issue that Eidsvoll 1814 can be used to illustrate is the development of democratic processes and institutions, and how the beginning of democracy in Norway was achieved peacefully, without bloodshed. In this context one can explore questions like: How does one organize nation-states? What does the state control? What do the individual or groups of individuals decide? To what extent should one centralize? Or de-centralize? A strong comparative perspective is highlighted here because the main objective is that the students should better understand their current situation, and not take for granted the social order they know.

The third issue is nationalism and identity. Per sees this as a critical issue for contemporary youngsters in the context of the rise of neo-Nazism in Northern Europe, which attracts youths who are alienated from the mainstream culture. He notes that his textbook uses the word *patriotism* rather than *nationalism*. Per links nationalism and identity to their positive aspects, for example, traditional family activities (skiing and hiking in the woods), language, culture, folklore, and identity, aspects of social life that contribute to a sense of belonging rather than alienation. He articulates the kind of "positive nationalism" exemplified in the so-called "Lillehammer Winter Olympics spirit" where every competitor was cheered, not just Norwegians, and not just winners.

Question 5: "Pedagogical Representations of the Ideas?"

As he moves from lesson to lesson, Per structures the topic more and more by means of questions that he either writes on the board or presents orally. These are intended to help the student focus on the topic for the day. At the start of the lesson dealing with the general background in Europe prior to 1814 (the first theme), he poses questions and the students work together in small groups to find the answers:

1. How was Norway affected by the general unrest in Europe at this time?

2. In 1807 Denmark/Norway were drawn into the war. Russia and France entered an alliance, trying to coerce all the other countries into joining the blockade of Great Britain. What options did Norway have in this situation, and what consequences would the various solutions have had? (a) What would have happened if we joined the French side? (b) What would have happened if we joined the British side?

3. What kind of relationships did we have to Europe previously?

The answers to these questions are not given directly in the textbook; rather, the students have to read and interpret the relevant section in the textbook. After groups have worked on the questions in class, Per initiates a dialogue in which he makes the groups relate and explain their conclusions. This pattern pervades the way Per examines almost all the topics that he teaches.

DISCUSSION

The voices of the founders of the sociohistorical school, researchers like Vygotsky and Bakhtin, ventriloquate through Shulman's model of pedagogical reasoning and action and Klafki's Didaktik analysis with its five questions. This occurs because both constructs promote and facilitate systematic reflection over specific ideas that have been around for a very long time, with the implication that the rationale for the inclusion of these ideas in a course needs to be reenacted. Such reflection involves a dialogue with voices from the past, voices that represent the arguments for including some cultural artifacts in the curriculum, and excluding others. According to sociohistorical theories, reflection is "dialogical," because to reflect is to enter into a dialogue with framework for Didaktik analysis, or the "Other," as promoted by Fenstemacher and Richardson (1993) in their analysis of the role of practical arguments. As Taylor (1985) proposed, the language of practice is the key to realizing the goals of Didaktik analysis. It is this language, Taylor claimed, that "marks distinctions among different possible social acts, relations, [and] structure" (p. 32).

As an example, let us take the game of chess. Like teaching, chess is a socially organized activity. There would be no such game without the specific chessboard, specific pieces (the pawns, queens, kings, rooks, knights, and bishops), and rules for moving them around the board. The vocabulary of chess, concepts such as "Sicilian defense," relates to a specific set of moves for specific pieces at particular times in a game. To learn to play chess, one has to master the moves and the language of the practice of chess, and not only know how to move the pieces in a way that reflects the "Sicilian defense," but also know in what contexts to use this defense in a game. To learn how to teach, and to develop as a teacher, mastery of the vocabulary of teaching a subject matter is necessary, along with the relevant practical activities. Without the activities the words labeling activities would have no meaning. Talking about "the exemplary value" of a topic, or exploring various possibilities to illustrate ideas, helps to clarify things, thus giving support to the claim that "changes in the language of practice . . . are to be seen as changes in the practice itself" (Phelan, McEwan, & Pateman, 1996). This makes teaching a mediated activity as this is seen in sociohistorical theory (Gudmundsdottir, in press).

Bruner (1996) claimed that education is a culture: Grossman and Stodol-sky (1995) asserted that school subjects are also subcultures. They observed that although different school subjects "share a common arena for practice," individuals teaching the same subjects interpret their subjects differently, as illustrated by Reinertsen's (1996) study of three teachers (in three differ-ent schools) teaching the same topic differently. Thus, teachers teaching the same subject in different schools have more in common with each other than with teachers teaching different subjects in their own school. This difference between teachers across subjects in the same school stems from the "beliefs that may help define the possibilities and constraints teachers perceive as they do their daily work and respond to innovations" (p. 6). Grossman and Stodolsky concluded that this creates a subculture within schools along the lines of school subjects.

School subjects differ by virtue of the status they have in a community and their inherent sequentiality, scope, and coherence (Grossman & Stodol-sky, 1995). These differences give rise to different beliefs and values relating to teaching and learning processes. Grossman and Stodolsky argued that the conceptions of school subjects held in the different contexts create a kind of subculture and it is language (and other social discourse) that creates and maintains cultures. Different practices, and/or conceptual con-texts, give rise to different issues and themes to reflect over—issues and themes that are the motivation and rationale for different "moves" in prac-tice. The language of practice for a school subject like Norwegian history is, therefore, more than just words; it is a cultural reservoir of beliefs, ideas, ways of doing and seeing, all embedded in a distinct social activity, a kind of heteroglossia, to invoke Bakhtin's (1994) term (see also Hoel, 1994, 1997).

According to Bakhtin (1981):

> {Heteroglossia is] a perception of language as ideologically saturated and strati-fied. The many social languages participating in heteroglossia at any specific moment of its historical existence are all specific points of view on the world, forms of "conceptualizing the world in words." (p. 292)

"Harry," a history teacher in California, expressed a similar "way of concep-tualizing the world in words" when he spoke of "Professor J" who turned him into a conflict historian. Harry says:

> I went to the University of Wisconsin at Madison and took a master's degree with specialization in the American Revolution. There I encountered Professor J [who] converted me to . . . a "neo-progressive" view of American history. I am convinced, as he was convinced and a lot of historians are, that what is important in American history are the differences, the conflict, not the con-sensus. So, I am what you would call a conflict historian. [In the classroom]

I consistently try to emphasize the differences whose resolutions lead to the next confrontation. That is why I gave this little group assignment today [where the students explored the differences between Jefferson and Hamilton]. (Gudmundsdottir, 1990b, p. 44)

In Per's reflection on his teaching of Eidsvoll 1814, we can also discern many voices, each ideologically saturated. We have the voice of Edvard Bull, who introduced social history to Per and to a whole generation of Norwegian history teachers. In a classroom in California, we hear the voice of J, who introduced Harry to neo-progressive history more than 37 years ago, ventriloquating through the activities that Harry organizes to emphasize conflict rather than consensus. We have the voices of the men who met at Eidsvoll speaking to the teenagers in Per's class through their diary entries and activities during that fateful month of May. In Norway we have the voices of the textbook authors, who are also history teachers socialized in a similar way as Per. In California we have the voices of the textbook authors whose view of history collides with Harry's, creating a "conflict" for the "conflict historian." We have the voices of those university teachers in Norway who have continued to include themes such as national independence, the constitution, and growth of democracy as topics in their research and scholarship. They speak through their ideas as these are included in textbooks used in classrooms. (Unfortunately, neo-progressivism is no longer on the agenda of the leading American historians, so Harry has to soldier on in solitude.)

In Norway we also have the voices of the writers of the national curriculum guidelines (who themselves are high school teachers and academics). Their voices impose restrictions on the freedom of history teachers. Finally, we have the voices of the students (when they speak out), their families, and peers. We hear these voices ventriloquate when the students interpret questions like Per's: "What do you think Christian Fredrik is up to? What would have happened if we had joined the French? What would have happened if we had joined the British?"

In a homogeneous culture like Norway, all of these voices represent slightly different ways of "conceptualizing the world in words." Thus the languages of practice produce meaning in the classroom, and create reality for Per and Harry and their students. Each language is associated with specific groups, as described earlier, or with "voices," whose collective belief systems ventriloquate through Per's, Harry's, and other teachers' practice (Hoel, 1994, 1997).

The notion of a language of the practice of teaching has implications for voice. Voice assumes a wide meaning related to a community of practitioners whose shared beliefs and practices ventriloquate through individual speech about practice. This is the case for both teachers reflecting on teaching (along the lines of Klafki's five questions) and researchers engaged in research on teaching. Voice is intimately interconnected with culture, meaning, and mediated activity; it is neither turned on nor created. "Voices are claimed because there is no singular voice; any claimed voice is a heteroglossia of culturally situated voices that ventriloquate through the singular voice that is claimed by an individual" (Gudmundsdottir, in press).

In a profession rich in traditions stretching as far back as teaching does, there are many voices to be claimed and developed into one's own through a process of interpreting curricular text, by answering the five questions Wolfgang Klafki asked of curricular materials. All such starting points have one major element in common—they invite teachers and student teachers to use and develop the language of practice through systematic reflection. This process of claiming voice is an interaction between an individual's beliefs and experiences and such external voices of practice as Klafki's questions: Individual meanings come into contact with external voices of practice through a structured interaction. The interaction becomes a site where a heteroglossia of voices is sounded and where the individuals who, like Per and Harry, are reflecting over their experiences, and student teachers who are preparing to teach cannot escape the voices and are compelled to claim several of them as their own. The implication is that the individual teacher's meaning is always multivoiced.

CONCLUDING REMARKS

Although Shulman's model of pedagogical reasoning and action has had limited impact on teacher education in the United States, and is no longer high on the agenda for educational researchers, Klafki's ideas are still very much alive in teacher education in Germany. They are widely used in teacher education as a guide for lesson planning by student teachers. As the sociohistorical approach to the study of teaching and learning gains ground, it is perhaps time to take a fresh look at the Shulman model and Klafki's questions. Both promote teaching as a moral and reflective activity that is primarily concerned with the search for meaning (Elbaz, 1997; Hansen, 1995).

ACKNOWLEDGMENTS

This chapter draws on the data from Reinertsen, A., Nordtømme, N., Eidsvik, R., Weidemann, E., and Gudmundsdottir, S. (1996) *Fagdidaktisk kunnskap i historie belyst gjennom undervisning i hendelene på Eidsvoll 1814: Tre kasusstudier av lærere i videregående skole* (Trondheim: Tapir). Nils P. Nordtømme is one of the three informants in the study.

We acknowledge the influence of Torlaug Hoel of the Department of Teacher Education, Norwegian University of Science of Technology, in this analysis.

REFERENCES

Bakhtin, M. (1981). Discourse and the novel. In M. Holquist (Ed.), *The diologic imagination: Four essays* (pp. 259–422). Austin: The University of Texas Press.

Ben-Peretz, M. (1974). The concept of curriculum potential. *Curriculum Theory Network, 5*(2), 151–159.

Bruner, J. (1996). *The culture of education.* Cambridge, MA: Harvard University Press.

Carter, K. (1993). The place of story in research on teaching and teacher education. *Educational Researcher, 22*(1), 5–12.

Doyle, W. (1997). Heard any stories lately? *Teaching and Teacher Education, 13*(1), 93–99.

Egan, K. (1988). *Teaching as storytelling.* London: Routledge.

Elbaz, F. (1997). Narratives as personal politics. *Teaching and Teacher Education, 13*(1), 75–83.

Fenstemacher, G., & Richardson, V. (1993). The elicitation and reconstruction of practical arguments in teaching. *Journal of Curriculum Studies, 25*(2), 101–114.

Grossman, P., & Stodolsky, S. (1995). Content as context: The role of school subjects in secondary school teaching. *Educational Researcher, 24*(8), 5–11.

Grossman, P., Wilson, S., & Shulman, L. (1989). Teachers of substance: Subject matter knowledge for teaching. In M. Reynolds (Ed.), *Knowledge base for the beginning teacher* (pp. 23–36). Oxford, England: Pergamon.

Gundem, B. B. (1980). Tradisjon, kritikk, syntese: En analyse av hovedtrekk ved samtidig tysk didaktikk med en relatering til aktuelle spørsmål i nordisk sammenheng. (Report No. 7). Oslo: Universitetet i Oslo, Pedagogisk forskningsinstitutt.

Gundem, B. B. (1991). *Skolens oppgave og innhold: En studiebok i didaktikk.* Oslo: Universitetsforlaget. (Original work published 1983)

Gudmundsdottir, S. (1988). *Knowledge use among experienced teachers: Four case studies of high school teaching.* Unpublished doctoral dissertation, Stanford University, Stanford, CA.

Gudmundsdottir, S. (1990a). Curriculum stories. In C. Day, P. Denicolo, & M. Pope (Eds.), *Insights into teachers' thinking and practice* (pp. 107–118). London: Falmer.

Gudmundsdottir, S. (1990b). Values in pedagogical content knowledge. *Journal of Teacher Education, 41*(3), 44–53.

Gudmundsdottir, S. (1991). Story-maker, story-teller: Narrative structures in curriculum. *Journal of Curriculum Studies, 23*(3), 207–218.

Gudmundsdottir, S. (in press). Narrative research on practice. In V. Richardson (Ed.), *Handbook of research on teaching* (4th ed.). New York: Macmillan.

Gudmundsdottir, S., Reinertsen, A., & Nordtømme, N. (1997). Eidsvoll 1814—en fallstudie i historie undervisning. In M. Uljens (Ed.), *Didaktik* (pp. 229–245). Lund: Studentlitteratur.

Hansen, D. T. (1995). *The call to teach.* New York: Teachers College Press.

Hoel, T. (1994). *Elevsamtaler om skriving i vidaregående skole: Responsgrupper i teori og praksis* [High school students' conversations about writing: Theory and practice of response groups]. Unpublished doctoral dissertation, Norwegian University of Science and Technology, Trondheim.

Hoel, T. (1997). Voices from the classroom. *Teaching and Teacher Education, 13*(1), 2–16.

Jank, W., & Meyer, H. (1991). *Didaktische Modelle.* Frankfurt am Main: Cornelsen Verlag Scriptor.

McEwan, H. (1987). *Interpreting the subject domains for students: Towards a rhetorical theory of teaching.* Unpublished doctoral dissertation, University of Washington, Seattle.

Morris, P. (Ed.). (1994). *The Bakhtin reader: Selected writings of Bakhtin, Medvedev, Voloshinov.* London: Arnold.

Phelan, A., McEwan, H., & Pateman, N. (1996). Collaboration in student teaching: Learning to teach in the context of changing curriculum practice. *Teaching and Teacher Education, 12*(4), 335–344.

Prichard, R. (1992). German classrooms observed: A foreigner's perspective. *Oxford Review of Education, 18*(2), 213–225.

Reinertsen, A., Nordtømme, N., Eidsvik, R., Weidemann, E., & Gudmundsdottir, S. (1996). Fagdidaktisk kunnskap i historie belyst gjennom undervisning i hendelsene på Eidsvoll 1814: Tre kasusstudier av lærer i videregående skole. Trondheim: Tapir.

Schwab, J. (1978). Education and the structure of the disciplines. In I. Westbury & N. Wilkof (Eds.), *Science, curriculum and liberal Education* (pp. 229–272). Chicago: University of Chicago Press. (Original work published 1961)

Shulman, L. (1987). Knowledge and teaching: Foundations of the new reform. *Harvard Educational Review, 57*(1), 1–22.

Taylor, C. (1985). *Philosophy and the human sciences* (Philosophical Papers 2). Cambridge, England: University of Cambridge Press.

Wilson, S., & Gudmundsdottir, S. (1987). What is this a case of? Exploring some conceptual issues in case study research. *Education and Urban Society, 20*(1), 42–54.

Author Index

Subject Index